The Bible In Modern English

Fenton, Ferrar, 1832-1920, Massachusetts Bible Society

THE

FIVE BOOKS OF MOSES.

THE
FIVE BOOKS OF MOSES

BEING VOLUME THE FIRST

OF THE

BIBLE IN MODERN ENGLISH.

TRANSLATED DIRECT FROM THE HEBREW, CHALDEE, AND
GREEK LANGUAGES, INTO ENGLISH

BY

FERRAR FENTON,

MEMBER OF THE CAMBRIAN ARCHÆOLOGICAL ASSOCIATION;

AUTHOR OF

" THE NEW TESTAMENT IN MODERN ENGLISH," " ST. PAUL'S EPISTLES IN MODERN
ENGLISH," " THE BOOK OF JOB IN ENGLISH AND IN THE ORIGINAL
METRE," ETC., ETC.

Copyrighted in England and the United States of America.

PUBLISHED FOR THE TRANSLATOR BY

MESSRS. S. W. PARTRIDGE & CO.,
8 & 9, PATERNOSTER ROW, LONDON, E.C.

BRADBURY AGNEW, & CO LD, PRINTERS,
LONDON AND TONBRIDGE

TO FIELD-MARSHAL

THE RIGHT HONOURABLE VISCOUNT WOLSELEY,

WHO THROUGHOUT HIS DISTINGUISHED CAREER HAS PROVED
HIMSELF A GOOD SOLDIER OF CHRIST AND OF
HIS COUNTRY,

THIS VERSION OF THE

Five Books of Moses is dedicated

BY HIS RESPECTFUL SERVANT

FERRAR FENTON (THE TRANSLATOR),

WHO HAS BEEN MUCH ENCOURAGED IN HIS WORK BY THE MANLY
APPROVAL OF THE PLAN OF PUTTING THE HOLY SCRIPTURES
INTO MODERN ENGLISH, WHICH HIS LORDSHIP EX-
PRESSED AFTER SEEING THE GOSPELS AND
EPISTLES PREVIOUSLY PUBLISHED.

PREFACE.

THE very favourable reception given by the most eminent Scholars, Divines, and the general Public, to my translations of St Paul's Epistles, the New Testament, and the Book of Job into Modern English, has removed all need for my making any apology for this First Volume of The Bible in Modern English, containing the Five Books of Moses The sale of the preceding portions has been extensive, St Paul's Epistles having reached a Sixth Edition, the Gospels two large issues, one of 3,000 and the second of 6,000 copies, and the Book of Job two editions

In the Books of Moses now presented I have followed my plan of making a translation direct from the Hebrew into English without any other version before me I do not consequently claim my work to be free from error, the more so as, owing to the severe illness of a very learned friend who had intended to revise it, I have had to make the translation single-handed, and not with the valuable assistance he gave me in my former portions of the Sacred Scriptures The loss of his help, however, has been partially supplied by the aid of that ripe Hebrew Scholar, the Rev JOHN BOWEN, B D , Rector of St Lawrence, Wolfs Castle, Pembrokeshire, whose critical knowledge of Oriental tongues, and all the Authorities upon Hebrew, has been of vital assistance to me, especially in the Books of Genesis and Deuteronomy

But in so entirely a new plan of Translation and Criticism as I have adopted many errors will no doubt be found, and if my readers will point out to me any parts where errors or omission of words may be discovered, I shall be grateful, and record them in my interleaved copy for a future edition

I am now old, but in my youth I pledged a resolve to God to use my talents and acquirements to establish the authenticity of the Sacred Scriptures as a Revelation from Him to Man, by making them intelligible, through the use of Modern English, to my Countrymen in all parts of the earth, and although I have been engaged in active commercial affairs for over forty years, I never ceased my studies to that end, and the progressive execution of it, in spite of conducting a business that extended to all parts of the world The Almighty has blessed my work so far, and I hope will enable me to accomplish the whole, and enjoy the pleasure of attaining the chief object of my existence,—to make the Books of the Bible as intelligible to my Race in the British Empire, and the great American Commonwealth, in spoken English, as they are to myself in the Oriental tongues, in return for His inspiration, through those Sacred Scriptures, having in early manhood taken me from the Mental Hell of Sceptical Doubt, to the Home of assured Rest in a knowledge of His Eternal Laws, which He revealed first in them, and is again in our days confirming by His fresh Revelation of them through the sciences of Physical Research Upon this fact the reader should consult my Introduction to St Paul's Epistles, in their sixth edition [1]

---

[1] Published by Horace Marshall & Son, Temple House, L.C.

Finally, I must note as to my spelling of the proper names of localities and men   As I made my translation from the Hebrew without any English version open before me, I have followed the now general plan of Oriental scholars, and simply transliterated those names, except a few, such as "Moses," "Joshua," etc, which are too fixed by popular use to be altered The Geographical Names I invariably retain in transliterated form, because the attempt of my predecessors in translation from the Septuagint and Vulgate, and their versionists, to render them into their supposed Greek equivalents territorially, has made such wild misplacing of Nations and Towns as to remind one of the dreams of a mapmaker gone mad, whole kingdoms often having been put thousands of miles away from their actual localities and these blunders have been incorporated in all our literature.

Hoping for the Divine blessing on my work,

I remain,

My Readers' servant,

FERRAR FENTON

315, CITY ROAD, LONDON, E C,
    ENGLAND,
       1901

THE FIRST BOOK OF MOSES, CALLED

GENESIS.

TRANSLATED DIRECT FROM THE HEBREW BY FERRAR FENTON.

BOOK THE FIRST.

The First Creation of the Universe by God = Elohim.

1 BY Periods[1] GOD created that which produced the Solar Systems, then that which produced the Earth

2 But the Earth was unorganised and empty, and darkness covered its convulsed surface, while the breath of GOD rocked the surface of its waters

3 GOD then said, "Let there be

4 light," and light came And GOD gazed upon that beautiful light, and GOD divided the light from the dark-

5 ness And to the light GOD gave the name of Day, and to the darkness He gave the name of Night This was the close and the dawn of the first period

6 GOD also said, "Let there be an expanse between the waters, and let it be a division between the waters

7 and the waters" And GOD made the expanse, and it divided the waters which were below the expanse from the waters which were above the

8 expanse, and that was done And GOD named the expanse the Heavens This was the close and the dawn of the second period

9 GOD then commanded, "Let the waters below the Heavens be collected in one place, and let dry land appear,"

10 and that was done And GOD named the dry land Earth, and the accumulated waters He named Seas, and

11 GOD admired their beauty GOD then said, "Let the Earth produce seed-bearing vegetation, as well as fruit trees according to their several species, capable of reproduction upon

12 the Earth," and that was done The Earth produced the seed-bearing herbage according to every species, as well as the different species of reproductive fruit trees, and GOD saw that they were good This was 13 the close and the dawn of the third period

GOD further said, "Let luminaries 14 appear in the expanse of the Heavens for a division between the day and the night, and let them serve to mark seasons, periods, and years, and let 15 them also illuminate the expanse of the skies so as to reflect their light upon the Earth," and that was done GOD had made two large luminaries, 16 the larger one to control the day, and the smaller one to control the night, accompanied by the stars And GOD 17 had fixed them in the heavenly expanse so as to illuminate the Earth, to control the day and to control the 18 night, and to mark the division between the light and the darkness, and GOD saw they were beautiful This was the close and the dawn of 19 the fourth period

GOD then said, "Let the waters be 20 swarming with animal life and let birds fly in the expanse of the skies above the Earth," GOD accordingly 21 produced the monsters of the deep, and the waters swarmed with every species of reptile, and also produced every species of flying bird And GOD admired their beauty And GOD, 22 in giving them His blessing, said, "Be fruitful and multiply, so as to fill the waters of the deep, and also let the birds multiply upon the Earth' This was the close and the 23 dawn of the fifth period

GOD then said, "Let the Earth 24 produce animal life according to its species, in quadrupeds, reptiles and all wild animals, answering to their species" and that was done GOD 25 accordingly made the various species of the animals of the Earth as well

---

[1] Literally "By Headships." It is curious that all translators from the Septuagint have rendered this word בראשית BARSHITH into the singular, although it is plural in th Hebrew So I render it accurately —F F.

as the several species of quadrupeds, and all the different species of reptiles, and GOD admired their beauty

Creation of Man under the Shadow of God.

26 GOD then said, "Let Us make men under Our Shadow, as Our Representatives, and subject to them the fish of the waters, and the birds of the sky, and the quadrupeds, as well as the whole of the Earth, and every reptile that creeps upon it"

27 So GOD created men under HIS own Shadow, creating them in the Shadow of God, and constituting them male

28 and female GOD then gave them His blessing, and GOD said to them, "Be fruitful and multiply so as to fill the Earth and subdue it, and rule over the fish of the sea, and the birds of the skies, and over every living animal that moves upon the Earth"

29 GOD also said, "See, I have given you for food every fruit and grain-bearing plant upon the surface of the whole Earth, as well as fruit and seed-bearing trees and all vegetation, so

30 that they may be food for you, and for every animal of the Earth, and for every bird of the skies, and for every reptile upon the Earth which possesses the life of animals,

31 and it was done And GOD gazed upon all that He had made, and it was very beautiful Thus the close came, and the dawn came of the sixth period

2 Thus the whole Host of the Heavens as well as the Earth were completed

2 And GOD rested at the seventh period from all the works which He had

3 made, therefore GOD blessed the seventh day, and hallowed it, because He then rested from all the work which GOD had arranged to do

The formation of Man from the Dust of the Ground by the Ever-living God.

4 The following were the productions for the Heavens and the Earth during their creation, at the period of their organization by the LORD GOD

5 of both the Earth and Heavens, and of every plant of the field before it was upon the Earth, and every herb of the field before He caused it to grow, even before the EVER-LIVING GOD had scattered them upon the Earth, and Man existed not to cultivate the Earth

A vapour then rose up from the 6 Earth, and moistened the whole surface of the ground

The EVER-LIVING GOD afterwards 7 formed Man from the dust of the ground, and breathed into his nostrils perception of life,[1] BUT MAN BECAME A LIFE-CONTAINING SOUL

The EVER-LIVING GOD then planted 8 a garden in Eden,—in the East,—and there He placed the man whom He had formed And out of the ground 9 the EVER-LIVING GOD caused to grow all the trees that were beautiful and good for food, as well as the Tree of Lives in the centre of the Garden; and the tree of the Knowledge of Good and Evil

A lake also sprang up in Eden to 10 supply the Garden with water, and from there it divided and became four sources The name of the first is 11 Pishon, and flows along the land of Havilah, where there is gold And 12 the gold of that land is pure, there are also bdellium and the onyx And 13 the second river is Jihon, it flows along all the land of Kush The name of 14 the third river is Hidikel, which flows through the east of Ashur, and the fourth river is the Frath [2]

The EVER-LIVING GOD then took 15 the man and placed him in the Garden of Eden for the purpose of cultivating and taking care of it And the LORD 16 GOD instructed the man, saying, "For food you may eat of the whole of the trees of the Garden, but from 17 the tree of the Knowledge of Good and Evil, you shall not eat, because in the day you eat from it dying you shall die"

The EVER-LIVING GOD also said 18 "It is not good for the man to be in solitude, I will make a comforter to live with him" Therefore the EVER- 19 LIVING GOD, who had formed out of the ground every animal of the field as well as every bird of the skies, took them to the man to see what he would name them And whatever the man with the Living Soul called them, that was their name So the 20 man gave names to all the quadrupeds, and all the birds of the skies, and to all the wild animals, but it was no comfort for the man to be with them

---

1 Or Reflective, or Intellectual life See
also Ch. II. 1
2 Euphrates

21 So the EVER-LIVING GOD threw the man into a stupor, and he slept And taking one of his ribs, He closed up
22 the flesh in its place And from the rib, which the EVER-LIVING GOD had taken out of the man, He constructed a woman, and brought her to the
23 man And the man said, "This form is bone of my own bone, and flesh of my own flesh This shall be named 'woman,' because she was
24 taken from man " Man shall therefore leave his father and his mother, and shall unite with his wife, and
25 they shall be one body And they were naked, the man and his wife, but they were not ashamed

The Temptation of Eve.

3 Now the Serpent was more impudent than any of the wild animals of the field which the EVER-LIVING GOD had made So he asked the woman, "Is it true that GOD has said, you may not eat of every tree of the
2 Garden?" And the woman replied to the serpent, "We may eat of the
3 fruit of the trees of the Garden, but of the fruit of the tree which is in the middle of the Garden, GOD has said, 'do not eat of it, and do not even
4 touch it, lest you die'" But the serpent answered the woman "You
5 will not die, but GOD knows that at the time you eat of it, your eyes will then be opened, and you will be like GOD, acquainted with both good and evil "
6 So the woman perceiving that the tree was good for food, and beautiful to the eyes, and a tree stimulating to the intellect, she took some of its fruit and ate it, and gave some to her husband with her, and he also ate it
7 Then the eyes of both of them were opened, and they became aware that they were naked They accordingly joined fig leaves together, and made aprons for themselves
8 They then heard the sound of the EVER-LIVING GOD moving in the Garden in the breeze of the day, and the man and his wife hid themselves from the presence of the LORD GOD among the trees of the Garden
9 But the EVER-LIVING GOD called to the man, saying, "Where are you?"
10 And he replied, "I heard Your sound in the Garden, and perceiving that I was naked, I hid myself"
11 Then He asked, 'Who told you that you were naked? Have you

eaten of the tree of which I commanded that you should not eat?"
12 And the man replied, "The woman whom You gave to me, she gave me of the tree, and I ate it " "Why
13 did you do that?" the LORD GOD asked the woman And the woman answered, "The serpent deceived me and I ate it "
14 The EVER-LIVING GOD accordingly said to the serpent, "Because you have done this you shall be accursed more than all the cattle, and more than all the wild beasts of the field, you shall crawl upon your belly, and eat dust all the days of your life I
15 will also cause antagonism between you and the woman, and between your progeny and her progeny HE shall wound your head, and you shall wound His heel "
16 But to the woman He said, "I will increase your sorrows and your joys You shall give birth to children with pain, but your love shall be for your husband, and he shall rule over you "
17 Then to Adam He said, "Because you have listened to the voice of your wife, and have eaten of the tree of which I commanded you, saying, 'Eat not of it,' I will set the ground apart for your cultivation, in sorrow you shall eat from it every day of
18 your life It shall grow thorns and briars for you, but you shall have
19 the plants of the field for food In the sweat of your brow you shall eat bread, until you return to the ground, from which you were taken For dust you are, and to the dust you shall return "
20 The man then gave to his wife the name of Eve, [1] because she was the mother of all life For Adam also
21 and his wife the EVER-LIVING GOD made clothing of skins, and dressed them
22 The LORD GOD also said, "Now the man was like one of Ourselves, acquainted with both good and evil, therefore it may be that he will stretch out his hand, and take also of the Tree of Lives and eat of it, and live
23 for ever " The EVER-LIVING GOD consequently expelled him from the Garden of Eden, in order to cultivate the ground from which he was taken
24 So He drove out the man, and He stationed at the east of the Garden of

---

[1] Khavah or life container

Eden the Divine Watchers, with the flaming sword to guard the path to the Tree of Lives.

The First Man Child—Births of Cain and Abel.

4 The man afterwards knew Eve his wife, and she conceived and gave birth to Cain, and said, "I have been given a man from the
2 EVER-LIVING" She afterwards gave birth to his brother Abel And Abel became a shepherd of sheep, but
3 Cain was a cultivator of the soil And during the harvest time Cain brought some of the produce of the ground as
4 an offering to the EVER-LIVING And Abel also brought of the best and the fattest of his sheep And the LORD looked favourably upon Abel and his
5 offering, but He did not regard Cain and his offering with favour Cain therefore was very angry, and his
6 countenance fell Then the EVER-LIVING asked Cain, "Why are you angry, and why has your countenance
7 fallen? If you do right, is there not approval? and if you do not do right, Sin crouches at the door and awaits you, but you should conquer it"

The Murder of Abel.

8 When Cain was afterwards talking with his brother Abel, and they were together in the field, Cain attacked his brother Abel, and murdered him
9 The LORD accordingly asked Cain "Where is your brother Abel?" But he replied, "I do not know,—am I my brother's keeper?"
10 The EVER-LIVING however answered, "What have you done? The voice of your brother's blood cries to
11 Me from the ground Therefore you are cursed from the ground, which has opened her mouth to take in your brother's blood from your hand
12 When you cultivate the ground it shall not yield up its wealth to you, you shall be a wanderer and vagabond upon the earth"
13 But Cain answered to the LORD, "My punishment is heavier than I
14 can bear Since You drive me to-day out on the face of the earth, I shall be deprived of Your presence, and be a wanderer and a vagabond upon the earth, and whoever meets me will kill me"
15 But the EVER-LIVING replied, "Not so whoever kills Cain shall be

punished sevenfold" Therefore the LORD put a mark upon Cain, so that he might not be attacked by anyone who met him
16 Cain accordingly went out from the presence of the EVER-LIVING, and lived in a land of exile on the eastern side of Eden, where Cain knew his
17 wife, and she conceived and gave birth to Enok, and he built a village, and named it after the name of his
18 son, Enok[1] And to Enok there was born Irad, and Irad produced Mehujael, and Mehujael produced Methusael, and Methusael produced Lemek
19 And Lemek took two wives for himself, the name of one was Ada, and
20 the name of the other Zillah And Ada gave birth to Jabal, who was the originator of tent-dwellers and merchants
21 And his brother's name was Jubal, he was the originator of all those who play the harp and wind instruments
22 Zillah also gave birth to Tubal-Cain, the improver of every work in copper and iron, and the sister of Tubal-Cain was Namah
23 And Lemek addressing his wives said

"Ada and Zillah listen to my voice,
Wives of Lemek listen to my speech,
For I killed a man who wounded,
And a youth who hurt me—
24 If Cain had sevenfold protection,
Seventy-seven should be that of Lemek!"

Birth of Seth.

25 And Adam knew his wife again, she gave birth to a son, and named him Sheth,[2] "for God," she said, "has given me another son in the place of Abel, who was murdered by Cain"
26 And to Sheth, a son was born, and he gave him the name of Enosh[3] Men then began to call upon the name of the EVER-LIVING.

The Genealogy of Mankind, who were created as Representatives of God.

5 This is the Birth-Book of Men From the time that GOD created men, He made them to represent
2 God, constituting them male and female, giving them His blessing and naming them by the name of Mankind, upon the day of their formation
3 Adam, when he was one hundred

---

1 Enok the dedicate B)
2 The "Second" or "Renewal"—F F
3 Enosh—"Mankind" or "a weakling"

and thirty years old, produced a representative of himself, like his own

4 shadow, and gave him the name of Sheth   And the lifetime of Adam, after the birth of Sheth, was eight hundred years, during which time sons

5 and daughters were born to him   So the whole lifetime of Adam was nine hundred and thirty years when he died

6   And Sheth was one hundred and five years old when Enosh[1] was born

7 to him   And Sheth, after the birth of Enosh, lived eight hundred and seven years, and had sons and daughters

8 born to him · And the whole lifetime of Sheth was nine hundred and twelve years, when he died

9   And Enosh lived ninety years,

10 when Kenan was born to him   And Enosh, after the birth of Kenan, lived eight hundred and fifty years, and had sons and daughters born to

11 him   And all the lifetime of Enosh was nine hundred and five years, and he then died

12   And Kenan lived seventy years when Mahalalel was born to him

13 And Kenan, after Mahalalel was born to him, lived eight hundred and thirty years, and had sons and daughters

14 born to him   So the whole lifetime of Kenan was nine hundred and ten years, and he died

15   And Mahalalel living until he was sixty-five years of age, had Jared

16 born to him   And Mahalalel, after the birth of Jared, lived eight hundred and thirty years, and sons and

17 daughters were born to him, and the whole lifetime of Mahalalel was eight hundred and ninety-five years, when he died

18   And Jared lived until he was one hundred and sixty-two years of age,

19 when Enok[2] was born to him   And after the birth of Enok, Jared lived eight hundred years, and had sons

20 and daughters born to him, and the whole lifetime of Jared was nine hundred and sixty-two years, and he died

21   And Enok lived until the age of

sixty-five years, when Methuselah was born to him   And Enok walked 22 with GOD, after Methuselah had been born to him, three hundred years, and sons and daughters were born to him   And the whole lifetime of 23 Enok was three hundred and sixty-five years   And Enok walked with 24 GOD, and he did not die, GOD having taken him to Himself

And Methuselah, having lived until 25 he was one hundred and eighty-seven years of age, had Lamek[1] born to him, and Methuselah, after Lamek 26 had been born to him, lived seven hundred and eighty-two years, having had sons and daughters born to him And the whole lifetime of Methuselah 27 was nine hundred and sixty-nine years, and he then died

And Lamek lived until he was one 28 hundred and eighty-two years of age, when a son was born to him, to whom 29 he gave the name of Noah,[2] saying, " He comforts in our labour, and in the trouble of our hands, upon the land which was denounced by the EVER-LIVING "   And Lamek, after 30 Noah was born to him, lived until the age of five hundred and ninety-five years, sons and daughters being born to him   And the whole lifetime of 31 Lamek was seven hundred and seventy-seven years, when he died And Noah was five hundred years 32 old, when Shem, Ham, and Japheth were born to him

The Corruption of Mankind.

But when corrupt Men increased 6 upon the surface of the Earth, and sons and daughters were born to them, then the sons of GOD admired 2 the daughters of Men who were beautiful, and they took to themselves wives from all they desired

Consequently the EVER-LIVING said, 3 " My spirit shall not call to man for ever, for he is sinful flesh, but they shall have a hundred and twenty years "

The Nephalim were upon the earth 4 in those days, and also afterwards when the sons of GOD came to the daughters of man, and they bore to

---

[1] Enosh, the son of Sheth, must not be confused with the Enok, the son of Cain, mentioned in Ch 4, v 17. They are totally different —F F

[2] This Enok is a different individual to the Enok, son of Cain, of Ch 4, v 17 The barbarous spelling of the old translators has confused the genealogies which I hope to clear —F F.

[1] This Lamek, son of Methuselah, is a totally different person to the Lemek, descended from Cain, and mentioned in Ch 4, v 23 —F F

[2] Noah, meaning Comfort —F F

them mighty men, who were men of renown of old.

5 And the EVER-LIVING saw that the sin of man increased upon the earth, and that every effort of the thought of his heart was to promote sin every

6 day And the EVER-LIVING sighed for the doings of man upon earth, and it

7 grieved His heart The LORD therefore said, "I will sweep away man whom I created from off the surface of the earth, from man to beast and reptile, and birds of the skies, for I regret that I made them"

8 But Noah found favour in the presence of the EVER-LIVING

The History of Noah.

9 The following are the children of Noah Noah was a good man, he was upright in his age Noah walked

10 with GOD And Noah had three sons given to him, Shem, Ham, and

11 Japheth But the Earth corrupted itself in the presence of GOD, and the

12 Earth was full of crime And GOD looked upon the Earth, and saw its corruption, for all men had corrupted their way upon the Earth

The Deluge Foretold

13 So GOD said to Noah, "I decide to cut off all men from My sight, for the earth is full of crime from their presence. I will accordingly sweep

14 them from the earth Make therefore for yourself an Ark[1] of pitch-pine Make the Ark with decks, and pitch

15 it inside and outside with pitch You shall make it thus,—it shall be three hundred cubits[2] long, fifty cubits

16 wide, and thirty cubits deep Make a ventilator to the Ark, and make it a cubit high, and place a door in the side of the Ark You shall make

17 second and third decks, for I Myself will bring a downrush of waters upon the earth to sweep off all beings possessing the breath of life, from under Heaven, all that move upon

18 the land Then I will establish My Covenant with you, and you shall go into the Ark yourself with your sons and your wife, and your sons' wives

19 along with you And from every animal of all kinds, two of each shall

go into the Ark to live with you, they shall be male and female of birds 20 by their species, and of animals by their species, and of reptiles moving in the field by their species, two of each shall accompany you, so as to preserve life And you shall take 21 with you all kinds of food which is eaten, and store it with you, and it shall be provision for yourself, and 22 for them" Noah accordingly did all that GOD commanded him He accomplished it

Noah ordered to enter the Ark, or Ship.

Afterwards the LORD said to Noah, 7 "Go yourself and all your household into the Ark, for I have seen that you have been righteous in the face of this generation Take with you of 2 all clean cattle, seven, male and female, and of beasts which are unclean two of them, a male and a female Also from birds of the sky 3 seven, seven male and female, so as to preserve a seed of life upon the surface of the land Because at the 4 end of seven days, I will pour on to the earth for forty days and forty nights, and I will sweep away every creature that I made from off the surface of the ground" And Noah did 5 all that the EVER-LIVING instructed him

Noah was six hundred years old 6 when the downrush of water came upon the earth Noah with his children and wife, and the wives of his 7 sons with them went accordingly into the Ark from the face of the waters of the deluge, with the clean cattle and 8 with the unclean cattle, and with the birds, and all that crawls upon the field, who came two by two to the 9 ark, male and female, as GOD had directed Noah

When the seven days had passed, 10 then the downrush of water came upon the earth In the six hundredth 11 year of the life of Noah, in the second month, on the seventeenth day of the month, on that day all the sources of the Great Ocean, and the belts in the heavens were broken, and 12 there was a downrush on to the earth for forty days and forty nights At 13 the close of that day,[1] Noah, along

---

[1] The Hebrew word הַתֵּבָה, THEBATH, really means a ship not a floating house, like the common child's toy —F F

[2] A cubit 〟 〟 ⋅ l 〟 ⋅ ⸳⋅⸳⋅⸳⋅⸳ and a fraction over — l l

---

[1] "That day" refers back to the 17th day of the month when Noah entered the Ark — F F

with Shem, Ham, and Japheth, sons of Noah, and the wife of Noah, and the three wives of Noah's sons along 14 with them entered the Ark, they themselves and all the animals according to their species, and all the cattle, according to their species, and all crawlers upon the earth by their species, and all birds by their species, every bird of every 15 wing There also came to Noah into the Ark two by two, from all creatures which have animal breath 16 Thus they came male and female of all creatures, as GOD had directed them, and the LORD shut him inside 17 The downrush continued forty days upon the earth, and the waters swelled and lifted up the Ark, and 18 raised it from off the land And the waters overwhelmed and rose greatly upon the earth and the Ark floated 19 upon the surface of the waters The waters rose very high above the earth, and covered up all the hills and mountains which are below the skies 20 The waters covered the hills fifteen 21 cubits And all animals that moved upon the land expired, with bird, and cattle, and wild animals, and every insect swarming upon the land, and 22 every man, all which breathed the breath of animals in its nostrils, with 23 all that was in the desert, died Thus He swept away the whole that He had made upon the surface of the ground, from man to cattle, and reptile, and birds of the skies, thus He swept them from off the earth, but Noah and those who were with him in the Ark remained And the waters overwhelmed the earth one hundred and fifty days

The Deluge Subsides.

8 But GOD remembered Noah, and all the animals and all the cattle which were with him in the Ark Therefore GOD passed a wind over 2 the earth, and the waters dried, and He closed the fountains of space, and the belts of the skies, and stopped 3 the torrents from the skies, and stayed the waters from going on to the earth, and so the waters retired and diminished from the period of one 4 hundred and fifty days The Ark then rested on the seventeenth day of the seventh month upon the

Mountain of the Peaks,[1] and the 5 waters were retreating and subsiding until the tenth month In the eleventh month the tops of the hills appeared Then at the end of forty days, Noah 6 opened the window which he had made in the Ark, and sent out a 7 raven, and it went, wandered and turned about until the waters dried away from off the earth Afterwards, 8 he sent out a dove from him, to see if the waters had lessened from the surface of the field, but the dove 9 found not a resting-place for the sole of her foot, so she returned to him in the Ark, for the waters were still on the whole surface of the earth, so he put out his hand and took her, and brought her to him into the Ark He 10 then waited seven days longer, and again sent out the dove from the Ark And the dove returning at dusk, 11 carried in her mouth an olive-leaf which had been broken off So Noah then knew that the waters were off the earth Waiting yet another seven 12 days, he sent the dove out again, and it did not again return to him At 13 the end of his six hundred and first year, on the first day of the month, the waters dried from off the earth Noah then loosened the upper deck of the Ark, and looking out, perceived that the surface of the ground was dry And in the second month, on 14 the twenty-seventh day of the month, the earth was dry

GOD then spoke to Noah saying 15 "Go from the Ark, yourself, your 16 wife, and your sons, and your sons' wives along with you All the animals 17 which are with you, of every kind, with bird, and cattle, and with every reptile that creeps upon the earth, bring it along with you, and let them breed plentifully on the land, and cover it, and increase over the earth"

So Noah went out, and his wife, 18 and his sons' wives with him, every 19 animal, every bird, and every reptile creeping upon the land, according to their species, went out from the Ark Noah then built an Altar to the 20

1 I translate the compound Hebrew word "Ararat," as by leaving it in the Hebrew as the current versions do it misleads the reader to fancy Ararat in Armenia is meant but the real resting place of the Ark, as the Sacred Record clearly proves was upon the Peaks of the Hymalavah Mountains in the Hindoo Koosh in the region of Kashgar, or North ru Afghanistan —I I

EVER-LIVING, and took from every clean beast, and from every clean bird, and offered burnt offerings upon the

21 Altar, and the EVER-LIVING perceived pleasant sweet perfume, and the LORD said in His heart, "Never again will I curse the ground to the labour of man, although the thought of the heart of man is wickedness from his youth, and never again will I cut off every

22 animal I have made During the whole existence of the earth, sowing and harvest, and cold and heat, and Winter and Summer, Spring and Autumn, and day and night, shall continue"

God's Blessing and Command to Mankind upon Noah leaving the Ark.

A Renewal of the Primeval Blessings

9 GOD also blessed Noah and his sons, and said, "Be prolific and

2 increase and fill the earth And the fear and terror of you shall be upon every animal of the land, and every bird of the sky, with all that swarm upon the ground, and all the fish of the waters, they shall be given into

3 your hand Every living animal that moves shall be food for you I have given the whole to you like the green

4 herbage But the flesh with its life,

5 its blood, you shall not eat And also the blood of your life I will require, from the hand of every animal I will require it, and from the hand of man, even from the hand of his brother, I will require the life of man

6 Whoever sheds the blood of man, by man his own blood shall be shed, because I made man in the likeness

7 of Gods And be prolific yourselves, increase and swarm on the earth, and multiply on it"

8 GOD also spoke to Noah, and to his

9 sons along with him, saying, "Now I Myself will fix a Covenant with you,

10 and your descendants after you, and with every living animal that is with you, with bird, and cattle, and with every animal of the earth with you, of all coming out of the Ark, and

11 with every wild beast of the earth I have fixed My Covenant with you, that all flesh shall never again be destroyed by a downrush of water and there shall ever again be a down-

12 rush to destroy the earth God also said "This is the attestation of the Covenant which I have made between Myself and you, and between all animal life which is with you for every generation I place My rainbow in 13 the clouds, and it shall be for an evidence of the Covenant between Myself and all the earth When there 14 is My cloud, covering the earth, and the rainbow appears in the cloud, I 15 shall remember My Covenant that is between Myself and you, and between all animal life and there shall never again be a downrush of water to sweep away all living The rainbow shall 16 be in the cloud, and appear as an eternal record of the Covenant between GOD and all animal life existing upon the earth" And GOD 17 repeated to Noah, "This is the Covenant which I have settled between Myself and all existence which is upon earth"

History of Noah after the Flood.

Now the sons of Noah who came 18 out of the Ark were Shem Ham, and Japheth, and Ham was the father of Canaan These three were the sons 19 of Noah, and from these three the whole earth was peopled

Noah then became a farmer, and 20 planted a vineyard, and drinking of 21 the wine, he became drunk, and was naked in his tent, and Ham the 22 father of Canaan, saw the nakedness of his father, and reported it to his two brothers, outside Shem and 23 Japheth, however, took a shawl, and spread it on their shoulders, and going backwards, they covered the nakedness of their father, and their faces were turned away, so that they did not see their father's shame So, 24 when Noah woke up from his wine, and knew what his younger son had 25 done to him, he said

"Cursed be Canaan
A servant of servants let him be to his brothers"
He also exclaimed 26
"The Living GOD bless Shem,
And let Canaan be a servant to him
GOD will extend Japheth, 27
But He will dwell in the tent of Shem,
And Canaan shall be his servant"

Noah lived after the deluge, for 28 three hundred and fifty years So

all the lifetime of Noah was nine
hundred and fifty years, when he died

History of Noah's Sons.

10 Now these are the registers of the
sons of Noah, Shem, Ham, and Japheth, for they had sons born to them
after the deluge

2 The sons of Japheth, Gomer, Magog,
and Madai, and Ion, and Thubal, and

3 Meshech, and Thiras And the sons
of Gomer, Ashkenaz, and Riphath,
and Thogarmah And the sons

4 of Javan (Ion) Elishah, and Thar-
shish, Kittim, and the Dodanim

5 From these they spread themselves
over the sea-coasts of the countries
of the heathen, each with their
language amongst the heathen tribes

6 And the sons of Ham, Kush, and
Mizraim, and Phut, and Canaan

7 And the sons of Kush, Seba, and
Havilah, and Sabthah, and Raamah,
and Sabtheka, and the sons of

8 Raamah, Sheba and Dedan To Kush
was born Nimrod Wild beasts began

9 then to infest the earth, so he became
a powerful hunter in the presence of
the LORD, therefore it is said, "Like
Nimrod, a mighty hunter before the

10 LORD" And the capitals of his kingdom were Babel,[1] and Ereck and Akad,
and Kalinah in the land of Shinar

11 From that land Asshur proceeded to
Assyria, and built Ninevah, and the

12 town of the plains, and Kalah, and
Resen, between Ninevah and Kalah,
which is a large city

13 The Mizraim also produced the
Ludim, and Anamim, and Lehabim,

14 and Naphtuhim, and Pathrusim, and
Kasluhim, from whom sprung the
Philistines and the Kaphtorites

15 And to Canaan were born Zidon,

16 his eldest, and Heth, and the
Jebusite, and the Amorite, and the

17 Girgashite, and the Hivite, and the

18 Arkite, and the Sinite, and the
Arvadite, and the Zemarite, and
the Hamathite, and each spread
themselves as the tribes of the

19 Canaanites And the boundaries of
the Canaanites are from Zidon by
the valley of Gerai to Gaza, along
the valley of Sodom and Gomorrah
and Admah, and Zeboim, to Lashar

20 These were the sons of Ham, in
their tribes and languages, in the
regions of the heathen

21 And Shem, the elder brother of
Japheth, also produced He was the

22 father of all the sons of Heber[1] The
sons of Shem were Elam, and Ashur,
and Arphaxed, and Lot, and Aram

23 And the sons of Aram Uz and Hul,

24 and Gether, and Mash And to
Arphaxed was born Shelah, and

25 to Shelah was born Heber, and to
Heber were born two sons, the name
of the first, Peleg,[2] because in his
days the Continent was split up, and
his brother's name was Joktan[3]

26 And to Joktan were born Almodad
and Sheleph and Hazarmaveth, and

27 Jereh and Hadoram, and Uzal, and

28 Diklah, and Obal, and Abimael, and

29 Sheba, and Ophir, and Havilah,
and Jobab, all these were sons of

30 Joktan, and they populated from
Mesha, by the valley of Sephar, a

31 mountain of the East These are
the sons of Shem, by their tribes and
by their languages in their countries
among the heathen

11 All the land was of one language

2 and they spoke alike But some of
them removing from the East, proceeded to the plain of Shinar, and

3 settled there There each said to
his neighbour, "Come, let us set to
work making bricks, and see that
they are properly burnt; and bricks
shall serve us for stone, and petroleum

4 for mortar." So they agreed, "We
will build here for ourselves a City
and a Tower whose top shall reach
the sky thus we will make a Beacon
for ourselves, so that we may not
be scattered over all the surface of

5 the country' But a Power came
down to inspect the city and the

1 The Babel mentioned here must not be
confused with the Babylon of the Nebuchad-
nezzars, which was built long after, as a
City probably really by Nebuchadnezzar
the First —F F

1 V, 21 Heber" in Hebrew signifies a
"coloniser" or "colonist," and it is an his-
torical fact that the Semitic nations have
been the greatest colonisers of the earth As
Baron von Humboldt says of the Arabian
branch, "They are the most mobile race in
the world,"- F F

2 V 25 "Peleg" means "split" in
Hebrew

3 V 25 "Joktan" means in the Hebrew
"Lessened," probably referring to the
"lessening" of the original continent by the
"splitting" away of the American continents.
See Prof C A L Totten's works upon this
great geological convulsion If we take a
map of the two Americas, in Mercator's pro-
position, and cut out the Atlantic, the inden-
tations of the Eastern Americas and Western
Europe and Africa fit into each other, as
they did before this convulsion —F. F.

tower which the sons of men had
6 built, and the Power said, "Now
they are one people, of one
language all of them, and having
began to do this they will not
be restrained from anything they
7 determine upon We will therefore
go down and confuse their language,
so that each will not understand his
8 neighbour's speech" So the Power
scattered them over the surface of
the whole country, and they aban-
9 doned the building of the city They
therefore called its name Babel [1]
because it was there that the Power
confused the language of all the
country Thus from there the LORD
scattered them over all the surface
of the land [2]

The History of Shem's Descendants.

10 These are the genealogies of Shem
Shem was one hundred years old
when Arphaxad was born to him two
11 years after the deluge, Shem then
lived after the birth of Arphaxad, five
hundred years, and had sons and
daughters born to him
12 And Arphaxad lived thirty-five
years, then had Shelah born to him,
13 and Arphaxad lived after the birth
of Shelah four hundred and forty-
three years, and sons and daughters
14 were born to him And Shelah lived
thirty years when Eber was born to
15 him, and after the birth of Eber,
Shelah lived four hundred and three
years, and sons and daughters were
16 born to him And Eber lived thirty-

four years, when Peleg was born to
him Eber lived after the birth of 17
Peleg four hundred and thirty years,
and sons and daughters were born
to him And Peleg lived thirty years 18
and Reu was born to him Peleg 19
lived after the birth of Reu two
hundred and nine years, and sons
and daughters were born to him
And Reu lived thirty-two years, when 20
Serug was born to him, and after 21
the birth of Serug, Reu lived two
hundred and seven years, and sons
and daughters were born to him
And Serug lived thirty years and 22
Nakhor was born to him Serug lived 23
after the birth of Nakhor, two hundred
years, and sons and daughters were
born to him And Nakhor lived 24
twenty-nine years, when Terah was
born to him, and Nakhor lived after 25
the birth of Terah, one hundred
and nineteen years, and sons and
daughters were born to him And 26
Terah lived seventy years, when
Abram, Nahor and Haran were born
to him

Now, these are the descendants of 27
Terah, Terah had Abram, Nahor,
and Haran born to him, and Haran
had Lot born to him Haran died 28
before Terah his father in his native
country in Ur of the Kaldees

Abram and Nahor then took wives 29
for themselves The name of the
wife of Abram was Sarai, and the
name of Nahor's wife was Milkah
the daughter of Haran, the father of
Milkah and father of Iskah Sarai 30
was sterile and had no child for herself Terah however took Abram his 31
son and Lot his grandson, the son of
Haran, and Sarai his daughter-in-
law, the wife of Abram his own son,
and departed from Ur of the Kaldees
to travel to the land of Canaan, and
arriving at Haran they settled there
The lifetime of Terah was two hundred 32
and five years, and Terah died in
Haran

---

[1] Confusion

[2] The word Jehovah, commonly translated
Lord, was originally used as a title of honour
for nobles or governors as shown in Genesis,
Ch xviii v. 13, and elsewhere, as in Exodus,
Ch iv v 24, where the title is given to the
chief of a tribe, who attempted to murder
Moses, and was not reserved as a synonym for
GOD until after the promulgation of the Law
from Sinai In this passage it is evident it did
not mean the Supreme Being, and to translate it as if it did misleads the reader —F F

NOTE —As Ch xi of Genesis forms a decisive period in human history, I think it well to
add a note to endeavour to remove a difficulty that has for generations puzzled students of
the Holy Scriptures, in regard to the age to which the men before Abraham are stated to
have lived Sceptics have delightedly used this point as a weapon of assault upon Biblical
history, and thus upon the Christian Faith But the difficulty, it appears to me, has arisen
from a want of knowledge amongst both the believers and sceptics of Europe and America
of the methods of expression used in the primæval literature of Asia, as Governor Holwell
pointed out a century and a half ago in his " India Tracts," and the modes of thought prevalent
among the earliest races of that continent, and which, at least in their religious affairs, continue
to this day, and have even been continued in the legal vocabulary of the British Constitution
to our own times Thus our constitutional lawyers and books tell us that, according to our

law, ' The King never dies,—he only vacates the throne," or demises the crown, yet no one imagines, or asserts by that expression, that the present reigning monarch is twelve hundred years of age, as he would be, dating from King Arthur, who is said to be his remote ancestor, or "father," as he would be called in the Hebrew, Arabic, or Chinese languages The phrase of our constitutional law is merely what we now call a "survival ' of a very ancient theory

That theory, and the linguistic idiom of the first eleven chapters of Genesis, as still used in the religious ideas and expression of them, amongst the Thibetans, Chinese, and kindred nations, is, that their Royal High Priest, the Great Lhama, and his subordinate high priests, equivalent to our archbishops of provinces, never die, but that their souls, their real selves, when their visible bodies grow old and inconvenient to them, go and select a son, or some beautiful child or youth into whom they enter, and through whom they continue to exercise their beneficent duties as kings and priests, and thus are thousands of years old

We know, from universal history, that the chief of every tribe was formerly always both priest and ruler, and as a fact in all organized states the chief magistrate, king, or president is actually so in our day, and decides with his advisers what doctrines or forms of religion shall be allowed amongst the citizens of the states over whom he, and they as his administrators, rule I refrain from quoting illustrations for want of space The fact is clear to every man who reflects

Using the above lamp of history by which to read the early chapters of Genesis, we may safely conclude that the patriarchs of such apparently incredible length of life were actually priest-chiefs of tribes, whose souls were believed to have passed from the first organizer of the tribe, or the man who as head of a family originated, as Abraham, Isaac, and Jacob did, a powerful house which developed into a nation, and who ruled it by their descendants until by internal revolution or by being unseated and expelled from their hereditary offices by some conqueror, were said to have " died " in the linguistic idiom of their times

This interpretation of that idiom was suggested to me when studying St Paul's argument founded upon the history of Abraham The Apostle, in the fourth chapter of Romans, quotes the fact that Abraham believed the promise of the Divine messenger that he should beget a son, when between 80 and 100 years of age, as a stupendous exhibition of " faith in God," when he believed that God could accomplish that promise by restoring to him, Abraham, procreative power, which the patriarch knew had ceased in himself by the natural decay of age, as it did in all men But if Abraham's ancestor, Arphaxad and his father, Terah, and all his contemporaries, had been accustomed to his own knowledge to produce " sons and daughters " from 35 years of age until 478 to 500 years, as recorded in Genesis, Ch xi, and his grandfather, Nakhor, who died young, to 148, and Terah, his father, when 205 years old, it would have needed no faith at all of an extraordinary kind for Abraham to believe he could do the same when only 80, or need any special restoration of his youth by Divine power to enable him, as the messenger and the Apostle both said it did It has long appeared extraordinary to me that neither the assailants of the Bible, nor its defenders, have seen this question in the light I now put it, and which is undoubtedly the right one

St Paul was a man of the most powerful and clear intellect, and from his splendid line of inductive reasoning relating to the subject he had in hand, proves that he was accustomed to read the First Book (or, as we call it now, Chapters) of Genesis in a very different sense to modern students, and evidently, from his studies of ancient Asiatic writers, now lost to us through the barbarian ravages and stupid illiteracy of the Romans, with a knowledge that the sense was different to the idiom of his day, and what my own researches in Oriental literature and history have shown to be the correct one, as above

My defence for making this long note is, that this matter has been brought to me so frequently by sincere Christians as a tormenting source of doubt and mental unrest, and by anti-Christians triumphantly as a weapon to assail all religion, that I have felt it absolutely necessary to present the religious and scientific publics with the only true and rational solution of the problem, a solution supported by history —F FENTON

GENESIS

BOOK THE SECOND.

History of the House of Abram.

12　The EVER-LIVING then said to Abram, "Depart from your native land, and from the home of your forefathers, to the land to which I
2 will direct you And I will make you a great nation, and I will prosper and ennoble your name, and you
3 shall be a benefactor, and I will bless those who benefit you, and

punish those who injure you, and all the nations of mankind shall become benefited from you " So Abram 4 departed, as the EVER-LIVING had told him, and Lot accompanied him, and Abram was seventy-five years old at his departure from Haran Abram also took Sarai, his wife, and 5 Lot the son of his brother, and the whole of his property which he possessed, and the slaves which he had acquired in Haran, and he proceeded to travel to the land of Canaan, and he came to the country of Canaan

6 Then Abram travelled in that country to the village of Shekhem, as far as Alon-Moreh, and the Canaanites

7 were still in the land The EVER-LIVING also appeared to Abram, and repeated, " I will give this country to your descendants" So he there built an altar to the EVER-LIVING Who

8 had appeared to him Afterwards he removed from there to the hills at the East of Bethel, and pitched his tent with Bethel at the west and Haai to the east There he also built an Altar to the EVER-LIVING, and called upon the name of the EVER-

9 LIVING Then Abram marched on his journey, and proceeded to the south

Abram's Visit to Egypt, or the Mitzeraim.

10 But a famine occurred in the land, and Abram went down to Egypt to stay there for a time, as the famine

11 was severe in the land And as they were approaching Egypt, he said to Sarai his wife, " See now, I know

12 you are a fair woman, and it may be that when the Egyptians see you they will say, ' This is his wife', and they may murder me, and keep you

13 alive Say, therefore, that you are my sister, so that they may show respect to me because of you, and my life may be saved by means of you "

14 And on Abram entering Egypt, the Egyptians noticed that the woman

15 was very fair The courtiers of the Pharaoh also observed her and sung her praises to Pharaoh The woman was accordingly taken to Pharaoh's

16 palace On her account he favoured Abram, and presented him with sheep, oxen, asses, slaves, and maids, as well as she-asses, and camels But

17 the EVER-LIVING disturbed Pharaoh and his household greatly on account

18 of Sarai, the wife of Abram So Pharaoh summoned Abram, and

19 asked, " Why have you done this to me ? Why did you not inform me that she was your wife ? Why did you say, ' She is my sister' ? For I might have secured her as a wife for

20 myself But now take your wife, and go " And Pharaoh ordered his men about him, and they sent him away, and his wife and all that he had along with him

So Abram went up from Egypt 13 with his wife, and all he possessed, and Lot accompanied him to the southern pastures And Abram was 2 very rich in cattle, silver, and gold Afterwards he marched from the 3 south towards Bethel, to the place where his tent had at first been pitched, between Bethel and Haai, to the place where he had formerly 4 built an Altar, and there Abram called upon the name of the EVER-LIVING Lot also, who journeyed with Abram, 5 possessed sheep, cattle, and camp-followers, so that the land could not 6 support them living together, for their flocks were so great that they could not live together A dispute 7 accordingly took place between Abram's shepherds and Lot's shepherds, and the Canaanite and the Perizzite, who inhabited the land

So Abram said to Lot, " Let there 8 be no quarrel between me and you, or between my shepherds and your shepherds, for we are both of us brothers Is not all the country 9 before you ? I ask you to separate yourself from me, if you take to the left, then I will take to the right, if to the right, I will go to the left "

Lot therefore looked up, and 10 observed all the district of the Jordan, that it was everywhere well watered, before the LORD swept away Sodom and Gomorrah, it was like a Garden of the LORD, from the land of Egypt to the valley of Zoar So the whole plain of the Jordan 11 pleased him, and Lot marched to the east, and they separated from each other Abram accordingly remained 12 in the land of Canaan, and Lot remained in the villages of the plain, but resided at Sodom The men of 13 Sodom, however, were very wicked and sinful in the presence of the EVER-LIVING

The EVER-LIVING said to Abram, 14 after Lot separated from him, " Look upward, and from the place where you are take a view northward, and southward, and eastward, and westward, for all the land which you see, I will 15 give to you, and to your race for ever [1]

---

[1] The reader should carefully guard against taking the words " for ever" as meaning " eternally" or " without any cessation," as popular commentators have been wont to do It is used in the Bible, as we use it in daily life to indicate only a long, or indefinite period —I F

16 I will also make your race like the dust of the earth, so that if a man is able to count the dust of the earth,

17 then he can number your race. Arise and march through the land, inspect both its length and its breadth, for I

18 will give it to you." So Abram struck his camp, and came and settled in the Oakwoods of Mamrah which is near Hebron, and there he built an Altar to the EVER-LIVING.

War of Abram with the Five Kings

14 It was now in the reign of Amrafel, king of Shinar,[1] Ariok, king of Ellassar, Kedarlaomer, king of Elam,[2] and

2 Thidal, king of the Golim,[3] and they waged war with Bera, king of Sodom, and with Bersha, king of Gomorrah, Shinab, king of Admah, and Shemeber, king of Zeboim, and king Bela

3 of Zoar. All these were defeated in the valley of Siddim (now known as

4 the Salt Sea). They served Kedarlaomer for twelve years, but in the

5 thirteenth year they rebelled. Accordingly, in the fourteenth year, Kedarlaomer and his allied kings defeated the Refaim at Ashteroth's Horn, and the Zuzim at Ham along with them, and the Emim at the Devil's Horns,[4]

6 and the Horites in the mountains of Seir, as far as the pastures which

7 adjoin the desert. They then returned and came to the Well of Justice[5] and conquered all the plain of Amalakites, and also the Amorites who inhabited

8 the palm groves. The king of Sodom accordingly went out with the king of Gomorrah, and the king of Admah, and the king of Zeboim, and king Bela of Zoar, and they commenced hostili-

9 ties in the valley of Siddim with Kedarlaomer king of Elam, and Thidal king of nations, and Amrafel king of Shinar, and Ariok king of Ellassar—four kings against five

10 The valley of Siddim, however, was full of petroleum pits, and the kings of Sodom and Gomorrah took flight and fell there, and the Hillmen pur-

11 sued, and seized all the wealth of Sodom and Gomorrah, and the whole

12 of their stores and marched off. They also took Lot, the nephew of Abram, and his chattels when they marched,

for he resided in Sodom. A fugitive 13 then came and reported to Abram, the Colonist, who had settled at the Oakwoods of Mamrah, the Amorite, the brother of Ashkol, and brother of Aner, who were confederate chiefs with Abram. When Abram heard 14 that they had taken captive his relative, he then mustered the trained youths of his own family, to the number of three hundred and eighteen, and pursued to punish them, and overtook them in the night-time, 15 and he and his followers defeated and pursued them to Hobah, which is on the north of Damascus. And he re- 16 covered all the property, as well as Lot his relative, and his property, together with the men and the people 17

The king of Sodom then met him to congratulate him after his return from defeating Kedarlaomer, and the kings who were with him at the Devil's valley.[1] Melkizedek, also, king 18 of Salem, came out to them with wine, and he was a priest of ALMIGHTY GOD. And he gave him his blessing, 19 and said

"ALMIGHTY GOD, Creator of Heaven and Earth, bless Abram, and 20 you thank the Most High who gave your enemies into your hand."

He then gave to him a tenth of all the spoil.

The king of Sodom also said to 21 Abram, "You have given me my life, so take all the wealth to yourself."

But Abram replied to the king of 22 Sodom, "I have lifted my hand to the EVER-LIVING GOD ALMIGHTY, the Maker of Heaven and Earth, against 23 taking even a shoestring, or from taking anything that is yours, so that you may not say, 'I have made Abram rich,' except what the soldiers have 24 eaten, and the share of the men who came with me, Aner, Ashkol, and Mamrah—allow them to take their share."

The Ever-living appeals to Abram, with a Promise.

It was after these events that the 15 EVER-LIVING spoke to Abram in a vision, saying, "Be not afraid Abram, I am your Shield, your abundant reward, I will greatly enrich you."

---

1 Mesopotamia, as we now call it.
2 Western Persia.
3 The heathen.
4 Hebrew, "Shava Qirmim."
5 Or the Fountain of Judgment, "Kadesh.

---

1 "(The same as the King's Valley)" is an inserted note of an ancient transcriber, not a part of the original text. I therefore put it at th foot of the page.—F. F.

2 But Abram replied, "Mighty GOD, why should You give to me, when I go childless? and the possessor of my house will be Eliezer of Damascus?"

3 And Abram continued, "Look at me, You have not given me offspring, so that the steward of my house will become my heir"

4 But the EVER-LIVING answered him, saying, "That man shall not be your heir, but one who shall owe his birth to yourself, shall become your heir"

5 Then He took him to the open, and said, "Look up to the sky, and count the stars,—if you are able to count them," telling him also,

6 "Thus shall your race be" And Abram believed in the EVER-LIVING, and it was repaid to him in righteous-

7 ness He also said to him, "I am the EVER-LIVING Who brought you from Ur of the Kaldees to give you this land as an inheritance"

8 But he replied "Mighty LORD, how am I to know that I shall inherit it?"

9 Who answered him, "Select for me a three-year-old heifer, a three-year-old goat, a three-year-old ram, a turtle dove, and a young pigeon"

10 Taking all these he split them in the middle, and placed each part opposite its neighbour, but he did not split the

11 birds Then the kites descended upon the carcases, but Abram

12 drove them away And, when the sun was sinking, a stupor fell upon Abram, and also a great and terrible

13 darkness oppressed him

HE then said to Abram, "Know this, and be assured that your race will be foreigners in a land not their own, and they shall enslave them and oppress them for four hundred years

14 The nation which enslaves them, however, I will punish, and after that I will bring them out with great

15 wealth But you shall go to your forefathers in peace, you shall be buried with beautiful grey hairs

16 And in several generations they shall return here, when the sins of the Amorites will be complete"

17 After the sun set, followed by thick darkness, a bright cloud appeared, a blazing fire, which passed between the

18 pieces At the same time the EVER-LIVING made a covenant with Abram, saying, "I will give this country to your race from the River of Egypt

19 to the great River Euphrates The

20 Kenite, the Kenit... of the Kadmonite,

the Hittite and the Perizzite, and the 21 Refaim, and the Amorite, and the Canaanite, and the Girgashite, and the Jebusite"

Sarai advises Abram to marry Hagar.

Sarai, Abram's wife, had given him 16 no children, but she had an Egyptian maid named Hagar So Sarai said to 2 Abram, "See, now, the EVER-LIVING has kept me childless, therefore go to my maid, perhaps she will have a son for me" And Abram listened to the voice of Sarai Therefore Sarai, the 3 wife of Abram, took Hagar the Egyptian maid, at the end of the tenth year of Abram's residence in the land of Canaan, and gave her to Abram her husband, as a wife So he went to 4 Hagar, and she conceived, when she saw that she had conceived, her mistress was despicable in her eyes Then Sarai said to Abram, "My 5 wrong came from you I gave my maid to you as wife, and she sees that she has conceived, and I am despicable in her eyes Let the EVER-LIVING decide between me and you"

Abram answered Sarai, "Well, 6 your maid is under your hand, do to her whatever you consider right" So Sarai persecuted her, and she fled from her presence A messenger of 7 the EVER-LIVING met her, however, at the Well of Waters in the Desert at the Well by the road to the Wall,[1] 8 and asked, "Hagar, servant of Sarai, where are you going, and what are you weeping for?"

And she answered, "I am flying from the hand of Sarai, my mistress" But the messenger of the EVER-LIVING 9 said, "Return to your mistress, and submit yourself to her" The EVER- 10 LIVING'S messenger further said to her, "I will greatly increase your race, so that they cannot be numbered for multitude" The EVER-LIVING'S mes- 11 senger also continued, "You are now with child, and you will give birth to a son, and you must call his name Ishmael,[2] for GOD heard your sorrow And he shall be a free man, his hand 12 shall be with every man, and the hand of every man with him, and he shall stand up in the presence of all his brothers"

---

1 The wall across the Isthmus of Suez built to protect Egypt from border raiders

2 He shall hear God ישמעאל = Ishmael in Hebrew

13 She accordingly called the name of the EVER-LIVING Who spoke to her " You are the GOD I saw, I can say this, for I have lived after He appeared to me " So the well was named " the Well of the Vision of Life " It is situated between Kadesh

15 and Bered And Hagar gave birth to a son to Abram, and Abram called the name of his son by her, Ishmael [1]

16 Abram was eighty-six years old when Hagar gave birth to Ishmael to Abram

The Second Appearance of Jehovah to Abram, and Promise of a Son to Sarai.

17 When Abram was ninety-six years old, the EVER-LIVING appeared again to Abram, and said to him, " I am GOD ALMIGHTY, walk before Me and

2 be perfect, and I will make a Covenant between Myself and you, and I will increase you very, very greatly "

3 Abram then fell on his face, and

4 GOD spoke to him saying, " I now make a Covenant with you, and you shall be a father of many nations,

5 so your name shall be Abraham, for you shall be the father of many

6 nations And I will make you very fruitful, and I will make nations and

7 kingdoms proceed from you I will also establish My Covenant between Myself and you, and with your descendants after you from generation to generation for ever, to be a GOD

8 to you and your race after you I will also give to you and your race this country where you are a foreigner, the whole land of Canaan for a possession for ever, and I will be their GOD "

9 GOD also repeated to Abraham, " Now this is the Covenant which you shall keep, as well as your race after

10 you, in their generations This is the Covenant which you shall keep between Myself and you, and your race after you, Circumcise every male of them, and they shall be circumcised in the foreskin of the body, for an attestation of the Covenant

12 between Myself and them And upon the eighth day every male shall be circumcised, in their generations, whether born of the family, or purchased for money, although he is

13 not of your race Whoever is the child of your own family, or bought for money, shall be circumcised, and it is My Covenant in your body as an everlasting bond But the degraded 14 male who has not been circumcised shall then become separated from My people, because he has broken the Covenant "

GOD further said to Abraham, 15 " Sarai, your wife, shall no more be called by the name of Sarai, for Sarah shall be her name, and I will bless 16 her, and also give you a son from her, and she shall become the mother of nations, and of kings of peoples "

Then Abraham fell upon his face 17 and laughed, and said in his heart, " When I am an hundred years old ? and will Sarah also, when ninety years of age, have children ? " Then Abraham said to GOD, " I wish that Ishmael might live in Your favour "

God repeats His Promise to Ishmael

And GOD replied, " Feeble Sarah 19 your wife, shall give you a son, and you shall call his name Isaac, [1] and I will fix My Covenant with him as an everlasting Covenant for his race after him And for Ishmael I have also 20 heard you For My Covenant is also with him, I make My Covenant with him and I will increase him very greatly He shall beget twelve princes, and I will grant him to become a great nation, but that other 21 is the covenant I will fix with Isaac, whom Sarah your wife will bear about this time next year " Then He ceased to converse with him, and 22 the Divine Messenger went up from Abraham

Abraham accordingly took his son 23 Ishmael, and all who were born in his family, and all bought with his money, every male of the people of the household of Abraham, and circumcised the foreskin of their bodies on that very day which God spoke to him And Abraham was ninety-nine 24 years old when he was circumcised in the foreskin of the body Ishmael 25 also was thirteen years of age when he was circumcised in the foreskin of his body On the very same day 26 Abraham and his son Ishmael were circumcised All the men born in his house, or bought with his money, and foreigners, were circumcised with him

God appears a Third Time to Abraham.

18 The LORD again appeared to him at the Oakwoods of Mamrah, when he sat at the door of his tent in the heat of the day

2 Then he raised his eyes and looked, and saw three men standing opposite to him, and he looked, and called to them from the door of his

3 tent, and bowing to the ground, said, "My masters, if now I have found favour in your eyes, will you not come

4 in to your servant? Take a little water, and wash your feet, and rest

5 under the wood, and take a bit of bread, and refresh your heart, and afterwards proceed, perhaps for this you passed near your servant?"

And they replied, "Do as you have

6 said" Abraham then hastened into his tent to Sarah, and said, "Hasten with three measures of fine flour kneaded

7 and make cakes" Abraham also ran to the fold, and took a fine, fat calf and gave it to a youth, who at

8 once dressed it Then he took cheese and milk, and the calf which he had dressed, and placed before them and he stood opposite them under the

9 trees while they were eating They afterwards asked him, "Where is Sarah your wife?" and he replied, "She is in the tent"

10 They then said, "I will restore you, as at the period of youth, and there shall come a son from Sarah your wife," and Sarah heard it at the door of the tent, where she was behind

11 him Now, Abraham and Sarah were old—advanced in years and feeble It was not with Sarah as

12 women are, so Sarah laughed in her apartment, saying, "After I am wasted, will there be pleasure for me, even when my master is old?"

13 The Lord[1] consequently said to Abraham, "Why did Sarah laugh? saying, 'Shall I suckle a child when

14 I am old?' Is it a great thing for the EVER-LIVING to say, 'At such a time, I will return to you the period of youth, and give a son to Sarah'?"

15 But Sarah denied, replying, "I did not laugh," for she was afraid

He, however, answered, "Yes, you did laugh"

[1] The word Lord here does not mean the Almighty, but all the Prime Messenger See note on Exd. (Ch. 11) —P. 1

The Doom of Sodom

The men then departed from there, 16 and faced towards Sodom, and Abraham walked with them to converse Then the LORD said, 17 "Shall I conceal from Abraham what I am about to do? When 18 Abraham is to become a great and mighty nation, and every nation of the earth to be blest through him? For I have instructed him in order 19 that he may command his sons, and the sons of his house after him, that they must keep to the path of the EVER-LIVING, and do right and justice, so that the EVER-LIVING may cause to come upon Abraham what He has promised to him" So the 20 LORD continued "Sodom and Gomorrah shriek, for their sins are many; and are very grievous I 21 have therefore come down and I will see what causes the shrieks that have come to Me have they full cause? if not I will know"

So the men turned from there, and 22 went towards Sodom, but Abraham stood firm in the presence of the LORD, and Abraham approached 23 and said, "Will You destroy the just along with the wicked? If there are 24 fifty just persons within the city, will You destroy it, and not raise Your hand from the place, because of the fifty just persons that are within it? Far be it from You to do as You have 25 said, thus to kill the just with the wicked, and to make the just and the wicked alike It is far from You Will not the Judge of the whole earth do justice?"

The LORD accordingly answered, 26 "If I find fifty just men in the whole city of Sodom, then I will for their sakes take off My hand from all the place"

Then Abraham answered and said, 27 "See, now, I began to speak to my LORD, although I am but dust and ashes If there should want five just 28 persons of the fifty, will You sweep away the whole city for want of five?"

And He answered, "I will not sweep it away, if I find there forty-five"

But he continued still to speak to 29 Him, and said, "If there are found forty there?"

He replied, "I will not do it for the sake of the forty

'Still,' he said 'let not my LORD 30

be angry now, and I will speak, if thirty are found there?"

And He answered, "I will not do it if I find thirty"

31 He continued however, "See, now, I will dare to speak to my LORD, if there are found twenty there?"

And He answered, "I will not destroy it for the sake of the twenty"

32 He then said, "Let not my LORD be angry now, and I will speak once more, if ten are found there?"

And He replied, "I will not destroy it for the sake of the ten"

33 Then the LORD went to do what He had told to Abraham, and Abraham returned to his own place

The Destruction of Sodom for Sin

19 And two of the Messengers came to Sodom at evening, when Lot was sitting at the gate of Sodom, and Lot saw and rose to invite them, and

2 bowed his face to the ground, and said, "See now my good sirs, turn aside to the house of your servant, and rest yourselves, and wash your feet, and quench your thirst, and you can then proceed on your journey"

But they replied, "No, for we must go further"

3 Then he pressed them much, so they turned with him, and came to his house, and he made them a repast with unleavened cakes, and

4 they partook of them It was not yet time for sleep, when the men of the city, the men of Sodom, surrounded the house, from youths to old men, in fact, all the people of the

5 neighbourhood, and called out to Lot, and said to him, "Where are the men who came to you to-night? bring them out to us, that we may ravish them"

6 Lot however went out to them to the porch, and the doors were closed

7 behind him, and he said, "My friends, do not commit such wickedness

8 Look now, I have two virgin daughters, I will bring them to you, and you can do to them whatever you like, only to these men do not such a thing, for as a protection from it, they came to the shelter of my roof"

9 But they replied, "Be off with that! This fellow came here a foreigner, and he dictates decisions, now it shall be worse for you than for them"

Then they rushed to the man Lot with a vengeance, and attempted to break the gates But the men put 10 out their hands, and brought Lot to themselves into the house, and closed the gates, and they struck the men 11 in front of the house with blindness, from the youngest to the oldest, so that they could not find the door-way

Then the men said to Lot, "Now, 12 who is with you here, relative, or son or daughter, or any one that you have in this city, let them go out from this place, for we shall destroy 13 this place, for its great shriek has come before the EVER-LIVING, and the EVER-LIVING has sent us to destroy it" Lot therefore went out 14 and spoke to his relatives, to the husbands of his daughters, and said, "Come let us go out from this place, for the EVER-LIVING will destroy the city"

But he was considered a fool in the eyes of his relatives So, when dawn 15 arrived, the Messengers said to Lot, 'Get up, take your wife and your two daughters, and go out, for the crimes of this city are completed"

But he hesitated, so the men 16 seized hold of his hand, and the hand of his wife, and the hands of his two daughters, from the pity of the LORD towards him, and brought them out, and placed them outside the city And when they had brought 17 them out, they then said, "Fly for your life! Look not behind you, and delay not, in all the plain, take flight to the mountains, take yourself there"

But Lot answered them, "Oh! my 18 Lords, let now your servant find favour in your sight, and increase the kindness which you have done to me, to enliven my soul, for I am not able to 19 escape to the hills before the disaster will overtake me, and I shall die See 20 now this city, it is easy to escape there, in a little time I can escape to there, is it not a trifle? and my life will be preserved"

So one replied to him, "Yes, I will 21 accept your presence, also for this thing, I will not destroy this town on behalf of which you have spoken Be 22 quick to escape there, for I am not able to do the thing until you arrive there" He accordingly called the name of that place Tzoar[1] The 23

---

[1] Truth

P ↳ C

sun had risen above the land when Lot entered Tzoar

24 The EVER-LIVING then rained upon Sodom, and upon Gomorrah, lightning and fire from the EVER-

25 LIVING from the skies, and overwhelmed those towns, them and all the plain, and all the inhabitants of the towns, and the produce of the

26 land But his wife looked back, and was transformed into a pillar of salt

27 And when Abraham went in the morning to the place where he stood

28 before the Lord, and looked out towards Sodom and Gomorrah and towards all the land of the plain, he saw and perceived a stench and smoke rise up from the country, like the smoke from a furnace

29 Thus it was that GOD destroyed the cities of the plain But GOD remembered Abraham, and sent Lot beyond the reach of the destruction with which he destroyed those towns

30 where Lot lived And Lot went up from Tzoar, and settled in the hills along with his two daughters, for he was afraid to stay in Tzoar, so he lived in a cave along with his two

31 daughters And the elder said to the younger, " Our father grows old, and there is not a man in the country to come to us as others do all the

32 world over Come on, let us make our father drunk with wine, and cohabit with him, and it may be that we shall have children by our father "

33 So they made their father drunk with wine that night and the elder went and lay with her father, but he was not aware of the fact when she lay down or rose up

34 It was some time afterwards that the elder said to the younger, " See, I went with my father the other night, let us make him drunk with wine also to-night, and you can go and lie with him, and it may be you will have

35 children by your father " So they made their father drunk also that night with wine, and the younger rose and went with him, and he knew not when she lay down or

36 when she rose up Thus both of the daughters of Lot conceived from

37 their father Then the elder gave birth to a son, and she called his name Moab, he was the ancestor of

38 Moab, of to-day And the younger also gave birth to a son, and she called I
the anc

Abraham and Abimelek.

Abraham then removed quietly **20** from there landward, and settled between Kadesh and the Wall, and resided in Gherar And as Abraham **2** said of Sarah his wife, " She is my sister," Abimelek the king of Gherar sent and took Sarah GOD, however, **3** came to Abimelek in a dream at night, and said, " Beware of death because of this woman whom you have taken, for she is a man's wife "

But Abimelek had not made advances to her, so he replied, " My **4** LORD, would you kill a just person ? Has not this man said to me ' She is **5** my sister ?' and did not she herself say to me, ' He is my brother ?' In the honesty of my heart, and the innocence of my hand, I have done this "

Then GOD said to him in a dream, **6** " I also know that in the honesty of your heart you have done this, so I restrained you, I also warned you from sin against Me , therefore I did not permit you to approach her So **7** now return the woman to her husband, for he is a Great Teacher, and will intercede for you But if you do not return her, know that you shall certainly die, and all that you have "

When Abimelek awoke in the **8** morning, he called his ministers, and related in their hearing the whole of these events, and the men were greatly afraid Abimelek con- **9** sequently called Abraham and asked him, " What have you done to us ? and what have I sinned against you, that you have brought on me and my kingdom this great danger for acts they have not done ? You have done us a wrong " And Abimelek continued to Abraham, " What have you seen that you have done this thing ?"

But Abraham replied, " I said that, **10** perhaps, there is no fear of GOD in this place, and they will kill me on **11** account of my wife And indeed she **12** is my sister, the daughter-in-law of my father, but not of my mother , and she was given to me for a wife But **13** when GOD caused me to be a wanderer from my father's house, then I said to her, ' This is the kindness which you shall show to me in every place where we come , say I am your brother '"

sheep, **14**
gave to

Abraham, and he returned Sarah his wife to him And Abimelek said,

15 " See my country is before you, stay wherever it is good for your eyes , " while to Sarah he said, " I have given a thousand gifts to this ' brother ' of yours, for he must be a covering of the eyes to all who are with you, and to all who meet you "

17 Then Abraham appealed for Abimelek to GOD and GOD made the wives of Abimelek fruitful, and his servants as well, and they gave birth to chil-

18 dren , because the EVER-LIVING had sterilized those of the household of Abimelek, on account of Sarah the wife of Abraham

The Promise fulfilled in Isaac.

21 The EVER-LIVING afterwards effected with Sarah what He had promised, and the LORD did for Sarah

2 that which He had said , and Sarah conceiving, gave birth to a son to Abraham in his old age, in the way

3 that GOD had promised him Abraham accordingly gave the son born to him

4 by Sarah, the name of Isaac , and Abraham circumcised Isaac on the eighth day, as GOD had instructed

5 him And Abraham was then one hundred years old when his son Isaac

6 was born to him Sarah then said,

"GOD has made a delight for me ,
For He has heard my laugh to Him,
All who hear will laugh with me , "

7 and she continued,

"For Abraham I am a flowing brook,
He has made me suckle children,
For I have borne a son to his age '

8 When the lad grew and was weaned, Abraham celebrated the weaning of

9 Isaac with a great feast Sarah also saw the son, which Hagar the Egyptian had borne to Abraham, playing ,

10 and said to Abraham, " Drive out my maid and her son, for the son of this slave shall not be an inheritor with my son Isaac "

The Renewed Promise to Ishmael

11 But in Abraham's view, this speech was very bad, in regard to his son ,

12 but GOD said to Abraham " Let it not be disheartening in your sight, do all that Sarah has said against the lad, and against his mother Listen

to what she says , for from Isaac I will nominate an Heir to you And also 13 from the son of your second wife I will found a great nation — for he is your heir "

Abraham accordingly rose up at 14 dawn , and taking bread and a skin of water, he placed them on the shoulder of Hagar, and the lad's, and sent her away , and she went and wandered in the desert of Beer-sheba 1 When the water in the skin was ex- 15 hausted, however, she placed the lad under a bush, and went and seated 16 herself on the other side, she said, " I shall not then see the lad's death ' So she rested on the other side, and she raised her voice and wept GOD 17 then heard the voice of the youth, and a Messenger of GOD called from the sky to Hagar and said to her, " What, Hagar, is the matter ? Be not afraid, for GOD has heard the voice of the lad from where he is Arise, 18 take the lad, and support him, for I will make from him a great Nation " Then GOD opened her eyes, and she 19 saw a spring of water, and she gave the lad a drink Thus GOD gave life 20 to the lad, and he grew, and dwelt in the desert, and became a mighty archer, and settled in the desert of 21 Paran , and she took a wife for him from the land of Egypt

Abraham's Treaty with Abimelek.

It was about this time that Abime- 22 lek, and Pikol the commander of his army, addressed Abraham, saying, " GOD is with you in all that you do So now take an oath to me before 23 GOD, that you may not deceive, and to my children and posterity, that the kindness which I have shown to you, you will show to me, and to the land where you have been a foreigner "

And Abraham replied, " I will take 24 the oath " Abraham then reproved 25 Abimelek about the affair of the well of water, which the servants of Abimelek had stolen

Then Abimelek answered, " I did 26 not myself know of that matter , and neither did you report it to me , and I never heard it until to-day "

Abraham then took sheep and oxen, 27 and gave to Abimelek, and the two entered into a treaty

Abimelek then asked Abraham, 28

---

1 The Well of the Oat

29 "What are these seven lambs for, which you have put by themselves?

30 "You take these seven lambs from my hand," he answered, "that they may be an evidence for me that I

31 dug this well." They accordingly called that place the Well of the

32 Oath,[1] and he entered into a treaty at the Well of the Oath, with both Abimelek and Pikol, the commander of his army. Then they returned to

33 the land of the Philistines. They also planted tamarisk trees by the Well of the Oath, and called there on the name of the EVER-LIVING ETERNAL

34 GOD. So Abraham remained in the land of the Philistines for many days

The Trial of Abraham's Faith.

22 After these events, GOD tried Abraham and said to him, "Abraham," and he replied "I am here"

2 Then He said, "Take your son, your peculiar one, whom you love—Isaac—and go to the Land of Vision, and offer him there as a burnt-offering upon one of the hills which I will point out to you"

3 When Abraham woke in the morning he saddled his ass, and took two youths along with him, and Isaac his son, and split up wood for a sacrifice, and they rose up and went to the

4 place which GOD had told him. On the third day, Abraham looked up, and saw the spot some distance off

5 Then Abraham said to his attendants, "Stay here by yourselves, with the ass, and the lad and I will go and worship, and will then return to you"

6 Abraham accordingly took the wood for the sacrifice and placed it upon Isaac his son, and took in his own hand the fire and the knife, and the two went together

7 Isaac then said to Abraham, his father, "My father,' and he replied, "I am here, my son' "There is fire and wood," he said, "but where is the lamb for the burnt-offering?'"

8 "GOD," answered Abraham, "will provide a lamb for Himself for a burnt-offering, my son," so they

9 went on together. When they came to the place that GOD had commanded him, Abraham built an altar, and arranged the wood, and bound Isaac his son, and laid him upon the altar,

10 upon the top of the wood. Then Abraham stretched out his hand, and

took the knife to slaughter his son;

11 but a Messenger from the EVER-LIVING called to him from the skies, and said, "Abraham! Abraham!" And he replied, "I am here"

12 "Stretch not your hand against the young man," he said, "nor do to him what you intended, for now I know that you reverence GOD, and would not withhold from Me your son, your special one"

13 Abraham then looked up and saw a goat caught in a bush by its horns. So Abraham went, and took the goat, and offered it as a burnt-offering,

14 instead of his son. Abraham therefore called the name of that place Jehovah-Irah[1]

15 Then the messenger of the EVER-LIVING called again to Abraham from the skies, and said to

16 him, "I promise," the LORD declares,

17 "that because you have done this thing, and not held back your special son, that when blessing I will bless you, and when increasing I will increase your race as the stars of the skies, and like the sand upon the sea-shore, and your race shall possess

18 the gates of its enemies, and I will benefit all the nations of the earth through your heir, because you have listened to My voice"

19 Abraham afterwards returned to his attendants, and they rose up and went back to the Well of the Oath

20 After these events a message was delivered to Abraham, "Your sister Milka has given birth to children to

21 Nahor your brother, Uz and his brother Buz, and Kemuel the father

22 of Aram, and Kesed, and Hazo, and Kildash, and Zidlaf, and Bethuel,

23 and Bethuel has produced Rebekka, these eight Milka has borne to Nahor your brother. And his second wife,

24 whose name is Raumah, she also has given birth to Tabakh, and Gaham, and Thahash, and Makah"

The Death of Sarah.

23 Now the life of Sarah was one hundred and twenty-seven years, the

2 whole of the life of Sarah, and Sarah died in Kirath-Arba,[2] in the land of Canan, and Abraham came to mourn and lament for Sarah

---

1 The Revealing LORD. The words, "It is said to this day, In the Hill of the LORD it can be seen,' are a note of an old copyist, not part of the text of Moses.—F F

2 . . . . . . an ancient

3 Then Abraham rose up from the presence of his dead, and spoke to
4 the sons of Heth saying, "I am a foreigner and wanderer with you, give me the possession of a grave among you, and I can bury my dead from my sight"

5 And the sons of Heth replied to Abraham, "We listen to my lord, who stands like a god among us
6 Choose from our tombs a grave for your dead None of us will deny his tomb to you, where you can bury your dead"

7 Then Abraham rose up, and bowed to the people of the land, to the sons
8 of Heth, and addressed them saying, "If it is in your minds to let my dead be buried from my sight, listen to me, and apply for me to Ephron, the
9 son of Tzohar, and let him sell to me the Cave of Macphelah, which is within the boundaries of his land He shall sell it to me for full value as a tomb possessed among you"

10 Now Ephron resided among the sons of Heth, and Ephron spoke after Abraham, in the hearing of the sons of Heth, to all who came to the
11 gates of the town, saying, "No, my lord, listen to me! I give you the field, and the cave that is in it, I give it to you in the presence of the sons of my people, I give it to you as a grave to bury your dead"

12 Then Abraham bowed to the people
13 of the land, and addressed Ephron in the hearing of the people of the land, saying, "Nay, if you are disposed to listen to me, I will pay you money for the field, so accept it from me and I will bury my dead there"

14 Then Ephron, in reply to Abraham
15 said, "My lord, listen to me, for four hundred shekels of money between me and you, the land is yours, and you can bury your dead

16 So Abraham listened to Ephron, and Abraham weighed to Ephron the money which he had agreed upon, in the sight of the sons of Heth, four hundred shekels of silver currency
17 Thus he bought the field of Ephron, that is in Macphelah, which is opposite Mamrah, the field and the cave which is in it, and all the trees which were in the field, with all the hedge
18 around it Thus Abraham bought it in the presence of the sons of Heth, of all who came to the gate of the
19 town, and after that, Abraham . buried Sarah his wife in the cave of

the field of Macphelah, opposite Mamrah,[1] in the land of Canan, and the field with the cave in it was 20 acquired by Abraham for a burial ground from the sons of Heth

The History of Isaac's Marriage.

Abraham however grew old, and 24 advanced in years, and the LORD had prospered Abraham in everything Then Abraham said to his servant, 2 the chief of his household, and steward over all he had "I wish you to put your hand under my thigh, and take 3 an oath to me by the EVER-LIVING, the GOD of Heaven, and the GOD of the earth, that you will not take a wife for my son from the Cananites, among whom I reside, but that you 4 will go to my old family, and take a wife for my son Isaac"

But the servant asked him, "If a 5 woman does not desire to come along with me to this country, shall I return and take your son to the land from which you came?"

When Abraham, in reply to him 6 said, "Be careful not to take my son there The EVER-LIVING, the GOD 7 of Heaven, who took me from my father's home, and from the land of my birth, and who spoke to me, and also took oath to me, saying, 'I will give this country to your race,' He will send His Messenger before you, and you will bring a wife for my son from there But if a woman does not 8 desire to come along with you, then you shall be free from this oath, except that you must never take my son there"

Abraham's servant accordingly put 9 his hand under the thigh of his master, and took an oath to him upon this matter The servant afterwards took 10 ten camels of his master, and plenty of his master's wealth in his hand, and rose up, and went to Aram-between-the-Rivers, to the town of Nahor, and he knelt the camels out- 11 side the town, at the well of water, in the evening, at the time when they came out to draw water, and prayed,— 12

"EVER-LIVING GOD of my master, Abraham, turn now Your face to-day, and do a kindness to my master

1 The words, "That is now Hebron," are th o t of m oie nt editic a t part of the origined ax t t He bro n had n e attained its name in the days of M s ——J P

13 Abraham I am here encamped at the spring of water, and the daughters of the men of the town will come out

14 to draw water, so let it be, that when the girl to whom I say, 'Hand me your jar, and I will drink,' if she replies, 'Drink, and I will also give drink to your camels,' let Your servant take her to Isaac, for by that I shall know that You will do a kindness to my master"

15 And it so happened, as he was coming to the end of his prayer, that Rebekka, who was the daughter of Bethuel, the son of Milka, wife of Nahor, the brother of Abraham, came out with a bucket upon her shoulder,

16 and the girl was very beautiful to look upon, a maiden, who had no sweetheart, and she ran to the well, filled

17 her bucket, and drew it up The steward was delighted, and spoke to her, and said, "Will you give me a drink of a little of the water from your bucket?"

18 "Drink, sir," was her reply, and she tripped on, and lowered her bucket to her hand and gave him a

19 drink When she had given him a drink, she added, "And now, I will draw for your camels, that they may

20 all have a drink" Then she ran and carried her bucket to the spring, and dipped it into the well to draw, and

21 she drew for all the camels The man watched her silently, to know whether or not the EVER-LIVING had granted prosperity to his journey

22 And when she had watered all the camels, then the man took a brooch of gold of half a shekel, and placed on her arms two bracelets of rich

23 gold of a shekel and said, "My girl, will you now ask the men of your father's house for a place for us to lodge in?"

24 And she answered him, "I am the daughter of Bethuel, the son of Milka,

25 whom she had to Nahor" And she continued, "We have plenty of straw and fodder, and room enough for you to lodge"

26 Then the man bowed, and thanked

27 the EVER-LIVING, and said, "Thank the EVER-LIVING GOD of my master Abraham, Who has not forgotten His goodness and truth to my master, for the EVER-LIVING has led me to the house of the brother of my master"

28 And the girl ran and reported to the house of her mother, as it is here

29 related And to Rebekka's brother

whose name was Laban Then Laban rose to go to the man who rested near

30 the well, when he saw the brooches and the bracelets on the hands of his sister, and heard the words of Rebekka his sister, "That the man said this to me," he went to the man, who re-

31 mained by the well with his camels, and said, "Come in, you blessed of the LORD Why do you stand out-

32 side, when I offer you the house, and a stable for your camels?" Then the man entered his house, and he unloaded the camels, and gave straw and fodder to the camels, and water to wash his feet, and the feet of the young men, who were

33 with him He also placed food before them

But he replied, "I will not eat until I have delivered my message"

"Speak," he said

34 "I am the servant of Abraham," he answered, "and the EVER-LIVING has prospered my master very greatly,

35 and has given to him sheep and oxen, and silver and gold, and men and women servants, camels and asses

36 Sarah also, my master's wife, had a son to my master, a son in his old age, and he will give him all he has

37 Now my master has pledged me to say, 'Take not a wife for my son from the daughters of the Cananites among whom I reside in their land,

38 but go instead, to the home of my father, and choose a wife for my son

39 from among my own family' I re-

40 plied to my master, 'Perhaps the woman will not come with me' Then he said to me, 'The EVER-LIVING Who has caused me to walk in His presence, will send His Messenger along with you, and He will guide you in your path so as to secure a wife for my son, from among the children of my own tribe, and from

41 the home of my father So take an oath to me that you will go to my tribe, and if they will not give to you, you shall be free from your oath to

42 me' And I came to-day to the well, and said, 'LORD the GOD of my master Abraham, if it pleases You,

43 point me to the path that I should follow See! I have arrived at this well of water, so let it be that when a young girl comes to draw, when I say to her give me a little water from your bucket and she answers to me,

Drink and I will also draw for the camels, she is the wife

the LORD will grant to the son of my
44 master' This speech had not come
to an end on my lips, when Rebekka
approached with her bucket upon
45 her shoulder, and she dropped it into
the well, and drew Then I said to
46 her, 'Pray, give me a drink,' and she
quickly lowered the bucket from off
her, and said, 'Drink, and I will
also water your camels' So I drank,
and she watered the camels as well
47 Then I inquired of her and asked,
'My girl, who are you?' And she
replied, 'The daughter of Bethuel,
the son of Nahor, whom Milka had
to him' So I placed the brooches
on her brow, and the bracelets upon
48 her hands Then I bowed to the
LORD and worshipped, and thanked
the EVER-LIVING GOD of my master
Abraham, Who had been kind to me,
leading me in the right way to the
house of the brother of my master,
49 for his son And now, if it is your
will to show kindness and truth to
my master, inform me, and if not,
tell me so, and I will turn to the
right or to the left"
50 　　Then Laban and Bethuel answered
and said, "This has proceeded from
the LORD, we are not able to say to
51 you either good or ill See, Rebekka
is before you, take her and go, and
she shall be a wife to the son of your
master, as the EVER-LIVING has
directed"
52 　　And when Abraham's steward heard
their words, he bowed to the ground
53 to the LORD The steward also
brought out ornaments of silver, and
ornaments of gold and clothing, and
put them upon Rebekka, and gave
treasures to her brother and mother
54 Then they ate and drank he and the
men with him, and rested, and rising
in the morning, he said, "I will now
55 return to my master" The brother
and mother, however, said, "Let the
girl remain with us a day or two,
after that she shall go"
56 　　He, however, replied, "If she will
not go with me, then the LORD will
prosper the way of return, and I
will go back to my master"
57 　　Then they said, "Let the girl be
58 called, and ask her own self" So
they called Rebekka, and asked her,
"Will you go with this man?" "I
59 will go," was her reply They, therefore, sent off Rebekka their sister,
with her nurse, and the steward of
60 Abraham and his attendants and

they gave Rebekka their blessing, and
said to her,
　　"You are our sister Increase to
thousands, and may your descendants
possess the gate of their enemies"
Then they lifted Rebekka and her 61
attendants, and placed them upon
camels and they rode after the man,
thus the steward took Rebekka and
departed
　　Now, Isaac was travelling towards 62
the Well of Vision, for he resided in
the south country, and he had come 63
out to meditate in the field at the
approach of the evening, and there
he raised his eyes and looked, and
saw camels coming Rebekka also 64
raised her eyes, and saw Isaac, and
dismounted from her camel, and asked 65
the steward, "What man is that who
walks in the field?" and the steward
replied, "He is my master" So she
took a veil, and put it on Then the 66
steward reported to Isaac all the
things that he had done, and Isaac 67
brought her to the tent of his mother
Sarah, so he took Rebekka, and she
was a wife to him, and he loved her,
and Isaac was comforted after his
mother

Abraham and Keturah.

Abraham prospered, and he took 25
a wife whose name was Keturah, and 2
she bore him Zimram, and Yokshan,
and Midan, and Midian, and Ishbak,
and Shuakh And Yokshan begot 3
Sheba, and Dedan And the sons of
Dedan were Ashurim, and Tushim,
and Lammim And the sons of 4
Midian, Aifah and Afer, and Hanok,
and Abida, and Aldaha, all were
descendants from Keturah Abraham 5
left all that was with him to Isaac,
but to the sons of the secondary wives 6
that Abraham had, Abraham gave
fortunes and sent them from his son
Isaac, during his own life, to the east
of the eastern country
　　These were the days of the life of 7
Abraham that he lived, one hundred
and seventy-five years, so Abraham 8
expired and died, a fine grey-headed
old man, and satisfied, and they placed
him with his people, and his sons 9
Isaac and Ishmael buried him in the
cave of Makphelah on the estate of
Ephron the son of Zohar the Khivite,
which is before Mamrah, the field 10
which Abraham bought from the sons
of Heth, there Abraham was buried

11 with Sarah his wife. After the death of Abraham GOD prospered Isaac his son, and he resided at the Well of Vision

The History of Ishmael

12 Now these are the sons of Ishmael, son of Abraham, whom Hagar, the Egyptian, the slave of Sarah, had by

13 Abraham These are the names of the sons of Ishmael, by the names of their families The eldest of Ishmael was Nebioth, and Kedar, and Abdal,

14 and Mibsam, Mishma, and Dumah,

15 and Masa, Khader, and Thema,

16 Zetur, Nafish, and Kadmah These were sons of Ishmael, and these their names, by their villages and towers, twelve men by their nations

17 The years of the life of Ishmael were a hundred and thirty-seven years, when he expired and died, and was

18 added to his people, and they took him from Havilah to the Wall which is between Egypt and the road to Ashur, laying him with all his relatives

History of Isaac

19 And these are the children of Isaac, son of Abraham, Abraham begat

20 Isaac And Isaac son of Abraham was forty years old when he took for his wife Rebekka the daughter of Bethuel the Aramite of Padan Aram, and sister of Laban the Aramite

21 And Isaac prayed to the EVER-LIVING about his wife, for she was childless, and the LORD answered him, for

22 Rebekka his wife conceived, and the children struggled together in her breast and she consequently said, "Why does this happen to me?" so went to enquire of the EVER-LIVING

23 And the LORD said to her, "Two nations are in your breast, and two peoples shall proceed from your womb, and one people shall be stronger than the other people, and the elder shall serve the younger"

24 When her days were full for her

25 delivery there were twins, and the first born boy came out covered with hair, and she called his name

26 Esau [1] Then after him came his brother, with his hand holding the heel of Esau, so they called his name Jacob [2]

Isaac was sixty years old at the birth of them

Esau sells his Birthright foolishly.

When the lads grew up, Esau was 27 a man skilful in hunting,—a man of the field, but Jacob was a quiet man,— a stayer in the tent So Isaac loved 28 Esau because he hunted with him, but Rebekka loved Jacob

Once when Jacob was boiling por- 29 ridge, Esau came from the field, and he was exhausted, so Esau said to 30 Jacob, "Feed me now with that red porridge, for I am exhausted", there- fore they called his name "Red-soup"[1]

But Jacob replied, "Sell me your 31 Birthright to-day"

Then Esau answered, "Now I am 32 going to die—what is that Birthright to me?"

So Jacob said, "Swear to me now 33 at once" And he swore to him, and sold his Birthright to Jacob

Then Jacob gave to Esau bread 34 and lentil porridge, and he ate, and drank, and rose up, and went Thus Esau was careless about his Birthright

Isaac during a Famine goes to Gherar.

Afterwards there was a famine in 26 the land, beside the former famine which was in the days of Abraham, so Isaac went to Abimalek, king of the Philistines of Gherar Then the 2 EVER-LIVING appeared to him in a vision and said, "Descend not to Mitzer,[2] dwell in the land that I promised you, remain in this land, 3 and I will be with you, and will bless you, for to you and your race I will give the whole of this country as a dwelling, and I will complete the oath which I swore to your father Abraham, and I will increase your race like the 4 stars of the sky, and I will give to your race the whole of this country for a home, and I will bless all the nations of the earth through your Heir In accordance with what I 5 promised to Abraham according to My words,—'if you will carefully keep My commands and statutes and 6 laws'" So Isaac remained in Gherar

When the men of the place asked 7 about his wife, he replied, "She is my sister," for he feared to say, "my wife," lest the men of the place should murder him for Rebekka, for she was beautiful to look on After he had 8 resided a considerable time, it hap- pened that Abimalek king of the Philis-

---

1 The Hair   2 Or Tirgum up   1 Edom   2 Egypt

tines was looking out of his window, when he saw Isaac sporting with his

9 wife Rebekka Abimalek therefore summoned Isaac, and said, "Now she is your wife!—then why did you say to me 'she is my sister'?"

And Isaac answered, "Because I said to myself, I fear they will kill me because of her"

10 "Why did you do so to us?" Abimalek said, "perhaps one of the people might have lain with your wife, and you would have brought sin

11 upon us" Abimalek, therefore, commanded to all his people, saying, "Whoever touches this man, he shall as surely die"

Isaac goes to Bashan and Elsewhere.

12 Isaac, however, removed from that country, and went to Bashan, he and his possessions, and the EVER-LIVING

13 prospered him Thus the man travelled about and increased until

14 he was very great He also had flocks of sheep and herds of cattle, and many servants, and the Philistines

15 were envious of him, so the Philistines filled with earth all the wells that the servants of his father Abra-

16 ham had dug in his days Abimalek, also, said to Isaac, "Go from among us, for you are much stronger than

17 we" So Isaac went from there, and encamped by the river Gherar, and

18 remained there Isaac, also, settled, and cleared out the wells of water which were dug in the time of his father Abraham, and he called them by the names they were called in the

19 days of his father The servants of Isaac also dug in the valley and discovered there a spring of living water

20 But the shepherds of Gherar contended with the shepherds of Isaac, and said, "The water is ours," so he called the name of the well Strife,

21 because they disputed with him He therefore dug another well, and they contended about that also, so he

22 called its name Contention He then removed from there, and dug another well, and they did not fight over it, so he called its name "Room-enough," for he said, "Now, LORD, You have given us room, and made us fruitful

23 in the land" Afterwards he arose from there and went to the Well of the Oath

24 And the EVER-LIVING appeared to him that night, and said, "I am the GOD of your father Abraham fear

not, I am with you, and will bless you and increase your race, because of My servant Abraham"

25 Then he built an altar at the place and called on the name of the EVER-LIVING and he pitched his tent there The servants of Isaac also dug a well

26 But Abimalek went to him from Gherar, with his chief herdsman, and

27 Pikol, the general of his army Isaac, therefore, asked them, "Why have you come to me? when you are my enemies, and have driven me from among you?"

28 And they replied,—"We are terribly afraid, because GOD is with you so we would say, let there now be an under-

29 standing between us and you, and let a treaty be made with you so that you will not do wrong to us, if we do not touch you, and as we have certainly done good to you, and sent you away in peace You are now The Blessed of the EVER-LIVING"

30 He therefore made them a feast,

31 and they ate and drank, and rose up in the morning when they swore each to his brother Then Isaac sent them away, and they went from him in

32 peace In the same day also the servants of Isaac came and informed him about the well which they had dug, and they said "We have found

33 water" He therefore called it "Satisfaction" Consequently the name of the village by that well is called Satisfaction[1] to this day

The History of Esau; and of Jacob's Deception.

34 When Esau was forty years old, he took as a wife Judith the daughter of Bari the Hitite, and Basmath the

35 daughter of Ailon the Hitite But they were a bitter wind to Isaac and Rebekka

27 And when Isaac was old, and his eyes dim that he could not see, he called his eldest son Esau, and said to him, "My son," and he replied,

2 "I am here" Then he said, "See now, I am old, and I know not the

3 day of my death, so now take up your spear, quiver, and bow, and go to the field and hunt venison for me,

4 and make me tasty food such as I love, and bring it to me, and I will eat it, so that my soul may bless you before I die"

5 But Rebekka heard the speech of Isaac to Esau his son and that Esau

1 Shiloh in Hebrew.—L T

had gone to the field to hunt venison

6 to bring in   Then Rebekka spoke to Jacob her son, and said, " I have just heard your father speak to your brother

7 Esau, saying, ' Bring to me venison, and make me tasty food, that I may eat it, and I will bless you before I die '

8 So now my son, listen to my voice to

9 do what I shall order you   Go to the flock, and select for me two good kids of the goats and I will make tasty food for your father such as he

10 loves, and you shall carry it to your father, when he will eat, and because of it he will bless you before his death "

11   But Jacob said to Rebekka his mother   " But my brother Esau is a hairy man, and I am a smooth man,

12 when my father feels me I shall be in his eyes like a swindler, and shall bring a curse on myself, and not a blessing "

13   His mother however said to him, " Let any curse for you come on me my son, only you go and do as I tell you '

14   He consequently went, and did it, and brought to his mother, and she made for him tasty food such as his

15 father loved   Then Rebekka took some of the clothes of her son Esau, which were in the house with her, and put them on her younger son

16 Jacob, and put the skins of the kids of the goats on his hands, and the

17 smooth part of his neck   Then she gave the dainties and the bread which she had made into the hand of her

18 younger son Jacob, and he went to his father, and said to him, "Father," and he replied, " I am here, who are

19 you ?" When Jacob answered, " I am your eldest son Esau, I have done as you asked me   Rise now, turn and eat of my venison, so that your soul may bless me "

20   Isaac, however, asked his son, " How is it you have been so quick in meeting with it my son ?"

  So he replied, " Because your EVER-LIVING GOD brought it before me "

21   Then Isaac said to Jacob, " Come near me, my son, and I will feel if you are really my son Esau, or no "

22   So Jacob approached to Isaac his father and he felt him, and said " The voice is the voice of Jacob, but the hands are the hands of Esau,"

23 therefore he did not detect him because his hands were like the hands of his brother Esau hairy

and he was thankful   Yet he asked, 24 " Are you really my son Esau ? " and he replied, " I am "

  Then he said, " Bring it to me and 25 I will eat of the venison of my son, so that my soul may bless you "

  He consequently presented it to 26 him and he ate, and he brought wine to him and he drank

  Then Isaac his father said, " Come 27 close now, my son, and give me a drink "   So he approached and gave him a drink, and he smelt the smell of his clothes and was satisfied, and said,— ' Yes ' the smell of my son is like the smell of a field which the LORD has blessed, so may GOD give 28 to you the dew from the skies, and the fatness of the earth, and increase and possession   Nations shall serve 29 you, and bow down to you, yes, a multitude of mighty peoples, with your brothers also shall pay tribute to you, my son   If any curses you, he shall be cursed, and if any blesses you, he shall be blessd "

  But it happened that as Isaac 30 finished blessing Jacob, and Jacob had gone away from the presence of Isaac his father, that Esau his brother came with his venison, and 31 he also had made dainties, and brought them to his father and said to his father, " Arise, my father, and eat of the venison of your son, so that your soul may bless me "

  Isaac his father however asked of 32 him, " Who are you ?" and he replied " I am your firstborn son Esau "

  Then Isaac was terrified with a 33 very great terror, and asked, " Who then is he who has hunted venison, and brought it to me, and I have eaten of all before you came, and I have blessed him ?—Yes and he must be blessd "

  When Esau heard the speech of 34 his father, then he cried with a very great and bitter cry, and said to his father, " Bless me, also me, my father "

  But he replied, " Your brother has 35 come with deception and stolen your blessing "

  And he answered, " He was 36 rightly named ' Tripper-up '[1] for he has tricked me this twice, to take my birthright, and also now to take my

1   Tripper-up   1   Hebrew Yakob = English [ ]

blessing " Then he asked, "Have you not a blessing left for me ?"

37 But Isaac replied and said to Esau, " Since I have made him your Master, and have given all his brothers to him for servants, and with increase and possession I have endowed him, —where now my son is there anything I can do ?"

38 But Esau said to his father, "Is there then only One Blessing with you my father ? Bless me also, my father," and Esau lifted up his voice and wept

39 Then Isaac his father answered and said to him,

"Yes ! in the most fertile land shall be your dwelling

And with the dew from the skies above

40 And you shall live by your sword, but shall serve your brother,

Yet when you extend, you shall break his yoke

From off your neck "

41 But Esau hated Jacob for the blessing with which his father had blessed him, and Esau said in his heart, " The day approaches for the mourning of my father, when I will kill my

42 brother " But the words of her elder son Esau were reported to Rebekka, so she sent and called her younger son Jacob, and said to him, "Now Esau, your brother, intends to

43 kill you, consequently my son listen to my voice, and arise and go away to Laban my brother, at Kharan,

44 and stay with him for some time, until the anger of your brother has

45 passed away When the rage of your brother against you has passed, and he forgets what you have done to him, I will send and fetch you from there Why should I be deprived of both in one day ?"

46 Then Rebekka said to Isaac, "I hate my life in the presence of these Hitite girls ! If Jacob should take a wife from among these Hitite girls— such girls as they are, in this country, —why should I live ?"

Jacob sent to Padan Aram.

28 Consequently Isaac called for Jacob and blessed him, and commanded him not to take a wife from the girls

2 of Canan "Arise, go to Padan Aram, to the house of Bethuel your mother's father, and take yourself a wife from there from the daughters

of Laban, your mother's brother
And may ALMIGHTY GOD bless you, 3 and make you fruitful, and increase, and may you become an assembly of nations, and may He give the bless- 4 ings of Abraham to you and your race with you, to inherit the land of your strangerhood, which GOD gave to Abraham " Thus Isaac sent off 5 Jacob, and he travelled to Padan Aram, to Laban, the son of Bethuel, the Arami, the brother of Rebekka, the mother of Jacob and Esau

But when Esau knew that Isaac 6 had blessed Jacob and sent him to Padan Aram to take himself a wife from there to comfort him,—and had ordered him saying, "Take not a wife from the girls of Canan," and 7 that Jacob had listened to the voice of his father and mother, and had gone to Padan Aram Then Esau 8 perceived that the girls of Canan were displeasing in the eyes of Isaac his father, so Esau went to Ishmael 9 and took Malath the daughter of Ishmael the son of Abraham, the sister of Nebaioth, besides his other wives, as a wife to himself

Jacob's History in Padan Aram.

Jacob, however, set out from the 10 Well of the Oath and travelled to Kharan And he arrived at a place, 11 and rested there, for it was sunset, so he took one of the stones of the place and put it for his pillow, and laid down in the spot Then he 12 dreamed and saw a ladder with its foot standing on the ground and its head reaching to the heavens, and there were MESSENGERS of GOD ascending and descending it And 13 he saw the EVER-LIVING stationed above it, Who said, "I am the EVER-LIVING GOD of your father Abraham, and the GOD of Isaac,—the land which you now lie upon I will give to you and your race, and your race 14 shall be like the dust of the earth, and shall spread West and East, and North and South, and all the Nations of the world shall be benefited by you and your Heir Be assured also 15 that I am with you, and will guard you wherever you go, and I will give you a quiet return to this country, for I will not forsake you until I have accomplished what I have promised to you

Then Jacob woke from his sleep, 16

and exclaimed, "The EVER-LIVING is certainly in this place, and I knew
17 it not," so he was afraid and said, "How terrible this place is! Is not this truly the House of GOD? and this
18 the Gate of Heaven?" Jacob, however, slept until morning, when he took the stone which he had placed for a pillow and set it upright, and
19 poured oil on the top of it, and called the name of that place "GOD'S House"¹ (but Andam-loz was its
20 former name) Then Jacob vowed a vow, saying, "If the EVER-LIVING GOD is with me, and will guard me in the way that I now go, and give to me bread to eat and clothing to
21 put on, and bring me back safely to the house of my father,—then the
22 EVER-LIVING shall be my GOD And this stone which I placed for a pillow shall be a House of GOD, and of all that You give to me, I will return a tenth part to You"

29   Then Jacob arose on to his feet, and went towards the land of the sons of
2 the East, and he looked and saw a Well in the field and there were by it three flocks of sheep lying down, for from that Well they watered the flocks,—but a great stone was on the
3 mouth of the Well So when all the flocks had collected there, they rolled away the stone and watered the sheep, and then returned the stone on to the mouth of the Well until
4 another time Jacob, therefore, asked them, "Brothers where do you come from?" and they replied, "We are from Kharan"
5   Then he asked them if they knew Laban the son of Nahor? When they answered, ' We know him"
6   He next asked them, "Is he well?" and they said, "He is well,—and here is Rachel his daughter coming with his sheep"
7   Then he asked, "Look! it is full day already,—is it not time to water the cattle and sheep that they may go and feed?"
8   But they replied, "We cannot, until all the flocks are collected, and they roll away the stone from off the mouth of the Well and water the sheep"
9   Whilst he was speaking with them Rachel came with her father's sheep,
10 for she shepherded them But it happened that when Jacob saw Rachel

the daughter of Laban the brother of his mother, and the sheep of Laban his mother's brother, that Jacob rolled the stone from off the mouth of the Well and watered the sheep of
11 his mother's brother Laban Then Jacob kissed Rachel, and lifted up
12 his voice and wept and Jacob said to Rachel, "I do it because I am a relative of your father, and because I am the son of Rebekka" So she ran and reported it to her father
13 When Laban had heard the report about Jacob, the son of his sister, he ran to invite him and embraced him, and kissed him, and brought him to his home, where he related to Laban all these events
14 Then Laban said, "You are my bone and my flesh"; so he stayed five days with him, when Laban said
15 to Jacob, "Since you are my relative, now serve me, and also inform me what wages I shall pay you?"

Jacob's Faithful Love.

16 Now Laban had two daughters the name of the eldest Leah, and the
17 name of the youngest Rachel But the eyes of Leah were timid, and those of Rachel perfect in form and
18 beautiful to see, and Jacob loved Rachel, so he replied, "I will serve you seven years for your youngest daughter Rachel"
19 Laban then replied, "Good, she shall be yours —I will give her for a wife after you have stayed with me"
20 So Jacob waited for Rachel seven years, but they were to him like a single day because of the love he
21 had for her Then Jacob said to Laban, "Give me my wife, for the time is up, and I will go to her"
22 Laban then collected all the men
23 of the place and made a feast, and when it was dark he took Leah his daughter and brought her to him,
24 and he went to her Laban also gave Zilfa his servant, to Leah to be her servant
25 But when it was morning he discovered it was Leah, and said to Laban, "Why have you done this to me? Was it not for Rachel that I served you? Then why have you cheated me?"
26 But Laban answered, "It is not our custom in this country to give
27 the younger before the elder Count the seven for this then I will give to you also the other and for her you

shall serve with me another seven years afterwards "

28 Jacob therefore agreed to it, that he would serve thus, so he gave Rachel his daughter to him for a

29 wife Laban also gave to Rachel Bilah his servant to be her servant

30 He therefore went to Rachel, and he loved Rachel completely, and served to him other seven years afterwards

31 But the EVER-LIVING saw that he hated Leah, so he opened her womb,

32 but Rachel was childless So Leah conceived and bore a son, and she called his name Reuben, for she said, that "The EVER-LIVING has looked on my sorrow, so that now my husband

33 may love me " And she conceived again and bore a son, and said, "Now the EVER-LIVING has heard that he hates me, so He has given to me also this," and she called his

34 name Simeon Then she conceived again and bore a son, and she said, "Now certainly my husband will cling to me, for I have borne him three sons," therefore she called his

35 name Levi She also conceived again and bore a son, and she said "This time I will praise the LORD," so she called his name Judah Then she ceased to bear children.

30 When Rachel saw that she bore no child to Jacob she envied her sister, and said to Jacob, "Give me children, and if not I shall die!"

2 But Jacob's anger fired at Rachel, and he answered, "Am I in the place of GOD, to hold back from you the fruit of your body?"

3 She therefore said, "See now my attendant Bilah,—go to her and she shall bear at my knee, so that I also myself shall have children from her,"

4 so she gave to him Bilah her servant for a wife And Jacob went to her, and she conceived and bore a son to

5 Jacob Then Rachel said, "GOD has done me justice, and also has heard my voice and given me a son," therefore she called his name Dan

7 Again Bilah the servant of Rachel conceived and bore a son to Jacob, when

8 Rachel exclaimed, "I struggled with GOD, I also struggled with my sister," so she called his name Naphthali

9 When Leah saw that she ceased to bear, she took Zilfa her attendant

10 and gave her to Jacob for a wife, so Zilfa the servant of Leah bore a son to Jacob Then Leah said, "D troop," and called his name G

Zilfa the attendant of Leah also 11 bore a second son to Jacob, and Leah 12 exclaimed, "I am blest, for the women will bless me," she therefore called his name Asher

Reuben once went out at the time 14 of wheat harvest, and found love apples in the field, and brought them to Leah his mother, when Rachel said to Leah, "Give me, I pray, some of your son's love apples "

But she said, "Is it a trifle that you 15 have taken my husband, and would you also take the apples of my son?"

When Rachel replied,—"Come, now,—he shall sleep with you to-night, in exchange for your son's apples "

When Jacob came from the field in 16 the evening, Leah met him, and said to him, "You must come, for I have hired you with the love apples of my son, so sleep with me to-night" And 17 GOD heard Leah, so she conceived and bore a fifth son to Jacob Leah 18 therefore said, "GOD has paid me wages, because I gave my servant to my husband" She therefore called his name Issakar [1]

Leah afterwards conceived again a 19 sixth son to Jacob Then Leah said, 20 "GOD has endowed me, even me, with a good dowry, so that my husband will live with me, for I have borne him six sons," therefore she called his name Zebulon [2] She after- 21 wards also bare a daughter, and called her name Dinah [3]

But GOD remembered Rachel, and 22 GOD listened to her, and opened her womb, and she conceived and bore 23 a son Then she said, "GOD has taken away my reproach" She 24 therefore called his name Joseph,[4] saying, "The EVER-LIVING has added to me another son "

But it occurred that when Rachel 25 had borne Joseph, Jacob said to Laban, "Send me away, and I will go to my own home, and to my own country Give me my wives and my 26 children, whom I have served you for, because I must go with them, for you know the wages for which I have served to you "

Laban persuades Jacob to become his Chief Shepherd.

But he replied, "Name your wages 28 to me and I will give you them "

M H —F F
Index J Increase

29 So he answered him, "You know how I have served you, and how your
30 herds have been with me, for they were small that were with you before me, and they have spread out to many, and the EVER-LIVING has blessed you at my feet Yet have I gained even a house of my own?"
31 But he replied, "What shall I give?"

Then Jacob answered, "You shall not give me anything If you will do this thing for me I will conduct your
32 sheep and guard them I will go over all your sheep to-day counting Every sheep speckled or spotted, and every black sheep among the lambs, and every spotted or speckled in the
33 rams, they shall be my wages, and you shall assign them justly to me from to-day forward, as my wages from you All that is not spotted or speckled in the goats, or black in the sheep, it shall be a theft with me"
34 And Laban replied, "It shall be exactly as you say"
35 He therefore separated on that day the marked and spotted rams, and all the marked and speckled of the goats from all that were white, and all the black sheep, and gave them to the
36 hands of his sons, and put a three days' journey between them and between Jacob's, but Jacob shepherded the other sheep for Laban his father-in-law
37 Jacob then selected young wands of willow, and almond, and sycamore, and peeled them, peeling to the white so as to show the whiteness of
38 the wands, and he stuck the wands which he had peeled near the watering troughs where the sheep came to drink, in the sight of the sheep, when they were hot for breeding after
39 drinking So the sheep were hot amongst the wands, and bore, and the sheep bore marked, and spotted,
40 and speckled Then Jacob separated the lambs and placed the faces of the sheep towards the striped, and gave all the black among the sheep of Laban to his own flocks, and did not assign them to the sheep of Laban
41 Thus when any of the strong sheep were hot for union, then Jacob placed the wands before the eyes of the sheep, near the troughs, to inflame
42 them among the wands Before the feeble of the sheep, however, he placed them not, so the feeble went to Laban and the strong to Jacob

Thus the man increased very much, 43 and he possessed many sheep, and women and men servants, and camels and asses

However he heard the sons of 31 Laban talking, saying, "Jacob will take all that our father has, and from what our father possessed he has made all his wealth" Jacob conse- 2 quently watched the face of Laban, and perceived it was not with him as formerly

Then the EVER-LIVING said to 3 Jacob, "Return to the land of your fathers and your birth, and I will be with you" So Jacob sent and called 4 Rachel and Leah to the field to his sheep, and said to them, "I see that 5 the face of your father is not with me as formerly,—but the GOD of my fathers is with me Now you know 6 that with all my strength I have served your father But your father 7 has deceived me, and changed my wages ten times, GOD however did not allow him to do evil to me For 8 when he said, 'The spotted shall be your wages,' all the sheep were spotted —but if he said, 'The streaked shall be your wages,' then all the sheep were streaked, so GOD took 9 away the flocks of your father and gave them to me

"It also happened in the season of 10 the heat of the sheep, that I raised my eyes in a dream and saw the rams leaping on the streaked, speckled and spotted sheep, and the Messenger 11 of GOD said to me in the dream, 'Jacob,' and I replied 'I am here' Then he said, 'Lift up your eyes 12 and see all the rams leaping on the streaked, speckled and spotted sheep, for I have seen all that Laban has done to you I am the GOD of the 13 HOUSE of GOD[1] which you consecrated there in the pillar which you dedicated to me,—where you vowed a Gift Go from this country, and return to the country of your birth'"

Then Rachel and Leah answered 14 and said to him, "What portion or inheritance is there to us in the house of our father? Are we not like 15 strangers and outcasts to him? for he sold us, and has eaten up our money For all the wealth which 16 GOD has stripped from our father

---

[1] Beth-el in Hebrew means "House of God —I I

that is ours, and our children's, so do all that God has said to you "

17 Therefore Jacob arose, and mounted his children and wives on camels,

18 and collected the whole of his herds, and the whole of the property which he had acquired by trading, property he had acquired in Padan Aram, to go to his father Isaac in the land of Canan

19 Laban, however, had gone to shear his sheep, so Rachel stole the Tera-

20 phim which were her father's   Thus Jacob stole away secretly from Laban the Arami, without informing him,

21 for he fled from him   So he fled, he and all he possessed, and they went up and crossed over the river, and he

22 set his face to Mount Gilad   But on the third day it was reported to Laban that Jacob had fled

23 Then he took his relatives with him and pursued after him—a seven days' journey, and came up with him at

24 Mount Gilad   But God appeared to Laban the Arami in a dream by night, and said to him, "Guard yourself in what you do to Jacob for either good

25 or ill "   Laban, however, overtook Jacob and had pitched his tent on the hill, but Laban with his relatives on Mount Gilad

26 Laban then said to Jacob, "What have you done?   You have carried away my daughters like captives,

27 desolate?   Why did you steal away to fly and deceive me, and not inform me, when I would have sent you away with pleasure, and with the sound of

28 drums and harps?   You have not even let me kiss my children, and your children   You have acted like

29 a fool!   Truly there is a God who guides me from evil in acting with you, for the God of your father last night said to me, ' Guard yourself in dealing with Jacob for good or ill,'

30 so go your journey, for you desire the house of your father,—but why have you stolen my gods?"

31 Then Jacob replied, "Because I was afraid, for I said he will certainly

32 steal his daughters from me   If, however, you find your Gods, it is not known to me   Go round what is with me, and take your own "   (For Jacob did not know that Rachel had stolen them)

33 Laban, therefore, went round the tent of Jacob, and the tent of Leah, and to the tents of the two mothers, and did not find them, consequently

he left the tent of Leah and went to the tent of Rachel   But Rachel had 34 taken the Teraphim and placed them under the camel-saddle, and sat upon them, so Laban searched all the tent and could not find   And she said to 35 her father "Let it not grieve your eyes my Lord that I am not able to rise before you, for the way of women is on me "   So he searched and did not find the Teraphim

Then Jacob was furious, and abused 36 Laban, and Jacob was savage and said to Laban, "What is my fault, and what is my sin?   that you have come after me?   Now you have 37 searched all my goods, what have you found of all the goods of your house?   Put it before my people and your people, and they shall decide between us   During the twenty years I have 38 been with you, I have not lost a sheep or a goat of yours, and I have never eaten a ram of your flock   I have 39 not brought you the maimed   I have borne the loss from my own hand   I have restored to you the stolen by day, and the stolen by night   I have 40 borne the heat by day, and the cold by night, and my eyes never rested   This twenty years I have been in 41 your house,—I served you fourteen years for your two daughters, and six years for your sheep, and you cheated me over my wage ten times   If the 42 God of my father Abraham, and the WORSHIPPED of Isaac, had not been with me, then you would have sent me away empty   But God saw my weary feet, and defended me last night "

But Laban answered, and said to 43 Jacob, "The girls are my girls, and the children my children, and the sheep my sheep, and all that you see is mine, and for the girls what shall I do for them or the children which they have borne?   However, now, 44 come on, and let you and I make a settlement, and let it be a witness between Myself and You "

Then Jacob took a stone and set it 45 up with both his hands, and Jacob 46 said to his father-in law, "Let them collect stones "   So they collected stones and made a heap   Then they feasted on the heap there, and Laban 47 called it for himself, "The Heap of Witnesses," but Jacob called it for himself "The Heap of Evidence "[1]

---

1 Gilad

48 Laban also said, "This heap is a Witness between me and between you to-day," therefore

49 they called its name Gilad[1] and a "Watch-tower," for he said, "Let the EVER-LIVING watch between me and between you to keep each from

50 evil. If you grieve my daughters,—and if you take wives beside my daughters, when we are not together, let GOD see the Witness between me

51 and you." Then Laban added to Jacob, "See this heap, and see the pillar which I have raised between me and between you,—Witness this Heap, and Witness this Pillar, if I should pass over to you beyond this Heap, or if you should pass over to me beyond this Heap, and this Pillar

53 for evil, the GOD of Abraham, and the GOD of Nahor judge between us, the GOD of our fathers."

Jacob then swore by the WOR-

54 SHIPPED of his father Isaac. And Jacob sacrificed a sacrifice on the Heap, and invited his relatives to eat bread. So they ate bread, and they rested on the Heap.

32 Laban then rose up in the morning, and kissed his sons and his daughters and blessed them, and went and

2 returned to his own place. But Jacob continued his journey, and a

3 Messenger of GOD met him. So Jacob said, "What a glorious encampment of GOD this place is!"—therefore he called the name of that place, "The Encampment."

Meeting of Esau and Jacob

4 Then Jacob sent messengers before himself to his brother Esau, at Mount

5 Seir, in the land of Edom, and he commanded them saying, "You shall say this to my Lord Esau,— 'Jacob, your servant, says thus,—"I have lodged with Laban, and stayed

6 until now, and there are with me bullocks, and asses, and sheep and serving men and women, so I have sent to inform my Lord, to find favour in your eyes."'"

7 When the messengers returned to Jacob they reported,

"We went to your brother, to Esau, and he is also coming to call upon you, and four hundred men with him."

8 Jacob, consequently, was very greatly afraid, and it distressed him,

so he divided the people who were with him, and the sheep and the cattle, and camels into two camps, "because," he said, "if Esau comes to the one camp, and assails it, then there will be the other to fly to."

10 Jacob also said, "GOD of my father Abraham, and GOD of my father Isaac, the LORD Who said to me 'Return to the land of your birth and I will be good to you.' I am un-

11 worthy of all the mercies and of all the support which You have shown to me when I, Your servant, passed over this torrent with my staff, and I

12 am returning as two camps. Grant me a deliverance from the hand of my brother, from the hand of Esau, for I fear that he will come and cut

13 off mothers with children. But You have said 'Supporting I will support you, and I will make your race like the sand of the sea, which cannot be counted for quantity.'"

14 So he rested there that night.

15 Then he took presents in his hand,—presents for his brother Esau. A hundred goats, and twenty he-goats, a hundred sheep, and twenty rams,

16 thirty suckling camels with their foals, forty cows and ten bulls,

17 twenty she-asses and ten asses, and he put them under the hands of servants separately, troop by troop, and said to his servants, "Go before me, and spread a space between

18 troop and troop." He also ordered the foremost, saying, "If you meet Esau, my brother, and he asks you 'Who are you? and where are you going? and whose are these before

19 you?' you shall reply, 'From your servant, from Jacob, a present he sends to my Lord, to Esau. And look also he is behind us!'"

20 He ordered the second also, with the third, with all the servants who followed after them, repeating, "You shall say the same words to Esau if

21 he meets with you, and you shall also say to him, 'See, your servant Jacob is behind us.'" For he remarked, "I will pacify him first by the presents that I send to him, and afterwards I will see by his face whether or no I can stand before him."

22 Thus he sent presents over before him, but he himself stopped that

23 night in the camp. However he ꞏꞏꞏ꞉ ꞏꞏꞏ his two wives, ꞏꞏꞏ and his

eleven lads and crossed the ford of Jabok

24　So he took them and passed them over the brook, and sent over all who

25　were with him　Jacob, however, was left alone by himself, and a man wrestled with him until the departure

26　of the darkness　He saw, however, that he was not equal to him, so he touched him in the hollow of the thigh, and struck the hollow of the thigh of Jacob whilst wrestling with

27　him　Then he said, "Release me, for the darkness is going '

　But he replied, ";I will not let you

28　go unless you bless me"　Then he answered, "What is your name?"

　And he said, "Jacob"

29　When he responded, "Your name shall no longer be called Jacob, but 'Israel',—for you have wrestled with a Divine Messenger, as with men, and been equal to it"

30　Then Jacob asked, and said, "Tell me your name?"

　And he replied, "Why do you ask my name?" but he then blessed him

31　Jacob, consequently, called the name of that place "Pen-i-El"—that is "GOD's face"—"for I have seen divinities face to face and preserved

32　my life"　And the sun arose on him as he crossed over from Peniel, but

35　he limped on his thigh　Therefore the children of Israel do not eat the sinew-nerve from the foot to the thigh until this day, for he struck Jacob in the sinew-nerve at the hollow of the thigh

Jacob and Esau Meet.

33　Then Jacob raised his eyes and saw that Esau approached, and four hundred men with him, so he separated the children of Leah and of Rachel, and of the two second wives,

2　and placed the second wives and their children in the front, and Leah and her children next, and Rachel

3　and Joseph behind, but he passed to the front of them and bowed to the earth seven times whilst approaching to his brother

4　But Esau rushed forwards, and called to, and embraced him, and fell on his neck and kissed him, and

5　wept　Then he lifted his eyes and saw the wives and children and asked, "Who are these with you?"

　And he replied, "The children which GOD has given me, your servant."

Then the second wives approached 6 with their children and they bowed.

Leah also came forward and her 7 children, and they bowed, and afterwards Joseph and Rachel, and they bowed

So he asked, "What is all this camp 8 with you which approaches me?"

When he replied, "To find favour in the eyes of my Lord!"

Esau, however, answered, "I have 9 plenty, my brother　let your own remain to yourself"　But Jacob said, 10 "Not so, if now I have found favour in your eyes, take a present from my hand, for certainly I have seen your face as if I had seen the face of GOD, and am delighted　Now do take the 11 thanks which I have brought to you, for GOD has favoured me, and because there is plenty for me as well"　So he pressed him until he took them

Then he said, "I will rise up and 12 travel and we will go along together '

But he answered him, "My Lord 13 knows that the children are many, and the sheep and the cattle with me are breeding, so if we drive them a single day, then all the sheep will die　But let my Lord now go before 14 me, and I will be travelling at my ease, according to the pace of the guide before me, and the pace of the children, until that I come to my Lord, at Seir"

But Esau said, "I will then assign 15 to you some of the people who are with me"

And he replied, "Why have I found this favour in the eyes of my Lord?"

So Esau returned that day on his 16 journey to Seir, but Jacob pitched 17 his tent, and built himself a house, and cattle yards, making an encampment, therefore he called the name of the place Skuth [1]

Afterwards Jacob went quietly to 18 the village of Shekhem, which is in the land of Canan, on his return from Padan Aram, and encamped before the village, and bought that 19 part of the land, where he pitched his tent, from the hand of the son of Hamor the father of Shekhem for a hundred kesitas　He also built an 20 Altar there and called on GOD, the GOD of Israel

---

1 "The Tents" when translated from the Hebrew　I　Γ

Shekhem's Outrage on Dinah.

34 But it happened that Dinah the daughter of Leah, whom she bore to Jacob, went out to visit the women

2 of the country, and Shekhem, the son of Hamor, the Chief of the country, saw, and seized her and violated her,

3 and disgraced her. But his soul was attached to Dinah the daughter of Jacob, and he loved the girl, and spoke to the girl's heart.

4 So Shekhem spoke to Hamor his father, saying, "Get me this girl for a wife."

5 Jacob, however, heard that he had defiled his daughter Dinah, but his sons were at the fold in the fields, so Jacob kept silence until their

6 return. Then Hamor the father of Shekhem came to Jacob to speak

7 with him. But the sons of Jacob returned from the field upon hearing it, and the men were grieved, and very angry at it, for he had done an outrage to Israel in violating the daughter of Jacob,—which ought not to be done.

8 But Hamor spoke to them saying, " My son Shekhem is attached by his soul to your daughter, therefore give

9 her to him for a wife, and you can give your girls to us, and we can give ours to you, to take for yourselves,

10 and you can dwell with us and the land shall be before you. Reside, and

11 travel about, and possess it." Then Shekhem said to her father and her brothers " Let me find favour in your eyes, and whatever you ask of me I

12 will give it. Heap upon me a great dowry and settlement, and I will give whatever you say to me, only give me the girl for a wife."

13 Then the sons of Jacob answered Shekhem and Hamor his father craftily, " because," they said, " he

14 has corrupted our sister Dinah." So they replied, " We are unable to do such a thing as to give our sister to an uncircumcised man, for that would

15 be a reproach to us. Yet if you will agree with us, that, like us, every male

16 of you should be circumcised, then we will give our daughters to you, and we will take your daughters to us, and we will reside with you, and be one people.

17 But if you will not listen to us, then we will take our sister and depart."

18 And the idea was good in the eyes

19 of Shekhem the son of Hamor :— so the youth did not delay to do the

thing, for he had an affection for the daughter of Jacob; and he was the most honoured of all his father's house. So Hamor and Shekhem his 20 son went to the gate of their village, and addressed the men of their town saying; " These men are peaceable 21 with us, and they travel in it, and the country lies open to their hands before them. We would wish to take their daughters to us for wives, and give our daughters to them. However 22 the men will only unite with us in this way, to reside with us and to be one people, by our circumcising every male of us, as they are circumcised. Their herds and possessions and all 23 they have—will they not be ours if we agree with them, and they reside with us ? "

All who sat in the gate of the village 24 listened therefore to Hamor and Shekhem his son, and they circumcised every male who came to the gate of the town. But on the third 25 day when they were in pain, Simeon and Levi, the two sons of Jacob, brothers of Dinah, each took his sword, and went into the village quietly and slew every male. They 26 also slew Hamor and his son Shekhem with the edge of the sword, and took Dinah from the house of Shekhem, and went away. Then the 27 sons of Jacob came on the booty, and plundered the town, which had defiled their sister. They took the 28 sheep, the cattle, and the asses, and the wealth in the village and the wealth in the field, and captured their 29 youths and little children, and wives, and plundered all the furniture in the houses. But Jacob said to Simeon 30 and Levi; " You are a sorrow to me ;—you have made me hateful to the inhabitants of the land, to the Cananites, and the Perizites, and I being few in number, they will outnumber me and assail, and destroy me and my house."

They however answered; " Ought 31 they to use our sister as a harlot ? "

GOD afterwards said to Jacob **35** " Arise ; go to Beth-el and reside, and make an altar there to the GOD who appeared to you in your flight from your brother Esau."

Jacob destroys the Idols of his Family and Servants.

So Jacob said to his family, and all 2 who were with him " Throw away

the strange Gods which are among
you, and purify yourselves, and change
3 your clothing, and let us be rising,
and we will go to Beth-el, and I will
there build an Altar to the GOD who
pitied me in the day of my distress,
and was with me in the journey that
I went "

4   They, therefore, gave to Jacob all
the strange Gods which were in their
hands, and the earrings that were in
their ears, and Jacob buried them
under the oak which was near Shek-
5 hem. Then they marched, and a
terror from GOD was upon their
neighbours and they did not pursue
6 after the sons of Jacob So Jacob
came to Luz in the land of Canan
(it is Beth-el), and his people with him
7   He also built an altar there, and
called the HOUSE of GOD, Beth-el,[1]
for there GOD appeared to him in his
flight from the presence of his brother
8 But Deborah the nurse of Rebekka
died, and he buried her between
Beth-el and Alon, and called the
name of the place "The Oak of
weeping "

Another Divine Appearance to Jacob. and Promises.

9   GOD also appeared another time to
Jacob, on his return from Padan Aram,
10 and spoke with him, when GOD said
" Your name shall no longer be called
Jacob, for Israel shall be your name ,"
11 so He called his name Israel, and
GOD said to him, " I am the ALMIGHTY
GOD Be fruitful and multiply A
Nation and an Assembly of Nations
shall come from you, and Kings shall
12 proceed from your loins, and the
land which I gave to Abraham and
Isaac, I will give to you, and the same
land I will give to you and your race
13 after you " Then the Divine Messenger went up from him from the place
14 where he spoke with him So Jacob
erected a pillar at the place where he
had spoken with him,—a pillar of
stone, and poured a libation upon it,
15 and poured oil upon it Jacob also
called the name of that place where
GOD spoke with him GOD'S HOUSE [3]
16   He afterwards marched from there,
and had gone some distance into the
country towards Ephrathah, when
Rachel was taken in labour, when
17 childing went hard with her, but
when she was delivered with hard

labour, the midwives said to her, " Be
not down-hearted, for this child is a
son " But she breathing out her 18
life—for she was dying—named him
Son-of-my-Anguish,[1] but his father
called him Benjamin [2] So Rachel 19
died, and they buried her at Ephrathah, which is near Bethlehem, and 20
Jacob erected a pillar over her tomb [3]

Then Israel marched from there, 21
and pitched his tent at the encampment of Migdal-Adar And it was 22
whilst Israel resided in that country,
that Reuben went and committed
adultery with Bilah his father's
second wife,—and Israel heard of it

Registers of Jacob's Sons

These are the twelve sons of Jacob 23
The first born by Leah to Jacob,
Reuben , then Simeon, then Levi,
then Judah, and Issackar, then
Zebulon

The sons of Rachel Joseph and 24
Benjamin And the sons of Bilah
the servant of Rachel, Dan and 25
Naphthali And the sons of Zilpha, 26
the servant of Leah, Gad and Asher,
these are the sons of Jacob, who were
born to him in Padan-Aram

Jacob afterwards went to his father 27
Isaac, at Mamra, near Kiriath Arba,[4]
where Abraham and Isaac dwelt And 28
the days of Isaac were a hundred and
eighty years Then Isaac expired, and 29
died, and was added to his people, old
and satisfied with years, and Esau and
Jacob his sons buried him

History of Esau continued

Now these are the descendants of 36
Esau, who is Edom —

Esau took wives from the women of 2
Canan , Ada the daughter of Ailon
the Hitite, and Ahlibamah, the
daughter of Zibaon the Hivite, and 3
Bashmath the daughter of Ishmael,
the sister of Benaioth

And Ada bore to Esau Ailifaz, and 4
Bashmath bore Rauel, and Ahlibamah 5
bore Jaish and Jamal, and Korah ,—
these are the sons of Esau, which
they bore to him in the land of Canan

Esau afterwards took his wives, and 6
his sons and daughters, and all the
persons of his house, and the flocks,
and all his cattle, and all property

---

1 Ben-oni   2 Son of my right hand
3 "This pillar at Rachel's grave still exists '
Editorial note by an Old Hebrew editor — F F
4 " The same as Hebron " is also an ancient
.por.ti. . ' . . .l

---

1 "God's hou . . .   1 . ' .c'

which he had acquired in the land of Canan, and left the land from the face
7 of his brother Jacob, for their possessions were too great to remain together, for the land was not able to lodge the both of them, because of
8 their herds   So Esau remained in
9 Mount Seir   (Esau is Edom —Esau was the father of the Edomites in Mount Seir)
10   These are the names of the sons of Edom
   Ailifaz the son of Ada, the wife of Esau , Rauel the son of Bashmath wife of Esau ,
11   And these are the sons of Ailifaz , Omar, Tzifo, and Nathan, and Kenez ,
12 and Thimna was secondary wife to Ailifaz, the son of Esau, and she bore to Ailifaz Amalek ,—these are the sons of Ada the wife of Esau
13   And these are the sons of Rauel , Nahath, and Zarath, Shama, and Mizah , these were the sons of Bashmath, wife of Esau
14   And these are the sons of Ahlibamah, the daughter of Anah, the daughter of Tzibaon, wife of Esau, which she bore to Esau —Jaish , and Jalam , and Korah
15   These were the chiefs from the sons of Esau and of the sons of Ailifaz, the eldest of Esau —
   Chief Thamar , Chief Omar , Chief
16 Tzifo , Chief Kenez , Chief Korah , Chief Nathan , Chief Amalek — These were the Chieftains of Ailifaz, in the land of Edom   They were the sons of Ada
17   And these were the sons of Rauel, the son of Esau —
18   Chief Nahath , Chief Zerah, Chief Shama , Chief Mizah ,—These were Chieftains of Rauel in the land of Edom   They were sons of Bashmath
19 the wife of Esau   These were sons of Esau, and were Chieftains in the land of Edom
20   These are the sons of Seir (the Horites who inhabited the country) Lotan and Shubal, and Zilaon, and
21 Anah , and Dishon and Azar, and Dishan   These were Chieftains of the Horites sons of Seir, in the land of Edom
22   And these were the sons of Lotan, Hori and Himam , and the sister of Lotan was Thimna
23   And these are the sons of Shobal ,— Alwan, and Manahath, and Aibal, Shefa, and Aonam
24   And these are the sons of Zibaon —

Aiah and Anah (he is the Anah who discovered mules in the desert while attending the asses of Zebaun his father)
   These are the children of Anah ; 25 Dishon, and Ahlibama, daughter of Anah
   And these are the sons of Dishon ,— 26 Hamedan , and Ashban, and Ithran and Keran
   These are the sons of Azan, Bilk- 27 han, and Zavan, and Akan ,
   These are the sons of Dishan, Aur, 28 and Aran
   These are the Chiefs of the Horites 29 —Chief Lotan , Chief Shubal, Chief Zibaon , Chief Anah , Chief Dishon , Chief Azer , Chief Dishan ,—These were Chiefs of the Horites, as Chieftains in the land of Seir [1]
   And these are the names of the 40 Chieftains of Esau by their families, with their Tribal names   Chief Thimnah , Chief Alva , Chief Ithath ; Chief Ahibamah , Chief Alah , Chief 41 Pinan , Chief Kana , Chief Theman , 42 Chief Mibzar , Chief Magdiel , Chief

[1] NOTE—The verses Ch xxxvi 31--39, are not a part of the text of Moses, but a note of an ancient editor   From internal evidence I conclude he was Ezra, who edited the Pentateuch after the return from Babylon, as the number of Kings named show ten generations of Monarchy, which the context indicates came after the Tribal Government under Chiefs, and as the Kings were clearly elective, the certainty of long wars between each election would extend the time too much for the Tribal Commonwealth and the succeeding Monarchical period to be contained in the epoch between the death of Esau and the conquests of Moses east of the river Jordan, during which he wrote Genesis

" And these are the kings which reigned 31 in the land of Edom (before a king reigned over the sons of Israel)   There reigned in 32 Edom Bela, the son of Baur, and the name of his city was Dinahba   And Bela died 33 and Jobab the son of Zerakh reigned instead of him in Bozrah   And Jobab 34 died and Hasham reigned instead of him from the land of the Thiman   And when 35 Hasham died, Hadad the son of Bedad reigned instead of him, in Makah of Midian, in the land of Moab, and the name of his city was Avith   And Hadad 36 died, and Shamlah, from Masrakah, reigned instead of him   And when 37 Shamlah died, Shaul from Rakoboth on the river reigned in his stead   And Shaul 38 died, and Bal the Mercyful, the son of Akkor, reigned instead of him   And Bal 39 the Mercyful, the son of Akkor died, and Hader reigned in his stead, and the name of his city was Pau, and the name of his wife Mehitabel the daughter of Matrod, the daughter of Mizahab   —E F.

Airam,—These were Chieftains of Edom, with the names of the districts they possessed Esau himself was the father of the people of Edom

Continuance of the History of Jacob and of Joseph

37 Jacob continued to reside in the land of his father's foreignhood—in the land of Canan

2   These are the progeny of Jacob Joseph a lad of seventeen years was attending to the sheep with his brothers, the young men who were sons of Bilah and sons of Zilfa two of his father's wives And Joseph reported their bad conduct to their

3 father Israel, also, loved Joseph more than all his children, because he was the son of his old age, so he made him a robe with long sleeves

4 And his brothers saw that their father loved him more than all his brothers, so they hated him, and would not let

5 him be in peace Joseph, however, dreamed a dream, and told it to his brothers, and they hated him the

6 more for it, for he said, "Listen now to the dream that I dreamed

7 We were binding sheaves in the middle of a field, when my sheaf arose, and stood up, and your sheaves turned, and bowed to my sheaf"

8   But they replied to their brother, "Reigning, would you reign, and ruling would you rule over us?" So they hated him the more, because of his dream, and his talk

9   Then he dreamed another dream, and related it to his brothers, and said," I have dreamed another dream, when the sun and the moon and eleven stars came and did homage to me"

10 He told it to his father and to his brothers, and his father reproved him, and said, "What is this dream which you have dreamed? Shall I and your mother, and your brothers, come and bow down to the ground to

11 you?" So his brothers envied him, but his father remembered the event

12   His brothers afterwards went to pasture their father's sheep in

13 Shekhem, and Israel said to Joseph, "Are not your brothers feeding the sheep in Shekhem? Go' I will send you to them"

And he replied, "I am ready"

14 Then he continued, "Go, then and see how your brothers are, and how the sheep are, and bring me word

They had gone, however, from the vale of Hebron, and removed to Shekhem.

And a man met him while search- 15 ing the field, and asked him, "What are you seeking?" When he answered, 16 "I am seeking my brothers Tell me where I can find them?"

So the man responded, "They 17 have marched from here, for I heard them say 'Let us go to the Two Wells'" Joseph consequently went after his brothers and found them at the Two Wells When they saw him 18 in the distance, and before he approached them, they determined to murder him, and each said to his 19 brother, "Here is My Lord the Dreamer' There he comes' So 20 now let us go and murder him, and fling him into one of these wells and we will say a wild beast caught him,— then we shall see what will come of his dreams'"

But Reuben heard it, and wished 21 to deliver him from their hand, so he said, "Let us not destroy his life" Reuben also said to them, "Let us 22 not shed his blood Let us fling him into this dry well," for he was desirous that they should not stab him, so that he might rescue him from their hands to return him to his father

Therefore when Joseph was come 23 to his brothers, they stripped the robe from Joseph ,—the long-sleeved robe which was on him,—and took 24 him and flung him into the empty well, with no water in it Then 25 they turned to eat bread. But looking up, they saw at a distance Ishmaelites coming from Gilad with their camels loaded with spices, and nuts and balm, who were going down to Mitzeraim [1]

Then Judah said to his brothers, 26 "What profit is it to us to murder our brother and dabble ourselves in his blood? Come on' Let us sell 27 him to these Ishmaelites, and that guilt will not be upon us, for he is our brother, and our own flesh ' so they listened to their brother Mean- 28 time those Midianite merchants came on, and approached, so they pulled up Joseph from out of the well, and sold Joseph to the Ishmaelites, for twenty shekels Thus Joseph was taken down to Mitzeraim therefore 29

[1] Lo'it

when Reuben returned to the well he did not find Joseph in the well, so he
30 tore his garments. When he went back to his brothers he said;—"The lad is not! and mourning, I shall grieve, and die of grief."

31 They, however, took and slaughtered a goat kid and dabbled his robe in its
32 blood, and sent the long-sleeved robe to their father with this message, "About this robe which we send you, send back and say if it is the
33 robe of your son or no?" And he replied, "It is the robe of my son. Some wild beast has torn and eaten
34 my son." Jacob consequently tore his garments, and put on sackcloth for his death, and mourned for his son many days.

35 Then all his sons and all his daughters arose to console him, but he refused their consolations, and said, "I know that I shall go mourning for my son to the grave;" so he wept for his son.

36 But the Midianites sold him in Mitzeraim to Potiphar, the General of Pharoh, Commander of his Guards.

History of Judah.

38 About this same time Judah went and separated from his brothers, and joined with an Adulamite, whose
2 name was Hirah. Whilst there he saw the daughter of a Cananite, whose name was Beth-Shua and he
3 took her and married her, and she
4 conceived and bore a son, and called
5 his name Ar. Then she conceived again and bore a son, and called his name Onan. She afterwards increased and bore a son and called his name Shelah; then she ceased to be child-bearing.

6 When Judah took a wife for his eldest son Ar, her name was Thamar.
7 But Ar, Judah's eldest son, was wicked in the presence of the EVER-LIVING, so the LORD caused him to
8 die. Judah consequently said to Onan, "Marry the wife of your brother, and raise up an heir for
9 your brother." But Onan knew that the heir would not be his own, therefore when he approached his brother's wife, he ejected on the ground, instead of giving seed to his brother.
10 What he did was, however, wicked in the eyes of the EVER-LIVING, and therefore He caused him to die.
11 Then Judah said to Thamar "Return as a widow to your father's

house until Shelah my son grows up," for he reflected "Perhaps she may also kill him like his brothers." Therefore Thamar went and returned to her father's house.

12 But time went on, and Beth-Shua the wife of Judah died and Judah grieved for her, and went up with Hirah the Adulamite, his partner,
13 to shear the sheep at Timnath; and it was reported to Thamar, that her father-in-law was going up to Tim-
14 nath to shear his sheep, so she put off her widow's weeds and concealed herself in her veil, and went down and sat at the opening by the wells which are on the road to Timnath, for she saw that Shelah was grown up, and he was not given to her as a husband:
15 Judah saw her, and he thought she was a harlot, for she had hidden her
16 face, so he turned from the road to her, and said, "Come on, go with me;"—for he knew not she was his daughter-in-law.

Then she asked, "What will you give to me, if I go with you?"
17 Then he replied—"I will send you a kid of the goats or sheep."

And she replied—"If you will give me a pledge that you will send them?"
18 He replied, "What is the pledge that I shall give you?"

And she answered "Your ring and the stick you have in your hand."

So he gave her them, and he went with her, and she conceived to him.
19 Then she arose, and went and put the veil from off her, and dressed herself in her widow's weeds. But
20 Judah sent the kid of the goats by the hand of his partner the Adulamite, who was to receive the pledge from the hand of the woman;—and he
21 could not find her. He therefore enquired of the men of the place asking, "Where is the whore of the wells by the road?" But they replied, "There is no whore by
22 there." So he returned to Judah and reported, "I cannot find her;—and the men of the place said 'there was not a whore there.'"
23 Judah, therefore, said; "You have taken it to her, therefore I cannot be abused by her; for I sent the kid, but you could not find her."
24 But three months after it was reported to Judah "Your daughter-in-law Thamar has prostituted herself, and she is also with child from

her fornication," and Judah replied, "Bring her here and burn her"

25 They brought her when she produced the ring and walking stick,—and said, "By the man that these belong to I am with child," and she continued, "To whom belongs this ring and its motto, and this walking stick?"

26 Then Judah replied and said, "You are more virtuous than I, for I did not give you Shelah my son" He therefore proceeded no further to examine her

27 When, however, the time for her delivery came, there were twins in her

28 belly, and it happened in her childing one put out his hand, so the midwife took it, and tied a scarlet thread upon its hand, remarking,

29 "This came the first" But it occurred that he drew back the hand, and then his brother was produced, when she said, "What? Have you broken?" The breach be upon yourself" therefore she called

30 his name Pherez,[1] and afterwards his brother was born, upon whose hand was the scarlet thread, so she called his name Zaiah[2]

History of Joseph continued.

39 Thus Joseph had been taken down to Mitzer,[3] and sold to Potiphar, Pharoh's General, Commander of the Guards, a Mitzerite, from the hands of the Ishmaelites who had

2 brought him there But the EVER-LIVING was with Joseph, and he became a prosperous man, and was steward to his master, the Mitzerite,

3 for his master saw that the EVER-LIVING was with him, and that all he did the LORD prospered it in his

4 hand Joseph therefore found favour in his eyes, for he was honest towards him, consequently he appointed him chief of his house, and entrusted all

5 his possessions to his control, with the result that from when he was appointed over the house and over all that belonged to him, the EVER-LIVING blessed the house of the Mitzerite under the administration of Joseph, and he was blessed by the EVER-LIVING in all his possessions,

6 in the house and in the field, so that all he had increased under the direction of Joseph, consequently he made no enquiry what he had, except for the bread which he ate Joseph

---

[1] Breaker   [2] Sunrise   [3] Egypt

was also handsome in form, and handsome in face

7 It happened, however, after these events, that the wife of his master lifted up her eyes to Joseph, and

8 said, "Lie with me!" But he refused, and said to his master's wife, "My master knows not what is in his house, and all that he possesses

9 he has placed in my control There is not a greater than I in this house, and he has withheld nothing from me, except yourself, because you are his wife Therefore I will not commit that great sin, and outrage, against GOD"

10 However she solicited Joseph day after day, but he would not listen to her to lie beside her, or be with her

11 But it happened that one day when he came to her apartment with a message for her, and there were none of the attendants of the house there

12 in the apartment, that she seized him by his wrapper, saying "Lie with me," but he let his wrapper slip off in her hand, and fled away naked

13 So when she saw that he had left his wrapper in her hand, and had

14 fled naked, she cried out to the attendants of her house and said to them, "Look! he has brought this foreign fellow to us to insult us! He came to me to violate me,—but I shrieked

15 out, and when he heard that I raised my voice and shrieked, then he left his wrapper beside me and fled

16 naked!" She also laid by the wrapper with her till her lord came

17 home when she spoke to him about all this matter, saying, "There came to me the Hebrew slave whom you

18 brought to us, to insult me, but when I raised my voice to cry out, he abandoned his wrapper near me and fled away naked"

19 And when his master heard the tale of his wife, which she told him, asserting, "Your servant acted towards me according to my statements," he was fired with anger,

20 therefore Joseph's master took and put him into the tower-house, the place where the prisoners of the king were imprisoned, and he was confined

21 in the tower-house But the EVER-LIVING was with Joseph, and gave him mercy, and gave him favour in the eyes of the commander of the tower-

22 house, so that the commander of the tower-house placed in Joseph's hands the whole of the prisoners who were in

the tower-house, and all that was
23 done there he directed it. The commander of the tower did not superintend anything. the whole was in his hands, because the EVER-LIVING was with him, and what he did the LORD prospered it.

40 But it occurred after these events, that the butler of the king of the Mitzeraim offended, and the king of
2 the Mitzeraim, his master, was angry. And Pharoh was enraged with two of
3 his officers, with the chief of the butlers, and with the chief of the cooks, and he ordered them to be confined in the house of the Commander of the
4 Guards — in the tower-house, — the place where Joseph was also imprisoned. The Commander of the Guards consequently remitted them to Joseph, and he kept them, and they were many days under restraint.

5 But they dreamed, both of them, a dream; each dream in the same night; each dream had a separate appearance, to the butler and to the cook whom the king of the Mitzeraim had imprisoned in the tower-house.

6 When Joseph came to them in the morning, he saw their pining gloom,
7 so he asked the officers of Pharoh who were in his custody in the house of his master, " Why are your faces sad and sorrowful to-day ? "

8 And they replied, " We have dreamed dreams, and we have not an interpreter."

But Joseph answered, " Is not GOD the interpreter of dreams ? Tell to me now."

9 The chief butler therefore told his dream to Joseph and said to him : " In my dream I saw a vine before
10 me, and on the vine three branches, and the berries grew on them, and
11 the clusters of grapes were ripe, and Pharoh's cup was in my hand ; so I took the grapes and crushed them into the cup of Pharoh, and put the cup into the hand of Pharoh."

12 Joseph then said to him, " This is the interpretation. The three branches
13 are three days : after three days hence Pharoh will raise your head, and restore you to your station, and you will give Pharoh's cup to his hand, as was appointed formerly,
14 when you were his butler.—Then remember me, because I was kind to you. Do me therefore a kindness and remind Pharoh of me, and cause him to bring me out of this house,

for by treachery I was dragged from 15 the country of the Hebrews, and also here I have done no crime that should put me in a dungeon."

When the chief baker saw that the 16 interpretation was good, he also said to Joseph : " I have dreamed as well ; and there were three baskets filled on my head, and in the highest 17 basket of all victuals for Pharoh, ready baked, but the birds ate them from the basket, from off my head."

Then Joseph answered and said, 18 " This is the interpretation. The three baskets are three days. Three 19 days from hence Pharoh will take your head from off you, and will hang you on a gallows, and the birds shall eat your flesh from off you."

It happened that three days after 20 was Pharoh's birthday, and he made a feast for all his officers, and raised the head of the chief of the butlers, and the head of the chief of the bakers among his officers, and restored the 21 chief of the butlers to his butlership, and he gave the cup to the hand of Pharoh ; but he hung the chief of the 22 bakers, as Joseph had interpreted the dream. The chief of the butlers, however, did not remember Joseph, but forgot him.

Some time after it occurred that **41** Pharoh dreamed, and seemed standing by the river, and saw seven cows 2 come up from the river, beautiful to see, and full fleshed, and they fed upon the rushes. Then he saw seven 3 other cows come up after them from the river, poor to look upon and lean in flesh ; and they approached the cows on the bank of the river, and 4 the cows that were poor to look upon and lean in flesh, ate up the seven beautiful looking and fat cows.—Then Pharoh awoke.

He slept again, and dreamed ; and 5 saw seven ears of corn spring up from one stalk very beautiful and good. He saw also seven ears of corn spring 6 up after them withered and blighted by the east wind ; and the seven 7 withered ears of corn swallowed the seven beautiful and good ears. Then Pharoh awoke ;—and it was a dream.

When morning came his spirit was 8 oppressed ; so he sent and summoned all the writers of Mitzeraim, and all her scientists, and Pharoh related his dreams to them. But there was not an interpreter among them for Pharoh.

9 Then the chief of the butlers spoke to Pharoh, saying, " I remember my
10 offence of the day when Pharoh was angry with his servant, and put me into custody in the house of the General of the Guard, and the chief of the
11 bakers was with me, and we dreamed a dream in the same night, I and he , each according to the form of the
12 dream we had dreamed But there was with us a Hebrew youth, a slave of the General of the Guard, and we related them to him, and he interpreted to us our dreams He inter-
13 preted to each his own dream And it happened to us exactly as he interpreted to us our dream "
14 Pharoh, therefore, sent and summoned Joseph, and they took him from the dungeon, and shaved him and changed his clothes, and brought him to Pharoh
15 Then Pharoh told Joseph the dream he had dreamed, and that none could interpret it to him , " but I have heard a report about you, that you heard a dream and interpreted it "
16 Joseph, accordingly answered to Pharoh, saying, " May GOD return an answer of peace to Pharoh "
17 So Pharoh related his dream to Joseph " I stood by the bank of the
18 river, and saw come up from the river seven cows, full fleshed and beautiful to see, and they pastured on the
19 rushes Then I saw seven other cows come up after them miserable and very bad to look at, and lean in flesh I never saw such wretched things in all the land of the Mitzeraim, they
20 were so bad But the lean and wretched cows ate up the seven former beautiful cows, and they came and approached me, and yet I noticed as they came and drew near, and could observe they were as poor as before Then I awoke
21 " Again I was in a dream and saw seven ears of corn spring from one
22 stalk, each full and good Then I saw seven ears blasted, poor, and withered by the east wind follow them , and the poor ears swallowed
24 the seven good ears, and I told it to the writers and they cannot inform me about it "
25 Then Joseph replied to Pharoh, " The dream of Pharoh is unique What GOD has determined to do, He
26 has related to Pharoh The seven good cows are seven years, and the seven good ears of corn are seven

years,—these dreams are unique And 27 the seven lean and poor cows that came up after them, are seven years , and the seven poor ears of corn, blasted by the east wind, they are seven years of famine This event 28 which I have stated to Pharoh GOD has made known to Pharoh The 29 seven years before us will be great years in all the land of the Mitzeraim , but they will be followed by seven 30 years of famine afterwards, and those seven shall be forgotten in the land of the Mitzeraim, for the famine shall desolate the land For those seven 31 shall not be recognized in the land before the presence of the famine that will follow them ,—for it will be very heavy As for the double dream 32 granted to Pharoh, that confirms the event from GOD,—and GOD will hasten to effect it Therefore let Pharoh 33 seek out a man, firm and skilful, and set him over the Mitzerites, and let 34 Pharoh act, and appoint officers over the land, and take a fifth part produced by the land of the Mitzerites in the first seven years of the sevens, and store up all that food in the seven good years that are coming, and 35 store up corn under the hand of Pharoh for food in cities and fortresses, so that there may be food to support 36 the land in the seven years of famine which will be in the land of the Mitzerites, so that the country may not be cut off by the famine "

And this advice was good in the 37 eyes of Pharoh, and in the eyes of his ministers Therefore Pharoh 38 commanded his ministers to select some man with the spirit of GOD in him Then afterwards Pharoh said 39 to Joseph, " I have perceived that GOD is with you in all this, and there is certainly no intelligence like yours, therefore you shall be over my house, 40 and by your mouth all my affairs shall be regulated , only in the throne will I be greater than you ' Pharoh 41 also said to Joseph, " See, I appoint you over all the land of the Mitzerites "

Then Pharoh took his ring from 42 his hand, and put it upon the hand of Joseph, and clothed him in a white robe, and put a golden chain on his neck, and mounted him in a hooded 43 chariot of his own, and they proclaimed before him the appointment given to him over all the land of the Mitzerites Pharoh also said to 44 Joseph, " I am Pharoh —but without your order no man shall move his hand or foot in all the land of the Mitzerites."

45 Pharoh consequently called the office of Joseph "The High Treasurership," and gave him Aseneth the daughter of Poti-Phara, priest of On, for a wife.

Joseph has Egypt surveyed and stores up Corn.

Joseph at once made a survey of the whole land of the Mitzerites.

46 Joseph was thirty years old on his appearance before Pharoh king of the Mitzerites, and Joseph went from the presence of Pharoh and organized
47 all the land of Mitzer. The earth also produced big loads in the seven
48 years of the sevens, and he collected much provision in the seven years, in the land of Mitzer, and stored up the provision. For every town he stored up provision from the fields
49 around it. Joseph consequently stored corn like the sand of the sea for quantity; the amount was so great that they ceased to measure it, because it was immeasurable.
50 Joseph also had two sons born to him before the years of the famine came. Aseneth the daughter of Poti-Phara the priest of On bore
51 them, and Joseph called the name of the eldest Manasseh,[1] "For GOD has made me forget all my troubles, and
52 all my father's house." But he called the name of the other Ephraim,[2] "For GOD has enriched me in the land of my wrongs."
53 Then the seven years of the sevens which were to be in the land of the
54 Mitzeraim came to an end; and at their end the seven years of famine began, according to the declaration of Joseph; and the famine was upon all the lands, but in the land of the Mitzeraim there was bread. At last the whole
55 country of the Mitzerites hungered, and the people called upon Pharoh for bread, but Pharoh replied to all the Mitzerites, "Go to Joseph, who
56 will tell you what to do." And as the famine was over the whole surface of the country, Joseph opened the stores which he had by him, and distributed to the Mitzerites. Although the famine raged in the land of the Mit-
57 zeraim, yet all the countries came to the Mitzeraim to buy corn from Joseph, for the famine raged over all the countries round.

---

1 Forgotten.   2 Fruitful.

Joseph's Brothers are sent to Egypt to buy Corn, and terrified by being called Spies.

Jacob also learnt there was corn in **42** Mitzeraim, so Jacob said to his sons, "Why do you look at each other?"
2 He also said, "I have heard that there is corn in Mitzeraim. Descend to there and buy for us from it, that we may live and not die."

Therefore ten brothers of Joseph 3 went down to buy corn from the Mit-
4 zeraim. But Jacob did not send Benjamin the own brother of Joseph with his other brothers, for he said, "I fear an injury might happen to him."

Thus the sons of Israel went down 5 to buy corn, together with other travellers, for there was a famine in the land of Canan.

Joseph was then Protector over all 6 the country, to distribute to all the people of the land, and Joseph's brothers came and bowed to him, face to the ground. When Joseph 7 saw them he scrutinized and recognized them, but spoke to them harshly, and asked, "From what country do you come?"

They replied, "From the land of Canan, to buy food."

Although Joseph recognized his 8 brothers they did not recognize him,—
9 but Joseph remembered the dream which he dreamed to himself, and said to them, "You are spies; come to survey the nakedness of the land."

But they replied to him, "No, my 10 lord, but your slaves have come to buy food; and all of us are sons of 11 one man;—we are honest men;—we are not spies."

However he replied, "No! but you 12 are come to see the nakedness of the country."

They then answered, "Your slaves 13 were twelve brothers. We are the sons of one man in the land of Canan. The youngest is at home to-day, and one is not."

But Joseph returned, "That is just 14 what I said to you, when I said you are spies. By this I will prove you. 15 By the life of Pharoh! you shall not go from here until you have brought your youngest brother here! Send 16 one of yourselves to take your brother, and return; then you will prove your words true about him, and if not, by the life of Pharoh, you are spies!"

And he further ordered them to be 17

18 imprisoned three days. But after the third day Joseph said to them,

19 "Do this and live;—for I fear GOD. I will select one of you brothers, whom I will put into confinement instead of you, and you others take corn for

20 your starving families. But you must bring your younger brother to me, and verify your statement, and live and not die." And they did so.

21 But each said to his brother. "We suffer for our sins against our brother, because we saw the anguish of his soul imploring us to have pity on him, and we would not listen. Therefore this distress has come upon us."

22 Then Reuben answered them, and said, "Did I not speak to you and say, 'Let us not sin against the lad,' and you would not listen to me? And now his blood is sought for!"

23 And they did not know that Joseph understood them, for he used an

24 interpreter with them. But he withdrew from them and wept. Then he returned to them and spoke, and selected Simeon from them and fettered him before their eyes.

25 Joseph afterwards commanded and their waggons were loaded with corn, but he caused their money to be returned into the load of each. Then he gave them leave to go,—and

26 showed politeness to them. They also loaded corn upon their asses,

27 and set out. But one of them opened a sack of his, to give fodder to his ass in the inn, and saw his money, which was placed openly in its mouth.

28 Then he said to his brothers, "He has caused my money to be returned, and here it is in my bag;" and their hearts stopped, and they trembled each at his brother, exclaiming, "What is this that GOD has done to us?"

29 They went, however, to Jacob in the land of Canan and reported to him all

30 these proceedings, saying, "The man who is master of the country spoke to us harshly, and took us for spies upon

31 the land. But we said to him, 'We

32 are honest, and are not spies, we are twelve brothers, sons of our father—one is not, and the youngest is now with our father in the land of

33 Canan.' But the man, who is master of the country, said 'By this I will discover if you are honest, I will select one of your brothers to remain with me, but take for your starving families, and go. But you shall bring me your youngest brother, that I may

be convinced you are not spies, when I will return the brother I have selected from you, and you may trade in the country.'"

35 When, however, they were emptying their loads, then each found his money in his cargo, and they were in fear at the finding of the money,

36 both they and their father were afraid, and Jacob their father said to them, "I am bereaved! Joseph is not, and Simeon is not, and you would take from me all there are!"

37 Then Reuben replied to his father, saying, "Kill my two sons, if I do not bring them back to you!—I now place them in your hands as a pledge that I will them return to you!"

38 But he answered, "My son shall not go down with you, for his brother is dead, and he alone remains, and an accident might happen to him in the journey that you are going —and you would bring down my grey hairs with sorrow to the grave."

43 But the famine oppressed the

2 country, and it arrived that when all the food they had bought from the Mitzeraim ended, that their father said to them, "Return, and buy us a little food."

3 When Judah replied to him saying, "The man swore to us, asseverating, 'You shall never see my face, unless

4 your brother is with you.' If you are wise enough to send our brother with us, we will return and buy food

5 for you to eat. But if you will not send, we will not go down, for the man said to us, 'You shall not see my face unless your brother is with you'"

6 Israel, however, answered, "Why did you wrong me by telling the man that there was another brother to you?"

7 And they responded, "The man demanded of us about our birth-place, asking, 'Have you a father living? Have you a brother?' and we told him straightforwardly about those things. How could we know he would say 'Bring your brother down with you'?"

8 Then Judah exclaimed to Israel, "Send the lad with me, and I will come up, and return him alive. and if not kill me, myself, as well as my

9 children! I pledge myself for him! From my hand seek him if I do not bring him back to you! then banish me from your face for I shall have

10 sinned against you all my days. If

you had not hesitated, we should already have returned before now."

11 Therefore Israel their father said to him, "If it must be, do this, take some of the productions of this country in your waggons, and go down to the man with a present,— some balsam, and honey, perfumes,

12 and myrrh, nuts and almonds Also take double money in your hands, and the money that was returned in the mouth of your bags, return with your

13 own hands to him again Take your brother also, and arise, go back to

14 the man, and may the Almighty GOD give you mercy before the man, and send your brother back with Benjamin For if I am to be bereaved, I shall be bereaved"

Joseph's Brothers' Second Journey to Egypt; and they Dine with him.

15 Consequently the men took the present, and took double money in their hands and Benjamin, and arose and went to Mitzeraim and appeared

16 before Joseph And Joseph saw Benjamin with them, and said to the chief of his house, "Invite those men to my house, and prepare a dinner, for those men shall eat with me at noon"

17 The man therefore did as Joseph ordered, and he brought the men to

18 Joseph's house But the men were afraid at being brought to Joseph's house, and said "It is on account of the money which was returned to our bags last time that we are brought, to have an excuse against us, and to fall upon us and to take us for his

19 slaves, with our asses" Therefore they approached the steward of Joseph's house, and spoke with him

20 in the verandah of the house, and said, "By the EVER-LIVING we came down for the purpose of buying food,

21 but when we returned to the inn and opened our bags, there was our money in the mouth of our bags, in full amount But we have returned

22 with it in our hands We have also brought other money with us to buy food We knew not that our money was there in our loads"

23 But he answered, "Be quiet, and fear nothing Your GOD and the GOD of your father has given you that money secretly into your loads Come with me" Then he brought Simeon

24 to them The man the steward of Joseph's house also went out and ordered water and they washed their feet Then he ordered fodder for

25 their asses They then prepared the present against Joseph's arrival at noon, for they heard they were to

26 dine with him When Joseph came to the apartment, they presented him the present which they had brought from home, and bowed to the ground before him

27 Then he asked them about their health, and said, "Is your father well?—the old man you told me of? Is he alive yet?"

28 And they replied, "Your slaves are well, and our father is yet alive," and

29 bent and bowed But he raised his eyes and saw Benjamin his brother, the son of his mother, and asked, "Is this your youngest brother, of whom you spoke to me?" Then he added,— "GOD show you mercy, my son"

30 Then Joseph hastened, for his affection burned for his brother, and he sought to weep, so he went into

31 his chamber and wept there But afterwards he washed his face and came again, and restrained himself, and ordered dinner to be served

32 They therefore served it for him, by himself, and to them apart, by themselves, for the Mitzerites dined by themselves, for the Mitzerites are not allowed to eat food with foreigners for that is disgusting to the Mitzerites

33 But they placed in his presence the eldest, according to his age, and youngest according to his youth, and arranged the men each by his relative,

34 and they took dishes from before him to offer to them but they offered to Benjamin more dishes than to any of the rest, presenting five, which they presented and left with him.

Joseph Discovers Himself to his Brothers

44 Afterwards he commanded his steward, saying, "Fill the loads of these men with food as much as they are able to carry, and put the money

2 of each on the top of the carts, and my cup, the cup of silver, place at the top of the load of the youngest, with the money for his corn" So they did as Joseph ordered

3 At morning-light the men went off

4 with their asses When they had gone not far from the city, Joseph said to his steward, "Mount and follow those men, secure them, and say to them, 'Why have you returned

5 evil for good? Where is that my lord

drinks from? He is very sharp-sighted He saw what you were doing!'"

6 So he pursued, and said this to them

7 But they replied, "Why has my lord spoken these words accusing your servants of having done such a

8 thing? You know we returned to you from the land of Canan the money which we found in the top of our loads We have not stolen silver or gold from

9 the house of your lord If it is found with any of your servants, kill him, and we also will be slaves to my lord"

10 And he replied, "It shall be as you say, Therefore with whoever of you it is, he shall be my slave, and you shall be innocent"

11 Then they hastened and each one

12 unloaded his load, and he searched beginning at the eldest to the youngest, and found the cup in Benjamin's

13 load Then they tore their garments, and mounted each man his ass and returned to the city

14 When Judah and his brothers came to Joseph's house, and were again brought in, they fell on their faces to

15 the ground While Joseph said to them, "How has this occurred that you have committed? Did you not know that I observe what happens around me?"

16 Then Judah replied, "What can I say to my lord? What assert? or how vindicate myself? God has found out the sin of your slaves in their hands, —alas! we are slaves to my lord! both we, and the one in whose hand the cup was found!"

17 But he answered and said, "Far be it from me to act thus The one in whose possession the cup was found, he shall be a slave to me, but you can go in peace to your father"

18 Then Judah approached him and said, "To me, my lord, grant now for your slave to speak to the ears of my lord, and let not your anger burn with your slave,—for you are to me

19 like Pharoh My lord asked of his slaves, saying, 'Have you a father, or

20 brother living?' and we replied to my lord, 'A father lives with us, an old man, and a lad of his old age, the youngest, but his brother is dead And beside him there is none from his mother, so his father loves him'

21 Then you said to your slaves, 'Bring him to me, that I may set my eyes

22 on him' But we replied to my lord, 'The youth is not able to leave his father, for if he leaves his father

then he will die You, however, said 23 to your slaves, 'If you do not bring down your youngest brother with you, you shall not again see my face'

24 And when we went up to your slave, my father, he was informed of the 25 demand of my lord, so that when our father said, 'Return and buy us a little food,' we replied 'We cannot 26 go down unless our youngest brother is with us Even should we descend, we cannot see the face of the man unless our youngest brother is with us' Then your slave, my father, said 27 to us, 'You know that my wife bore me two lads, and one went from me, 28 and I said, alas! he has been torn to pieces, and I shall see him no more And if you take this one from my 29 face, and an accident should happen to him, you will bring my grey hairs with sorrow to the grave' So now if 30 I should go to your slave, my father, and the youth is not with us, whose life is bound to his life, it will be then 31 when he sees that the youth is not with us, he will die, and your slave will cause the grey hairs of your slave, our father, to go down in agony to the grave Besides, your slave pledged 32 himself for the youth to my father, saying, 'If we do not bring him back to you, then let me be banished from my father all my days' So now, I 33 pray, let your slave remain, instead of the youth, a slave to my lord, and let the youth return with his brothers, for if I go up to my father, 34 and the youth is not with me, then I shall see the misery that will come upon my father!'"

Then Joseph was not able to re- 45 strain himself before all the officers around him, and cried,—"Every man go out from me!" So not a man remained with him while Joseph made himself known to his brothers Then Joseph discovered his language 2 to his brothers, and the Mitzerites heard, and it was reported to the house of Pharoh, and Joseph said to 3 his brothers, "I am Joseph Does my father yet live?" But his brothers were not able to answer him, for they were terrified, at the sight of him

Joseph, therefore, said to his 4 brothers, "Come near to me" So they approached, when he said, "I really am Joseph, your brother, whom you sold to go to Mitzer And I know 5 that with fury and rage in your eyes, you sold me however God sent me

6 before you to preserve life , for these two years the famine has encircled the earth, and for five years more there will not be ploughing or harvest,

7 therefore GOD has sent me before you to preserve to you a posterity in the earth, and a secure refuge for

8 your lives Consequently it was not you who sent me, but GOD who appointed me as a Father to Pharoh, and an Administrator of all his house, and a Governor for all the land of

9 the Mitzeraim Therefore arise and go up to my father, and say to him , 'Your son Joseph says thus —GOD has appointed me as Administrator of all the Mitzerites, so come down

10 to me Do not delay You shall reside in the land of Goshen, and be near to me,—you, your children, and your children's children, with your sheep and your oxen and all that you

11 have, and I will provide for you there, for there are five years of famine yet , therefore come down, yourself and your family, and all that you have ,

12 so that my eyes may see you and the eyes of my brother Benjamin, and that my mouth may also speak with

13 you ' You must also inform my father of all my power among the Mitzeraim, and all that you have seen, and cause your father to mount and come down to here "

14 Then he fell upon the necks of his brothers and wept, and Benjamin

15 wept upon his neck He also kissed all his brothers, and wept over them, and afterwards his brothers con-

16 versed with him And a report was communicated to the Palace of Pharoh saying, " Joseph's brothers have come " and it was good in the eyes of Pharoh, and of his ministers

17 Pharoh therefore said to Joseph, " Say to your brothers thus,—' Load up all of you from the city and go to

18 the land of Canan, and take your father and your families and come to me, and I will give you the best of the land of the Mitzeraim, and you shall be fed on the fat of the land '

19 You, yourself, also command this to be done,—' Take from the land of Mitzer waggons for your little children and wives, and your father, and bring

20 them Care nothing also for the abandonment of your goods, for the best of the land in Mitzer shall be yours '"

21 The sons of Israel accordingly did so, and Joseph gave them waggons from Ph... h ... and provided

provisions for the journey He also 22 gave all of them a suit of clothes, but to Benjamin he gave three hundred pounds, and five suits of clothes To 23 his father he sent in addition ten he riding asses the best in Mitzer, and ten she riding asses besides, with bread and meat for his father on the way Thus he sent off his brothers, and said 24 to them, " Do not quarrel on the road "

They accordingly went from the 25 Mitzeraim and ascended to the land of Canan, to Jacob their father, and 26 reported to him saying, " Joseph is yet alive, and he is also Governor of all the land of the Mitzeraim " Then his heart failed, for he could not believe them Then they related all 27 that Joseph had said to them ,—but when he saw the waggons which Joseph had sent to carry himself, then the spirit of Jacob their father revived, and Israel said, "It is enough ! 28 my son Joseph does live ! I will go and see him before I die ! "

Israel consequently marched, and **46** all that were with him, and went to the Well of the Oath, and offered offerings to the GOD of his father Isaac Then GOD appeared to Israel 2 in a vision at night, and said " Jacob ! Jacob ! "—and he replied " I am here " When He answered, " I am GOD, the 3 GOD of your father Isaac , fear not. Go down to the Mitzeraim, for you shall become a great nation there I, THE MIGHTY, will be with you in 4 Mitzer, and I will support you, and Joseph shall place his hands upon your eyes "

Jacob afterwards arose from the 5 Well of the Oath, and the sons of Israel carried Jacob their father, and their children and wives in the waggons which Pharoh had sent to carry them in They also took their 6 herds, and the property they had purchased in the land of Canan, and went to the Mitzeraim —Jacob and all his race with him his sons and sons 7 of his sons with him , his daughters and his daughters' sons and all his race went with him to the Mitzeraim

The Roll Call of the Patriarchs.

Now these are the names of the 8 sons of Israel who went to the Mitzeraim —

Jacob , and the eldest son of Jacob, Reuben and the sons of Reuben, 9 Hanok, and Phelwa and Hetzon and Karmi.

10 The sons of Simeon, Jemuel, and Jamin, and Ahad, and Jakin, and Tzokhar, and Shaul ben Cananith

11 And the sons of Levi, Gershan, Kehath and Merari,

12 And the sons of Judah, Ar, and Onan, and Shelak, and Pherez, and Hetzeon, and Hamal:

13 And the sons of Issackar, Tholah, and Phurah, and Job, and Shimron

14 And the sons of Zebulon, Sered, and Alon, and Jakhlal,

15 These were children from Leah, which she bore to Jacob in Padan Aram, beside Dinah his daughter, and the persons of her sons and daughters were thirty-three

16 And the sons of Gad, Tzifion, and Hani, Sheni, and Atzbon, Ari, and Arodi and Akheli;

17 And the sons of Asher were, Jamna, and Ishnah, and Ishur, and Beriah, and Sirakh, his twin brother, and the sons of Beriah, Heber, and Malkiel,

18 These were the children of Zilfa, whom Laban gave to Leah his daughter, and who bore them to Jacob, six and twenty persons

19 Sons of Rachel, wife of Jacob, were

20 Joseph and Benjamin But there were born to Joseph in the land of the Mitzeraim whom Aseneth the daughter of Poti-Para priest of On bore,—Manasseh, and Ephraim

21 And the sons of Benjamin, Bela, and Beker, and Ashbol, Ghera and Namen, twins, and Rash with the twin Muphi, and twin Khuphi, and Arad,

22 These were the sons of Rachel which she bore to Jacob, fourteen persons in all

23 And the son of Gad was Kushan,

24 And the sons of Naphthali, Jakhzel, and Guni, and Jetzer, and Shilam

25 These were the children of Bilah, whom Laban gave to Rachel his daughter, and she bore these to Jacob, —in all seven persons

26 And the souls who went with Jacob to Mitzer, who sprung from his loins, being men only, sons of Jacob,—all the persons were seventy

27 But the sons of Joseph, who were born to him in Mitzer were two persons, men, so all the persons of the family of Jacob who came down to Mitzer were seventy

Jacob and Joseph Meet

28 But he ~ ... re ...

to invite Joseph to meet him in Goshen, when he arrived in the land of Goshen Joseph accordingly at 29 once mounted his chariot, and went to meet Israel his father in Goshen Whom he looked at, and fell upon his neck, and wept on his neck for a long time, and Israel said to Joseph, 30 "Let me die at once,—after I have seen your face' Why should I live longer?"

Joseph afterwards said to his 31 brothers, and to the family of his father, "I will go and inform Pharoh, and tell him that my brothers, and the family of my father who were in the land of Canan have come to me, and that the men feed sheep, they 32 have lived with people of the fold, and their sheep and cattle and all that they have they have brought But it must be that when Pharoh 33 calls you and enquires 'What can you do?' you must say, 'Your slaves have lived as cattle-men from their youth, until now, both we and our fathers,—grant us to settle in the land of Goshen,' for the Mitzerites hate every shepherd of sheep"

Joseph accordingly went and re- 47 ported to Pharoh, and said, "My father and brothers, and their sheep and cattle, and all that they have, are come from the land of Canan, and are in the land of Goshen" Then 2 he selected five from his brothers to take and present to Pharoh, and 3 Pharoh asked his brothers, "What is your business?' When they replied to Pharoh, "Your slaves are shepherds of sheep,—as we are, so were our fathers" They also said to 4 Pharoh, "We have come to reside in the land, for there is no pasture for your slaves' sheep, because the famine is heavy in the land of Canan, so allow your slaves to live in the land of Goshen'

Pharoh therefore in reply said to 5 Joseph, "Your father and your brothers have come to you, the land 6 of the Mitzeraim is before you, so fix your father and brothers on the best of it Let them settle in the land of Goshen, and if you know also a skilful man amongst them, appoint him superintendent of my farms"

Joseph afterwards took Jacob his 7 father and presented him before Pharoh, and Jacob blessed Pharoh, and Pharoh asked Jacob, "How many 8 ... life?"

9   When Jacob replied to Pharoh, "The days of the years of my stay have been one hundred and thirty years Few and evil have been the years of the days of my life ' and they have not reached to the days of the years my fathers lived in the days

10 of their stay" Then Jacob blessed Pharoh, and retired from the presence of Pharoh

11   Joseph afterwards settled his father and his brothers, and gave them possession in the land of the Mitzeraim in the best district in the country of Ramases, as he was commanded

12 Joseph also provided food for his father and brothers, and all their families, according to their children

History of Egypt's Famine continued.

13   Bread failed in all the country, for the famine was very severe, and the land of the Mitzeraim and the land of Canan fainted before the famine,

14 therefore Joseph gathered up all the money he found in the land of Mitzer, and in the land of Canan, and all the Mitzerites came to Joseph for the corn which they bought, and Joseph brought the money to the treasury of

15 Pharoh Thus he collected the money from the land of Mitzeraim and the land of Canan

Then all the Mitzerites came to Joseph to say, "Provide bread for us, so that we may not die before you, for our money is exhausted"

16   Joseph, however, answered them "Bring your cattle, and I will give you it for your cattle, instead of for money"

17   Consequently they brought their cattle to Joseph and he gave them bread, for horses and cattle and sheep, for herds of oxen and asses he supplied them with bread, in exchange for all their cattle for that year

18   But that year ended, so they came to him in the next year, and said to him, "We have kept back nothing from my lord We have nothing left before my lord, except our bodies,

19 and our land Why should we ourselves die before your eyes? Buy to yourself our land for bread, and we and our land will be slaves to Pharoh"

20   Thus the Mitzerites sold every one his farm, for the famine was cruel upon them —and the land became

21 Pharoh's But he transferred the

people upon it to fresh villages, from the one extreme boundary of Mitzer to the other extreme of it, except 22 that he did not buy the lands of the priesthood, for he protected the priesthood by laws from Pharoh, and they were fed from rations provided for them, therefore he did not buy their lands

Then Joseph proclaimed to the 23 nation, "You see I have bought you to-day, and your land for Pharoh I will supply seed to you, and you can sow the land But of its produce 24 you shall give one-fifth to Pharoh, and four-fifths shall be for yourselves, to sow the fields and to feed you, with those you employ, and as food for your children"

They thereupon replied, "Our 25 lives have found favour in the eyes of my lord, and we will be slaves of Pharoh"

So Joseph made it the constitution 26 to this day,—that the land of the Mitzerites was Pharoh's for the fifth tax, except the lands of the priesthood, which were not to become Pharoh's

Joseph also settled Israel in the 27 land of the Mitzeraim in the district of Goshen, and they possessed there, and flourished, and increased greatly.

The Sickness and the Death of Jacob.

Jacob, however, lived seventeen 28 years in the land of the Mitzeraim, and all the days of the years of Jacob were one hundred and forty-seven years But the day approached 29 for Israel to die, and he called his son Joseph to him, and said to him, "If now I have found favour in your eyes, put your hand under my thigh, and do to me a true kindness, and bury me not among the Mitzeraim, but lay me to sleep with my fathers, 30 and carry me from Mitzer, and bury me in their burial place"

And he replied, "I will do as you 31 have said"

But he answered, "Swear to me," and Israel was reclining on the surface of his bed

But it was after these events that **48** it was reported to Joseph, "Your father is ill," so he took his two sons, Manasseh and Ephraim, with him, and Jacob was told, "Your son 2 Joseph has come to you'

Then Israel exerted himself and sat up in his bed, and Jacob said to 3

Joseph, "The ALMIGHTY GOD appeared to me on my departure from the land of Canan, and blessed me,

4 and said to me, 'I will make you flourish, and increase your family, and make you an assembly of nations, and I will give this land to your race after you as a possession

5 for ever!' But now for your two sons, who have been born to you in the land of the Mitzeraim before I came to you in Mitzer,—let then Ephraim and Manasseh be mine, as

6 Reuben and Simeon are mine. But your children whom you have begot after them they shall be yours They shall not be called by the name of their brothers in their inheritance

7 "When I came from Padan, Rachel died from me in the land of Canan, on the journey, in Kibrath-artz, near the pass of Ephratha, and I buried her there by the road at Ephratha "[1]

8 Then Israel looked at the sons of Joseph, and said, "These are mine!"

9 But Joseph said to his father, "They are the sons which GOD gave me here!"

He, however, replied, "I will take them now for myself, and bless them."

0 But the eyes of Israel were heavy from age He was not able to distinguish, so he drew them to him and kissed them, and embraced them

1 Afterwards Israel said to Joseph, "I have seen your face unexpectedly, and now GOD has shown me also your heirs "

2 Then Joseph brought them for his blessing and they bowed before his

3 face, earthward [2] Then Joseph took both of them, Ephraim in his right hand for the left hand of Israel, and Manasseh in his left, for the right hand of Israel, and approached him But Israel

4 stretched out his right hand and placed it upon the head of Ephraim, who was youngest, and his left hand upon the head of Manasseh, intentionally,

although Manasseh was the eldest Then he blessed Joseph, and said 15 "The GOD in the presence of Whom my fathers Abraham and Isaac walked,

The GOD Who appeared to me from of old until this day,

The MESSENGER Who redeemed 16 me from all misfortune,

Bless the lads, and give them my Power,

The Power of my fathers Abraham and Isaac,

And pour out their increase to the bounds of the earth!"

Joseph then discovered that his 17 father had placed his right hand on the head of Ephraim, and it was unpleasing in his eyes, so he took hold of his father's hand to change it from off the head of Ephraim to the head of Manasseh Joseph also said 18 to his father, "Not thus my father, for this is the eldest, place your right hand on his head "

But his father refused, saying, "I 19 knew it my son, I knew it He also shall be a nation,—and he also shall be great, — but nevertheless his younger brother shall be greater than he, and his race shall be a multitude of nations, and when bless- 20 ing in that period they shall say, 'The Blessing of Israel be upon you! May GOD make you like Ephraim and like Manasseh,' and they will place Ephraim above Manasseh "

Then Israel said to Joseph,—"I 21 shall die, but GOD will be with you, and will return you to the land of your fathers Therefore I give to you She- 22 kem alone, above your brothers, which I took to me by my hand, from the Amorites, by my sword and my bow "

Jacob's Blessings to his Sons.

Jacob afterwards called his sons 49 and said,

"Assemble and I will inform you 2 What will befall you in future times; Collect and listen, sons of Jacob, Yes, list to your father Israel,

To Reuben.

Reuben! The first of my vigour,— 3 You are the crown of my passion, Excelling in beauty, excelling in strength!

Boiling like water, you lost command,— 4*

For mounting your father's bed, Yes! defiling my honour's abode

---

1 Ch 48, v. 7 The words, "Which is Bethlehem," are a comment of a Rabinical copyist, not part of the Text, so I put it at the foot of he page —F F

2 V. 12. A learned Jewish gentleman hearing of my work sent to ask how I rendered the 12th verse of the 48th of Genesis—"for," he said, "it is translated totally wrong in both the Authorized and Revised Versions, and all others " I copied out from my MSS my translation as above, and my enquirer declared I was correct, as well as in another passage of which he had asked my translation My readers can see the value of the correction by consulting the A V. and R V —F. F

To Simeon and Levi.

5   Simeon and Levi are brothers;
     Cruel weapons are hidden with
       them :

6   To their plottings go not my soul !
     My honour, join not their clan !
     For they murdered guiltless men,
     And joyfully murdered a prince.

7   Curse their crime, as great, and
       their transgression,
     For it sorely troubled Jacob, and
       Israel shamed.

To Judah.

8   Judah you shall direct your
       brothers;
     Your hand shall be on the neck of
       your foes ;
     To you shall the sons of your father
       bow !

9   A young lion, Judah, for plunder !
     My son springs from his couch like
       a lion—
     And as a lioness,—who dare rouse
       him ?

10   The sceptre shall not depart from
       Judah,
     Or the Giver of Law from between
       his feet,
     Till peace arrive, and the nations
       obey him.—

11   Bound to the vine like an ass,
     And a colt the son of a stepper,
     He washed his garments in wine,
     And his clothes in the blood of
       clusters !

12   His eyes shall be bright with wine,
     And his teeth be white with milk !

To Zebulon.

13   Let Zebulon dwell on the shore of
       the sea,
     On the shore of the ships,
     And extend his legs to the fishery !

To Issakar.

14   A strong ass, Issakar, lies in the
       stall ;—

15   And he saw that rest was good,
     And the land, that it was pleasant,
     So he gives his back to the load,
     And becomes a servant for hire !

To Dan.

16   Dan shall govern his people,
     As a sceptred Prince of Israel !

17   Dan is a snake in the path,—
     An adder laid in the road,—
     He will bite the heels of the horses,
     Who will throw their riders back-
       wards.
     For your victory trust on the LORD !

To Gad.

Gad,—A troop !—He shall troop,— 18
But a troop shall deceive him !   19

To Asher.

For Asher, his food shall be rich,   20
And his are the royal pleasures.

To Naphthali.

Naphthali is a nimble stag,   21
Has the gift of eloquent speech !

To Joseph.

Joseph ! a fruitful plant !   22
A fruitful plant by a well,—
With branches spread on the wall !
But the master of arrows provoked, 23
And shot, and pierced him ;
But he turned to his powerful bow, 24
And the hands of his arms were
     quick
By the hands of the mighty GOD of
     Jacob,
From Whom is Israel's guardian
     stone.
May the GOD of your father guard 25
     you ;—
And the ALMIGHTY bless you !
With blessings from the sky above,
With blessings below of dancing
     water,
With the bliss of the breasts, and
     love !
May the blessings of your father 26
     strengthen,
With the bliss of the fertile vales. —
May the wealth of the ancient hills
Be heaped on the head of Joseph ;—
More nobly crowned than his
     brothers !

To Benjamin.

Benjamin ! a wolf, shall eat plunder 27
     at morn,
And at night shall divide his spoil."

All the offshoots of Israel were 28
twelve. And their father said this to
them, and blessed each with his blessing : with blessings adapted to each.
Then he addressed them and said ;— 29
" I shall be added to my people.
Bury me with my fathers, in the cave
which is in the field of Ephron the
Hitite ; in the cave which is in the 30
field of Makphelah, which is near
Mamra in the land of Canan, which
field Abraham bought from Ephron
the Hitite for a place of burial,
Abraham is buried there, and Sarah 31
his wife. Isaac is buried there, and
Rebekka his wife, and there I buried

32 Leah   The field was bought, and
the cave in it, from the sons of Heth "

33   Jacob thus finished instructing his
sons, and stretched out his legs upon
the bed, and expired, and was added
to his people

50   Then Joseph fell upon his father's
face and wept, and kissed him

Embalming and Burial of Jacob

2   Joseph afterwards ordered his servants the physicians to embalm his
father   The physicians accordingly

3 embalmed Israel   When the forty
days were completed, which the
embalming occupies, then the Mitzer-

4 ites wept for him yet forty days, and
at the conclusion of the forty days of
mourning, Joseph addressed the court
of Pharoh and said —

    "If, now, I have found favour in
your sight, speak, I request to the ears
of Pharoh, and say,

5   " My father made me swear, saying,
'When I die, bury me in the tomb
which I cut out for myself in the land
of Canan.' so now I wish to go up
and bury my father, and will return "

6   Pharoh then replied, "Go up and
bury your father, as he made you

7 swear " Joseph therefore went up to
bury his father, and there went up
with him all the ministers of Pharoh,
the nobles of his court, and all the
nobles of the land of the Mitzeraim,

8 with all the family of Joseph and his
brothers, and the families of his
father, except the children, and except the sheep and cattle which were

9 left in the land of Goshen   There
also accompanied him chariots and
horsemen, making a very large army

10 All these marched to Goren-Hatar
which is over the Jordan,[1] and
mourned there with a great and very
heavy mourning, and made a lamentation for his father for seven days

11   And when the inhabitants of the
land of Canan saw the lamentation
at Goren-Hatar they said, " This is
a great grieving, for the Mitzerites , "
Therefore they called its name " Mit-
zers-lament " It is beyond the Jordan [1]

Thus his sons did for him as he 12
commanded them

So they, his sons, carried him to 13
the land of Canan, and buried him in
the cave in the field of Makphelah ,
which field Abraham bought to be a
burial place, from Ephron the Hitite,
opposite Mamra

Then Joseph returned to Mitzer, 14
himself, and his brothers, and all
who had accompanied him to bury his
father, after he had buried his father

But when Joseph's brothers saw 15
that their father was dead, they said
to one another, " Joseph will hate us ,
and will return upon us all the wrong
which we heaped upon him "

They therefore sent to Joseph and 16
said, " Our father commanded us
before he died , ' Say to Joseph this, 17
forgive, I pray, your brothers' fault
and sin in the wrongs they heaped
upon you '   Consequently we beg of
you to forgive the fault of the servants
of the GOD of your father "

Joseph, however, wept at their
address to him

Then his brothers went and fell 18
before his face, and said, " We are
your slaves "

But Joseph replied to them , " Fear 19
nothing ! For I am subject to GOD
Although you set upon me for injury, 20
GOD turned it to good, in order that
I might make this nation, to give life
to many peoples   Go now do not 21
fear me   I will protect you, and
your children "   Thus he comforted
them and spoke to their hearts

This was after Joseph returned to 22
Mitzeraim, he and his father's family

And Joseph lived one hundred and
twenty years

And Joseph saw his great-grand- 23
children from Ephraim   Sons also
of Makir the son of Manasseh were
fondled on the knees of Joseph

At last Joseph said to his relatives, 24
" I shall die   However the EVER-
LIVING will visit you and take you up
from this country to the land which
He swore to Abraham, to Isaac, and
to Jacob "

Then Joseph administered an oath 25
to the sons of Israel to say , " When
your GOD visits you, take up my
bones from here " Thus Joseph died 26
a hundred and twenty years old , and
they embalmed him, and placed him
in a coffin in Mitzeraim.

---

[1] This means on the West of the Jordan,
and is an internal proof that Genesis was
written upon the Eastern side, and by Moses,
during the Exodus   If it were a forgery of
some unknown scribe of Jerusalem of a few
centuries before Christ, he would have made
" beyond Jordan " lie on the East —F. F

END OF THE BOOK OF GENESIS

THE SECOND BOOK OF MOSES, COMMONLY CALLED

EXODUS.

(ALA SHAMOTH.)

The Names of the Twelve Patriarchs.

1 THESE are the names of the sons of Israel who came to Mitzer-aim.

The Chief Jacob, and his family with him :—Reuben, Simeon, Levi, 2 and Judah ; Issakar, Zebulon, and 3 Benjamin ; Dan and Naphthali ; Gad 4 and Asher ; all the persons proceeding from the loins of Jacob, were 5 seventy individuals ; Joseph was already in Mitzeraim.

6 Now Joseph and all his brothers 7 died, and all their children. But the sons of Israel were fruitful and bred and increased, and became very, very powerful and the land was filled with them.

A Foreign Conqueror rules Egypt and fears Israel.

8 Then a Foreign Conqueror arose over the Mitzeraim who knew nothing 9 of Joseph, and said to his nation, "This people, the sons of Israel, are more in number and stronger than 10 ourselves, therefore let us deal skilfully with them, to prevent them increasing, for it is possible they might turn upon us in war and conquer, for they hate us, and may be fighting against us and expel us from the land."

11 They consequently placed labour masters over them to force them to build, and they built fortresses for 12 Pharoh—Pithom and Ramasses. But the more they oppressed them the more they increased ; therefore they trembled and feared before the 13 sons of Israel. Consequently the Mitzerites endeavoured to crush the 14 sons of Israel, so they embittered their lives by cruel labour in the forges, and in the brick-kilns, and in

every labour upon the land, by every means possible trying to crush them. The king of the Mitzeraim also 15 summoned the midwives of the Hebrews, of whom the name of the chief was Shifra, and the name of her lieutenant Phua, and decreed ; 16 "When you deliver the Hebrew women examine their children ; if it is a son, kill him ; but if a daughter, let her live."

But the midwives feared GOD, and 17 did not do as the king of the Mitzeraim ordered them, but preserved the children alive. The king of the 18 Mitzeraim therefore summoned those midwives again and enquired from them, "Why have you not executed the law, but have preserved the children's lives ?"

When the midwives replied to 19 Pharoh, "Because they are not like Mitzerite women when in labour, but lively, so that before the time the midwives have come to them they are delivered." Therefore 20 GOD showed kindness to those midwives.

So the people increased and were very strong ; and seeing that the mid- 21 wives were GOD-fearing he imprisoned them. Pharoh then commanded this 22 people, saying, "Every boy that is born throw him into the river, but let the girls live."

The Birth of Moses, and Adoption by Pharoh's Daughter.

But there was a man of the family 2 of Levi, who married a Levite woman. And his wife conceived and bore a 2 son. When she looked on his beauty, she hid him for three months. But 3 being no longer able to hide him, she made a boat of bulrushes and pitched it with pitch and resin and placed it in the reeds on the bank of the

4 river　But his sister stood at a distance to see what would happen

5 to him　Then the daughter of Pharoh came down to bathe in the river, and her maids walked along the bank of the stream, and they noticed the boat amongst the rushes So she put out her hand and took it

6 When she opened it she saw the lad, and he cried, and she grieved over him, and said, "It is one of the Hebrew children"

7 Then his sister asked the daughter of Pharoh, "Shall I go and seek for you a nursing woman of the Hebrews, so that she may nurse the lad for you?"

8 And the daughter of Pharoh replied to her "Go", so she went immediately and called the mother of

9 child, to whom Pharoh's daughter said, "Take this child and nurse it for me, and I will pay you the cost" Its mother therefore took the child and nursed it

10 When the lad grew up he was taken to the daughter of Pharoh as a son, and she called his name Mosheh,[1] for she said "I drew him out of the water"

The Prince Moses thinks of his Nation.

11 But it was long after this, when Moses had become great, that he went out to his brothers, and examined into their condition　Then he saw a Mitzerite strike a Hebrew,

12 who was related to him　Then he turned this and that way, and not seeing anyone, he struck the Mitzerite, and concealed him in the sand

13 At another time when he was inspecting, there were two men, Hebrews, quarrelling, so he said to the wrong-doer, "Why do you strike your neighbour?"

14 But he replied, "Who appointed you as foreman and judge over us?— Are you going to murder me as you murdered the Mitzerite?"

Then Moses was afraid and said to himself, "That affair is known

15 then?"　The matter was also reported to Pharoh who endeavoured to execute Moses　But Moses fled from the presence of Pharoh, and turned to the land of Midian, where he rested beside a well

Moses and the Priest of Midian.

It happened that the Priest of 16 Midian had seven daughters, and these girls came to draw and fill the watering troughs to give drink to their father's sheep　Then the 17 shepherds came and drove them away, but Moses arose and prevented them and watered their sheep　So 18 when they returned to Rauel, their father, he asked, "How is that you have returned so quickly to-day?"

They answered him, "A Mitzerite 19 protected us from the hand of the shepherds and also drew and gave water to our sheep"

Then he replied to his daughters, 20 "Where is he?　Why have you left the man there?　Invite him, and let him eat bread"

Thus Moses began to stay with the 21 man, who gave Ziforah his daughter to him, and she bore a son, and he 22 called his name Ghersham,[1] "for," he said, "I am a stranger in a foreign land"

A New Tyrant arises in Egypt.

A long time after these events, that 23 king of the Mitzeraim died　But the children of Israel were still oppressed in their servitude, and their cries from their slavery reached GOD GOD therefore heard their groaning, 24 and GOD remembered His covenant with Abraham, and with Isaac, and with Jacob, therefore GOD looked 25 upon the children of Israel, and GOD revealed Himself

God's Revelation in the Burning Bush

Moses, however, was shepherding 3 the sheep of Jethro his father-in-law, the priest of Midian, and he had led the sheep to the far side of the desert, and came to the mountain of GOD, in Horeb, where a Messenger of the 2 EVER-LIVING appeared to him, in a flame of fire, in a bush　When he looked, he saw that the bush burnt with fire, yet the bush was not consumed!

Then Moses said, "I will draw 3 near and examine this great wonder, why the bush is not burnt up." But 4 the LORD saw that he approached to examine it, so GOD called to him from the midst of Sinai, and said, "Moses! Moses!" and he answered, "I am here

---

[1] Moses = "From the Water"　—F. F.

[b] A stranger here　—F. F.

5　　Then He said, "Approach not! Put off your shoes from your feet, for the place upon which you stand is
6　Holy!" Then He continued, "I AM the GOD of your fathers,—the GOD of Abraham, and the GOD of Isaac, and the GOD of Jacob!"

Then Moses hid his face, for he feared to gaze upon GOD

7　　The Lord then said, "I have seen the suffering of My PEOPLE who are in Mitzeraim and I have heard their shrieks before their drivers, and I
8　have understood their sorrows, and I have come down to deliver them from the hand of the Mitzerites, and to take them up from that country to a good land, and a spacious, to a land flowing with milk and honey,—to replace the Cananites, and the Hitites, and the Amorites, and the Perizites,
9　and the Ivites, and Jebusites　For the cries of the children of Israel have now come to Me, and I have seen the oppression with which the Mitzerites
10　oppress them, therefore you must go, and I will send you to Pharoh, to bring My PEOPLE, the children of Israel, up from the Mitzeraim"
11　　But Moses replied to GOD, "Who am I, that I should go to Pharoh? and that I should lead the children of Israel up from among the Mitzeraim?"
12　He answered, however, "Because I will be with you,—therefore go For I have sent you to lead the people from the Mitzeraim, and they shall serve GOD upon this mountain!"
13　　Then Moses said to GOD, "Supposing I should go to the children of Israel, and should say to them, 'The GOD of your fathers has sent me to you,' and they should ask me, 'What is His name?'—what am I to say to them?"
14　When GOD responded to Moses, "I AM WHAT I AM! Therefore say 'I
15　AM' has sent me to you" And GOD further spoke to Moses, "You shall say thus to the children of Israel.— 'The EVER-LIVING GOD of your forefathers,—the GOD of Abraham, and the GOD of Isaac, and the GOD of Jacob, has sent me to you This is My Name from Eternity, and I remember this from generation to
16　generation　Go and assemble the Chiefs of Israel, and say to them, The EVER-LIVING GOD of your fathers has appeared to me, the GOD of Abraham Isaac, and Jacob, and said, I have visited you and I will save

you from the Mitzerites　Therefore 17 I command you to go from among the Mitzerites to the land of the Cananites, and the Hitites, and the Amorites, and the Perizites, and the Hivites, and the Jebusites, to a land flowing with milk and honey,' and 18 they will listen to your voice　Then go, you and the Chiefs of Israel, to the king of the Mitzeraim, and say to him, 'The EVER-LIVING GOD of your servants has commanded us, therefore we pray let us go a three days' journey into the desert and offer sacrifice to our EVER-LIVING GOD' But I know that the king of the Mit- 19 zeraim will not permit you to go, except by a strong hand　Conse- 20 quently I shall stretch out My hand and strike the Mitzerites with all the wonders that I will do within their bounds, and afterwards he will send you away　Then I will give this 21 People favour in the eyes of the Mitzerites, so that it shall be when they march, they shall not march unprovided, but every woman shall demand 22 of her neighbour and from the guests in her house, ornaments of silver, and ornaments of gold, and clothing, and put them upon her sons and daughters, and shall strip the Mitzerites"

Then Moses answered and said, 4 "But they may not trust me, and not listen to my voice; for they may say, 'We have never seen your GOD, the EVER-LIVING!'"

GOD, however, asked him, "What 2 is in your hand?" and he replied, "A stick"

And He then said, "Throw it on 3 the ground!" So he threw it on the ground, and it became a serpent, and Moses fled from before it

But the EVER-LIVING said to 4 Moses "Stretch out your hand and seize it by the tail" So he stretched out his hand and seized it, and it became a stick in his hand　"Be 5 certain they will believe because of that, that the EVER-LIVING GOD of their fathers appeared to you,—the GOD of Abraham, the GOD of Isaac, and the GOD of Jacob" And con- 6 tinuing the EVER-LIVING said to him, "Put your hand now into your bosom," so he put his hand into his bosom, and when he drew it out his hand was leperous like snow!

Then He said, "Replace your hand 7 in your bosom, so he replaced his hand in his bosom, and took it out again from his bosom, and it returned like his other flesh

8   "And it shall be if they will not trust you, and not listen to your voice at the first evidence, yet they will trust to your voice after the second

9 sign But if they do not trust you even for this second evidence, and do not listen to your voice, then take some of the water from the river and pour it out on the dry land, and there the water which you have taken from the river shall become blood on the dry ground '

10 • Moses, however, replied to the EVER-LIVING, "But yet, LORD, I am not an eloquent man, I have not been so in the past, nor in this speaking between You and Your servant, for I am slow of mouth and heavy of tongue "

11 But the EVER-LIVING replied to him, "Who gave a mouth to man? or who makes dumb, or deaf? or blind, or seeing? Is it not I, the LIVING

12 ONE? So now go, and I will be with your mouth and show you what you shall say "

13 But he answered , " Indeed, my LORD, send I pray You by some other hand ' "

14 Then the EVER-LIVING was angry with Moses, and He said , " Have you not a brother, Aaron the Levite? I know that he can talk—and he is even now coming to seek you See that you

15 can go cheerfully with him, and speak to him, and put words into his mouth, for I will be with your mouth, and in his mouth, and will show you what

16 you are to do, and he shall speak for you to the people He shall be like a mouth for you, and you shall be to

17 him in place of GOD And that staff, —take it in your hand, for you shall perform wonders with it "

18 Moses therefore went and returned to Jethro his father-in-law, and said to him , " I wish to go now and rejoin my relatives who are in Mitzeraim and see if they are alive " When Jethro replied to Moses, "Go in peace "

19 The EVER-LIVING afterwards said to Moses, in Midian , " Go! Return to the Mitzeraim, for all the men are dead who sought your life "

20 Then Moses took his wife, and his sons, and mounted them upon asses and turned towards the land of the Mitzeraim Moses also took the Rod of GOD in his hand

21 The LIVING ONE also said further to Moses " During your journey to

the Mitzeraim, regard all the signs which I put unto your hand, and do them before Pharoh But I shall harden his heart, and he will not let the People go Then you shall say 22 to Pharoh, 'Thus said the EVER-LIVING,—Israel is My eldest son, and 23 I say to you, Allow My son to go to serve Him , and if you will not allow him, then I will slay your eldest son ' "

But while he was upon the road at 24 a resting place, a Chieftain [1] met him and attempted to kill him , but 25 Zifoiah took a razor and cut off the foreskin of her son and threw it at his feet, and said, "You make a blood-marriage for me " So he re- 26 tired from them, when she said, " It is a marriage circumcision "

Now the EVER-LIVING had said to 27 Aaron, "Go and seek Moses in the desert," so he went and met him at the Mount of GOD, and kissed him

Then Moses related to Aaron all 28 the instructions of the EVER-LIVING which He had sent to him, and the whole of the miracles which He had commanded Then Moses and Aaron 29 proceeded and collected all the Magistracy of the children of Israel And 30 Aaron repeated all the matters which the EVER-LIVING had addressed to Moses, and produced evidences before the eyes of the People, and the people 31 were convinced, and acknowledged that the EVER-LIVING had visited Israel, and that He had looked upon their sufferings ,—so they honoured and worshipped Him

Then Moses and Aaron went and 5 said to Pharoh ,—"Thus says the EVER-

---

1 The Hebrew word used is יְהוָֹה, Jehovah, and is translated " The LORD " in former versions I, however, use Chieftain, as the word was a title of honour, as much as our vocable of "Lord" for a Parliamentary Peer, and was used in the sense of Chief, as in Genesis, ch xviii , v 35, by the Divine Messengers sent to Sodom, when they conversed with Abraham After the Giving of the Law it seems to have been almost entirely reserved as a title or synonym for the Supreme Being, GOD It means "The EVER-LIVING" by its innate sense, therefore GOD commanded (ch iii , v 14) that from that time His Name should be " The EVER-LIVING GOD, to distinguish Him from heathen imaginary deities, whom their deluded votaries believed could die, be murdered, or dethroned, and hence they were no basis for eternal Law or moral life The reader thus can see the object of the name was to show the unchanging nature of the Laws of all that sent us in to the a Being of Eternal life

LIVING GOD of Israel; 'Send out My People that they may hold a festival to Me in the desert.'"

2 But Pharoh replied, "Who is the EVER-LIVING that I should listen to His voice, to send out the Israelites? I know nothing of the EVER-LIVING; and I shall not send the Israelites out!"

3 They, however, replied; "The GOD of the Hebrews has summoned us. Let us go therefore three days' journey into the desert, and sacrifice to our EVER-LIVING GOD, for fear He should assail us with plague or fever."

4 The King of the Mitzeraim said to them; "Why do you, Moses and Aaron, break off the people from their work? Go yourselves to the 5 buildings! And," Pharoh went on to say, "the people are now too many for the land, yet you would take them away from building!"

6 Pharoh consequently commanded, on that day, to the drivers and over-7 seers, saying,—"You shall not continue to give straw to these people for the bricks they make, as heretofore; but let them go and collect 8 straw for themselves. Yet the number of the bricks which they had to make heretofore lay upon them; you shall not diminish from them, for they are idle, therefore they cry out saying, 'Let us go and sacrifice to 9 our GOD.' Increase the work upon these men, and make them do it, and not listen to absurd speeches."

10 The drivers and overseers of the people consequently went and reported it to the people, saying thus; 11 "Pharoh has ordered us no more to give you straw. Therefore go, collect straw for yourselves wherever you can find it, for there is to be no diminution of your labours whatever."

12 So the people were scattered all over the land of the Mitzeraim to seek 13 stubble instead of straw. Yet the drivers ordered them, saying, "Complete your appointed work day by day in the production of bricks."

14 And the overseers who were set over the children of Israel were flogged by the drivers of Pharoh, who demanded; "Why have you not completed the stipulated number of bricks as formerly was done, before this?"

15 Then the overseers of the children of Israel appealed to Pharoh, asking; "Why have you done this to your 16 slaves? No straw is given to your slaves, yet they say to us, 'Make the

bricks,' and your slaves are beaten, and your people injured."

17 He, however, replied, "You are idle! you are idle! Therefore you say, 'Let us go and sacrifice to 18 the EVER-LIVING.' So now be off, you slaves, for straw shall not be given to you, but you shall make the number of your bricks!"

19 Consequently the overseers of the children of Israel saw they were in a bad position, when he said, "You shall not diminish from the number of bricks day by day;" so they assailed 20 Moses and Aaron for inciting them to go to present themselves to Pharoh, and said to them; "May the EVER-21 LIVING look upon you, and decide how you have made our breath stink in the opinion of Pharoh, and in the opinion of his ministers, and have put a sword into their hands to slay us!"

22 Then Moses turned to the EVER-LIVING and said; "ALMIGHTY! why have You caused suffering to this People, and why have You sent me 23 thus? And why have You sent me to Pharoh saying 'I will take this People from their suffering?' when You have not delivered them?"

Then the EVER-LIVING replied to **6** Moses, "Now you shall see what I will do to Pharoh, so that with a strong hand he shall send off, and with a strong hand he shall drive them from this country."

Appropriation of the Name Jehovah to God.

2 Afterwards the EVER-LIVING spoke to Moses and said to him; "I am THE EVER-LIVING. And I appeared 3 to Abraham, and to Isaac, and to Jacob, as GOD ALMIGHTY; and by My name of the EVER-LIVING [1] I did not make Myself known to them; but however I made a covenant 4 with them to give to them the land of Canan, the land of their foreignhood, when they were foreigners in it. I have also heard the groaning 5 of the children of Israel who are enslaved by the Mitzerites, and I have remembered My covenant;

1 V. 3. "Johvah." See on this name of the Almighty Prof. Lee's Hebrew Lexicon, voc. יהוה, Jehovah, where it is shown to indicate Christ, as the Manifestation of GOD Who spoke with the Patriarchs, Moses, and the Prophets, and that it was first used as a Divine name, to Moses at the bush. See also my note on ch. iv. v. 24.—F. F.

6 therefore say to the children of Israel, I AM, the EVER-LIVING, will cause you to come out from among the burdens of the Mitzerites, and I will deliver you from your slavery, and will redeem you with a directing 7 arm, and with great judgments, and will take you to Myself for a People, and will be a GOD to you, and you shall know that I, your EVER-LIVING GOD, have brought you out from among the burdens of the Mitzerites

8 I will, also, bring you to the land which I raised My hand to give to Abraham, and to Isaac, and to Jacob, and grant you its possession I AM, the EVER-LIVING "

9 Consequently Moses repeated this to the children of Israel, but they would not listen to Moses for their anguish of spirit, and from their hard slavery

The Repeated Message to Pharoh.

10 The EVER-LIVING again spoke to 11 Moses, saying, " Go! tell to Pharoh King of Mitzer that he must dismiss the children of Israel from his country "

12 But Moses replied against the EVER-LIVING, and said , " The children of Israel themselves would not listen to me , so certainly Pharoh will not listen to me I am, also, dull in speech "

Reiterated Command to approach Pharoh.

13 The EVER-LIVING, however, commanded Moses and Aaron again, and sent them to the children of Israel, and to Pharoh King of the Mitzeraim to demand the release of the children of Israel from the land of the Mitzeraim [1]

---

[1] The verses from 14 to 25 are clearly inserted here by mistake of an old transcriber, or were a note of some editor I therefore append them at the foot of the page —F F.

The Ancestral Chiefs of Israel.

14 These are the heads of the Ancestral Houses of the sons of Reuben, the eldest of Israel —
Hanok, and Hazran, and Karmi,—these were of the families of Reuben

15 And the sons of Simeon, Imuel, and Iman, and Ahad, and Jakin, and Zokhar, and Shaul, the son of the Cananitess,— these were the families of Simeon

16 And these were the names of the sons of Levi,—by their order of birth,—
Ghersham, and Kahath, and Merari,— and the years of the life of Levi were a hundred and thirty-seven years —

17 The sons of Ghersham, Libni, and

Thus the EVER-LIVING spoke to 26 Aaron and Moses to lead the children of Israel out of the land of the Mitzeraim by their armies He caused 27 them, Moses and Aaron, to demand from Pharoh King of the Mitzeraim to allow the children of Israel to go out of Mitzeraim The EVER-LIVING 28 was speaking daily to Moses in the land of the Mitzeraim

Thus the LORD commanded Moses, 29 " I am the EVER-LIVING ! Speak to Pharoh King of the Mitzeraim all that I command you "

But Moses replied, in the face of the 30 EVER-LIVING, " I am only slow of tongue, so Pharoh will not listen to me ! "

The Plagues of Egypt.

The EVER-LIVING, however, an- 7 swered Moses, " See, I will make you like a GOD to Pharoh, and Aaron your brother shall be your Reciter Therefore you must say all that I 2 command you to your brother, and he shall repeat to Pharoh that he must send the children of Israel from his country But I will make Pharoh's 3 heart obstinate, and I will multiply evidences and wonders in the land of the Mitzeraim But Pharoh will not 4 listen to you, so I will lay My hand upon the Mitzerites, and will bring out My People, the children of Israel, from the land of the Mitzeraim with

---

Shimai, with their families And the sons 18 of Kahath were Amram, and Itzar, and Habron, and Azriel, and the years of the life of Kahath were a hundred and thirty-three years.

And the sons of Merari were Mahli, and 19 Mushi, these were the families of Levi by their birth

When Amram married he took his 20 cousin Jokabad to him, and she bore to him Aaron and Moses, and the years of the life of Amram were a hundred and thirty-seven years

And the sons of Izachar were Korah, 21 and Nafag, and Zikri, and the sons of 22 Azuiel Mishael and Alzaphan, and Sithri

But Aaron married as his wife Alishama 23 the daughter of Aminadab, the sister of Nahashon, and she bore him Nadab and Abihud , Eliezar and Aithamar

And the sons of Korah were Asir, and 24 Alkanah, and Abiasaf These were the families of Korahites

But Eliezar the son of Aaron took a 25 wife from the daughters of Putiel, and she bore to him Finehas These were the chief fathers of the Levites by their families

5 Great Judgments, so that the Mitzerites may know that I am the EVER-
LIVING, when I stretch out My hand
over the Mitzeraim and bring up
the children of Israel from among
them."

6　So Moses and Aaron did as the
EVER-LIVING commanded them.

7 They did it. But Moses was eighty
years old, and Aaron eighty-six years
old, when they spoke to Pharoh.

8　Thus the EVER-LIVING spoke to

9 Moses and to Aaron, saying ;—" Since
Pharoh has said to you 'Give us an
Evidence' instruct Aaron,—Take your
rod and throw it down before Pharoh
and it shall become a serpent ! "

10　Moses and Aaron therefore went
to Pharoh, and did as the EVER-
LIVING commanded, and he threw
down his rod before Pharoh, and
before his ministers, and it became a
serpent.

11　But Pharoh summoned the scientists and chemists, and they also did
it, assisted by the engineers of the

12 Mitzeraim, by their delusions. For
each of them threw down their rods !
and they became serpents, but the
rod of Aaron swallowed their rods.

13 However the heart of Pharoh was
hardened, and he would not listen
to them ;—as the EVER-LIVING had
foretold.

14　The EVER-LIVING then said to
Moses, " The heart of Pharoh is decided not to let the people depart.

15 Confront Pharoh in the morning,
when he goes to the bath, and stand
to meet him at the bank of the river,
and take the rod which turned to a

16 serpent in your hand. Then say to
him ; " The EVER-LIVING GOD of
the Hebrews has sent me to you to
say, ' Let My People go and serve
Me in the desert. But if you will

17 not listen to that, thus says the EVER-
LIVING, by this you shall learn that I
am the MASTER :—When I strike
with the rod which is in my hand
upon the waters which are in the

18 river, they shall turn to blood ! And
the fish which are in the river shall
die ; and the river shall stink ; and the
Mitzerites shall loathe to drink of the
water of the river ! "

19　The EVER-LIVING also said to
Moses ; " Say to Aaron ; Take your
rod and extend your hand over the
waters of Mitzer ;—over the streams,
over the brooks, the pools, and over
all the reservoirs of water : and they

shall become blood ; and they shall
be blood in all the land of the Mitzerites, both in wood and in stone."

20 Therefore Moses and Aaron did as
the EVER-LIVING commanded, and
splashed with the rod, and the hand,
the waters which were in the river
before the eyes of Pharoh, and before
the eyes of his ministers, and all the
waters in the river turned to blood ; and
the fish which were in the river died,

21 and the river stank, and the Mitzerites
were not able to drink of the water
from the river, for it became blood
in all the land of the Mitzerites.

22 The engineers of Mitzer, however,
did the same by their delusions ;
therefore the heart of Pharoh was
hardened, and he would not listen to
them—as the EVER-LIVING had fore-

23 told. Pharoh, therefore, turned his
face and went to his palace, and did
not alter his heart even for this.

24 But all the Mitzerites dug pits along
the river for water to drink, for they
were not able to drink the waters

25 from the river. This continued for
seven days after the EVER-LIVING
had struck the waters of the river.

26 Then the EVER-LIVING said to
Moses ; " Go to Pharoh and say to
him ;—' Thus says the EVER-LIVING !
Send My People away to serve Me ;

27 but if you will not send them, then I
will plague all your dominions with

28 frogs, and the river shall swarm with
frogs, and they shall crawl up, and
come into your palace, and to your
chamber, to your couch, and up to
your bed ; and to the palaces of your
ministers, and of your people, and to

29 your daughters. In this way the
frogs shall come up upon your people,
and ministers.' "

8 Then the EVER-LIVING said to
Moses, " Command your brother
Aaron ; ' Extend your hand with your
rod over the rivers, and streams, and
lakes, so that the frogs may come up
over the land of Mitzer.' "

2 Aaron consequently extended his
hand over the waters of Mitzer, and
frogs came up and plagued the land
of the Mitzeraim.

3 The scientists, however, did the
same by their engineering, and also
brought up frogs upon the land of the

4 Mitzeraim. Pharoh, however, summoned Moses and Aaron, and said ;
" Entreat the EVER-LIVING, that He
may turn away the frogs from my
sight, and from my touch, when I

will release the People, and they shall sacrifice to the EVER-LIVING "

5 But Moses replied to Pharoh; "You threatened me you would kill me! Why should I pray for you, and your ministers, and your people, to drive away the frogs from you, and from your palace, except that there may be a few in the river?"

6 He however entreated, "Do it to-morrow"

And he returned, "It shall be done as you say, so that you may know that there is no LORD except our

7 GOD   Therefore the frogs shall turn back from you, and from your palace, and from your ministers, and from your people—except that in the river there shall be a few"

8 Then Moses and Aaron went out from Pharoh, and Moses cried to the EVER-LIVING about the frogs, as he

9 had promised to Pharoh, and the EVER-LIVING did as Moses had said and killed the frogs in the houses,

10 and in the streets, and in the fields, and the heaps of them corrupting, rotted,—and the country stunk

11 But when Pharoh perceived the smell of them, then he hardened his heart, and would not listen to them,—as the EVER-LIVING had foretold

12 Consequently the EVER-LIVING said to Moses, "Say to Aaron, 'Extend your rod, and beat the dust of the earth, and it shall become lice in all the land of the Mitzeraim'"

13 And he did so

When Aaron extended his hand with his rod in it and struck the dust of the earth, it became lice in all the land of the Mitzeraim

14 The scientists also tried by their contrivances to produce the same, and bring forth lice, but they were not able   These lice assailed both men and beasts

15 Then the scientists reported to Pharoh —"This is the product of GOD," but Pharoh hardened his heart and would not listen to them—as the EVER-LIVING had foretold

16 Therefore the EVER-LIVING said to Moses, "Arise at daybreak and stand before Pharoh, when he goes to bathe, and say to him —'Thus says the EVER-LIVING, Release My

17 People that they may serve Me! for if you do not release My People, I Myself will release against you, and your ministers, and your people, and your daughters, gad-flies, and the gad-

flies shall fill the houses of the Mitzerites, and also the land upon which they are   But at the same 18 time it shall be different in the land of Goshen, where My People dwell, for the gad-flies shall not be there, so that you may know that I am the EVER-LIVING in the midst of the earth

"'I will also make a distinction be- 19 tween My People and your People   This shall occur to-morrow'"

And the EVER-LIVING did it   For 20 swarms of gad-flies came into the palace of Pharoh, and the palaces of his ministers, and to all the land of the Mitzeraim   The gad-flies spread over all the country

Then Pharoh summoned Moses 21 and Aaron and said, "Go! Sacrifice to your GOD in this country"

But Moses replied, "We were not 22 instructed to do so   For if we were to sacrifice the idol of the Mitzerites in their sight, would they not stone us? We must go three days' journey 23 into the desert, and sacrifice to our EVER-LIVING GOD as He has commanded us"

Then Pharoh answered,—"I will 24 send you, and you shall sacrifice to your EVER-LIVING GOD in the desert, only in separating go not a long journey —Now pray for me!"

And Moses answered, "I will go 25 out from you and pray, and entreat the EVER-LIVING, and He will turn away the gad-flies from Pharoh, and from his ministers, and from his people, to-morrow   Nevertheless Pharoh will continue to oppose, and will not allow the People to go away to sacrifice to the EVER-LIVING"

Moses accordingly went out from 26 the presence of Pharoh and prayed to the LORD, and the EVER-LIVING 27 answered Moses and removed the gad-flies from Pharoh, and from his ministers, and from his People, and none remained   Pharoh, however, 28 hardened his heart even after this, and would not release the People

Consequently the EVER-LIVING 9 said to Moses, "Go to Pharoh, and tell him, Thus says the EVER-LIVING GOD of the Hebrews,—Let My People go and serve Me   However, if you 2 are unwilling to release them, and you are again obstinate with them, then the hand of the EVER-LIVING 3 shall bring upon your herds that are in the field and upon your horses, and asses, and camels, and cattle, and sheep, a very severe punishment.

4 But the EVER-LIVING will distinguish between the herds of Israel, and between the herds of the Mitzerites, and in all the herds of Israel nothing shall die."

5 The EVER-LIVING, however, fixed a period, "After a while the EVER-LIVING will do this thing in the
6 country." The EVER-LIVING accordingly brought the event at the period, and killed a number of the cattle of the Mitzerites, but of the cattle of the Israelites not any died.
7 Pharoh, also, sent to examine, and discovered that of the cattle of the Israelites none had died, yet Pharoh hardened his heart, and would not let the People go.

8 Subsequently the EVER-LIVING said to Moses and Aaron; " Take up for yourselves hands full of ashes from the smeltery furnaces, and let Moses fling them to the sky in the
9 sight of Pharoh, and they shall become a fine dust over all the land of Mitzer, and it shall settle upon man and beast, to inflame and produce boils in all the land of the Mitzeraim."
10 They took, therefore, ashes from a smeltery, and presented themselves before Pharoh, and Moses flung them skyward, and they produced inflammatory boils upon man and beast,
11 and the scientists were not able to stand before Moses, for the inflammation came upon the scientists, as well as upon the other Mitzerites.
12 But the EVER-LIVING hardened Pharoh's heart; so he would not listen to them;—as the EVER-LIVING had foretold to Moses.

13 Afterwards the EVER-LIVING said to Moses; "Arise at dawn, and go and stand before Pharoh, and say to him; Thus says the EVER-LIVING GOD of the Hebrews, 'Release My
14 People to serve Me! Or else, this time, I will fling with all My might upon your heart, and on your ministers, and on your people, so that they may learn that there is none, except MYSELF, in the whole earth.
15 For now I will send My hand against, and strike you; yourself, and Your People, with the object of destroying
17 you from the earth. If you oppose yourself to My People, to prevent
18 them from going, I will rain, at the date appointed in the future, very fierce hail, such as has not been in Mitzer from the day it was founded

until now. Therefore send your 19 cattle to shelters, and all that you have in the field. Every man and beast that remains in the field, and is not gathered into houses, the hail will come down upon them, and kill them."

Those of the ministers of Pharoh 20 who feared the message of the EVER-LIVING, collected their servants, and their cattle into the houses, but those 21 who did not lay the message of the EVER-LIVING to heart, left their servants and cattle in the field.

The EVER-LIVING afterwards said 22 to Moses, "Extend your hand to the skies, and there will come hail in all the land of the Mitzeraim, upon man, and upon beast; and upon all that is in the field, in the land of the Mitzeraim."

So Moses extended his rod to the 23 skies, and the EVER-LIVING uttered His voice; and fire ran along the ground, and the EVER-LIVING poured hail upon the land of the Mitzeraim. And there was hail, and continuous 24 fire mixed with the hail, very cruel, such as had never been like it in all the land of the Mitzeraim from when it became a nation. The hail also 25 struck in all the land of the Mitzeraim whatever was in the field, from man to beast, and all the vegetation of the field was struck by the hail, and all the trees of the field broken, except in the 26 land of Goshen where the children of Israel were,—there the hail was not.

After this Pharoh sent and invited 27 Moses and Aaron, and said to them; "I have sinned this time! The EVER-LIVING has done right, and I and my people have done wrong. Pray to the EVER-LIVING; for mighty 28 are the utterances of GOD,—and the hail;—and I will release you, and no more continue to prevent!"

But Moses answered him, "When 29 I am outside of the city, I will spread out my hands to the EVER-LIVING, when the voices will cease, and the hail will not continue; so that you may learn that the earth belongs to the EVER-LIVING, and that you and 30 your ministers may learn at last to fear before the presence of the EVER-LIVING GOD."

So the flax and the barley were 31 cut up, for the barley was in ear and the flax in flower; but the wheat and 32 rye were not cut up, for they were of later growth.

When Moses went from the 33 presence of Pharoh outside the city, he spread his hands before the EVER-LIVING ; and the voices ceased, and the hail storm poured not earthward

34 But when Pharoh perceived that the rain and hail and voices had ceased, he continued to sin, and hardened his heart,—he and his

35 ministers So Pharoh's heart was obstinate, and he would not release the children of Israel,—as the EVER-LIVING foretold, by the hand of Moses.

10 Therefore the EVER-LIVING said to Moses, "Go to Pharoh, for I will strike his heart, and the heart of his ministers, with two other evidences in

2 their midst, that you can record for the ears of your sons and your sons' sons, how I brought you up from the Mitzeraim, and the evidences that I produced among them, that they might know that I am the EVER-LIVING "

3 Moses and Aaron consequently went to Pharoh and said to him, "Thus says the EVER-LIVING GOD of the Hebrews; ' Until when will you refuse ? resisting to My face to release My people to serve Me ?

4 However if you continue refusing to release My people, I will bring locusts shortly into your dominions, and they shall hide the sight of the ground, so that you shall not be able to see the

5 ground, and they shall eat the remains of the fragments of what has been left to you from the hail, and shall eat all your fruit trees from the field,

6 and shall fill your palace, and the palaces of your ministers, and the houses of all the Mitzerites, in such a way as you have never seen, or your fathers, or the fathers of your fathers from the day they lived upon the earth to this day.' "

Then he ceased and went away from Pharoh.

7 Then Pharoh's ministers said to him, "How long is this thing to go on with us, to ensnare us ? Release these men to serve their EVER-LIVING GOD —Do you not know that Mitzer is already destroyed ? "

8 Moses and Aaron were brought back to Pharoh, and he accordingly said to them,—"Go ! Serve the EVER-LIVING, your GOD—Who, and what do you wish should go with you ? "

9 So Moses replied, "With our young, and our old, we shall go, with our sons and our daughters, with our sheep, and our cattle, we shall go, so that we may hold a holy festival to our GOD."

He however exclaimed, "The 10 EVER-LIVING must be with you, then, when I let you go with your children,—look out ! for evil is before you ! It shall never be so !—But you may 11 go now, and make a pilgrimage, and serve your EVER-LIVING—for that is what you asked "

And they were driven from the presence of Pharoh

Then the EVER-LIVING said to 12 Moses, " Stretch out your hand over the land of the Mitzeraim for the locusts, and they shall come up upon the land of Mitzer, and shall eat everything green in the country, all that the hail has left "

So Moses extended his rod over 13 the country of the Mitzeraim, and the EVER-LIVING drove an east wind over the country all that day and all the night until the morning came, and the east wind carried the locusts, and the locusts came up over all the 14 country of the Mitzeraim, and seized upon all the dominions of the Mitzeraim very grievously Before them there were no such locusts, and never since have there been such They even hid the ground from 15 sight, and blackened the earth, and ate every green thing upon the ground, and all the fruit of the trees which the hail had left, and no verdure was left on the trees, or grass on the fields, in all the land of the Mitzeraim

Then Pharoh hastened, and sum- 16 moned Moses and Aaron, and said, " I have sinned against the EVER-LIVING GOD, and against you ! There- 17 fore pardon now my sin, only this once, and entreat the EVER-LIVING GOD to turn from me also this death "

So they went out from Pharoh and 18 entreated the EVER-LIVING, and the 19 LORD caused a very strong west wind to blow, and it swept off the locusts and blew them into the Red Sea. There was not a locust in all the dominions of the Mitzeraim But the 20 EVER-LIVING strengthened the heart of Pharoh, and he would not release the children of Israel

Afterwards the EVER-LIVING said 21 to Moses, " Stretch your hand towards the sky, and darkness shall come upon all the land of the Mitzeraim, and a darkness that may be felt "

Therefore Moses stretched his 22 hand to the skies, and thick darkness came upon all the land of the Mitzeraim for three days No one 23 saw his brother, and no one rose from his place for three days. But to all the children of Israel there was light for their operations.

24 Then Pharoh sent for Moses and said; "Go! Serve the EVER-LIVING. Only your sheep and cattle must stay; your children, also, may go with you."

25 But Moses replied; "You must also give to our hands sacrifices and offerings that we can make to our

26 EVER-LIVING GOD, and therefore our herds must go with us; not a hoof must be left; for we must take from them to serve our EVER-LIVING GOD. And we cannot be knowing what we must serve the EVER-LIVING with until we arrive there."

27 The Lord, however, hardened the heart of Pharoh, and he was not

28 willing to release the People. Therefore Pharoh replied to him, " Get off from me! and take care to yourself never again to see my face! for on the day you look again on my face you shall die !"

29 When Moses answered; " As you have spoken right, I never will look on your face again!"

11 Then the EVER-LIVING said to Moses; "I will bring yet another blow upon Pharoh, and upon the Mitzeraim, after which he will release you. They all will release you,

2 driving you from here. Therefore privately instruct the People that they must demand every man from his neighbour, and every woman from her neighbour, articles of silver and

3 articles of gold." The EVER-LIVING also gave the People favour in the eyes of the Mitzerites; for the man Moses was very powerful in the land of Mitzer, in the eyes of the ministers of Pharoh, and in the eyes of the People.

4 After that Moses proclaimed; "Thus says the EVER-LIVING, At midnight I will pass through the

5 land of the Mitzeraim, and kill all the first-born in the land of Mitzer, from the first-born of Pharoh, who sits upon the throne, to the first-born of the slave who sits behind the mill; as well as the first-born of the cattle;

6 and a great cry will go up from all the land of Mitzer, when these are

7 not; and those are perished. But from all the children of Israel there shall not be hurt a dog's tongue, that you may know that the EVER-LIVING distinguishes between the Mitzerites

and Israel. Then all your ministers 8 shall descend, and bow down to me saying, 'Go away, you, with all the People who are following you,' and after that I will depart."

Thus he went from before Pharoh in burning anger. Then the EVER- 9 LIVING said to Moses; " Since Pharoh will not listen to you, I will increase my evidences in the land of the Mitzeraim." Therefore Moses and Aaron 10 effected all these evidences before Pharoh; yet the EVER-LIVING hardened the heart of Pharoh, and he would not release the children of Israel from his country.

Consequently the EVER-LIVING 12 spoke to Moses and to Aaron in the land of the Mitzeraim, commanding;

" This month shall be to you the 2 Chief Month; it shall be the first month of the year to you,

Institution of the Passover.

" Speak to all the families of Israel 3 commanding that in the tenth month they shall take for themselves each one a lamb for a father's house, a lamb for a family. But if the family 4 is too small for a lamb, then let him and the neighbour to his house, according to the number of persons who are to eat, share in the lamb. It must be a perfect he lamb of a 5 year. You may take it from the sheep or from the goats; and you 6 must keep it by you until the fourteenth day of this month, then kill it. All the Assembly of the Families of Israel must kill it between the dusks.[1] Then they shall take of the blood and 7 sprinkle upon the two door-posts, and upon the lintel of the houses where they eat it. And they shall eat the 8 flesh in that night, roasted with fire. They shall eat it with unfermented 9 bread and bitter herbs. They shall not eat any of it parboiled, or boiled in a boiler, but only roasted with fire, its head, and limbs, and ribs; and 10 they shall not reserve any of it till the morning, but what is left of it at the morning they shall consume with fire. And they shall eat it in this 11 way;—girt with their belts, their shoes on their feet, and their sticks in their hands; and they shall eat it rapidly. It is a Passing-over to the EVER- LIVING, for I will pass through the 12

---

1 The dawn and twilight. — F. F.

land of the Mitzeraim in that night, and strike all the first-born of the Mitzerites from man to beast Upon all the gods of the Mitzerites also I will execute judgment I the EVER-

13 LIVING But the blood upon your houses shall be a safeguard to you, that you are there, when I see the blood, then I will pass over you, and there shall not be a life injured in my destruction of the land of the

14 Mitzeraim Therefore this day shall be to you for a Remembrance, and a Festival It shall be a Festival to the EVER-LIVING in your generations, an ordinance for ever You shall sanctify it

15 "You shall eat unfermented bread for seven days, that is in the first day you shall remove ferment from your houses, for all who eat fermented bread, then, that person shall be excommunicated from Israel, from the

16 first day to the seventh day So the first day shall be proclaimed holy, and the seventh day shall be proclaimed holy for you You shall not do any work upon them, except for what every person must eat, you shall

17 only do that Therefore, guard these days of unfermented bread, for on these days I led out your armies from the land of the Mitzeraim with power, consequently keep this period as an everlasting institution in your

18 generations, beginning at the fourteenth day of the month at the dusk to eat unfermented bread, until the twenty-first of the month at dusk

19 During seven days, ferment shall not be brought into your houses, for everyone eating of fermented bread, that person shall be excommunicated from the families of Israel, whether a foreigner or a native of the country

20 You shall not eat of any in your dwellings You shall eat biscuits"

21 Moses therefore proclaimed to all the magistrates of Israel, saying, "Blow the trumpet, and select for yourselves a lamb for your families,

22 and kill the Passover, and take a bunch of hysop and dip it in the blood which ensues, and sprinkle the lintel and the two door-posts with the blood which ensues, and none of you shall go out from the door of his

23 house until daybreak, for at dusk the EVER-LIVING will strike the Mitzerites, but when he sees the blood on the lintel, and upon the two door-posts, then the EVER-LIVING

will pass over the door, and will not allow injury to come to that house to strike it

"You shall also keep this com- 24 mand as an Institution for you and your sons for ever Also when you 25 have arrived at the land which the EVER-LIVING will give you, as He promised, you shall there also regard this service And when your children 26 shall say to you, 'What is this service for?' you shall reply, 'This is the 27 sacrifice of the Passover to the EVER-LIVING, Who passed over the houses of the children of Israel in Mitzer. when He struck the Mitzerites, and protected our houses Therefore, the People shall bow down and worship'"

So the children of Israel went and 28 did as the EVER-LIVING commanded to Moses and Aaron — they did it

When that midnight came, the 29 EVER-LIVING struck all the first-born in the land of the Mitzeraim, from the first-born of Pharoh, who sat upon the throne, to the first-born of the prisoner in the dungeon, and all the first-born of cattle Then Pharoh 30 and all his ministers arose in the night, with all the Mitzerites, and there was a great shriek among the Mitzeraim, for there was not a house in which there was not someone dead!

Consequently he sent to Moses and 31 Aaron by night, and said, "Rise up! Go away from among my People,— both yourselves and the children of Israel Go! serve the EVER-LIVING, as He has commanded you And 32 take your sheep and your cattle, as you demanded, and march But therefore bless me!"

The Mitzerites also pressed on the 33 People to hasten them to go out from the country, "for," they said, "we shall all be dead!" So the People 34 took up the dough before it was fermented with yeast, rolled up in their knapsacks on their shoulders

The children of Israel also had 35 done as Moses ordered, and had demanded from the Mitzerites ornaments of silver and articles of gold, and clothing, and the EVER-LIVING 36 gave them favour in the eyes of the Mitzerites Thus they demanded from them, and escaped from the Mitzeraim

Then the children of Israel marched 37 from Ramases to the Encampment,

about six hundred thousand men,
38 beside children ; many strangers also went up with them, and very great
39 herds of sheep and cattle. They also baked the dough which they had brought from the Mitzeraim into biscuits, before it was fermented, for the Mitzerites drove them, and they were not able to ferment it, as well as also being ordered not to do it.

Period of Israel's Residence in Egypt.

40 Now the period of the residence of the children of Israel, during which they stayed amongst the Mitzerites, was four hundred and thirty years.
41 And it was at the end of the four hundred and thirtieth year, upon the self-same day, that all the armies of the EVER-LIVING came out from the
42 land of the Mitzeraim ; it is a night to be observed to the EVER-LIVING ; for He brought them out from the land of the Mitzeraim. It is the Night, the Night of observance to the EVER-LIVING, for all the children of Israel and their descendants.
43 The EVER-LIVING had said to Moses and Aaron ; " This is the Feast of the Passover ; any son of a foreigner
44 shall not eat of it ; but every person
45 bought with money when he has been circumcised may eat of it.
46 " It shall be eaten by single families ; they shall not carry any of its flesh outside of the house ; and a bone of
47 it shall not be broken. Every family
48 in Israel shall offer it ; and if there resides with you a foreigner, and he would offer the Passover to the EVER-LIVING, let him cause every male to be circumcised. He may then approach to offer it, when he shall be like a native of the country, but any uncircumcised person shall not eat
49 of it. One law shall be for the native, and for the foreigner, who is among you."
50 So all the children of Israel did as the EVER-LIVING commanded to Moses and Aaron ; they did it.
51 Thus it was on the self-same day the EVER-LIVING caused the children of Israel to go out from the land of the Mitzeraim, with their armies.
13 The EVER-LIVING also commanded
2 to Moses ; " Consecrate to Me every first-born proceeding from every womb of the children of Israel, both of man and beast. It is Mine."

Therefore Moses said to the people, 3 " Remember this day when you came out of the land of the Mitzeraim, from the house of bondage ; for with a strong hand the EVER-LIVING brought you from there :—so you shall not eat fermented bread. The time 4 when you came out was in the month of harvest ; consequently, when the 5 EVER-LIVING brings you to the land of the Cananites, and the Hitites, and Amorites, and the Hivites, and the Jebusites, which He swore to give to you ;—a land flowing with milk and honey ;—then you shall perform this service in this month. For seven 6 days you shall eat biscuits, and on the seventh day shall be a festival to the EVER-LIVING. You shall eat 7 biscuits for seven days ; and fermented bread shall not be seen with you ; nor shall ferment be seen in all your boundaries. You shall inform your 8 children of this day, saying, ' This is for the Passing-over the EVER-LIVING made for us, in bringing us out from the Mitzeraim.' Thus it will be to 9 you like a mark on your hand, and as a remembrance between your eyes, so that the reverence for the EVER-LIVING may be before you ; for with 10 a strong hand the EVER-LIVING led you out from the Mitzeraim ; therefore you shall observe this institution for a witness for ever and ever.

" And when the EVER-LIVING has 11 brought you to the land of Canan, which He promised to you and to your fathers that He would give you, then you shall devote every first-born 12 of the womb to the EVER-LIVING ; and every first offspring of cattle which shall come to you as a male, to the EVER-LIVING. But every 13 first-born of an ass, you shall redeem with a lamb ; or if you do not redeem it, then break its neck. Every eldest male, however, of your children you shall redeem.

" When any of your sons, then, 14 shall ask you hereafter, saying : ' Why is this ?' You shall reply to him, The EVER-LIVING brought us out from the Mitzeraim with a strong hand, from the house of bondage. And when Pharoh refused to release 15 us, then the EVER-LIVING slew all the first-born in the land of the Mitzeraim, from the first-born of man, to the first-born of beast,—therefore I sacrifice to the EVER-LIVING all the first male offspring of the womb, and all

16 the first-born of men I redeem. Thus they will be like marks upon your hand, and as frontlets between your eyes, that with a strong hand the EVER-LIVING brought you from Mitzer."

History of the Exodus continued.

17 However, when Pharoh had released the People, GOD did not conduct them out by way of the country of the Philistines, although it was the nearest, for GOD said, "If I should conduct the People to the sight of war, they will return to the Mitze-

18 raim." Therefore GOD turned the People to the way by the desert of the Sea of Weeds. The children of Israel, however, marched in readiness for battle from the land of the Mitzeraim.

19 Moses also took the bones of Joseph with him, for he had administered an oath to the children of Israel saying, "The EVER-LIVING will visit you, and you shall carry up my bones from here with you."

20 So they marched from the Encampment, and pitched on the borders of

21 the desert, and the EVER-LIVING went before them by day in a pillar of cloud, to direct them on the way, and in a pillar of fire by night, to light them in the way by

22 day and night. The pillar of cloud never departed by day, nor the pillar of fire by night from before the People.

14 Then the EVER-LIVING spoke to Moses, saying,—

2 "Command the children of Israel, that they must turn and encamp before Pi-Hakhiroth [1] between Migdol and the sea, in front of Bal-zephon. You shall encamp directly opposite the sea!

3 "Upon which Pharoh will exclaim, 'The children of Israel have confused themselves as to the country!' The

4 desert shuts them in'" And I will embolden the heart of Pharoh and he will pursue you, and then I will be honoured by Pharoh and by all his forces, and the Mitzerites shall know that I am the EVER-LIVING."

They accordingly did it.

5 When it was reported to the king of the Mitzeraim that the People had

fled, then the heart of Pharoh and of his ministers changed about the People, and they said, "What is it that we have done? Why have we released the People from serving us?"

6 Consequently he had his own chariot harnessed, and took his forces with

7 him, and took six hundred officers' chariots, and all the chariots of the Mitzeraim with three men upon each of them.

8 Thus the EVER-LIVING emboldened the heart of Pharoh king of the Mitzeraim, and he pursued after the children of Israel. But the children of Israel went out with a high hand.

9 The Mitzerites, however, pursued after them, and came up with them encamped by the sea —all the horse chariots of Pharoh and his forces,— at Pi-Hakhiroth, before Bal-zephon.

10 As Pharoh approached, the children of Israel raised their eyes, and saw the Mitzerites marching after them, and they were terrified, so the children of Israel cried out to the EVER-LIVING,

11 and they said to Moses, "Because there were no graves among the Mitzeraim, have you brought us out from Mitzer into the desert to die?

12 Was not this what we said to you in Mitzer, 'Let us alone and we will serve the Mitzerites'? For it is better for us to serve the Mitzerites, than that we should die in the desert!'"

13 Moses, however, replied to the People, "Fear not! Stand still! and you shall see the victory of the EVER-LIVING, which He will effect for you to-day! For although you see the Mitzerites to-day, you shall not see them again for ever and ever!

14 The LORD will fight with them, and you shall keep silent!'"

15 The EVER-LIVING then said to Moses, 'Why do you cry to Me? Command the children of Israel to march. And you, raise your staff,

16 and extend your hand over the sea, when it will divide itself, and the children of Israel can go through it as upon dry land. But I, Myself, will

17 embolden the hearts of the Mitzerites, and they shall follow after them. Then I shall be honoured by Pharoh and by all his forces, by his charioteers and horsemen, and the Mit-

18 zerites shall learn that I am the EVER-LIVING by My conquering over Pharoh and his horsemen.

---

1 "The gorge of the caves" when translated —F. F.

19   Then the Messenger of GOD who went before the camp of Israel marched, and went behind them, and the pillar of cloud also marched from before them and stood at their rear,

20 and went between the camp of the Mitzerites, and the camp of Israel, and became a cloud and darkness—even of the light of the night,—so that the one approached not to the other all the night.

21   When Moses stretched his hand over the sea, the EVER-LIVING caused a strong east wind to blow and rolled back the waters all that night, and made the sea like dry land,

22 and made a plain in the waters. Then the children of Israel passed through the sea on the dried-up part, and the waters were to them a protection[1] on their right hand and upon their left.

23 The Mitzerites also pursued and went after them; all the horse chariots of Pharoh, and his horsemen,

24 into the midst of the sea. But when the morning-watch arrived the EVER-LIVING looked down from the Pillar of Fire and Cloud on to the army of

25 Mitzeraim and broke off the wheels from their chariots, and confused the ranks of the drivers, so that the Mitzerites exclaimed; "Let us fly from the presence of Israel, for the EVER-LIVING fights for them against the Mitzerites."

26   Then the EVER-LIVING said to Moses, "Stretch out your hand over the sea, and the waters shall return upon the Mitzerites, over their chariots and over their horsemen."

27   So Moses extended his hand over the waters, and the waters returned at the beginning of the morning to their regular flow, and the Mitzerites fled from their approach. Thus the EVER-LIVING overwhelmed the Mit-

28 zerites in the midst of the sea, and the waters returned and struck the chariots and the horsemen, and all the forces of Pharoh that went after them into the sea;—not one of them remained.

29   But the children of Israel went along upon the dry land in the midst of the sea, and the water was a protection to them on the right and on

30 the left. Thus the EVER-LIVING

saved Israel at that time from the hand of the Mitzerites, and Israel saw the Mitzerites dead on the shore of the sea; and Israel also saw the 31 great power by which the EVER-LIVING dealt with the Mitzerites, therefore the People feared the EVER-LIVING, and trusted in the LORD, and Moses His servant.

Song of Moses.[1]

Then Moses and the children of **15** Israel sang this song to the EVER-LIVING and said in chorus :—

STANZA I.

"I will sing to the LORD,
For with splendid power,
He has flung the horse and his rider
    Into the sea!

STANZA II.

"I shout and sing to my GOD,   2
For from Him comes my salvation!
He is my GOD, and I rest upon Him!
The GOD of my Fathers, and I will exalt Him!

STANZA III.

"The LORD is a warrior;   3
His name is JEHOVAH,—
He whelmed Pharoh's cars and 4 his force in the sea!
And his generals sank in the Sea of the Weeds!
The breakers sucked in to the 5 deeps like stone!

STANZA IV.

"Your right hand, LORD, is strong 6 and glorious,
Your right hand, LORD, has crushed Your foes,
And with grandeur destroyed 7 Your opponents!
You shot Your fire ;—it consumed them as chaff!
And the sea was filled by the 8 breath of Your mouth!
And they lay like heaps for the plunderers;
They curdled the waves in the heart of the sea!

---

1 Or "Circumvalation"—that is, like a moat or ditch on each side of the shallow from which the wate . . . . b . . . driv . . off by the east wind.—F . . .

1 I render this into the metre as I read the Hebrew original to run; and add another metrical version by my accomplished friend Henrik Borgström.

STANZA V.

9   " 'I will pursue,' said the foeman,
     ' O'ertake, and plunder and sate
       my lust,
     Draw my sword and my hand
       shall destroy them ! '—
     You blew with Your wind, and the
       sea overwhelmed,
     And their Princes sank like lead
       in the seas !

STANZA VI

" Who is like to the LORD among
     Gods ?
Who like Him in His Holy
     splendour,
In brightness, and honour, and
     powerful acts ?
You extended Your hand and
     the earth was shaken,—
You led in Your love this people
     free,
And will bring in Your might to
     Your Holy Home

STANZA VII

14   " The Nations hearing it trembled,
     Terror seized on Philistia's men,
15   The Chiefs of Edom were also in
     terror,
     The Princes of Moab shook in
     their fear,
     And the people of Canan dis-
     solved like a cloud,
     Dread and terror upon them fell
16   At Your Mighty power they stood
     like a stone,
     Until Your People, LORD, passed
     over,
     Until Your Race had passed out
     redeemed !
17   Whom You brought and fixed as
     Your own on Your Hill,
     The place You had chosen, LORD,
     for Your work,
18   To the Temple, ALMIGHTY, Your
     hands had made

STANZA VIII.

19   " The LORD will reign for ever and
     ever,
     For the horse of Pharoh went
     with his chariot,
     And with his horsemen, into the
     sea,
     Where the LORD turned on them
     the flood of the waters,
     But the children of Israel walked
     on the dry,—
     Thro' the midst of the sea !

20 Miriam the Poetess, also, the sister
of Aaron, took the timbrill in her
hand and all the women followed her
with timbrills and dances, and Miriam 21
responded to them,

The Chorus of Women.

" Sing to the LORD for gloriously
     triumphing,
He has flung the horse and his
     rider,—
       Into the sea ! "

THE SONG OF MOSES [1]

By Henrik Borgstrom.

The Exaltation.

" I will now sing to Him Who is
     the Force of Life,
For in strength He is strong ex-
     ceedingly,
Horse and his chariot hath He
     precipitated into the sea.
My trust and exaltation was JAH,
For He, to me, was Salvation
This is my GOD, and I will praise
     Him—
The GOD of my fathers—and I
     will extol Him
The Living One is a Man of War,—
     I THAT AM, His Name.

The Death of Pharoh.

" The chariots of Pharoh, and his
     army,
Are thrown into the sea,
And the chosen of each three
     charioteers
Are sunk in the Sea of Weeds
The billows covered them,—
They went down in the deep like
     stone

The Revelation of Strength.

" Thy Right Arm, O Burning Fire,
     is revealed in strength,
Thy Right Arm, O Life of Life,
     has shattered the enemy,

The Force of God.

" And with the force of Thy
     Majesty
Hast Thou scattered those that
     stood against Thee

---

[1] By Mr Henrik Borgstrom, of Helsingfors,
Finland, and which on account of its power
had I was I include with my own version,
by his permission.—f. I

Thou hast let loose Thy wrath.
Thy anger devoured them as
  stubble,
And at the breath of Thy mouth
  The waters stormed!

The Coagulation in the Sea.

"Th' unstable waves stood as a
  wall;
In the heart of the sea
Did the billows coagulate.

The Lust of the Enemy.

"The enemy spake:—
'I will pursue them,
Overtake, divide the spoil,
Will flesh my sword, will fill my
  hand!'"

The Avenging Lord.

"Thou didst blow with Thy wind,
The sea was troubled,—
As lead they rolled
  Into the mighty waters.

Who is like to God?

"Who is like unto Thee,
Among the gods,
O Eternal One?
Who is like unto Thee,
Transfigured in holiness,
Terrible in Praise,
Working Wonder?

The Guidance of God.

"Thou stretchest out Thine arm,—
The earth was vastated;
Thou guidest in Love,
The people Thou hast redeemed;
With Thy strength Thou leadest
  them
To the mansion of Thy Holiness.

The Trembling Nations.

"The Nations hear and they
  tremble;
Fear commands the dwellers in
  Pelashet;
Terror unnerves the Dukes of
  Edom:
The Princes of Moab are smitten
  with dread,—
    They cower!
All the inhabitants of Canaan,—
Anguish is fallen upon them,
They shrink away,
At the awe of Thy Captaincy
  They stood as a stone!

The People's Redemption.

"Until Thy Race come out,
O Thou, Who art from Eternity,
Until Thy Race come out,
Whom Thou hast made Thine
  own;—
Till Thou shouldst bring in, and
  plant them,
On the mountain, which Thou
  possessest,—
The place that Thou hast made
  for Thy habitation,
    O Centre of Being;
The Seat of Holiness,—
    O Ruler,—
That Thy hands have con-
  structed.

Jehovah's Eternal Reign.

"Then shall JEHOVAH reign
Over the all,
And over the Infinitude."

March from the Wall to the Desert of Marah.

Moses afterwards marched the 22
children of Israel from the Red Sea,
and departed from the Desert of the
Wall, and advanced three days into
the desert, but found no water. Then 23
they came to Marah, but were unable to drink the waters of Marah,
for they were bitter; therefore Moses
called it Bitterness. Then the people 24
came to Moses to say; "Why have
you done this?"

So he cried to the EVER-LIVING, 25
and the EVER-LIVING showed him
a tree, which he put into the water
and it sweetened it. He gave it
therefore the name of the Pit of
Calamity, and named it Trial. But 26
he said;

"If you will listen to the voice
of your EVER-LIVING GOD, and do
what is right in His eyes, and
give your ears to His commands,
and keep all His institutions, all
the plagues which I laid upon the
Mitzerites I will not lay upon you,
for I am your EVER-LIVING,
Restorer."

After that they came to Ailim, 27
where there were twelve springs of
water, and several palm trees, so they
encamped there by the springs.

𝕸𝖆𝖓𝖓𝖆 𝕲𝖎𝖛𝖊𝖓

16   Then the children of Israel marched from Ailim and came to Arath, in the Desert of Sin, which is between Ailim and Sinai, on the fifteenth day of the second month from their departure out of the land of the
2 Mitzeraim But all the families of the children of Israel complained
3 against Moses and Aaron in the Desert, and the children of Israel said to them,—

"Why do you kill us by the hand of the EVER-LIVING ? In the land of the Mitzeraim we sat by the flesh pots to gorging ! Why have you brought all the congregation to this Desert to die of hunger ? "

4   Therefore the EVER-LIVING said to Moses, "I will rain bread for them from the skies, and the people shall go out to collect it day by day, so that I may try if they
5 will walk in My laws or no But upon the sixth day they must prepare what they bring in, which shall be twice as much as the daily portion "

6   Moses and Aaron consequently said to all the children of Israel, " To-morrow morning you shall know that the EVER-LIVING brought you
7 out of the land of the Mitzeraim, for in the morning you shall see the power of the LORD by His listening to your complaints against the EVER-LIVING, and us, regarding what you
8 have complained against us And," Moses continued, " the EVER-LIVING will give you flesh to eat in the evening, and bread in the morning to your fill, because the EVER-LIVING has heard your complaints, that you have complained against Him and us, — for you not only complain against us, but against the LORD "

9   Then Moses said to Aaron,— " Command all the families of the children of Israel to appear before the EVER-LIVING, for He has heard their murmurs "

10   Consequently Aaron commanded all the families of the children of Israel, and they presented themselves in the desert, and saw the splendour of the EVER-LIVING appear in the cloud

11   Then the EVER-LIVING spoke to Moses, saying,—

12   " I have heard the complaints of the children of Israel Speak to them and say, ' In the evening you shall eat flesh, and in the morning you shall be filled with bread —so that you may know that I am your EVER-LIVING GOD ' "

When evening arrived therefore 13 quails came up and covered the camp, and in the morning a layer of dew surrounded the camp But when the 14 layer of dew exhaled from the surface of the desert, grains like scales, — grains like hoar-frost,— covered the ground

When the children of Israel saw 15 it, they said each to his brother,— " Man hoa ? " [1] for they did not know what it was But Moses said to them, " This is the bread which the EVER-LIVING has given for you to eat And this is the thing that He com- 16 mands, You are to collect each of you according to his requirements a homer for each individual member of the living persons, that you entertain in your tents "

The children of Israel accordingly 17 did so, and collected it from the desert much and little But when 18 they measured by the homer there was no excess to the much, or deficiency to the little, each had according to the consuming mouths, for Moses had said to them, " Let not 19 any remain until the morning " But 20 some listened not to Moses, but reserved it by them until the morning, when it bred worms, Moses however was angry with them Therefore they collected it morning 21 by morning, according to the consuming mouths, for when the sun arose it melted But when the sixth day 22 came they collected a double quantity of bread, two homers, to each, and all the heads of families came to Moses and reported it When he re- 23 plied to them, " That is what the EVER-LIVING commanded, ' You shall rest a Holy Rest to the EVER-LIVING to-morrow What you have to bake, bake it, and what you have to boil, boil it, and all the remainder 24 keep by you until the morning ' "

So they laid it up until the morn- 25 ing, as Moses commanded, and it did not stink and worms were not in it Then Moses said, " Eat it to-day, for to-day is a rest to the EVER-LIVING,

—you shall not go out into the field.

26 You shall collect it six days, but the seventh day is a rest; you shall not

27 do it then." Yet it happened that on the seventh day a man went out to collect,—but he found none.

28 The EVER-LIVING therefore said to Moses, "Until when shall I entreat them to observe My com-

29 mands and laws? Let them see that the EVER-LIVING has given them the rest, for He has given to them on the sixth day bread for two days. Let each stay at his home. Let none go out from the camp on the seventh day."

30 So the People stayed at home on the seventh day.

31 Thus the House of Israel called it "Man,"[1] and it was like a seed of coriander, white; and the taste of it like cakes and honey.

32 Moses also said, "This is the rule that the EVER-LIVING commands to be practised continually, to be kept for your generations, so that you may see the bread which I caused you to eat in the desert, whilst I brought you out from the land of Mitzer."

33 Therefore Moses said to Aaron; "Take a basket, and put into it a full homer of Mana, and place it before the presence of the EVER-LIVING, to preserve for their pos-

34 terity." So as the EVER-LIVING commanded to Moses, Aaron laid it up in the presence, as a witness, in the treasury.

35 And the children of Israel ate the mana for forty years. Until they came to the land to rest, they ate the mana; until they came to the border of the land of Canan.[2]

Marching in Thirst.

17 Afterwards the whole body of the children of Israel marched from the

2 Desert of Sin by stages at the command of the LORD, and encamped in exhaustion, for there was no water to quench the people's thirst. There the people contended with Moses, saying, "Give us water, and quench our thirst."

Moses, however, replied; "Why do you mutiny against me? Why do you try the EVER-LIVING?"

But the People thirsted then for 3 water, and the People complained against Moses, and said; "Why did you bring us out from Mitzer, to kill us, with our children and cattle, with thirst?"

Then Moses cried to the EVER- 4 LIVING, saying; "What shall I do with these People? For they are ready to stone me!"

But the EVER-LIVING answered 5 Moses; "Pass along before the face of the People and take with you the Magistrates of Israel. Take also in your hand the rod with which you struck the river, and march. I will 6 stand before your face there at the Rock in the Waste, and you shall strike upon the rock, and water shall come out from it, and quench the people."

And Moses did so in sight of the nobles of Israel, and named 7 the spot "Trial" and "Strife,"[1] because of the dispute with the children of Israel, and because of their trial of the EVER-LIVING, saying, "Does the EVER-LIVING exist with us, or not?"

The Amalekites attack Israel.

The Amalekites at this time came 8 with the Rephidites and made war with Israel. Consequently Moses said 9 to Joshua, "Choose your own men and go out to fight with the Amalekites to-morrow, and I will stand on the top of the hill with the rod of GOD in my hand."

Joshua, therefore, did as Moses 10 said to him, and fought with Amalek. But Moses and Aaron and Hur went up to the top of the hill; and when 11 Moses held up his hand, Israel became victorious, but when he lowered his hand, Amalek was victor. So when the hand of Moses became 12 weary, they took a stone and placed it under him and he rested upon it, and Aaron and Hur supported his hand, first one and then the other, so that his hand was stretched out until sunset, when Joshua defeated Amalek 13 and his people, by the edge of the sword.

The EVER-LIVING afterwards said 14 to Moses; "Write this and record it in a book, and instruct Joshua that I

---

1 "What is it?"—F. F.

2 36 (But a homer is the tenth part of an epha) is an old editor's note, not part of the original text.—F. F.

1 Masah and Meribah.

will blot the memory of Amalek from under the skies "

15 Moses then built an altar, and called its name " The Throne of the
16 EVER-LIVING," [1] and he said,—

"With the hand upon the throne of JACOB,
Fight Amalek for the LORD from age to age ! '"

Jethro meets Moses.

18 When Jethro, the priest of Midian, the father-in-law of Moses, heard all that GOD had done for Moses, and for Israel, His People ,—how the EVER-LIVING had led Israel out of
2 Mitzer,—then Jethro, the father-in-law of Moses, took Zifora, the wife of Moses, who had sent her back,
3 and her two sons,—(the name of the first was Gershom, for he said, " I have been a stranger in a strange
4 land, —and the name of the other Aehazer,—"For the GOD of my fathers has been a comfort and refuge to me
5 from the sword of Pharoh ,")—so Jethro, the father-in-law of Moses, brought his two sons and his wife to Moses in the desert, where the Mount
6 of GOD is   And he said to Moses, " I, Jethro, your father-in-law, have come to you with your wife and two sons with me "
7 Then Moses went out to meet his father-in-law, and bowed to him and kissed him, and they mutually enquired after their health   Then
8 they came to the tent   Moses there related to his father-in-law all that the EVER-LIVING had done to Pharoh and to the Mitzeraim on account of Israel ,—all the troubles which met them on the road, and how the EVER-LIVING delivered
9 them   And Jethro was glad at all the good which the EVER-LIVING had done to Israel, and His redemption of them from the hand of the
10 Mitzeraim   So Jethro said, " Bless the EVER-LIVING Who has delivered you from the hand of the Mitzeraim and from the hand of Pharoh, and Who has delivered this People from under the hand of the Mitzerites
11 Now you can perceive how much greater the EVER-LIVING is, than all their Gods, by the events with which He overwhelmed them "
12 Then Jethro, the father-in-law of

Moses, took burnt offerings and sacrifices to GOD, and Aaron and all the nobles of Israel came and dined with the father-in-law of Moses before GOD [1]

Moses administering Justice.

The next day, however, Moses sat 13 to administer justice to the People, and Moses remained from morning to evening   And the father-in-law of 14 Moses saw all that he did for the People, and said, " What is this business that you do for the People ?   Why do you sit alone, and all the People standing before you from morn till night ?"

When Moses replied to his father- 15 in-law , " Because all the People come to me to enquire of the EVER-LIVING   Whoever among them has 16 a dispute comes to me and I decide between man and man, and I make known the decision of GOD, and His laws "

Advice of Jethro on it.

But the father-in-law of Moses 17 answered him, " The practice that you follow is not good   You are not 18 prudent, nor are this people who are with you, for their affairs are more than you are able to bear alone   Therefore listen to my voice   I will 19 advise you, and GOD will be with you   Let now the People appear before GOD, and bring their affairs to GOD, and instruct them in the decisions of 20 His laws, and inform them the way they should walk in, and the acts they should do   Also choose for 21 yourself, from all the People, strong men, who fear GOD and hate bribes, and place over them as chiefs of thousands, chiefs of hundreds, chiefs of fifties and chiefs of tens, and let 22 them judge the People at all times, and let only all the great affairs be brought to you but let them judge all the little matters, and thus ease your-self,—for they load you

" If you do this and GOD confirms it, 23 then you can appoint it, and all these people can arrange their affairs with ease "

---

1 V 12   It is evident from this record that the exile of Moses in Arabia had been a period of spiritual education under Jethro, and that the Arabs had preserved the Faith of Abraham in greater purity than the Egyptians or Hebrews. —F I.

1 Yohvah Nisi

24   Moses, consequently, listened to the suggestion of his father-in-law,
25   and did all that he said. Moses therefore chose strong men from all Israel, and placed them as heads over the people; chiefs of thousands and chiefs of hundreds and chiefs of tens,
26   and they judged the people at all times in their affairs;—bringing the difficult matters to Moses,—but in the small affairs they decided for themselves.
27   Moses afterwards took leave of his father-in-law who went to his own country.

Israel arrives at Sinai.

19   At the third month from the coming out of the land of the Mitzeraim, on that day they came to the desert of
2   Sinai. Then the Rephidim also marched and came to the desert of Sinai, and encamped in the desert. Israel also encamped there near the hill.

God appears to Moses.

3   Then Moses went up to GOD, and the EVER-LIVING called to him from the hill saying;—"Say this to the House of Jacob, and inform the
4   children of Israel, 'You have seen what I did to the Mitzeraim, and lifted you on the wings of eagles, and
5   brought you to Me, so now if you will listen to My voice, and keep My laws, then you shall be to Me a peculiar People, more than all the
6   Peoples of the earth. And you shall be to Me a Royal Priesthood, and a Holy Nation.'—These are the words you shall speak to the children of Israel."
7   Moses consequently went and assembled the nobles of the People, and set before them the whole of these promises as the EVER-LIVING
8   commanded. And all the People answered at once, and said, "We will do all the EVER-LIVING commands." Then Moses reported the declaration of the People to the EVER-LIVING.
9   And the EVER-LIVING replied to Moses, "Now I will come to you. In a cloud of fire I will pass by. The People shall hear Me talk with you, and also I will remain with you always." Then Moses reported the declaration of the People to the EVER-LIVING.

When the EVER-LIVING replied to 10 Moses; "Go to the People and sanctify them to-day, and to-morrow, and wash their clothes, and on the 11 third day let them assemble; for on the third day the EVER-LIVING will descend in the sight of all the People upon Mount Sinai. But you shall 12 keep the people at a distance around, by ordering, 'Take care that you do not go up to the Hill, or touch its skirts. All who touch the Hill shall die! Whether a beast or a man, let 13 them not touch it with the hand! or they shall be stoned with stones, or pierced with a dart; they shall not live who approach to ascend the Hill!'"

Consequently Moses descended 14 from the Hill to the People, and sanctified the people, and they washed their clothing. And he said, 15 "Restrain yourselves for three days, not to touch a woman."

The Divine Manifestation on Sinai.

When the third day came to the 16 day-break, there were voices and lightnings, and a heavy cloud over the Hill, and the sound of a powerful trumpet, so that all the people in the camp trembled. Then Moses brought 17 out from the camp all the people to meet GOD, and stationed them below the Hill. And the Hill of Sinai smoked 18 all over its surface, when the EVER-LIVING descended upon it in fire; and its smoke went up like the smoke of a smelting furnace, and the whole hill trembled greatly; and there was 19 the continuous sound of a trumpet; but Moses very boldly spoke, and GOD answered him by voice. Then 20 the EVER-LIVING descended on to the Hill of Sinai, on to the top of the Hill, and the EVER-LIVING called Moses to the top of the Hill, and Moses ascended.

Then the EVER-LIVING said to 21 Moses, "Descend at once to the People for fear they should break through to see, and numbers fall before Me. Let the Priests also who 22 sacrifice to the EVER-LIVING sanctify themselves, lest the LORD afflict them."

But Moses replied to the EVER- 23 LIVING; "The people cannot ascend the Hill of Sinai, for You commanded us, saying, 'Go a distance from the Hill, and sanctify yourselves.'"

24 The EVER-LIVING, however, answered him, "Go! Descend! and return, you, and Aaron with you. But the Priests, and the people must not attempt to ascend to the LORD, lest He afflict them."

25 So Moses descended to the people and spoke to them.

The Ten Commandments.

20 Then the EVER-LIVING dictated all these commands, and said,

COMMANDMENT I

2 "I am your EVER-LIVING GOD, Who brought you out from the Mitzeraim, from the house of bond-
3 age. There shall be no other GOD to you, except MYSELF."

COMMANDMENT II

4 "You shall not make for yourselves any image, or likeness of anything that is in the heavens above, or that is upon the earth beneath, or that is in the waters lower than the earth,
5 you shall not worship them or serve them, for I, your EVER-LIVING GOD, am a jealous GOD, visiting the sins of the fathers upon the children to the third and fourth generation of those
6 who hate Me, but I show mercy for thousands, to those who love Me and keep My commandments.

COMMANDMENT III

7 "You shall not take the Name of your EVER-LIVING GOD in vain, for the LORD will not hold guiltless the taking of His Name in vain.

COMMANDMENT IV

8 "Remember the seventh day to
9 keep it holy. Six days you may
10 labour, and do all your business, but the seventh day is a Rest to your EVER-LIVING GOD. You shall not then do any business, you, or your son, or your daughter, your man-servant, or your maid servant, or your cattle, or your stranger who is within
11 your gates, for in six periods the LIVER-LIVING made the heavens and the earth, the sea and all that is in them, but rested at the seventh period, therefore the EVER-LIVING blessed the seventh period and hallowed it.

COMMANDMENT V

12 "Honour your father and your

mother, that your days may be long in the land which the EVER-LIVING GOD will give to you.

COMMANDMENT VI

"You shall not murder.   13

COMMANDMENT VII

"You shall not commit adultery   14

COMMANDMENT VIII

"You shall not steal   15

COMMANDMENT IX

"You shall not bear false witness 16 against your neighbour

COMMANDMENT X

"You shall not covet your neigh- 17 bour's house, you shall not covet your neighbour's wife, or his man-servant, or his maid-servant, or his ox, or his ass, or anything that is your neighbour's"

The Terror of Israel.

And all the People perceived the 18 sounds and the flamings, and the trumpet voice, and the smoke from the mountain,—so the people feared and shook in themselves, and stood at a distance, and said to Moses, 19 "You speak with us, and we can listen but let not GOD speak with us, for fear we should die."

Moses, however, answered to the 20 People, "Fear not! for GOD has come to you to try you, and to test whether you will fear Him henceforward, and not sin."

So the People stood afar off, but 21 Moses approached the thick darkness where GOD was.

Then the EVER-LIVING said to 22 Moses, "Say this to the children of Israel, you have seen that from the heavens I have spoken with you. Never make for yourselves a God of 23 silver, or a God of gold. You shall not make them for yourselves. You 24 shall make an altar of earth for Me, and you shall offer upon it your sacrifices and your thank offerings, your sheep, and your oxen. In every place where I record MY NAME, I will come to you and bless you. But 25 if you make an altar of stone to Me, it shall not be of cut stones, for if you carve with a cutter upon it, then it will be polluted. And you shall not 26 pile up pyramids for an altar, so that

your nakedness may not be discovered when you go up to it "

The Law of Social Life.

21 " Now these are the decrees which
2 you shall put before them A servant
shall serve six years' servitude, and in
the seventh he shall go out to free-
3 dom If he is single, he shall go out
single, if he has a wife, his wife shall
4 go out with him But if his master has
given him a wife, and she has borne
sons or daughters to him, the wife
and her children which she has borne
shall belong to the master, and he
5 shall go away single If, however,
the servant says, ' I like my master,
my wife, and my children,' he shall
6 not go into freedom, but his master
shall present him to the magistrates,
and station him at the door, or at the
door-posts, and his master shall pierce
his ear with an awl, and he shall
serve continuously

Law of Marriage.

7 " If a man sells his daughter to be
a mother, she should not go as if
8 going into slavery If she is not
pleasing in the eyes of her master,
when he has not known her, then he
shall free her to her own people without a payment, he shall not have
power to sell her because of his
9 treachery to her But if she has
borne a child to him, then he shall
treat her according to the law about
wives
10 " If he takes another to her, he
shall not diminish her share for
11 clothing, and conjugal rights And
if a third to these, he shall not send
her away destitute, without money "

Law of Murder.

12 " Whoever assails a man and he
13 dies,—He shall be put to death But
if he did not lie in wait, but his
stroke came from GOD, then you
shall provide a place where he may
14 fly If, however, a man plans against
his neighbour to murder him, then
you shall take him from My altar to
kill him
15 " And whoever assaults his father
or his mother, He shall be killed
16 " Whoever steals a man and sells
him, when he is caught he shall be
put to death

" Whoever curses his father or 17
mother, he shall be put to death
" And when men contend, and a 18
man assaults his neighbour with a
stone or a clod, but he does not die,
yet is reduced to his bed, if he re- 19
covers and can walk out upon his
crutch, and he escapes from the
injury, except his loss of time, he
shall be compensated, and the phy-
sician paid for his cure
" And if a man strikes his slave, or 20
his maid-servant, with his stick and
he dies under his hand, they shall be
avenged Yet if these continue a 21
day, or some days, they shall not be
avenged, for they were his property.
" And when two persons quarrel, 22
and they strike a pregnant woman,
and her child comes out, and mischief does not ensue, he shall be
fined, according to what is laid upon
him to compensate the woman, and
that shall be fixed by the judges
But if mischief ensues, you shall 23
inflict life for life eye for eye, tooth 24
for tooth, hand for hand, foot for
foot mark for mark mutilation for 25
mutilation. wound for wound. blow
for blow
" And if any man strikes his slave 26
in the eye, so that his eye becomes
blind, he shall let him go free instead
of his eye
" And if a tooth from his slave, so 27
that the tooth is destroyed, in com-
pensation he shall set him free,
instead of his tooth
" And if a bullock butts a man and 28
the man dies, you shall stone the
bullock, and not eat of its flesh, but
destroy the bullock for nothing But 29
if the bullock were accustomed to
butt formerly, and his owner knew it,
and did not guard it, and it kills a
man, or a woman, the bullock shall
be stoned and the owner put to
death
" But if a fine is laid upon him, he 30
shall pay it, and his life be free from
all, because of the fine laid upon
him Whether a man or a woman 31
is butted, it shall be done according
to this decree
" If a slave man or woman is butted 32
by a bullock, thirty shekels of silver
shall be given to their master, and the
bullock be stoned.

Laws of Accidents and Thefts.

" And if a man opens a well, or 33
digs a well, and does not cover it,

and an ox or an ass shall fall into it, because of the well he shall pay a money fine to its owner, and the dead shall be his

34 "And if the bullock of a man gores the bullock of his neighbour, and it dies, then they shall sell the living bullock, and divide the money, and

35 they shall also divide the dead But if its master know that the bullock gored formerly, and he did not guard it, he shall compensate with a bullock for the bullock, and the dead shall be to him

36 "If a man steals a bullock or a sheep, and slaughters it, or sells it, he shall compensate with five bullocks in place of the ox, or four sheep in place of the sheep

22 "If a thief is found breaking in, and is struck and dies, there is not

2 blood-guilt for him If the sun was shining on him, he may redeem his blood If he has nothing then he shall be sold for stealing

3 "If you find his theft in his hand, as a bullock, or an ass, or sheep, alive, he shall be fined by two

The Laws of Property.

4 "If the farm or vineyard of a man is burnt, and ruffians from his village burn his farm, or part of his farm, or a part of his vineyard, it shall be compensated

5 "If you make a fire, and it fires the bushes, and consumes the standing corn, or a homestead, or a farm, it shall be compensated from the burner to the burnt

6 "Whoever places with his neighbour money or goods as trustee, and they are stolen upon the premises of that person, if the thief is discovered

7 he shall repay twice as much If the thief is not found, then the master of the premises shall approach the House of GOD and swear he has not put his hand upon the property of

8 his neighbour, upon anything lost, upon ox, or ass, or sheep, or clothing, or anything strayed, and shall say that as a witness to GOD, he brings twice as much as was lost to GOD He shall recompense his neighbour double

9 "If a man entrusts to his neighbour an ass, or ox, or sheep, or any cattle, to take care of, and it dies or is torn

10 or tears, out of his sight, there shall be an oath to the LORD between the

two, that he has not put his hand upon the property of his neighbour, and its owner shall take it, and not

11 be compensated But if it has been stolen from him, he shall compensate

12 its owner If it is torn he shall bring the torn pieces as a proof He shall not compensate

13 "And if a man hires it of his neighbour, and it is broken or dies, and its owner is not with it, he shall be com-

14 pensated If its owner is with it, he shall not be compensated, if it was hired, he went for the wages

Laws of Morality.

15 "And if a man seduces a girl who has not been betrothed to him, and lies with her so that she conceives,

16 she shall be his wife But if her father is unwilling to give her to him, he shall pay money as a dowry for

17 the girl She shall not live as a slave

18 "Whoever lies with a beast shall be put to death

19 "No sacrifice shall be burnt to gods, except to the EVER-LIVING only

20 "You shall not persecute or oppress foreigners, for you were foreigners in the land of the Mitzeraim

21 "You shall not annoy any widow or

22 orphan If you wrong them, so that they cry to me, I shall hear their cry,

23 and My anger will burn, and I will slay you by the sword, and your own wives shall be widows, and your own children orphans

24 "If you lend money to My People, My poor among you, you shall not be to them like a usurer You shall

25 not put upon them usury If your neighbour deposits with you as a pledge a garment, at the setting of the sun you shall return it to him,

26 for it is his only covering with which he clothes his body, in which he lies down, and it may be he will cry to Me, when I will hear, for I am merciful

The Laws of Reverence towards God.

27 "You shall not blaspheme GOD, and shall not curse the princes of your nation

28 "You shall not delay to give to Me the first produce of your farm, and

29 vineyard You shall do the same with your cow, and your sheep It shall be seven days with its mother, and on the seventh day you shall give it to Me

30 "As you shall be holy men to Me, you shall not eat of torn flesh, that has been torn in the field   You must throw it to the dogs

23 "You shall not make a false oath   You shall not set your hand to commit fraud   You shall not be a false witness

2 "You shall not go with the powerful to do wrong, and you shall not plead for the powerful to make excuse

3 for their wrong-doing   And you shall not turn away from the poor man when he pleads

4 "When you meet with the cow, or ass of your enemy straying, you shall take it back to him

5 "When you see the ass of your enemy fallen under its load, and you can ease and free it for him, you shall help to free it with him

6 "You shall not pervert justice from the destitute when he pleads

7 "Keep far off from false pretence   You shall not kill the innocent, and the righteous, for I will not acquit

8 the wicked   And you shall not receive bribes, for bribes blind open eyes, and pervert the words of the righteous

9 "And you shall not oppress a foreigner, for you know the feelings of a foreigner, since you were foreigners in the land of the Mitzeraim.

Laws of Agriculture.

10 "For six years you shall sow the
11 earth, and gather its produce, but in the seventh you shall manure it, and spread it out, and the destitute of your people shall eat, and the rest the animals of the field shall eat   You shall do the same with your
12 vineyards and olive plantations   Six days you shall do all your business, but the seventh day you shall rest, so that your ox and your ass may take comfort, and your servants and foreigners refresh themselves
13 "And all that I say to you you shall regard, for you shall not remember a name of other Gods, and it shall not be heard from your mouth

Laws about Sacred Festivals.

14 "Three times in a year you shall make a festival to Me
15 "The feast of unfermented bread [1] you shall keep for seven days   You

shall eat biscuits, as I commanded you, at the season of the month of harvest,[1] for in it you came out of Mitzer, and you did not see My presence in vain

"And you shall make the feast of 16 the first-fruits of harvest, when you sow in the field, and the feast of harvest-home at the end of the year when you gather in your produce from the fields

"Three times in the year all your 17 men shall come before Me, the ALMIGHTY LORD

"You shall not sacrifice with fer- 18 mented bread a blood-sacrifice to Me, and the fat of My feast shall not be kept till the morning

"The best of the first-fruits of your 19 ground you shall bring to the hand of your EVER-LIVING GOD

"You shall not boil a kid in its mother's milk

"Then I will send My Messenger 20 before your face to guard you in your way, and to bring you to the place where I will fix you   Regard his 21 presence, and listen to his voice   Grieve him not, that he may not rise to punish you, for My POWER is around him   But if you listen to 22 his voice, and do all that I shall command, then I will love you, but I will distress your distressers   For 23 My Messenger shall march before you, and bring you to the Amorites, and the Hitites, and the Perizites, and the Cananites, and the Hivites, and the Jebusites, and destroy them

Prohibition of Paganism and Idolatry.

"You shall not worship their Gods, 24 and not serve them, and you shall not make like them, but you shall destroy, and you shall break their pillars, and you shall serve your 25 EVER-LIVING GOD, and He will bless your bread, and your water, and will turn war away from around you   You shall not be childless, and 26 sterile in your land   You shall fulfil your days.

Promises to the Faithful.

"I will send My terror before your 27 face, and will terrify every Nation when you arrive at them, and I will make all your enemies to turn their back to you.   And I will send the 28

---

1 Biscuits   1 Abib.

Destroyer before you, and drive out the Hitites and the Cananites and the Hivites from before your ap-

29 proach I will not drive them away in a year from before you, lest the earth should become waste, and the beasts of the field should increase

30 upon you I will drive them out little by little before you, until you multiply and can inherit the country

31 And your two boundaries shall be from the Sea of Weeds at the Sea of Philistia through the desert to the River,[1] which I will give to your hand, and I will drive the inhabitants of the country from before you

32 You shall not make a treaty with them, or a covenant with their Gods

33 They shall not reside in your land, for fear they would cause you to sin against Me, so that you would serve their Gods, for I am the EVER-LIVING, for you to reverence "

Moses and Aaron and the Princes ascend Sinai.

24 Then it was commanded to Moses, " Go up to the LORD, you and Aaron, Nadab and Abihu, and seventy of the princes of Israel, and let them worship

2 at a distance But Moses shall approach alone to the EVER-LIVING, for they must not approach, nor the people go up with him "

3 So Moses went and reported to the people the whole of the commands of the EVER-LIVING, and the whole of His decrees, when all the people answered with one voice, and said, " All the commands which the EVER-LIVING commands, we will do "

Moses records these Laws.

4 Moses afterwards wrote down all the commands of the LORD and arose in the morning, and built an altar under the hill, and twelve pillars for

5 the twelve tribes of Israel And he commissioned representatives of the children of Israel who went out and offered burnt offerings, and sacrificed peace-offerings to the EVER-LIVING

6 Moses also took part of the blood and put it in basins, and part of the blood he sprinkled upon the altar

7 Then he took the book of the Cove-nant, and read it in the hearing of the People, and they said, " All that the EVER-LIVING has commanded, we will do and listen to "

1 Luph ...

Moses consequently took the blood 8 and sprinkled it upon the People, and said, " This is the blood of the Covenant which the EVER-LIVING has settled with you, in all these commands "

The Chiefs ascend Sinai.

Afterwards Moses, Aaron Nadab, 9 and Abihu, and the seventy princes of Israel went up, and saw the GOD 10 of Israel, and under His feet was like the dazzle of sapphire stones, and the splendour of the clear sun , but upon 11 the nobles of the children of Israel, He did not extend His hand They however gazed upon God , and they ate and drank.

Moses called to Sinai.

Then the EVER-LIVING said to 12 Moses , " Come up to the mountain to Me, and stay there, and I will give you stone slabs, with the Laws and Commandments which I have written for your instruction "

Therefore Moses arose with Joshua 13 his attendant, and Moses went up the mount to GOD But the princes 14 said, " Let us remain here, until you return to us, and also Aaron and Hur with us,—Why should the words of the EVER-LIVING come to us ? "

Consequently Moses ascended the 15 hill, and a cloud covered the hill, 16 and the splendour of the EVER-LIVING rested upon the hill of Sinai , and the cloud covered it six days Then He called to Moses on the seventh day out of the cloud, and the 17 glory of the EVER-LIVING appeared like a consuming fire on the head of the mountain to the eyes of the children of Israel

Moses, therefore, went into the 18 midst of the cloud, and ascended the hill And Moses was upon the hill forty days and forty nights

The Instructions on Sinai.

There the EVER-LIVING spoke to 5 Moses and said, " Tell the children of Israel that they must bring offer-ings to Me From anything their heart induces them, they may offer And these are the offerings they may 2 offer for themselves, gold, silver, and brass, and blue, and purple, and 4 scarlet, and red , spun goats' hair, and red ram skins, and badgers' skins, and acacia wood , oil for the light for 6 t ...   and
" c ... to ...   e for 8

Me a Sanctuary, and I will dwell

9 amongst them   Exactly according to the pattern I have shown you, you shall form the dwelling, and form all its furniture,—thus you shall make it

10   "You shall also make an ark of acacia wood, of two cubits and a half long and two cubits and a half breadth, and a cubit and a half high,

11 and you shall plate it with pure gold inside and out, and wreathe and make

12 a border of gold around it   You shall also cast rings of pure gold, and place on the four corners of it   That is, two rings on one side of it, and two rings on the other side of it

13 And you shall make staves of acacia

14 wood, and plate them with gold, and put the staves into the rings on the sides of the ark, to carry the ark by

15 them   The staves shall remain in the rings ;—they shall not be removed

16 from them.   You shall then put into the ark the evidences that I will give

17 to you   You shall also make a cover of pure gold of two cubits in length and a cubit and a half in breadth

18 You shall besides make two covers of gold, shaped as dishes, in two divisions

19 for the covers   Make the cases thus ,—one for each side, and a kerub for that division of the cover   You shall make it with kerubim upon the

20 two divisions   Thus the kerubim will be stretching their wings as over-shadowing the covers with their wings with the wings of each towards his brother over the covers   The kerubim shall be face to face

21   "Then you shall place the covers upon the top of the ark, and you shall put into the ark the evidences that

22 I will give to you   Then I will instruct you there, and I will speak to you from off the covers, from between the two kerubim, which are upon the ark, all that I command you for the children of Israel

23   "You shall also make a table of acacia wood, two cubits long and a cubit broad, and a cubit and a half

24 high, and plate it with pure gold, and make a border of gold around it

25 Construct thus a border like a coping around it, and make points of gold

26 upon the surrounding border   Also make for it four staves of gold, and put the staves in the four sockets

27 which are above the legs   These four sockets shall be above the border, for the [...]

28 So you shall make the staves of

acacia wood, and plate them with gold, to carry the table   You shall

29 also make dishes, and spoons, and bowls, and the cups in which the wine is, of pure gold, and place upon

30 the table the shewbread before Me continually

  "You shall also make lamps of

31 pure gold   Make the lamp with spreading branches, with a stalk rising upwards like a blossom, with a bowl on it   Let there be six stalks

32 going from the sides of it   Three stalks for lamps on one side of it, and three stalks for lamps on the other side of it   Three nobs with

33 almonds on each stalk, a flower and a bowl, the same for each of the three stalks that are provided for the lamps, and for the fourth lamp a

34 nob with an almond, a nob and a bowl, and a nob under two of the stalks between them, and a nob under two

35 of the stalks between them, and a nob under two of the stalks between them, for the six branches that come from the lamp   The nobs and the

36 stalks between them shall be, all of them, each one, turned from pure gold

  "You shall also make seven re-

37 flectors to throw the light in front of themselves   And dishes and snuffers

38 of pure gold   You shall use a talent[1]

39 of pure gold for it, and all its instruments   And be careful to make them

40 according to the pattern I showed you on the mountain

  "You shall also make for the tent

26 ten curtains of twisted linen, and azure, purple, and blue, ornamented artistically with two kerubs   The

2 width of each curtain shall be eighteen cubits, and the height of it four cubits   The extent of each curtain shall be the same to all the curtains   Two curtains shall be

3 attached one to the other, and five curtains attached one to the other You shall also make loops of azure

4 on the edge of each of the curtains in the selvage to join them, and make

5 the same in the selvage of the two curtains to join them   Make five loops to each curtain   thus make five loops on the selvage of the two curtains that are joined by the opposite loops to the first one   And make five

6 golden hooks to unite the curtains,

---

1 £s 17s sterling at £1 per oz   But the pur-h sing power of gold was at that period at l ast forty or fifty times what it is now —F F

each to the other by hooks, so that they may be one tent

7 "Also make curtains of goat-skin as a covering for the first tent Make

8 eleven curtains of them The length of the first curtain to be thirty cubits, and the breadth four cubits Make each one of the eleven curtains the

9 same Then join five of the curtains together, and six curtains together, for the doublings of the sixth curtain

10 in the front of the tent You shall also make fifty loops upon the edge of the first curtain, upon the selvage at the juncture, and fifty loops upon

11 the edge of the second curtain. And make hooks for the loops and unite them for the pavilion and let it be

12 one But part of the curtains must hang down from the roof of the pavilion, half the curtains of the roof you shall hang over the back

13 part of the tent, with a cubit on this side, and a cubit on that side, for the fold in the length of the curtains of the pavilion shall hang down over the sides of the tent on this side,

14 and that side, to conceal it You shall in addition, make a covering to the tent of red ram skins, and a covering of skins of badgers all over it

15 "You also make the boards of the Sanctuary of acacia wood, planed, ten cubits the length of each board, and a cubit and a half the breadth of

16 each plank You shall set clasps upon the first plank at the edges of

17 each of its counterparts You shall do the same to all the planks of the

18 Sanctuary And make the planks for the Sanctuary twenty planks for the

19 face to the right, with forty sockets of silver to fix under the twenty planks Two sockets under each plank to fix the clutches into

20 "And upon the second side of the Sanctuary, to face the north, twenty planks, and forty sockets of silver, two sockets under each plank, and two clutches under each plank

22 "And to the breadth of the Sanc-

23 tuary, westward, you shall make six planks, with two planks made for a

24 corner of the Sanctuary at its lengths And there shall be rings to fasten them for the one shall have a ring on the top of it, to meet the ring of the other This shall be for the two

25 corners that is eight planks, with their sockets of silver, sixteen sockets, two sockets for each plank

26 "Make also cross-bars of acacia

wood, five to a plank at one side of

27 the Sanctuary, and five cross-bars for the second side of the Sanctuary, and five cross-bars to the planks at the side of the Sanctuary stretching west, and fix the cross-bars in the middle of the planks, with bolts from one junction to the other junction

29 And overlay the planks and their rings with gold Make also of gold, rests for the cross-bars, and plate the cross-bars with gold And erect

30 the Sanctuary according to the plan I showed you in the mount

31 "Make besides a veil of azure, and purple and blue, and red, and twisted linen Ornament it with an em-

32 broidery of kerubim, and place it upon four supports of acacia, over-layed with gold, with pins of gold, upon four sockets of silver And

33 hang the veil below the hooks, and bring there, within the veil to the Holy of Holies, the Ark of the

34 Witnesses Then put the covers upon

35 the ark in the Holy of Holies And place the table outside the veil, and put the lamp upon the table at the south side of the Sanctuary, and place the table towards the north side

36 "Then make a skreen for the door of the tent, of azure and purple, and blue, and have it embroidered with

37 spun flax Also make five standards of acacia for the skreen, and plate them with gold, and have pins of gold, and cast for them five sockets of brass

27 "Make besides an altar of acacia wood, five cubits long and five cubits broad The altar shall be square,

2 and its height three cubits And make horns to it upon its four sides The horns shall project from it You

3 shall also sheathe it in brass And make buckets for the ashes, and shovels, and brushes, and tongs Make all its instruments of brass

4 Make also a net like a lattice of brass, and form on the network four pro-jections of brass, on its four corners, and fix it below the fire-place of the altar by its projections, so that the grating may be in the centre of the altar

6 "Make also staves for the altar, staves of acacia wood, and plate them

7 with brass, so that the staves may go into projections, and let the staves be upon the two sides of the altar to

8 carry it by Made it with hollow panels such as were shown to you in

the mountain. You shall make them the same.

Form of the Sanctuary.

9   "Make the court of the Sanctuary to face towards the south. The curtains of the court of spun linen, one hundred cubits in length on one face,

10   with twenty standards, and twenty sockets, of brass, with spikes to the standards, and hooks of silver.

11   "And then on the length of the north side one hundred cubits of curtains, and twenty standards, with their twenty sockets of brass, with spikes for the standards, and hooks of silver.

12   "Let the breadth of the court to face the west be fifty cubits of curtains, ten standards, and ten sockets.

13   "And the breadth of the court to face the east, towards the sun-rise, fifty cubits, with fifteen cubits of curtains to the gateway, with three standards, and three sockets. And from the other shoulder fifteen cubits with three standards, and three

16   sockets. But for the gate of the court let there be a mask of twenty cubits, made of azure, and purple, and crimson, and blue, and red, and embroidered spun linen, with four

17   standards and four sockets. All the standards around the court shall have silver connecting rods and pins of

18   silver, and sockets of brass. The length of the court a hundred cubits, and the breadth fifty by fifty: and the height five cubits of spun linen

19   with standards of brass; with all the furniture of the Sanctuary, and all the service, and all its nails, and all the nails of the court of brass.

20   "You shall further command the children of Israel that they must bring to you pure pressed olive oil for

21   the lamps, for a continual offering, in the pavilion of the Testimony, outside the veil which is over the evidences, providing it for Aaron and his sons to serve till the morning before the EVER-LIVING, as an everlasting institution for their descendants, among the children of Israel.

The Institution of a Priesthood.

28   "And you shall separate to yourself Aaron your brother, and his sons with him from among the children of Israel, to be Priests to Me; Aaron Nadab, and Abihu Eleazar, and Ithamar,

the sons of Aaron. Also make sacred 2 robes for Aaron, your brother, to honour and beautify him. And speak 3 to all the skilful-minded, who have a skilful intellect, that they should make those robes for Aaron, to consecrate him as a Priest to Me. And these 4 are the robes which they shall make; a breastplate, and ephod, and a cloak, and a cape of embroidery; with a turban and girdle.—These are the sacred robes to be made for Aaron your brother, and for his sons, as Priest to Me.

"They must also bring gold and 5 azure, and purple, and blue, and red, and thread.

"Make the ephod of gold, azure, 6 purple, blue, red, and spun linen embroidery. The two shoulder pieces 7 shall be joined to it on the two sides, and fastened; and the embroidery, 8 which they work upon the ephod, shall be of gold, azure, and purple, and blue, red, and spun flax. Then 9 you shall take two onyx stones and engrave upon them the names of the sons of Israel; six of their names 10 upon one stone, and the names of the other six of them upon the second stone, in order of their birth. You 11 shall make the engraving like a seal. Having engraved the two stones with the names of the sons of Israel, you shall cause them to be surrounded with settings of gold; and set the two 12 stones upon the two shoulders of the ephod, as stones of remembrance for the sons of Israel, and Aaron shall carry their names before the EVER-LIVING upon his two shoulders for a remembrance.

"Make, as well, settings of gold, 13 and two chains of pure gold. Make 14 them with edgings, as a wreath is made, and fix the chains on to the settings.

"Also make a breastplate of Justice, 15 of embroidery like the ephod. Make it of gold, azure, and purple, and blue, red, and spun linen combined. It shall be square; a double span long, 16 and a span wide, with settings in it; 17 a setting of four stones in a row.

"A ruby, a topaz, and a diamond for the first row.

"The second row, an emerald, a 18 sapphire, a jasper.

"The third row, a ligure, an agate, 19 and an amethyst.

"The fourth row, an amber, an 20 onyx and pearl.

"They shall be in settings of gold
21 with their fastenings and the stones
shall have the names of the twelve
sons of Israel, their names engraven
like a seal, each shall have one name
of the twelve tribes

22   "Also make for the breastplate
linked chains, of pure gold, as a
23 wreath   Also make for the breastplate two buttons of gold, and fix the
two buttons on the two edges of the
24 breastplate, and fix the two wreaths
of gold upon the two buttons at the
25 edges of the breastplate, and the two
ends of the two wreaths you shall
fasten on to the two settings, and put
them upon the shoulders of the ephod,
upon its front face

26   "Also make two buttons of gold,
and place them on the two sides of
the breastplate, upon its edges, where
the ephod turns over to its inside
27 Besides, you shall make buttons of
gold and fix them upon the two
shoulders of the ephod, extending
from the front of it to the juncture at
the top of the girdle of the ephod,
28 and shall bind on the breastplate by
its button to the hook of the ephod,
so that the breastplate shall not fall
29 from off the ephod   Thus Aaron
will carry the names of the sons of
Israel, upon the breastplate of justice,
upon his heart, when he goes to the
Sanctuary, as a remembrance before
GOD continually

30   "Also fix on to the breastplate the
Urim and Thumim,[1] so that they
may be over the heart of Aaron when
he goes before the EVER-LIVING, and
Aaron shall carry justice for the
children of Israel before the EVER-
LIVING continually

31   "Also make for the cape of the
32 ephod loops of azure, and let there be
eyelets at the middle of the edge, at
the seam around it, made like the
weaving for the eyelets of a coat of
mail, so as not to tear away

33   "Also make upon the hem pomegranates of azure, and purple, and
blue, and red, on the hems around,
and bells of gold beside them around,
34 a bell of gold and a pomegranate, upon
35 the hem of the cape around   And
they shall be upon Aaron when
ministering, so that their sound may
be heard at his going into the

Sanctuary before the EVER-LIVING,
and coming from Him, so that he
may not die

"Make also a Flower of pure gold, 36
and engrave upon it like the engraving of a seal, 'Holiness to the LORD,'
and fasten to it an azure cord, that it 37
may be held upon the turban, in the
front of the turban, and be above the 38
brow of Aaron, so that Aaron may
carry their weaknesses to the Sanctuaries when he sanctifies the children
of Israel, sanctifying them with every
offering so it shall be above his brow
continually, to bring favour to them
from the EVER-LIVING

"Also embroider a robe of white 39
linen, and make a turban of white
linen, and make an embroidered sash

"Make also robes for the sons of 40
Aaron, and make for them sashes,
and make them mitres, to honour and
adorn them   And clothe with them 41
Aaron your brother, and his sons with
them   Then consecrate them, and
put a ring on their hands and sanctify
them, and they shall be My Priests
Also make drawers for their legs, to 42
cover their naked body from the waist,
and to extend down the thighs These 43
shall be worn by Aaron and his sons
when they go into the Tent of the
Congregation, or to clothe them at
the altar, when serving religion, so
that they may not excite passion and
die   This is a perpetual order to him,
and his descendants after him

The Method of Consecrating Priests.

"And these are the things you shall 29
use in consecrating them to be Priests
to Me —

"You shall take an heifer from the
cows, and two perfect rams, and un- 2
fermented bread, and unfermented
cakes mixed with oil, and then unfermented wafers buttered with oil,
which you shall make of wheaten
flour, and put them in a basket, and 3
offer them in the basket, with the
heifer and the two rams

"Then Aaron and his sons shall 4
approach the door of the Hall of
Assembly and you shall wash them
with water

"Next you shall take the garments 5
and clothe Aaron with the robe, and
the cape of the ephod, and the ephod,
and the breastplate, and you shall
invest him with the adjuncts of the
ephod   Then you shall place the 6

---

1 "Light and Truth" is the meaning when
translated, the less not which have not dwelt
upon —F F

turban upon his head, and the Crown of Righteousness upon the turban.

7 "Afterwards take the Oil of Consecration and pour it upon his head, and consecrate him.

8 "Then bring forward his sons and

9 clothe them with their robes, and gird Aaron and his sons with the sashes and bind the mitres on them, which shall indicate the priesthood, as a perpetual institution. Appoint Aaron, and appoint his sons in this manner.

10 "Next you shall bring forward the heifer before the Hall of Assembly, and Aaron and his sons shall strike their hands upon the head of the

11 heifer. Then slay the heifer before the EVER-LIVING at the door of the

12 Hall of Assembly, and take of the blood of the heifer and put upon the horns of the altar with your finger, and the rest of the blood pour out at

13 the foundation of the altar. Then take all the fat of the caul of the bowels, and the caul over the liver, and two kidneys, and the fat which is about them, and burn them before

14 the altar. But the flesh of the heifer, and its skin, and the dung, you shall burn with fire outside the camp, as a sin offering.

15 "Then you shall take one of the rams, and Aaron and his sons shall strike their hands upon the head of

16 the ram. Afterwards slay the ram, and take its blood and sprinkle upon

17 the altar all round. But divide the ram into portions, and wash its entrails and its legs, and lay them upon

18 the portions with its head, and burn all the ram upon the altar. It is a whole burnt offering to the EVER-LIVING, it is a sweet odour to the EVER-LIVING.

19 "Afterwards take the second ram, and let Aaron and his sons strike their hands upon the head of the ram.

20 Then slay the ram, and take some of its blood and put upon the tip of the right ear of Aaron, and on the tip of the ears of his sons, and upon the thumb of their right hands, and upon the great toe of their feet, and sprinkle

21 the blood all around the altar. Next take some of the blood which is upon the altar, and some of the oil of consecration, and sprinkle upon Aaron, and upon his robes, and upon his sons, and upon their robes with him, and sanctify him and his robes, and his sons, and their robes as well.

22 "Afterwards take from the ram the fat, and the suet; and the fat of the caul of the bowels, and the lobe of the liver, and the two kidneys, and the fat that is over them,—for it is a ram of consecration,—and one round 23 loaf of bread; and one loaf buttered with oil; and one thin cake from the basket of unfermented cakes that are before the EVER-LIVING, and place 24 the whole on the hands of Aaron and the hands of his sons, and they shall wave them before the EVER-LIVING. Then take them from their hands and 25 burn with incense upon the altar for a whole offering, as a sweet smell before the EVER-LIVING. They shall be for the EVER-LIVING. Next take 26 the breast of the ram of consecration, which was for Aaron, and you yourself shall wave it before the EVER-LIVING, and it shall be to yourself for a portion. And sanctify the breast of 27 the wave-offering, and the legs of the wave-offerings which were raised up from the Ram of Consecration, which was for Aaron and for his sons, and 28 they shall be for Aaron and his sons to take always from the children of Israel;—a sacrifice of thanks—you shall raise them to the EVER-LIVING.

"And the sacred robes that are for 29 Aaron shall be for his sons after him to be consecrated in, and to serve with their hands in them. The priests from 30 his sons after him, who come to the Hall of Assembly for the holy service, shall be clothed in them seven days.

"Next take the Ram of Consecra- 31 tion and boil its flesh in the holy place, and Aaron and his sons shall eat the 32 flesh of the ram, and the bread which was in the basket at the door of the Hall of Assembly. They shall eat it 33 as a protection to them in the work of their hands,—in the Sanctuary alone: and a stranger shall not eat that holy thing with them. But if 34 there remains any of the flesh of the consecration, or of the bread until the morning, you shall burn the remnants by fire. They shall not be eaten, because they are holy.

"Do this with Aaron and his sons, 35 exactly as I have commanded. Thus for seven days you shall fill their hands, and offer a bullock for a sin 36 offering daily, as a protection for them, with a sin offering upon the altar to protect yourself; and you shall consecrate it to sanctify it. You 37 shall protect for the altar seven days and sanctify it. Then the altar shall be holy of holies, all approaching to the altar shall be sacred

The Ritual of the Altar.

38 " This is what you shall offer daily upon the altar, two lambs of a year

39 old, continually Offer the first lamb in the morning, and offer the second

40 lamb between the dusks, with a tenth of flour mixed with a quarter of a hin of olive oil, and a quarter of a hin of wine with the first lamb as a drink offering

41 " And offer the second lamb between the dusks, like the offering in the morning, and offer a similar drink offering with it, a sweetmeat to the EVER-LIVING, as continuous offerings from your posterity before the EVER-LIVING at the door of the Hall of Assembly, at the place He indicates to you, where He will speak to you

43 For I will show Myself to the children of Israel, and will sanctify them by

44 My Majesty Thus you shall sanctify the Hall of Assembly and the altar for Me, but I will sanctify Aaron, and

45 his sons to Myself as Priests, and I will dwell in the midst of the children

46 of Israel, and be their GOD, and they shall know that I am the EVER-LIVING, the GOD Who brought them from the land of the Mitzeraim, and dwell in the midst of them I am the EVER-LIVING GOD

30 " Make also an altar for incense of

2 acacia wood It shall be square, a cubit long and a cubit wide, and two

3 cubits high, from the base of it And you shall plate it with pure gold, its top and its sides all round, and round its top make battlements of gold

4 You shall also make two projections of gold on it, below the battlements Make also two golden rings below the battlements, you shall form them upon both sides, as sockets for two

5 staves to carry it by Make the staves of acacia wood, and plate them

6 with gold And place it before the veils which are over the Ark of the Witnesses, before the veils which are over the Witnesses that give evidence to you there

7 " And Aaron shall offer incense of spices upon it evening by evening He shall burn the incense at the

8 lighting of the lamps When Aaron's sons light the lamps between the dusks, he shall burn the incense perpetually, before the EVER-LIVING,

9 among your descendants You shall

not offer upon it scattered incense, or whole burnt offerings, or gifts, nor shall you pour a drink offering upon

10 it, but Aaron shall expiate once a year upon its horns with blood, he shall expiate upon it with a sin-offering of expiations once in a year, for your descendants It is the Holy of Holies to the EVER-LIVING "

The Law of the Census

11 Afterwards the EVER-LIVING spoke to Moses, saying.—

12 " When you take a conscription of the children of Israel, to regiment them, then each shall give an expiation for his life to the EVER-LIVING for conscripting them, so that the LORD may not punish them for con-

13 scripting This is the offering for everyone passing to the conscription, half a shekel, by the sacred shekel, twelve gheras to the shekel You shall offer half a shekel to the EVER-

14 LIVING Everyone passing to the conscription, from the age of twenty years old and upwards, shall give this offering to the EVER-LIVING

15 The rich shall not add, and the poor shall not diminish from the half shekel, given as an offering to the EVER-LIVING, as a protection for

16 their lives And you shall take the protection money from the children of Israel and give it to the workers in the Hall of Assembly, and it shall be as a remembrance for the children of Israel before the EVER-LIVING, to protect their lives "

The Apparatus of the Tabernacle.

17 Another time the EVER-LIVING spoke to Moses, saying —

18 " Make a bath of brass, with a base of brass, for washing, and place it between the Hall of Assembly and

19 the altar, and put water in it. and Aaron and his sons shall bathe themselves in it, both their hands and

20 their feet Upon coming into the Hall of Assembly they shall wash with water, so that they may not die, when they approach the altar to offer sweet perfumes to the EVER-LIVING

21 They shall wash their hands and their feet, so that they may not die, and this shall be a perpetual order to him, and to his descendants, in their generations "

Composition of the Oil of Consecration.

22　Again the EVER-LIVING spoke to Moses, saying;

"Now take to you perfumes; of heads of flowering myrrh five hundred, of sweet cinnamon one hundred and twenty-five; and of sweet cane one 24 hundred and twenty-five: of sweet cassia five hundred shekels weighed by the sacred shekel, and a hin of 25 olive oil, and make from them the holy consecrating oil; a compound of compounds. It shall be a perfumed Holy Consecrating oil, to consecrate the Hall of Assembly and 27 the Ark of Witnesses: and the table, and all the instruments of the altar, 28 and its furniture, and the altar of incense: and the altar of burnt offerings, and all its furniture; and the 29 bath, and its appliances. Consecrate them thus, and they shall be holy.

30　"Consecrate Aaron and his sons, also. Consecrate them to be priests to Me.

31　"Then you shall speak to the children of Israel saying:—

"This is the Holy Oil of Consecration to Me, in all your generations. 32 It shall not be poured upon a man's body; nor shall you make any of similar ingredients. It is Holy of Holies for you to the EVER-LIVING. 33 The man who compounds like it, and whoever puts it upon a foreigner shall be excommunicated from his people."

Compound for Sweet Powder.

34　The EVER-LIVING also said to Moses;—"Take to yourself sweet drops, and scented shell, and sweet galbanum, and pure frankincense of 35 equal weights, and make of them a sweet compound, seasoned with pure 36 holy salt, and pound it very fine. Lay some of it before the witnesses in the Hall of Assembly, where I will meet you. It shall be Holy of Holies for you. 37　"And this perfume that you make by weight they shall not use for themselves. It is sacred to you and the 38 EVER-LIVING. The man who uses it as a personal perfume shall be excommunicated from his people."

Skilled Workmen Appointed.

31　The EVER-LIVING also spoke to Moses, saying:

2　"See I have called by name Bezalal, the son of Auri, the son of Hor, of the tribe of Judah. I have also filled 3 him with a divine spirit of skill, and understanding, and knowledge, and with constructive ability, and with inven- 4 tive genius to work in gold, and silver, and brass; and to cut stone for all 5 works, and to cut timber to work for any purpose. I have also given him 6 Ahaliab the son of Ahisamak of the tribe of Dan. And I have endowed him also with intelligence and science, so that they may construct all I have commanded you:—

"The Hall of Assembly and the Ark 7 of Witnesses, and the covers which are upon it, and all the furniture of the Tabernacle, with the table and 8 its appurtenances, and the lamps of purity, and all their appliances, and the altar of incense; and the altar of 9 burnt offerings, and all its furniture; with the bath and its bases; and the 10 robes for service, and the sacred robes of Aaron, the priest, and the robes of his sons to officiate in, besides the oil of 11 consecration and the sweet perfumes, to sanctify all, as I commanded you."

Order to Keep the Sabbath.

Afterwards the EVER-LIVING spoke 12 to Moses saying:—

"Now speak to the children of Israel and say, 'Take care and keep My Sabbaths, for they are a witness between you and Me in your generations, that I am the EVER-LIVING Who sanctifies you. Therefore you shall 14 keep the Rest, for it is sacred to you. Whoever curses it, he shall die; and whoever does work in it, that person shall be excommunicated from the community of his people.

"You may do your business upon 15 six days, but on the seventh is the day of rest; it is a Holy Rest to the EVER-LIVING. All who do business upon the day of Rest, shall die.

"The children of Israel shall keep 16 the Sabbath to make a rest for their posterity, as an everlasting covenant. It is a sign between Me and the 17 children of Israel for ever; for in six periods the EVER-LIVING made the solar system and the earth, but upon the seventh period, He rested and refreshed."

Tables of the Law given to Moses.

Then He gave to Moses when He 18 had finished His commands to him upon Mount Sinai, two tablets of stone, with the evidence written by the finger of GOD

The Revolt.

The People make an Idol.

32 When the People saw that Moses delayed to descend from the mountain, they called upon Aaron, and said to him, " Rouse up, and make us gods who may go before us '—for as for this fellow, Moses, who brought us up out of the land of the Mitzeraim, we know not what has become of him ! "

2 Then Aaron replied to them, " Pull off the earrings of gold that are in the ears of your wives, sons, and daughters, and bring them to me "

3 All the people pulled off the rings of gold which were in their ears and

4 brought them to Aaron, and he took them from their hands, and modelled for it with a tool, and made a calf by casting, and said ,

" Israel ! these are your Gods who brought you up out of the land of the Mitzeraim "

5 Then Aaron paid it reverence and built an altar before it Aaron also proclaimed and said

" A feast to the POWER to-morrow "

6 So they arose early on the morrow and offered sacrifices, and presented thank offerings Then the People sat down to eat and drink, and got up to play

7 The LORD however said to Moses, " Go ' Descend '—For your People whom you led out of Mitzer have cor-

8 rupted themselves ' They have soon turned from the path which I commanded them ' They have made for themselves a cast-metal calf and they are worshipping it ' And they sacrifice to it, and say , ' This is your God, Israel ' that brought you up from the

9 land of the Mitzeraim ' " And the LORD said to Moses, " I fear for this People , for it is a people of stiff

10 neck —So now let Me alone, and My anger will burn against them, and consume them, and I will make from you a great nation "

11 But Moses fell upon his face before his EVER-LIVING GOD, and said , " Why, LORD, should Your anger burn against Your people, whom You have brought up out of the land of the Mitzeraim with great power and

12 with a strong arm ? Why should the Mitzerites say He brought them out

for evil, to kill them among the mountains, and to exterminate them from the face of the earth ? '—Turn away Your anger and forgive Your people Remember Abraham, and 13 Isaac, and Israel, Your servants, what you swore to them by YOURSELF, and promised them that their race should be as numerous as the stars of heaven , and also of this land which You promised to give to their descendants to inherit for ever " So the 14 EVER-LIVING had compassion upon the sin which His people had done against Him

The Laws of God Broken

Then Moses turned and descended 15 from the hill, with the two tables of the Law in his hands,—both tablets written upon both sides with writing And GOD had made those tablets, and 16 GOD wrote the writing that was engraved upon the tablets

When Joshua heard the voice of the 17 people at sin, he said to Moses, " There is the sound of war in the camp "

But he replied , " It is not the sound 18 of contention with swords ,—nor is it the sound of contention in charging, that I hear the roar of ' "

And when they approached the 19 camp, and saw the calf, and the dancing, then the anger of Moses burnt, and he flung the two tablets from his hands, and broke them under the mountain

[1] (He afterwards took the calf which 20 they had made and burnt it in the fire, and ground it until it was like dust, and threw it upon the face of the water, and made the children of Israel drink it)

Then Moses demanded of Aaron, 21 " What have this People done to you, that you should bring upon them this great sin ? "

But Aaron replied, " Let not my 22 Prince's anger burn ' You know this people, how bad they are ' and they 23 said to me, ' Make Gods for us, who can go before us — for as for this fellow Moses, who brought us up from the land of the Mitzeraim, we know not what has become of him '

---

1 V 20, in parentheses, does not refer to the immediate act of Moses, but to his subsequent action It is q, res tis, her olt The narrative carries us on at 2 So V , Ch xxii —F 1

24 So I said to them, 'Bring me gold,' and they brought it, and gave me it, and I threw it into the furnace, and this calf was produced!"

25 Then Moses saw that the People were in revolt, and had involved

26 Aaron in their insurrection. Therefore Moses stood up at the gate of the camp, and cried; "Who is for my EVER-LIVING GOD?" when all the sons of Levi joined him.

27 And he said to them, "Thus says the EVER-LIVING, the GOD of Israel; 'Let every man bind his sword upon his thigh! Go through and return from gate to gate of the camp and kill every man his brother, and every man his neighbour, and every man his friend!'"

28 So the sons of Levi did it, as Moses commanded, and there fell of the people in that day three-thousand men.

29 Moses afterwards said; "Your hands to-day have worked for the EVER-LIVING; thus each man has gained for himself a blessing through his son, and through his brother."

30 Some days afterwards, however, Moses said to the people themselves; "You have sinned a great sin; so now I will offer to the EVER-LIVING a ram as an expiation on account of your sin."

31 Therefore Moses turned to the EVER-LIVING and said; "Certainly this People have sinned a great sin, when they made a god of gold for

32 themselves; but yet remove their sin; and if not, strike me out of Your Book which You have written."

33 Then the EVER-LIVING answered Moses, "What is their sin to ME? I

34 will strike them from My Book. But now go, lead the People to where I command you, and My Messenger shall go before your face, and in the day of visitation I will visit upon them their sin."

35 Thus the EVER-LIVING punished the People for what they had done, regarding the calf that Aaron had made.

33 Then the EVER-LIVING said to Moses; "Go from here; you and the people whom you brought up from the land of the Mitzeraim to the land which I promised to Abraham, and to Isaac, and to Jacob, saying, 'To your

2 descendants I will give it.' And I will send My Messenger before your face, and drive out the Cananites, the Amorites, the Hitites, the Perizites,

3 the Hivites, and the Jebusites, from the land flowing with milk and honey.——Yet I shall not bring you straight to it, for you are a stiff-necked people, therefore I shall march you by a journey."

4 When the people heard this hard command they grieved; and many men would not put on their armour.

5 Therefore the EVER-LIVING spoke to Moses, "Say to the children of Israel, 'You are a stiff-necked people; —a rebellious one. If I came a single moment into your midst I could destroy you. However, strip off your arms, and I will make known what I will do to you.'"

6 So the children of Israel quickly stripped off their armour.

Moses carries off the Tabernacle of Witnesses and the Word Appears.

7 Then Moses seized the tabernacle, and pitched it for himself outside the camp, at a distance from the camp, and named it his Hall of Meeting, so that all who wished to inquire of the EVER-LIVING were obliged to come to him to his Hall of Assembly that was

8 outside the camp. But when Moses had gone away with the tabernacle, all the people rose in insurrection, and every man stood at the door of his tent and looked after Moses as he

9 went off with the tabernacle. And when Moses went with the tabernacle, the cloud tremblingly descended and stood at the door of the tabernacle,

10 and the WORD was with Moses. When all the people saw the trembling cloud standing at the door of his tabernacle, then all the people arose and everyone bowed down towards that tent.

11 There the EVER-LIVING spoke with Moses face to face, as a man speaks with his friend; — Then he turned towards the camp, and watched it; but Joshua the son of Nun, his attendant, did not depart from the inside of the tabernacle.

12 And Moses said to the EVER-LIVING: "See, You spoke to me to bring up this people, but yet You have not instructed me as to whom You will send with me. You have, however, said, 'I know you by name, and you have found favour in My eyes.' So now, if

13 I have found favour in Your eyes, teach me Your path that I may know You, since I have found favour in

Your sight, and perceive that Your People are this Nation."

14 Then He replied, "Turn their advance back, and I will support you."

15 But he answered to Him, "If Your PRESENCE is not with our marches,

16 do not take us from here. And by what can it be possibly known that I have found favour in Your sight, I and Your people? Would it not be by Your marching with us? and distinguishing me and Your People from every nation upon the face of the earth?"

17 Then the EVER-LIVING answered Moses, "I will grant also this request which you have made, for you have found favour in My eyes, and I have made MYSELF known to you by a NAME."

18 He therefore replied —"Show me, I pray, Your Majesty."

19 And he was answered, "I have passed all My beauty before your face, and I made MYSELF known to you openly by My Name of the EVER-LIVING. I show favour to those I love, and compassion to those I

20 compassionate — But," He added, "you are not able to see My face, for

21 no man can see Me and live. However," said the EVER-LIVING, "mount

22 up to Me and sit on the rock, and My Majesty shall pass over, and I will place you in a cleft of the rock, and shade you with My hand over you,

23 until I pass over, so that upon removing My hand you may see My back, for you cannot look upon My face."

Command to make New Tablets for the Commandments.

34 The EVER-LIVING afterwards said to Moses, "Cut for yourself two tablets of stone, like the former ones, and I will write upon them the Commandments which were upon the

2 first that you broke, and when dawn comes, go up at dawn to the Mount Sinai, and sit with Me upon the top of

3 the hill. But no man shall come up with you, for no man must be seen in all the hill, nor sheep, or beast approach to the hill."

4 Moses accordingly cut two tablets of stone like the former, and arose at morning, and ascended Mount Sinai, as the EVER-LIVING commanded him, and took in his hands the two tablets

5 of stone. Then the EVER-LIVING descended in the cloud and sat there

with him, and he called on the Name of JEHOVAH, when the EVER-LIVING 6 passed over before his face, and he cried out "EVER-LIVING! LIVING GOD of GENTLENESS and PITY, SLOW to ANGER, but GREAT in MERCY and TRUTH, preserving 7 mercy to thousands, taking away passion, and rebellion, and forgiving sin,—but not ceasing to visit the passions of the fathers upon their children, and upon the children of their children to the third and the fourth generation!'"

Then Moses hastily rose and fell to 8 the earth and worshipped, and said 9 "If now I have found favour in Your sight, ALMIGHTY, come, I pray, ALMIGHTY, near to us, for they are a stiff-necked People, and pardon our passions and sins, and give us our inheritance.'

And He replied, "Now I make a 10 covenant with all your People. I will produce wonders such as have not been from creation in all the earth, or in any nation, and every people among whom you are, shall see the work of the EVER-LIVING, for what I will do by you will be splendid. Attend to what I have communicated 11 to you to-day,—Then I will drive before you the Amorites, the Cananites, the Hitites, the Perizites, the Hivites, and Jebusites.

"Keep yourselves from making 12 treaties with the residents of the land when you come to it, for fear they should be a snare in your midst. Therefore overthrow their altars, and 13 break down their pillars, and cut down their shrines, for you shall not 14 worship another god, for the EVER-LIVING is jealous of HIS NAME, He is a jealous GOD.

"Beware of making alliances with 15 the inhabitants of the land, for fear you whore after their gods, and sacrifice to their gods, and approach to eat at their altars, or take from 16 their daughters for your sons, for their daughters will whore after their gods, and your sons whore after their gods. Nor shall you make a metallic 17 god for yourselves.

Repetition of Social Law.

"You shall keep the feast of un- 18 leavened bread for seven days. You shall eat biscuits as I have commanded you, at the assembly in the harvest month,[1] for in the month of harvest I brought you from among the Mitzeraim.

19 "All breaking the womb is Mine; and every male of your possessions, 20 of cattle or sheep bursting it; but an ass bursting it, you shall redeem with a sheep; and if you do not redeem it you shall break its neck.

"All your eldest sons you shall redeem, for you shall not see My presence empty-handed.

21 "You shall labour six days, but on the seventh you shall cease from 22 ploughing, and rest in harvest. You shall also make a festival of rest for yourselves at the first fruits of the wheat harvest; and a festival at the completion of the solar circuit of the year.

23 "Three times in a year all your men shall appear before the Presence of the LORD, the EVER LIVING GOD 24 of Israel, for I will drive out the heathen before you, and will extend your boundaries, therefore no man of your land shall neglect to go up three times in a year to see the Presence of your EVER-LIVING GOD. 25 You shall not shed the blood of My sacrifices away from it; and you shall not leave until the morning the 26 sacrifice of the Passover. You shall also decorate the house of your EVER-LIVING GOD with the first fruits of your fields when you come up.

"You shall not boil a kid in its mother's milk."

27 Finally the EVER-LIVING said to Moses;—"Write these commands, for upon the basis of these Commands I have made a covenant with you, and with Israel."

The Time Moses stayed on Sinai.

28 And he was there with the EVER-LIVING forty days and forty nights, and ate no bread, nor drank water, but wrote upon the tablets the commands of the Covenant;

THE TEN COMMANDMENTS.

The Splendour of the Face of Moses.

29 Then Moses descended from Mount Sinai with the Tables of the Testimony in the hands of Moses. On his descent, however, from the hill, Moses did not know that blinding rays of light[1] from his face, prevented their speaking to him!

But Aaron, and all the children of 30 Israel saw those rays of light from his face, and they were afraid to approach him.

Moses, however, called to them, 31 when Aaron turned to him, with all the leaders of the Assembly, and Moses addressed them; and after 32 that all the children of Israel approached, and he communicated all that the EVER-LIVING had commanded him in Mount Sinai.

But that Moses might speak to 33 them, he put a veil over his face. But when Moses went to speak with 34 the EVER-LIVING he removed the veil from his face, until he returned, and came and related to them what he had been commanded. So the 35 children of Israel feared in the presence of Moses, for rays of splendour preceded Moses, therefore Moses placed the veil over his face when he went to speak with them.

Moses addresses the Parliament of Israel.

Then Moses assembled all the **35** parliament of the children of Israel, and said to them;

"These are the Commandments which the EVER-LIVING has commanded you to practise:—

"You shall do your work for six 2 days, but the Seventh Day shall be a Holy Rest for you. You shall rest to the EVER-LIVING. Every one doing business on it shall die. No 3 man shall labour in all your habitations upon the Day of Rest."

Moses continued to speak to all 4 the parliament of the children of Israel, saying;—

"This is also a commandment 5 which the EVER-LIVING commanded, saying:—'Let everyone of willing heart bring an offering from themselves to the EVER-LIVING!'"

Gifts to God from the People.

All of free heart consequently brought an offering from themselves to the EVER-LIVING of gold, silver, and brass; and azure and purple, 6 and blue, red, and spun linen; and 7 ram skins, dyed red, and badger skins, and acacia wood; and oil for 8

Abib   [1] Literally "Horns of Light."—F. F.

the lamps, and perfumes for the Oil of Consecration, and incense for the 9 veils, and onyx stones, and stones for the settings of the ephod, and 10 breastplate Whilst those of skill among them came and made all that 11 the EVER-LIVING commanded The enclosures of the tent, and its veils, the hooks, and the planks, the cross-bars, the standards and the bases, 12 the ark and the staves for it, the 13 covers, and the covering veil, the table, and its staves, and all its ap-14 purtenances, and the Shewbread and the reflectors for the lamps, and the appurtenances for them, and the burners, and the oil for the lights, 15 and the incense altar, and its staves, and the Oil of Consecration, and the perfumes for the aromatics, and the veil for the door, at the opening of 16 the sanctuary The altar of burnt offering, and its base of brass, the staves and the whole of the instru-17 ments, the bath and its bases The curtains for the court and its stan-dards, and their bases, and the 18 skreen for the gate of the court The stakes for the sanctuary, and the stakes for the court, and the rest 19 The robes for the service, when serving in the Holy-place, the sacred robes for Aaron the priest, and the robes for his sons, the priests

20 Then the whole of the chiefs of the children of Israel came before Moses, 21 and brought whatever their heart suggested, and all that their spirit dictated to them, they brought as an offering to the EVER-LIVING, to sup-ply the Hall of Assembly, and its appurtenances, and for the sacred 22 robes Thus the chiefs coming to Moses,—all who were of liberal heart, —brought ear and nose rings, and brooches, and beads and all things made of gold, and everything which was adorned with gold to the EVER-23 LIVING Every man, also, who pos-sessed azure, and purple, and blue-red, and spun linen, and red goat skins, and badger skins brought them 24 Many nobles brought gifts of silver and brass, as presents to the EVER-LIVING, or of anything they pos-sessed Some brought acacia wood 25 for the works And the skilful women brought yarn in their hands, azure yarn, and purple, and blue-26 red, and linen All the men also who were skilful in spinning, their ...... their hearts gave ....

Other men brought precious stones 27 to set the ephod and the breastplate, and perfumes, and oil for the lights, 28 and for the Consecration Oil, and perfumes for the incense Every 29 man and woman with a liberal heart brought all the things that the EVER-LIVING commanded, by the hand of Moses, to be made as gifts to the EVER-LIVING

Appointment of Architects and Mechanics for the Sanctuary

Then Moses said to the children of 30 Israel, "The EVER-LIVING has called Bezalal, the son of Auri, the son of Hor of the tribe of Judah, and has 31 filled him with genius, skill, intelli-gence and knowledge, and a mecha-nical mind, and inventive faculties 32 for working in gold, and silver, and brass, and to cut stones for jewellery, 33 and to shape timber for use, and for all engineering work He has also given as a fitting assistant to him, Ahaliab the son of Ahhismak, of the tribe of Dan, filling them with in- 35 telligence to work in every kind of contrivance, in jewellery, and em-broidery, in azure, and purple, in blue, and red, and flax, and to weave all materials, and to make patterns "

Bezalal and Ahaliab consequently 36 worked, with all the skilful men to whom the EVER-LIVING had given intelligence and understanding, to assist them in their operations, for the production of all the furniture for the sanctuary, which the EVER-LIVING had commanded Thus 2 Moses appointed Bezalal and Ahaliab, and all the skilful men to whom the EVER-LIVING had given an intelli-gent mind, with everyone whose mind invited them to go to the work to effect it, and they received in the 3 presence of Moses all the offerings that the children of Israel had brought to make the appliances for the ser-vices of the sanctuary They fetched their part from the treasury morning by morning, and every skilled worker 4 brought back the articles for the sanctuary which he had made from his workshop, until they reported to 5 Moses, saying, "The material which the people have brought is more than the requirements for the furniture that the EVER-LIVING commanded ....

Moses therefore ordered not make 6

a proclamation in the camp to inform every man and woman not to bring further material to offer for the sanctuary. So the people ceased to 7 bring it, for the material was sufficient for all the appliances that had to be made, and in excess.

8 So the workmen made the furniture for the tent; Ten curtains of spun linen, and azure, and purple, and blue-red, with pictures of Kerubim formed in damask. The length 9 of the curtains was eighteen cubits each, and the width four cubits, each curtain ;—the same to each curtain ; 10 and the end of one curtain was joined to the other, and the next curtain's edge was joined to the 11 following ; for they made loops upon the selvage of each of the curtains at the end of the edges. Thus they made the curtains with attachments 12 to join the two. They made fifty loops on each curtain ; and fifty loop attachments were made upon the second curtain which joined it to the next, opposite to the loops, one for 13 one. They also made fifty hooks of gold to join the curtains one to the other, so as to form one tent.

14 They also made curtains of goatskins for the canopy over the tent, which were divided into twenty curtains. 15 The length of each curtain was thirty cubits, and four cubits broad for each curtain ; all the twenty 16 curtains were made equal ; and they joined five of the curtains together, 17 and six of the curtains together ; and made fifty loops on the lip of a curtain, at its edge to fasten with, and made fifty loops upon the lip of the 18 second curtain for fastenings. They also made hooks of brass to join the canopy to form it into one piece. 19 Then they made the Hall of Assembly of red ram-skins, with a verandah of badger skins over all of it.

20 They also made the planks for the tabernacle of acacia wood planed. 21 The length of a plank was ten cubits, and a cubit and a half broad, for 22 each plank. There were two hands to each plank at the joinings on one side and the other. They made the same to all the planks of the taber- 23 nacle. Twenty planks were made for the tabernacle on the side towards 24 the south. And forty bases of silver were formed under the twenty planks ; —two bases under a plank with two hands on them

And for the opposite side towards 25 the north, they made twenty planks, with forty bases of silver, two bases 26 for each plank. But the width of the 27 tabernacle to the west was six planks ; and two planks made the corners of 28 the tabernacle at the corners. And 29 there were clutches fitting together and uniting them. Thus both were 30 fastened at their edges. Thus there were eight planks, and sixteen silver bases, two bases, and two bases, under each plank. They also made 31 bars of acacia wood, five bars for the planks at the first side of the tabernacle ; and five bars to the planks at 32 the other side of the tabernacle, and five bars to the planks of the tabernacle at its length towards the west ; and the bars were made for shoots in 33 the middle of the planks from side to side. The planks, however, were 34 plated with gold, and their buttons were made of gold with lock-holes to each one, and the bars were plated with gold.

The veils also were made of azure, 35 and purple, and blue-red, and spun linen, with damasked Kerubims worked on them. They also made 36 four posts of acacia, and plated them with gold, with pins of gold, and cast for them four bases of silver. They 37 also made a skreen for the door of the sanctuary of azure, and purple, and blue-red, and spun linen, worked as embroidery. And the five pillars 38 and the pins, with the chapiters on their heads, and the rods were of gold, but the five bars were of brass.

Bezalal himself made the ark of **37** acacia wood. Its length two and a half cubits, and its breadth a cubit and a half, and a cubit and a half its height ; and he plated with pure gold 2 within and without, and made it a wreath of gold around ; and cast 3 four knobs of gold for its four feet ; two knobs at the one side, and two knobs at the other side. He also 4 made staves of acacia wood and plated them with gold, so that they 5 could put the staves into the ears upon the sides of the ark to carry the ark by.

He also made covers of pure gold, 6 two cubits and a half in length and a cubit and a half in width. Besides 7 he made two Kerubim of gold. They were made standing at the two ends of the covers ; one Kerub at this end, 8 and the other at that. But the 9 kerubim were extending their wings like a protection from above with their wings over the covers, with the face of each towards the other over covers —the kerubim faced each other

10 He also made the table of acacia wood, two cubits in length and a cubit and a half in breadth, and a 11 cubit and a half in height, and plated it over with pure gold, and made a 12 coronal round about it of gold He also made a ridge of a handbreadth around it, with rays of gold upon the 13 ridge all round, and cast four tabs of gold, and fixed the tabs upon the four 14 sides where its feet were The tabs were fixed near the ridge for the 15 staves to carry the table with He made the staves, to carry the table, of acacia wood and plated them with 16 gold, as well as the instruments that were upon the table,— the dishes and the snuffers, and the cups and the plates which covered them,—of pure gold

17 He also made the lamp of turned work of pure gold, its shank, upright stalk, its branches, its cups, and 18 blossoms were made of it And there were six branches going from the sides,—three branches from one side, and three branches from the 19 other side There were three almond cones and flowers upon one branch, a cup and a blossom,—and three almond cones and flowers on an alternate branch, a cup and a blossom, thus six branches rose up for the 20 lamps And upon the lamp four cones like almonds, a cup, and a 21 blossom But there was a ball between two of the branches mutually, and a ball between two of the branches mutually, and a ball between two of the branches mutually, for the six branches that rose up 22 from them There were balls and branches for them mutually, all the 23 appliances were of pure gold. He also made seven reflectors, and holders, and snuffers of pure gold 24 a talent weight of pure gold made these, and all the instruments

25 Afterwards he made the Altar of Incense of acacia wood Its length was a cubit, and its breadth a cubit, square, and its height two cubits,

with its horns, and he covered the 26 top of it with pure gold, and around its sides, and its horns, and made a coronal of gold around it He also 27 made two tabs of gold for it, between the coronal, upon the two sides, upon its opposite sides, to insert the two staves to carry it by He made the 28 staves also of acacia wood, and plated them with gold He also 29 made the Holy Consecration Oil, and the incense of pure spices for perfume

Then he made of acacia wood the 38 Altar of Burnt Offerings Its length was five cubits, and its breadth five cubits, square, and its height three cubits He also made horns upon 2 its four faces, its horns were all alike and he plated them with brass Besides he made all the instruments 3 for the altar, the cauldrons, and the brushes, and the sprinklers, and the rakes, and the shovels, he made of brass He also made for the altar a 4 netted sieve of brass under its fireplace, with projections at its edges, and he cast four tabs of brass for the 5 borders of the sieve—as receptacles for staves, which he made of acacia 6 wood, and covered them with brass, and placed the staves in the tabs at 7 the sides of the altar, to carry it by, —he made them to fit into valves

He also made the bath and its 8 pedestals of brass, with the mirrors for the use of whoever served before the Hall of Assembly

He also made the court at the side 9 towards the south The curtains for the court were a hundred cubits of spun linen The pillars twenty, and 10 the bases twenty The spikes of the pillars and the pins were of brass, but the rods of silver And on the 11 north face it was a hundred cubits, with twenty pillars and twenty bases The spikes of the pillars were brass, but the rods of silver But on the 12 west face, the curtains were fifty cubits, ten pillars and the bases, with spikes for the pillars, but the rods were of silver And upon the eastern 13 face, the sun rise, fifty cubits fifteen 14 cubits of curtains to the gate-posts, six pillars and six bases, but from 15 the other gate-post, on this side and that, to the gate of the court curtains for fifteen cubits, six pillars and six

16 bases. All the curtains around the
17 court were of spun linen, and the
bases of the pillars were of brass,
but the spikes of the pillars and the
rods were of silver, and the capitals
of the pillars of silver; with rods of
silver for all the pillars of the court.
18   The skreen for the gate of the
court, however, was made of embroidery of azure, and purple, and
blue-red, and spun linen; and its
length was twenty cubits, and in
height at the fold-back five cubits, to
the juncture with the curtains of the
19 court; with four pillars and four
bases of brass; but the pins of silver,
and the capitals of the heads of the
20 pillars of silver, with all the other
things for the tent and the court
around of brass.

The Officials of the Tabernacle.

21   These were the officers of the tent,
—the Hall of Assembly—which were
appointed by the mouth of Moses, for
the service of the Levites, under
Aithamar, the son of Aaron the priest,
22 with Bezalal the son of Auri, the son
of Hor of the tribe of Judah to make
everything that the EVER-LIVING had
23 commanded by Moses; and with
them Ahaliab the son of Ahhismak
of the tribe of Dan, to engrave, and
damask, and embroider, in azure,
and purple, and blue, and red; and
in spinning.

Amount of Gold and other Metals used in the Tabernacle.

24   The whole of the gold that was
used in the furniture of the sanctuary
was twenty-nine talents, and nine
hundred and thirty shekels, by the
25 sacred weight. And of silver from
the chiefs of the congregation one
hundred talents and one thousand
seven hundred and fifty-seven shekels
by the sacred weight.
26   The half shekel poll-tax by the
sacred weight, from who were passed
into the regiments, from twenty years
of age and over that, was six hundred
and thirty thousand, five hundred,
27 and fifty. And there were used one
hundred talents of silver in casting
the bases of the sanctuary; and the
bases of the doors;—a hundred bases
from a hundred talents:—a talent to
28 a base. They ..... used .... thousand
seven hundred .... seventy-five for

the spikes to the pillars, and the
capitals on their heads, and the rods
for them.
    Besides, the brass offered was 29
seventy thousand talents, and four
hundred shekels, which were used 30
for the bases of the doors of the
Hall of Assembly and the brass of
the door-posts, and the Brazen Altar,
and the lattice work of brass for it,
and the whole of the instruments of
the altar, with the bases of the court 31
around, and the bases of the gates of
the court, and all the rest of the
tent, and the remainder of the court
around.
    And of the azure, and purple, and **39**
blue-red, they made the service
robes, to serve in the sanctuary, as
well as the holy robes for Aaron, as
the EVER-LIVING commanded to
Moses.
    They also made the ephod of gold, 2
azure, purple, and blue-red, and
spun linen. And there were strips of 3
gold and wire twisted in the working
among the azure, and among the
purple, and among the blue-red, and
among the linen threads that made
the damasking. They made shoulder 4
pieces that joined upon the two
halves by a seam. They also made 5
the breast-plate of the ephod, to be
worn over it, of gold, azure, and
purple, and blue-red, and spun linen,
as the EVER-LIVING commanded
Moses.
    Besides they made two onyx stones 6
surrounded with gold settings, engraved like the engraving of a seal
with the names of the sons of Israel;
and placed them upon the shoulders 7
of the ephod as memorial stones for
the sons of Israel,—as the EVER-
LIVING commanded to Moses.
    They also made the breast-plate of 8
damasked work, as they made the
ephod, of gold, and azure, and purple,
and blue-red, and spun linen. The 9
breastplate was made a square
doubled,—a span long and a span
broad, doubled; and it was filled 10
with four rows of stones:
    The first row was;
    A ruby, a topaz and a diamond.
    The second row was: 11
    An emerald, a sapphire and an
opal.
    The third row was: 12
    A ligure, an agate and an amethyst;
    And the fourth row was: 13
    A tarshish, an onyx, and a jasper.

Surrounded by settings of gold to
14 fix them; thus there were twelve
stones with the names of the sons of
Israel; with the names engraven like
a seal; each with one name of the
twelve tribes.

15 They also made for the breastplate
chain borderings of plaited work of
16 pure gold. Beside which they made
two gold fastenings, and two buttons
of gold, and fixed the two buttons
upon the two sides of the breastplate,
17 and placed the two chains of gold upon
the two buttons at the sides of the
18 breastplate, and the two ends of the
two chains they fixed upon the two
buttons, and fastened them upon the
two shoulders over the front of them.
19 They also made two gold buttons and
placed them upon the two edges of
the breastplate, upon the lips which
20 went over the ephod inwards. Besides
they made two buttons of gold and
fixed them upon the two shoulders
of the ephod before and behind to
unite together at the top of the ephod
21 with the breastplate; and they laced
the breastplate, from button to button
to the ephod with laces of azure, to
secure the breastplate to the ephod,
so that the breastplate might not
fall off from the ephod;—as the
EVER-LIVING had commanded to
Moses.

22 They also made a mantle for the
23 ephod, of azure woven velvet; and
the mouth of the mantle was in the
middle of it, like a coat of mail, with
a binding around it so that it might
24 not tear. And they made on the hem
of the mantle pomegranates of azure,
and purple, and blue-red, with em-
25 broidery; and also made bells of pure
gold, and fixed the bells between the
pomegranates, upon the hem around
the mantle between the pome-
26 granates; a bell and a pomegranate
upon the hem around the mantle;—as
the EVER-LIVING commanded
Moses.

27 They also made vests of woven
linen work for Aaron and his sons,
28 and turbans of linen, and mitres of
linen, and white drawers of spun
29 linen; with girdles of spun linen, and
azure, and blue-red, as the EVER-
LIVING commanded Moses.

30 They also made the flower of the
Holy Crown of pure gold, and engraved upon it, with the engraving of a
seal, "Holiness to the EVER-LIVING,"
31 and fixed a cord of azure upon it to

fasten it upon the top, as the EVER-
LIVING commanded to Moses.

32 Thus were completed all the
appliances for the Hall of Assembly.
They were made in the manner that
the EVER-LIVING commanded to
Moses.

33 Therefore they brought the tent to
Moses;—the sanctuary and all its
furniture, its hooks, its planks, its
bars, its pillars and bases; and the
34 awning of red ram skins, and the
awning of badger skins, and curtains
for the screen; with the Ark of
35 Witnesses, and its staves, and its
covers; and the table, and all its
36 furniture; and the Shewbread,[1] with
37 the Lamp of Splendour, and its reflectors, and its series of lamps, and
the whole of its appliances; and the
oil for the lamps; with the altar of
38 gold, and the Oil of Consecration,
and the sweet incense; and the skreen
of the veil of the pavilion. The
39 brazen altar; and the brass grating
for it; its staves, and all its instruments; the bath and its buckets; the
40 curtains of the court, its pillars and
their bases; and the skreen for the
gate of the court; its ropes and pegs,
and the rest of the appliances for the
uses of the tent of the Hall of Assembly.
41 The ornamented robes for service in
the sanctuary; the sacred robes for
Aaron, the priest, and the robes for
42 his sons, the priests; according to
all that the EVER-LIVING commanded
to Moses, the children of Israel made
the whole for the service.

43 Then Moses inspected all the
work, to see if they had made all of
it according to the command of the
EVER-LIVING. They had done so,
and Moses blessed them.

Command to Erect the Tent.

40 Then the EVER-LIVING spoke to
Moses, saying:—

2 "To-morrow is the first month.
Upon the first of the month you shall
set up the tent of the Hall of Assembly,
3 and place there the Ark of Witnesses,
and cover the ark with the veil.
4 Then you shall bring the table, and
arrange its appliances, and bring the
Golden Lamp, and set up its re-
5 flectors; and place the golden altar
of incense before the Ark of the
Witnesses, and fix the skreen of
6 the doors to the tabernacle. Then

---

1 Bread of the Presence.—1 F.

place the altar of burnt-offering opposite the door of the Hall of Assembly, 7 and set the bath between the Hall of Assembly and the altar, and put water 8 in it. Afterwards fix up the court around, and put the skreen to the 9 gate of the court ; and then take the Oil of Consecration and consecrate the tent, and everything in it, and sanctify it, and the whole of its furniture ; when it shall be sacred.

"The altar shall be Holy of Holies.
11 "Next consecrate the bath and its
12 buckets, and sanctify it. Then present Aaron and his sons at the door of the Hall of Assembly, and wash
13 them with water, and clothe Aaron in the sacred robe, and consecrate him. Thus you shall make him holy, and
14 he shall be a priest to ME. Afterwards present his sons and clothe
15 them with vests, and consecrate them, as you consecrated their father, and they shall be priests to ME ; and the consecration shall be an appointment of them as priests for ever in their descendants."

16 Moses consequently did all that the EVER-LIVING commanded him. He effected it.

17 Thus it was in the first month, in the second year, on the first of the
18 month, they erected the tent. And Moses set up the tent, and fixed its bases, and placed its planks, and fixed its curtains, and erected its pillars,
19 and spread the canopy over the Tabernacle, and put the awning of the Tabernacle over its roof; as the EVER-LIVING commanded him.

20 Then he took and put the witnesses into the ark, and placed the staves to the ark, and put the covers upon the
21 top of the ark, and brought the ark to the tent, and hung the veil of the skreen, and veiled off the witnesses ; as the EVER-LIVING commanded Moses.

22 Then he placed the table in the Hall of Assembly, at the north side
23 of the Tabernacle outside of the veil, and arranged upon it the prepared bread before the EVER-LIVING ;—as the EVER-LIVING commanded to Moses.

Next he placed the lamp in the 24 Hall of Assembly, upon the table opposite at the south side of the Tabernacle, and raised the lights 25 before the EVER-LIVING; as the EVER-LIVING commanded Moses.

Then he placed the golden altar in 26 the Hall of Assembly before the veil, and offered sweet incense upon it ;— 27 as the EVER-LIVING commanded Moses.

Then he put the skreen to the 28 door of the Tabernacle, and set the 29 altar of burnt-offering at the door of the tent of the Hall of Assembly, and offered upon it the burnt offering, and the gift ;—as the EVER-LIVING commanded Moses.

Then he placed the bath between 30 the Hall of Assembly and the altar, and put water in it to wash with, and 31 Moses washed himself his feet and hands there, with Aaron and his sons, before going into the Hall of 32 Assembly, and approaching the altar, they washed themselves ;—as the EVER-LIVING commanded Moses.

They also erected the court around 33 the Tabernacle, and the altar and fixed the skreen at the gate of the court.

Then Moses ceased from his labours.

Then the cloud covered the Hall of 34 Assembly, and the splendour of the EVER-LIVING filled the tabernacle, and Moses was not able to go into the 35 Hall of Assembly for the cloud rested upon it, and the splendour of the EVER-LIVING filled the tent. After- 36 wards when the cloud arose from off the Tabernacle, the children of Israel marched in all their marches ; and if 37 the cloud did not arise, then they did not march until the day when it arose ;—for the cloud of the EVER- 38 LIVING was upon the Tabernacle by day, and there was a fire by night. It was in the sight of the house of Israel in all their marches.

END OF THE BOOK OF EXODUS.

THE THIRD BOOK OF MOSES, COMMONLY CALLED

LEVITICUS.

(VA IKRA AL MOSHEH=AND HE CALLED TO MOSES.)

The Ritual of Sacrifices.

1 THEN the EVER-LIVING called to Moses and spoke to him from the Hall of the Assembly, saying,—

Ritual of Burnt Offerings.

2 "Speak to the children of Israel and say to them, A man of you who would offer an offering to the EVER-LIVING, can offer it from the herd, or from the fold, or from the flock

3 "If they offer a burnt offering from the fold, it shall be a perfect male It shall be offered at the door of the Tent of Assembly, as a pleasure to

4 him before the EVER-LIVING Then he shall lay his hand upon the head of the sacrifice and present it before the EVER-LIVING to expiate for

5 himself, and he must slay the son of the fold before the EVER-LIVING Then the sons of Aaron the priest shall approach the blood, and sprinkle some of the blood around over the altar, that is at the door of the Hall

6 of Assembly Afterwards he shall skin the sacrifice and divide it into

7 parts Then the sons of Aaron the priest shall lay the parts of the head and fat in order upon the wood and

8 put fire upon the altar, and arrange wood upon the fire that is on the altar, after washing the inwards and

9 the feet in water, and the priest shall burn the whole of them on the altar as a sweet delightful perfume to

10 the EVER-LIVING But if he offers from the sheep or from the lambs, or from the goats, he shall offer as a burnt

11 offering a perfect male, and slay it at the north side of the altar before the EVER-LIVING, and the sons of Aaron the priest shall sprinkle some of its

12 blood around the altar Then he shall divide it into parts, and the priest shall arrange its head and its fat upon the wood that is upon the

13 fire that is on the altar Then he shall wash its inwards and legs in

water, and the priest shall offer the whole of them with incense upon the altar of burnt offering, as a sweet breath delightful to the EVER-LIVING

14 "But if he sacrifices a gift from the birds to the EVER-LIVING let him offer his gift from the turtle doves or

15 the young of pigeons, and the priest shall take it to the altar and wring off its head, and perfume the altar, and present its blood at the side of the

16 altar, and pull out its crop and feathers, and throw them to the eastern side of the altar into the

17 receptacle for the fat Then the priest shall cleave it,—not separate— and perfume the altar for it, offering it upon the wood which is on the fire, —it is sweet smell delightful to the EVER-LIVING

2 "And the soul that gives a present to the EVER-LIVING, let it be of fine flour, and pour oil upon it, and put

2 frankincense on it, and bring it to the sons of Aaron, the priest, and the priest shall grasp a handful from the fine flour and the oil, with all the frankincense, and shall burn as a remembrance on the altar,—a sweet perfume delightful to the EVER-

3 LIVING But the rest of the offering shall be for Aaron and his sons, holy of holies from the fire of the EVER-LIVING

4 "But if he would offer a present baked in the oven, let it be of fine ground flour biscuits mixed with oil, or wafer biscuits buttered with oil

5 "If, however, your gift is a present of baked bread, it shall be of fine

6 flour with oil, unfermented and broken in pieces with oil poured upon it It is a present

7 "But if you give a boiled present, let it be made of fine flour with oil

8 And you shall bring the present that you have made from it to the EVER-LIVING, and approach to the priest, and he shall carry it to the altar

9 Then the priest shall lift up the

present as a remembrance, and perfume the altar; a sweet smell
10 delightful to the EVER-LIVING. But the rest of the present shall be for Aaron and his sons;—holy of holies from the fire of the EVER-LIVING.

11   "Any present which they offer to the EVER-LIVING shall not be made with ferment, for not any ferment or any honey shall be burnt with it as a
12 delight to the EVER-LIVING. You shall bring them as an offering of the best kinds to the EVER-LIVING; they shall not be burnt upon the altar as a
13 breath of delight. Every offering presented by you shall be salted with salt; and you shall not withhold the salt of the Covenant of your God from your presents; upon every offering you shall offer salt.

14   "And if you offer a present from your crops to the EVER-LIVING, it shall be ears of wheat or oats,[1] from the field, as a present from your
15 crops. You shall also put upon it oil, and add along with it frankin-
16 cense. It is a present; therefore the priest shall burn the remembrance from the corn and from the oil, with all the frankincense as a perfume to the EVER-LIVING.

3   "But if anyone offers a thank-offering, let it be offered from the herd;—only a perfect spotless male may be
2 offered to the EVER-LIVING; and he shall lay his hand upon the head of his offering, and slay it at the door of the Hall of Assembly, and the sons of Aaron, the priest, shall sprinkle some of the blood around upon the
3 altar. He shall offer on the altar the thank-offering as a delight to the EVER-LIVING;—the fat of the caul, the chest, and the whole of the fat
4 that is upon the chest; with the two kidneys, and the fat that is upon them; and on the viscera; but the rest on the liver, and upon the kid-
5 neys he shall put aside; for the sons of Aaron shall offer them upon the altar of burnt-offering, with wood and fire, as a sweet breath to the EVER-LIVING.
6   "But if he offers a sacrifice from the flock as a thank-offering, let him
7 offer a perfect male or female. If he offers a lamb as his gift, then he shall
8 bring it before the EVER-LIVING, and lay his hand upon the head of the gift, and slay it before the Hall of

Assembly, and the sons of Aaron shall sprinkle some of its blood around the altar, and shall carry to 9 the altar—from the thank-offering made by fire to the EVER-LIVING,—the entire fat of the rump cut near the backbone, and the fat of the caul, and of the chest, and all the fat that is upon the chest, and the two 10 kidneys and the fat which is upon them, with that upon the bowels, and the remainder that covers the kidneys he shall put aside; and the priest 11 shall offer them upon the altar as a sweet scent to the EVER-LIVING.

"But if he offers a gift of a goat 12 before the EVER-LIVING he shall lay 13 his hand upon its head, and slay it before the Hall of Assembly; and the sons of Aaron shall sprinkle some of its blood around the altar, and offer 14 of the gift as a sweet scent to the EVER-LIVING, the fat of the caul, and the chest, and the whole of the fat that is upon the chest, and the two 15 kidneys, and the fat that is on them, with that upon the bowels, but the remainder, covering over the kidneys, he shall put aside. Thus the priest shall 16 burn them on the altar, consuming as a sweet breath, delightful to the EVER-LIVING, all the fat.

"It is an Institution for ever, for your descendants, in all your dwelling-places, that you shall not eat any fat or any blood."

The Law of Involuntary Sins.

Then the EVER-LIVING spoke to 4 Moses saying;

Sins of a Priest.

"Speak to the children of Israel, to 2 command;—

"The soul that sins by ignorance in any of the commands of the EVER-LIVING, through not having done, or doing it unconsciously;—If a con- 3 secrated priest shall sin to the injury of the People;—then he shall offer for the sin which he has sinned a perfect bullock from the fold, to the EVER-LIVING for his sin. And he 4 shall bring the ox to the door of the Hall of Assembly before the EVER-LIVING, and lay his hand upon the head of the ox, and slay the ox before the EVER-LIVING. Then the con- 5 secrated priest shall take some of the blood of the ox and carry it into the Hall of Assembly; where the priest 6 shall dip his finger into the blood

---

1 Heb.: "Fire-corn." For oats are roasted previous to . . . . . or husks.—? ?

seven times before the EVER-LIVING opposite the door of the sanctuary,

7 and the priest shall put some of the blood upon the horns of the altar of perfumed incense which is before the EVER-LIVING in the Hall of Assembly, and the rest of the blood of the ox shall be poured at the side of the altar which is at the door of the Hall

8 of Assembly. Then he shall remove the whole of the fat of the ox of the sin-offering from it,—the fat of the caul, with the chest and all the fat

9 upon the chest, and the two kidneys, and the fat which is upon them, with the fat of the bowels, and the remainder covering the kidneys he

o shall put aside, exactly as it is taken from the ox sacrificed as a peace-offering. Then the priest shall burn it upon the altar of burnt offering.

I But all the skin of the ox, and the whole of the flesh, with its head and

2 chest, and dung, he shall also cause to be brought, the whole of the ox, to the outside of the camp, to a clean place, to burn the fat upon wood with fire. It shall be burnt where the ashes are poured out.

Sins of Members of the Parliament

3 "But if any of the fathers of Israel goes and secretly commits out of the sight of the public, a breach of one of the commandments of the EVER-LIVING,—which they should not do,—

4 and he sins, then he shall confess the sin that he has sinned, and shall offer Publicly an ox from the fold for his sin, and bring it to the front of

5 the Hall of Assembly, where the elders of the Parliament shall lay their hands upon the head of the ox before the EVER-LIVING, and slay

6 the ox before the LORD. Then the consecrated priest shall bring some of the blood of the ox to the Hall of

7 Assembly, where the priest shall dip his forefinger into some of the blood, and sprinkle it seven times before the EVER-LIVING at the front of the

8 veil. But he shall put some of the blood upon the horns of the altar, that is before the EVER-LIVING in the Hall of Assembly, and all the rest of the blood he shall pour out at the side of the altar of burnt-offerings, at the door of the Hall of Assembly.

9 He shall then remove the whole of the fat from it, ... the

o altar, and do with . . . .

with the ox for a sin-offering, he shall do the same. Thus the priest shall expiate for him, and forgive him.

21 "Next, he shall cause the ox to be brought outside of the camp and burn it, as he burnt the former ox. It is a Public offering.

Sins of Ordinary Men.

22 "When a man sins, and breaks one of all the commandments of his EVER-LIVING GOD,—which he ought not to do—by ignorance, and has

23 sinned. or if he is informed of his sin that he has sinned, then he shall offer as a gift a perfect ram of the

24 goats, and lay his hand upon the head of the ram, and slay it in the place where the burnt-offerings are slain before the EVER-LIVING. It is

25 a sin-offering. Then the priest shall take some of the blood upon the tip of his forefinger and put it upon the horns of the altar of burnt-offerings, and pour the rest of the blood at the side of the altar of burnt-offerings,

26 and offer all the fat on the altar, like the fat of the thank-offering, and expiate for him for his sin, when it shall be forgiven to him.

Sins of the Working Classes.

27 "But if any of the people of the land break a commandment of the EVER-LIVING,—which ought not to

28 be done,—and transgresses, or he is informed that he has sinned some sin, he shall then bring a perfect she goat as an offering for the sin he has

29 sinned, and lay his hand upon the head of the sin-offering, and slay the sin-offering in the place of burnt-

30 offerings. Then the priest shall take some of the blood upon his forefinger and put on the horns of the altar of burnt-offerings, and pour out the rest of the blood at the side of the altar,

31 and remove the whole of the fat, as he removed the fat from off the thank-offering. Then the priest shall offer it upon the altar, as a breath delightful to the EVER-LIVING, and the priest shall expiate for him, and he shall be forgiven.

The Law of Absolute Wilful Sins.

32 "But if a person brings his gift for . . . . -fect

33 . . . . the

head of his sin-offering, and slay it in the place where the burnt-offerings 34 are slain. Then the priest shall take some of the blood of the sin-offering on his forefinger and put it on the horns of the altar of burnt-offerings, but pour out all the rest of the blood 35 at the side of the altar, and remove all the fat, as he removed the fat of the lamb offered for thanks, and the priest shall consume it upon the altar as a perfume to the EVER-LIVING, and the priest shall expiate for him for his sin that he sinned, and it shall be forgiven to him.

The Law of Expiation for Perjury.

5 "When a person who is a witness sins when he has taken the declaration of an oath, about an event he saw, or knew, if he does not relate it, he shall 2 bear his crime. Or a person who has touched anything unclean, or a corpse that is unclean; or carcase of an unclean beast; or an unclean reptile; and it was unknown to him; 3 he is unclean and guilty; or if he touches uncleanness of blood, or any uncleanness that may defile him, and he did not know it, yet he is 4 guilty; or a person listening to a libel injurious to his neighbour, or who delights in anything which injures the man by being reported, and hides it, when he knew it,—then he is guilty 5 by it; and as he has offended in this, he shall make confession that he has 6 sinned over it, and shall bring to the EVER-LIVING for his fault that he has sinned, a female lamb from the sheep, or a female goat for a sin-offering, and the priest shall expiate 7 for his sin. But if he did not personally participate with the fault, then he shall bring for the fault that he has sinned two turtle-doves, or two young pigeons, to the EVER-LIVING;— one for a sin-offering, and one for a 8 burnt-offering. Let him bring them to the priest, and offer that which is for the sin-offering first, and wring off its head from its neck, but not separate 9 it, and sprinkle some of the blood of the sin-offering at the side of the altar, and throw the rest of the blood to the side of the altar for sin-offerings. 10 But make of the second a burnt-offering for judgment, and the priest shall expiate for him for the sin he has committed; and it shall be forgiven to him.
11 "But if he does not possess the

two turtle-doves or two young pigeons, then let him bring, as his gift for the sin he has sinned, the tenth of an epha of fine flour. He shall not pour upon it oil, nor put frankincense with it, for it is a sin-offering, but bring it to the priest, and the priest 12 shall grasp a handful of it for a remembrance, and burn it on the altar, for a perfume to the EVER-LIVING. It is a sin-offering. Then 13 the priest shall expiate for him over the sin which he has sinned, and it shall be forgiven to him. But the gift shall belong to the Priest."
The EVER-LIVING also spoke to 14 Moses saying;—

The Law about Intentional Sins.

"A person who perversely sins in 15 what is holy to the EVER-LIVING, shall bring for his guilt to the LORD a perfect ram of the sheep, of the value of two shekels by the sacred shekel, for his fault, and that in which 16 he has sinned, in what is holy, he shall restore fivefold as much for it, and give it to the priest, and the priest shall expiate with the ram for his fault; and it shall be forgiven to him.

Involuntary Wrong-doing.

"But if a person has sinned and 17 broken one of the commandments of the EVER-LIVING,—which should not be done,—and did not know it, yet he is faulty, and shall bear his fault and bring a perfect ram of the sheep on account of his fault to the priest, and the priest shall expiate for him 18 over his error which he has erred, when he knew it not;—and it shall be forgiven to him. It is a fault 19 offering for error to the EVER-LIVING."
The EVER-LIVING also spoke to 20 Moses saying;—

Law of Perverse Criminality.

"A person who sins, with wilful per- 21 versity against the EVER-LIVING by deceiving his neighbour in a contract, or in a confidential trust; or robs; or betrays his neighbour; or retains 22 a find, and lies about it; and swears with falsehood about anything which may injure the man, sins by it. But 23 if it be that he has sinned and done wrong; but returns the theft that he has stolen; or the deception that he has sinned in, or the trust that was entrusted to him, or the strayling

24 that he has found, or in anything where he has sworn about it to deceive, and rectifies it, on the head of it he shall add fivefold to what he took to himself, they shall be given

25 in place of his fault. Then the guilty man shall bring for the EVER-LIVING a perfect ram of the sheep to the

26 priest, because of his fault, and the priest shall expiate for him before the EVER-LIVING, and he shall be forgiven at once, for all that he has done wrong in it."

6 The EVER-LIVING also spoke to Moses saying,—

The Law for National Offerings.

2 "Command Aaron, and his sons, saying—These are the laws of the burnt-offerings,—that is the offerings for burning upon the altar. All the night, until daybreak, fire shall burn upon the altar for it.

3 "The priest shall be clothed with his garments upon his limbs, and his frock on to cover his flesh, and he shall rake out the ashes that the fire upon the altar produces, and supply

4 wood to the altar. Then he shall strip off his clothes, and put on other clothes, and carry the ashes outside

5 the camp to a clean place. The fire of the altar must burn unextinguished upon it. None shall quench it, but the priest shall lay wood upon it every morning and lay upon it the burnt-offering, and incense with the

6 fat of the peace-offerings. The fire shall always burn upon the altar. It shall not be quenched.

7 "And these are the laws of the food gifts, that the sons of Aaron shall offer before the EVER-LIVING

8 in front of the altar. They shall take some from the flour of the gift and put upon the altar, with the whole of the frankincense which is with the gift, and burn as incense upon the altar, as a delightful breath of remembrance to the EVER-LIVING

9 But the rest of it Aaron and his sons shall eat. They shall eat it unfermented in the Holy Place in the

0 court of the Hall of Assembly. They shall not bake their portion with ferment. I give it to them for a flavour. It is Holy of Holies, like the sin-offering, and like the trespass-

1 offering. Any male of the children of Aaron may eat of it. This is a

perpetual constitution, for their descendants. As it is a flavour of the EVER-LIVING, let all be holy who touch it."

12 The EVER-LIVING further spoke to Moses saying —

The Law of Gifts at the Consecration as Priests

13 "This is the gift that Aaron and his sons shall offer during the period of their consecration. The tenth of an epha of flour, as a perpetual offering between daybreak and even-

ing, or half at the daybreak, and half

14 at the dusk. Let it be made saturated with oil in a pan, bring it in baked flat cakes, a delightful breath to the

15 EVER-LIVING. The consecrated priest of that course shall make it. It is a perpetual constitution to the EVER-LIVING, to be totally burnt. Every

16 food offering from a priest shall be burnt—you shall not eat it."

The Law of Sin-offerings.

17 The EVER-LIVING also spoke to Moses, saying—

18 "Speak commanding Aaron and his sons,—

"These are the laws of the sin-offering,—in the place where you slay the burnt-offering, you shall slay the sin-offering before the EVER-

19 LIVING. It is Holy of Holies. The priest that offers it for sin shall eat it in the Holy Place. Eat it in the

20 court of the Hall of Assembly. All who touch the flesh shall be holy. And whoever is sprinkled with the blood upon his garments, whatever is sprinkled with it shall wash his cloth-

21 ing in the Holy Place. Any vessel of pottery, also, in which it is boiled shall be broken; and if it is boiled in a vessel of bronze it shall be scoured, and washed with water. Every male

22 of the priests may eat of it. It is Holy of Holies. But any sin-offering

23 that is brought to the Hall of Assembly for a holy expiation you shall not eat—it shall be consumed by fire.

The Sacrifices for Trespass.

7 "These are also laws of the trespass-offerings. They are Holy of Holies.

2 "In the place where they slay the sacrifices for sin, they shall slay the trespass-offerings, and their blood shall be sprinkled around the altar,

3 and all the fat of it shall be offered up, the fat of the tail and the fat of

4 the caul, and of the chest; but the two kidneys with the fat that is upon

5 them, he shall put aside. Then the priest shall burn them with incense at the altar, as a flavour to the EVER-

6 LIVING. It is a trespass-offering.

7 As with the sin-offering, so with the trespass-offering; there is one law for them; the priest who has expiated with it shall have it for himself.

Perquisites of the Priests.

8 "The priest who offers up the burnt-offering for a man, the skin of the burnt-offering that he has offered,

9 shall belong to the priest. Every food offering which is baked in an oven, and all made in a pan, or upon a pan, it shall belong to the priest

10 who presents it. But every food offering mixed with oil, or dry, shall belong to all the sons of Aaron, each one as brothers.

The Law of Thank-offerings, and against Insanitary Food.

11 "And these are the laws of the sacrifices of thanks which may be

12 presented to the EVER-LIVING. If a man offers for thanksgiving; let him offer as a sacrifice of thanksgiving, cakes of unfermented bread mixed with oil, and unfermented wafers buttered with oil, and flour saturated

13 by rolling in oil. Let him offer no cakes of fermented bread with his gift upon the altar when thanksgiving

14 for a benefit. And let him offer the same with every offering lifted up to the EVER-LIVING. It shall belong to the priest who sprinkles the blood of the thank-offering for him to the

15 EVER-LIVING. But the flesh of the sacrifice of the thank-offering shall be eaten that day; none of it shall be left till the next morning.

16 "But if he gives a sacrifice for a vow, or a free-will gift, he may eat of it the day it is offered in sacrifice, and what remains of it he may eat to-

17 morrow. But the remainder of the flesh of a sacrifice shall be burnt

18 with fire on the third day; and if he eats of the flesh of a sacrifice for a benefit on the third day, it shall not be accepted as an offering from him; it shall not benefit him. It will be unclean, and the person who eats of it shall bear his punishment.

19 "Flesh also that has touched anything unclean shall not be eaten;—

it shall be burnt with fire; but the flesh of everything clean may be eaten

20 as food. But the person who eats the flesh of a sacrifice made to the EVER-LIVING for a benefit, and defiles himself over it,—that person shall be excommunicated from his people.

21 The person, also, who touches anything defiled by the defilement of blood; or by an unclean beast, or by any unclean reptile; and yet eats of the flesh as a sacrifice of thanksgiving to the EVER-LIVING:—that person shall be excommunicated from his people."

Eating Fat Prohibited.

22 Again the EVER-LIVING spoke to

23 Moses, saying;—"Any of the fat of an ox, or sheep, or goat you shall

24 not eat; but the fat of a carcase, and the fat of a torn animal may be used for any work;—but you shall not eat

25 of it, for whoever eats the fat of a beast which is offered to the EVER-LIVING;—that person shall be ex-

26 communicated from his people. Nor shall you eat any blood in any of your dwelling places, either of bird

27 or beast. Every person who eats any blood; that person shall be excommunicated from his people."

The Law of Thank-offerings.

28 The EVER-LIVING spoke further to Moses, saying:—

29 "Speak to the children of Israel, saying;—Whoever offers at the altar his thank-offering to the EVER-LIVING, let him bring his gift to the altar of the EVER-LIVING for his benefit.

30 He shall bring in his hand the present to the EVER-LIVING. Bring the breast with its fat to be waved, for

31 waving before the EVER-LIVING, but the priest shall burn the fat upon the altar, and the breast shall be for

32 Aaron and his sons. The raised leg also you shall give to the priest who lifts it up as a sacrifice for a benefit.

33 Whoever of the sons of Aaron offers the blood of the thank-offering, shall

34 have the right leg for a gift. For the waved breast, and the raised leg I have taken from the children of Israel, from their sacrifice of thanks, and I give them to Aaron the Priest and to his sons to be taken by them for ever from the children of Israel.

35 "They are the portion of Aaron, and the portion of his sons from the gifts to the EVER-LIVING during the time

36 they offer them as priests to the EVER-LIVING; which the EVER-LIVING commanded to be given to them at the time He consecrated them, as an endowment from the children of Israel, and their posterity for ever."

37 This is the law for burnt-offerings, and for sins, and for trespasses, and for consecrations, and for sacrifices of

38 thanks, which the EVER-LIVING commanded to Moses upon Mount Sinai, at the time He commanded the children of Israel to offer gifts to the EVER-LIVING in the desert of Sinai.

The Ritual of Priestly Consecration.

8 The EVER-LIVING also spoke to Moses, saying:—

2 "Take Aaron, and his sons with him, with the robes and the oil of consecration, and the bull for a sin-offer-ing, and the two rams, and the basket

3 of biscuits, and the whole of the chiefs of the Parliament to the door of the Hall of Assembly."

4 Moses consequently did as the EVER-LIVING commanded him; and summoned the chiefs to the door of

5 the Hall of Assembly. Then Moses said to the chiefs, "The EVER-LIVING commands this to be done."

6 Then Moses took Aaron and his

7 sons and washed them in water, and put the vests upon them, and girt them with the girdle, and clothed them with the mantle; and put the ephod on him, and girt him with the embroidered belt of the ephod, and

8 ephoded him with it. Then he put on the breastplate of the Urim and

9 Thumim;[1] and put the turban upon his head, and fastened upon the turban, at the front of it, the golden flower consecrated to holiness; as the EVER-LIVING commanded to Moses.

10 Moses next took the oil of consecration and consecrated the Tabernacle and all that was in it, and

11 sanctified them, and sprinkled with it seven times on the altar, and consecrated the altar, and all its instruments; and the bath, and all its cans,

12 to sanctify them; and poured the oil of consecration on the head of Aaron, and consecrated him, to sanctify him.

13 Then Moses brought forward the sons of Aaron and dressed them with vests, and girt them with girdles, and

---

[1] The breastplate of "Light and Truth" when translated from the Hebrew—I. F.

bound upon them the mitres; as the EVER-LIVING commanded to Moses.

14 Next he brought up the bull for a sin-offering, and Aaron and his sons laid their hands upon the head of the

15 bull for a sin-offering. Then he slew it; and Moses took some of the blood, and put it around the horns of the altar with his forefinger, to purify the altar from sin; and he poured out the rest of the blood at the side of the altar, and sanctified it with an expia-

16 tion for it. He also took the fat which is on the chest, and the other fat of the liver, and the two kidneys, with the fat upon them, which Moses burnt upon the altar. But the bull and its

17 skin, and its flesh, and its dung he burnt with fire; as the EVER-LIVING commanded to Moses.

18 Then he took the ram for the burnt-offering, and Aaron and his sons laid their hands upon the head of the ram.

19 Then Moses slew it, and sprinkled some of the blood on the altar around,

20 and divided the ram into parts. Moses then burnt the pieces of the

21 head, and its fat; but the chest and the feet Moses washed in water, and burnt the whole of the ram upon the altar, as a whole burnt offering. It was a pleasant breath given to the EVER-LIVING; as the EVER-LIVING commanded Moses.

22 Then he took the ram—the second ram—of consecration, and Aaron and

23 his sons laid their hands upon the head of the ram. Moses afterwards slew it, and took some of its blood and put it on the tip of Aaron's right ear, and on his right thumb, and on his right great toe; Moses also sprinkled the blood upon the altar

24 around. Next Moses took the sons of Aaron, and put some of the blood on the tips of their right ears, and on the thumbs of their right hands, and on the great toes of their right feet. Moses afterwards sprinkled some of the blood around the altar.

25 He also took the fat, and the tail, and the whole of the fat that is on the chest, and the rest of the fat, and the two kidneys with their fat, and the

26 right leg, and some from the basket of biscuits which was before the EVER-LIVING;—he took one biscuit, and one oil-bread cake, and one wafer, and placed them with the fats upon the

27 right leg, and put the whole into the hands of Aaron and the hands of his sons; and they waved them before the

28 presence of the EVER-LIVING. Then Moses took them from their hands, and offered them as a whole burnt-offering on the altar, as an appointment of them. It was an offering of pleasing flavour to the EVER-LIVING.

29 Moses then took the breast of the ram of consecration and waved it before the EVER-LIVING.—It was as a portion for Moses; as the EVER-LIVING commanded to Moses.

30 Moses afterwards took some of the oil of consecration, and some of the blood from the altar, and sprinkled upon Aaron, upon his sons, and upon his robes and upon the robes of his sons with him, and sanctified Aaron and his robes, and his sons, and the robes of his sons with him.

31 Moses also said to Aaron and his sons, "Boil the flesh at the door of the Hall of Assembly, and sit to eat it, with the bread that is upon the basket of consecration, as I have been commanded to instruct Aaron and his

32 sons that they should eat. But what is left of the flesh and bread burn

33 with fire. You shall, however, not quit the Hall of Assembly for seven days, until the days are fulfilled;— the days of your consecration;—for seven days will complete their

34 number. What has been done to-day, the EVER-LIVING commanded to

35 be done, to expiate for you. You shall remain at the door of the Hall of Assembly day and night for seven days, and guard the trust of the EVER-LIVING; and not remove; for so I have been commanded."

36 Aaron and his sons consequently did all the things that the EVER-LIVING commanded by the hand of Moses.

9 But when the eighth day came Moses summoned Aaron and his sons,

2 and the judges of Israel, and said to Aaron and his sons;—"Select for yourselves a perfect heifer from the fold for a sin-offering, and approach to the presence of the EVER-LIVING."

3 Then he addressed the children of Israel, saying;—

"You must take a ram from the goats for a sin-offering; and a lamb and bullock of a year old both perfect,

4 for a burnt-offering, with a bull and a ram for a thank-offering, to sacrifice before the EVER-LIVING; and a food-offering mixed with oil, for to-day the EVER-LIVING will appear to you.

5 They consequently brought what

Moses ordered to the front of the Hall of Assembly, and all the chiefs approached and stood before the EVER-LIVING.

Then Moses said;   6

"This is the thing that the EVER-LIVING commanded you to do; now the majesty of the EVER-LIVING will appear to you."

Moses next said to Aaron; "Advance 7 to the altar and offer the sin-offering, and the burnt-offering for yourself, and expiate first on account of Yourself, afterwards on account of the People; and make a gift for the People, and expiate on account of them; as the EVER-LIVING has commanded."

Aaron consequently advanced to 8 the altar and slew the calf that was for his sin-offering. The sons of 9 Aaron also advanced to the blood of it, and dipped their forefingers into the blood of it, and placed upon the horns of the altar, and poured the rest of the blood at the side of the altar. But the fat, and the kidneys, 10 and the rest from the breast of the sin-offering, he burnt on the altar;— as the EVER-LIVING commanded to Moses;—but the flesh, and the skin, 11 and dung he consumed in fire outside the camp.

Then he slew the burnt-offering; 12 and the sons of Aaron took some of its blood, and poured it upon the altar around.

Then he took the whole burnt- 13 offering to him to divide it, and burnt its head upon the altar. Afterwards 14 he washed the chest, and the feet, and burnt them as a burnt-offering on the altar.

Then he offered the gift for the 15 People, and took the goat for the sin of the People, and made a sin-offering, like the former sin-offering. Next he 16 presented the burnt-offering, and did as with the offering for righteousness. Afterwards he presented the food- 17 offering, and filled his hand from it, and burnt it upon the altar, besides the burnt-offering of the morning.

Then he slew the bull, and the ram, 18 as a sacrifice of thanks from the People, and the sons of Aaron brought some of the blood and sprinkled it around upon the altar, with the fats from the bull, and the 19 fat from the tail of the ram, the caul, and the kidneys, and the rest of the breast; and they piled up the fats 20

upon the chest, and burnt the fats
1 upon the altar, but the breast, and
the right leg Aaron waved before the
EVER-LIVING,—as the EVER-LIVING
commanded Moses

2 Then Aaron raised his hands and
blessed the People, and came down
from making he sin-offering, and
the burnt-offering, and the thank-
offering

3 Moses and Aaron next entered
the Hall of Assembly, and went and
blessed the People, — when the
splendour of the EVER-LIVING
4 appeared to all the People, the fire
came from the presence of the EVER-
LIVING and consumed the burnt-
offering on the altar, and the fats
When all the People saw it they
cheered, and fell upon their faces

Nadab and Abihu slain for Dis-
obedience to God.

0 But the sons of Aaron, Nadab and
Abihu, each took a fire-pan, and
placed on them fire, and put incense
upon it, and presented strange fire
before the EVER-LIVING, which they
2 were not commanded, therefore fire
came out from the presence of the
LORD and consumed them, and they
died before the LORD

3 Consequently Moses said to Aaron,
"What was it that the EVER-LIVING
spoke, saying, 'In approaching Me I
will be sanctified, and respected
before all the People'?" And Aaron
was silent

4 Then Moses called to Mishal, and
to Altzaphan, sons of Azial, the uncle
of Aaron, and said to them,—
"Approach! and take up those
from the presence of the sanctuary
to the outside of the camp"

5 So they approached, and carried
them in their vestments to the outside
of the camp, as Moses had ordered

6 Then Moses said to Aaron and to
Aliazar, and to Aithamar, his sons,
"You shall not uncover your heads,
and you shall not strip off your
robes, lest you should die, and anger
come upon all the congregation, but
your relatives of all the house of
Israel, shall weep for the burning that
7 the EVER-LIVING has burnt You
shall also not come out of the
Hall of Assembly, lest you should
die,—for the oil of consecration to
the EVER-LIVING is upon you

So they did as Moses ordered

The Priests forbidden to Drink
Intoxicants before going to
the Sanctuary

Then Moses spoke to Aaron and 8
commanded,—

"You or your sons with you shall 9
not drink of wine or an intoxicant
when you are going to the Hall of
Assembly,—so that you may not die
This is an everlasting institution for
your posterity

"For you shall distinguish between 10
the Sacred and the Common, and
between Sin and Purity, so that you 11
may teach the sons of Israel all the
Institutions which the EVER-LIVING
dictated to them by means of Moses"

Moses also spoke to Aaron, and 12
Aliazar, and Aithamar, his sons,—
"Take again another food-offering
for a present to the EVER-LIVING,
and eat it with biscuits at the side of
the altar, for it is Holy of Holies,
therefore you shall eat it in the Holy 13
Place, for it is a portion to you, and a
portion to your sons from the presents
to the EVER-LIVING, for so I have
been commanded But you may eat 14
the waved breast, and the raised leg
in a clean place, you and your sons,
and your daughters with you, for they
are given from My altar as a portion
to you and to your children as thank-
offerings from the children of Israel
The raised leg and the waved breast, 15
with the presents of the fats which
they bring to be waved, you shall
wave before the EVER-LIVING, and
they shall be for you and your children
for a perpetual portion,—as the
EVER-LIVING has commanded"

But when Moses inquired for the 16
goat for the sin-offering, he found it
had been burnt, therefore he was
angry with Aliazar and Aithamar the
sons of Aaron, again, and said,—
"Why have you not eaten the sin- 17
offering in the Holy Place?—for it is
Holy of Holies,—and it was given to
you to bear the frailty of the congregation, to expiate for them before the
EVER-LIVING Look! its blood was 18
not brought into the sanctuary You
ought to have eaten it in the sanctuary
as I commanded"

Then Aaron spoke to Moses, "On 19
the day they presented their sin-
offering, and their burnt-offering
before the EVER-LIVING you instructed me about it and I ate the

sin-offering that day. Let that compensate in the eyes of my Lord."

20   So Moses listened and it compensated in his eyes.

Clean and Unclean Foods.

11   Then the EVER-LIVING spoke to Moses and to Aaron saying to them ;—

2   "Speak to the children of Israel to command ;—

"These are what you may eat of all the animals that are upon the earth : —

The Laws of Animal Food.

3   "All that have hoofs, and divide the hoofs, and chew the cud ;—you may eat those beasts :—

4   "But you shall not eat those that chew the cud, and do not divide the hoof ;—

"The camel ; for it chews the cud, but has not divided the hoof. It is unclean to you ;—

5   "And the jerboa, for it chews the cud, but has not a divided hoof ; it is unclean to you ;

6   "And the Leaper,[1] for it chews the cud, but has not a divided hoof ; it is unclean to you :

7   "And the swine ; although it has hoofs, and divides the hoof, but it does not chew the cud ; it is unclean to you ;—

8   "You shall not eat of their flesh, nor touch their carcases ; they are unclean to you ;

Clean Fish.

9   "You may eat of all these that are in the waters ;—

"All that have fins and scales, in the waters, and the seas, and the rivers ; you may eat them.

10   "But all that have not fins and scales on them in the waters, and rivers, of all the swarms of the waters, and of every form of life that is in the waters, they must be loathsome to

11 you ; and their flesh shall be loathsome to you. You shall not eat of their carcases ; you shall loathe them.

12 All in the waters that have not fins and scales, shall be loathsome to you.

Unclean and Clean Birds.

13   "And these shall be loathsome to you among birds. You shall not eat them ; they are loathsome. The eagle, and the osprey, and the fish-

14 hawk ; the kite, and the vulture

[1] In Hebrew "Arnabeth" means a Leaper usually rendered "hare" but more probable the Kangaroo.—E. F.

species ; and all the raven species ; 15 and the ostrich, and the goatsucker, 16 and seagull and the buzzard species ; and the pelican, and the gannet, and 17 the owl ; and the crested owl, and 18 the turkey buzzard, and the carrion-eagle ; and the stork, and snorter 19 species ; and hoopoo, and the bat ; and every winged reptile that crawls 20 shall be loathsome to you.

21   "However you may eat of these ; of all the swarms of wing that crawl, that have knees above their feet to leap upon the earth, you may eat 22 these from among them ; the locust kind, and the cockchafer kind ; and 23 the grasshopper kind ; but all the winged-breed that crawls on its feet shall be loathsome to you, and they 24 defile. All who touch their dead bodies are unclean until the evening. And anyone who carries their carcases 25 shall wash his clothes and be unclean until the evening.

26   "Besides every beast that has hoofs, but does not divide its hoofs, and does not chew the cud ; they are unclean to you. All who touch them are unclean.

27   "And everything that walks upon its paws ; every insect that goes on all fours ;—they are unclean to you : everyone who touches their dead bodies is unclean, and whoever carries 28 their dead bodies shall wash his clothes and be unclean until the evening. They are unclean to you.

Unclean Vermin.

29   "These also are unclean to you of the species breeding upon the earth ; the mole, and the mouse, and the 30 lizard species ; the groaner, and the panter, and the shrew, and the iguanodon, and the camelion. These are 31 unclean to you in all their breeds ; all touching them when dead shall be unclean until the evening ; and all 32 who eat of them when dead are unclean ; and all upon which any of them may fall, and any vessel of wood, or clothing, or skin, or a sack,—any article that is made use of,—shall be put into water, and be unclean until the evening ;—then pure. And 33 any vessel of earthenware that they fall into, all that they fall into, is unclean, and it shall be broken ; and 34 all food that they have gnawed, or their water falls upon, is unclean ; and any cup from which they drink, 35   And any

thing upon which their dead bodies may fall is unclean ,—pan, or tub— it shall be broken They are unclean

36 and shall be unclean to you Except a spring, or well, or reservoir of water ,—they shall be pure —but all touching their dead bodies are un-

37 clean But if their dead bodies fall upon any grain to be used for seed

38 that is to be sown, it is pure Also if you have put water upon the seed, after their dead bodies fall upon it, it is clean to you

Cattle Dying of Disease Unclean.

39 " And when any of the cattle, that you possess for food dies, whoever touches its carcase is unclean until

40 evening , and whoever eats from its carcase, shall wash his clothes and

41 be unclean until the evening, and whoever carries the carcase shall wash his clothes and be unclean until the evening

All Reptiles are Unclean.

" All vermin, also, of the vermin on the earth shall be loathsome , it shall not be eaten

42 " Everything going upon its belly , and everything going by crawling upon many feet, of all the vermin of the vermin of the earth, you shall not eat, for they are loath-

43 some You shall not make your-selves loathsome with the bodies of any of the spawn of the vermin, and you shall not defile yourselves with them, nor be defiled by them ,

44 for I am your EVER-LIVING GOD, Who sanctifies you, and you shall be healthy for I am HOLY, and you shall not defile yourselves or your lives by any of the vermin that crawls

45 upon the earth , for the EVER-LIVING brought you up from the land of Mitzer to be a GOD to you , so you must be healthy , —for I am HOLY

46 " These are the laws about cattle, and birds, and every animal life that crawls in the waters, and every animal life that spawns upon the

47 land , with the difference between the unclean and the pure, and between the animals for food, and the animals that are not for food "

12 The EVER-LIVING also spoke to Moses saying ,—

Sanitary Laws for Women.

2 " Speak to the children of Israel commanding —-

" A woman who is delivered and bears a boy is unclean for seven days, as though she were unclean with the uncleanness of menstruation , and at

3 the eighth day his fore-flesh shall be circumcised But for a period of

4 thirty-three days she shall be secluded for her purification She shall not approach anything sacred, and shall not come to the sacred place until the days of her purification are completed

5 " But if she bears a girl, then she shall be separated as unclean for twice seven, as in menstruation , and for a period of sixty-six days she shall be secluded, for purification from her blood But upon the completion

6 of the days of her purification for a son or for a daughter, she shall bring a lamb of one year for a burnt-offering, and a young dove or a turtle dove, as a sin-offering to the door of the Hall of Assembly, to the priest, and he shall present them before the

7 EVER-LIVING, and expiate for her, and purify her for the flow of her blood —These are the laws about the childbirth of a boy or girl

8 " But if she does not possess a she lamb, then she shall take two turtle doves, or two young pigeons, one for a burnt-offering, and the other for a sin-offering, and the priest shall ex-piate for her, and she shall be pure "

Sanitary Laws of Contagious Diseases

13 The EVER-LIVING also spoke to Moses and Aaron saying ,—

2 " When a man has on the skin of his flesh a swelling or scab, or scurf, and there is on the skin of his flesh an irritation, he shall go to Aaron the priest or to one of the medical priests,

3 and shall show the priest the spot on the skin of his body, and the hair in the spot turned white Should the spot appear hollow under the skin of his body, it may be a contagion, and the priest shall diagnose it, for it is a disease

4 " But if a white scurf is upon the skin of his body, which does not appear to be below the skin, and the hair is not changed to white, then the priest shall isolate the patient for

5 seven days, and upon the seventh day the priest shall examine the patient, and if the mark appears to him to stand still without the spot spreading, the priest shall isolate

6 him for a second seven days, but the priest shall examine him on the seventh day the second time, and if the mark is mitigated, and the spot has not spread on the skin, then the priest shall cleanse off the scurf from it, and he shall wash his clothes, and

7 be clean But if the eruption spreads, and with scabs on the skin, after he has shown himself to the priest to be pronounced clean, then he shall show

8 himself again to the priest, and the priest shall examine him, and if the eruption has spread on his skin, the priest shall declare him diseased with a contagion

9 "When a man has been attacked by a contagion, he shall go to a priest,

10 and the priest shall examine him, and if he sees a white swelling in his skin, and if the hair has turned white, and corrupting flesh lives in the

11 swelling, it is chronic leprosy on the skin of his body, and he is unclean The priest shall not isolate him, but he is unclean

12 "But if the disease spreads on the skin, and the irritation covers the whole of his skin with an attack from his head to his feet, he shall show all

13 to the eye of the priest, and the priest shall examine it, and if the irritation covers the whole of his body, and the eruption is bright, all of it, turned

14 white,—he is clean, but if at any time raw flesh appears, he is con-

15 tagious, therefore he shall show the raw flesh to the priest, and be declared contagious,—the raw flesh is a

16 contagion,—it is contagious But if the raw flesh ceases and turns white,—

17 he shall also go to the priest, and the priest shall examine it, and if the eruption has turned white and bright, the priest shall declare him free from contagiousness

18 "When there is on the body a burn-

19 ing ulcer to be cured, and there may be on the inflamed part a white swelling, or a white-reddish scurf, it shall

20 be shown to the priest, and the priest shall examine it, and if he sees a sinking of the skin and the hair turning white, the priest shall declare him unclean with a contagion of spreading inflammation

21 "But if when the priest examines him, there is no white hair, and there is no sinking in the skin, but there is degeneration, then the priest shall

22 isolate him for seven days and if it spreads in the skin then the priest

shall declare him diseased by a contagious attack But if after- 23 wards, the inflammation abating, the irritation ceases to burn in the ulcers the priest shall declare him clean

"When there is in the flesh an 24 acute inflammation, and there is rawness on the inflammation, with white scurf, and red and white pimples, when the priest examines 25 him, and observes the hair to be turning white, on the scurf, and he observes pitting in the skin, it is an attack of inflammatory ulceration, and the priest shall pronounce him diseased It is a contagious disease

"But if on examining it, the priest 26 does not perceive white hair on the inflammation, nor a pitting in the skin, but it is fiery,—then the priest shall isolate him for seven days, but 27 when the priest shall re-examine him on the seventh day, if it is spreading over the skin, the priest shall declare him unclean It is a contagious disease But if afterwards the inflam- 28 mation abates, and does not spread on the skin, but the inflammation of the swelling is relaxed, then the priest shall pronounce him clean, for it is only an attack of inflammation

"And when a man or woman may 29 have spots on the head or chin, the 30 priest shall examine the spot, and if he sees on examining it a sinking in the skin, and with it a small yellow hair, then they are unclean, until the priest has extirpated it It is a disease of the head or chin

"But when the priest examines, if 31 the attack is extirpated, and discovers after examination that there is no depression on the skin, and strong black hair on it, then the priest shall isolate the patient he has cured seven days But the priest shall examine 32 the patient on the seventh day, and if it has not spread during the seclusion and there is not on him a yellow hair, and he observes not upon the isolated person a depression in the skin, the priest shall cause the patient 33 to be shaved, and the priest shall isolate the patient for a second seven days But the priest shall examine 34 the patient on the seventh day, and if it has not spread upon the patient's skin, and he observes that there is not a pitting of the skin, then the priest shall pronounce him clean, and he shall wash his clothes and be clean

35 "But if it spreads upon the patient's skin, after he has been pronounced

36 clean, the priest shall re-examine him, and if he observes a spreading on the skin of the patient, the priest need not examine for the yellow hair;

37 he is unclean But if when the patient stands for re-inspection and black hair has sprung up on him, the patient is cured The priest shall pronounce him clean

38 "And if a man or woman has in the skin of their body a bright shining

39 with whiteness, then the priest shall examine, and if he observes in the skin of their body a bright shining, with whiteness, it is an eruption flowering in the skin It is clean

40 "And if a person is sprinkled with
41 baldness on his head he is clean And if at the front of his face his head is sprinkled, it is fore-baldness He is
42 clean But if there should be upon his bald head or forehead, a whitish-red outbreak, it is an ulcerous attack, whether on the crown or the forehead;

43 so the priest shall examine it, and if he observes a rising white-reddish eruption upon the crown or the forehead when he examines the scurf

44 on the skin of the body, the man is diseased,—he is unclean—the priest shall declare him unclean by a

45 disease of the head; but the attack is constitutional His clothes shall be torn, and his head shall be uncovered, and he shall not curl his beard; but shall cry Unclean, Un-

46 clean! all the time he is suffering it, he is unclean He must be isolated, outside the camp, must be made to remain outside

47 "The clothing, also, that may be upon him is infected by the disease,— whether woollen clothing, or cotton

48 clothing, whether warped and wefted with wool or cotton, or of skin, or of

49 any preparation of skin; and if there is a greenish or reddish stain, on the clothing, or skin, whether of warp or weft, or any article of skin is marked by the discharge, it shall be examined

50 by the priest The priest who examines the patient shall then isolate

51 the sufferer for seven days, but shall re-examine the patient on the seventh day, when if the infection has discharged upon the clothing, whether in warp or weft, or on the skin of any article made of skin for use, it is an

attack of itch [1] It is unclean Conse- 52 quently he shall burn that clothing whether warped and weft, whether of wool or cotton, or of any article of skin, in which the infection may be, for it is infected with itch,—it must be burnt in fire But if when the priest 53 examines it, he observes that the infection has not spread in the fabric of warp and weft, or in the leather or any article of leather, then the priest 54 shall order them to wash whatever has the infection upon it, and isolate them for a second seven days But 55 the priest shall examine the infected articles after the washing, and if he observes that the infection has not disappeared from sight, and the stain has not gone, it is unclean They shall consume it in fire It is corroded by vermin or microbes

"But even if when the priest ex- 56 amines, and observes a mitigation of the attack, after the washing of it, yet there is a wearing away from the garment, or from the skin, or from the warp, or from the weft, and he 57 perceives that the garment of warp and weft, or any article of leather, is still fretted, they shall burn in fire everything in which the infection remains But the clothing of warp 58 and weft, or any article of leather which has been washed and the infection has departed from them, shall be washed a second time, and be clean

"These are the laws respecting in- 59 fection in clothing of wool or cotton, of warp and weft, or any article of skin, as to cleanness or uncleanness."

Sanitary Laws for Convalescents.

The EVER-LIVING also spoke to 14 Moses, saying,—

"These are the laws about sufferers 2 from infectious diseases at the time they are cured, and submitted to the priest

"The priest shall go to the outside 3 of the camp, and the priest shall examine, and look at the patient recovered from infection Then the 4 priest shall prepare, and take for purification two clean living birds, and cedar wood, and scarlet wool, and hysop,—and the priest shall 5 prepare and slay the first bird into a vessel full of living water, then 6 take the living bird to him, and the

---

[1] Literally "with irritation an attack."— F

cedar wood, and the scarlet wool, and the hysop, and sprinkle them and the living bird in the blood of the slain

7 bird and the living water, and also upon the man cleansed from the infection, seven times, and declare him clean, and send the living bird

8 out into the open field. Afterwards the cleansed man shall wash his clothes, and shave his head, and bathe in water, and be clean, and after that go into the camp. He shall however keep out of his tent for seven days

9 But on the seventh day he shall shave the whole of his head, both the head and his beard, and his eyebrows, he shall also shave the whole of his hair, and wash his clothes and bathe his

10 body in water, and be clean. Upon the eighth day he shall also take two perfect he lambs, and a perfect ewe lamb of one year, and three tenths of flour mixed with oil as a food-offer-

11 ing, and one log of oil, and the priest shall station the cleansed man, or the cleansed woman, before the presence of the EVER-LIVING, at the door of the Hall of Assembly

12 "Then the priest shall take one of the he lambs and present it as a tres-pass-offering, with the log of oil, and wave them before the EVER-LIVING,

13 and slay the lamb in the place where they slay the sin-offering, and the burnt-offerings, in the Holy Place, for, as a sin-offering, the trespass-offering shall be Holy of Holies to the priest

14 The priest shall also take some of the blood of the trespass-offering and place upon the tip of the right ear of the recovered man, and upon the thumb of his right hand, and upon

15 the great toe of his right foot. Then let the priest take some of the log of oil and pour it into the palm of the

16 priest's left hand, and dip the right hand of the priest in the oil that is in his left hand palm, and sprinkle the oil seven times with his finger before

17 the EVER-LIVING, and from the rest of the oil that is in his palm, the priest shall put some upon the tip of the right ear of the restored person, and upon the thumb of his right hand, and upon the great toe of his right foot, with some of the blood of

18 the trespass-offering. And the rest of the oil that is in the palm of the priest, he shall put upon the head of the recovered person —Thus shall the priest expiate for him before the EVER-LIVING.

19 "The priest shall also make a sin-offering, and expiate for the re-covered man for his sins, and slay

20 a burnt-offering for him. Thus the priest shall offer up the burnt-offering, and the food-offering on the altar, and expiate for him. The priest shall afterwards declare him clean.

21 "But if he is poor, and has no pro-perty, then he shall take a single he lamb for a trespass-offering to wave, to expiate for himself, and a tenth of flour mixed with oil for a food-offering,

22 and a log of oil, or two turtle-doves or two young pigeons, whichever he may possess, and one shall be for a sin-offering, and the other for a burnt-

23 offering. He shall bring them upon the eighth day after his recovery to the priest, at the door of the Hall of Assembly, to present to the EVER-

24 LIVING. Then the priest shall take the lamb for a trespass-offering, and the log of oil, and the priest shall wave them before the EVER-LIVING,

25 and slay the lamb for a trespass offer-ing. Then the priest shall take some of the blood of the trespass-offering and put it upon the tip of the right ear of the recovered person, and upon the thumb of the right hand, and upon the great toe of the right foot.

26 The priest shall also pour some of the oil into the priest's left hand

27 palm, and the priest shall sprinkle with his right forefinger some of the oil which is in his left palm, seven

28 times before the EVER-LIVING. Then the priest shall put some of the oil that is in his left palm upon the tip of the right ear of the recovered per-son, and upon the thumb of his right hand, and upon the great toe of his right foot, on the place for the blood

29 of the trespass-offering. But the rest of the oil that is in the palm of the priest he shall put upon the head of the recovered person, to expiate for

30 him before the EVER-LIVING. Or he shall take one of the turtle-doves, or young pigeons, which he possesses,

31 —which he holds in his hand,—the one for a sin-offering, and the other for a burnt-offering, with the food-offering —Thus the priest shall ex-piate for the recovered person before the EVER-LIVING.

32 "These are the laws about those attacked by contagious disease, who do not possess enough for the regular purification.

The Sanitary Law for Dwelling Houses.

33　The EVER-LIVING also spoke to Moses and to Aaron, to command,—

34　"When you arrive in the land of Canan, which I shall give to you to possess, and find a contagious disease in a house in the land you

35　possess, then the owner of the house shall go to the priest and inform him, saying that a contagious disease

36　has appeared in his house, and demand that the priest should visit the house The priest shall at once go and enquire the nature of the disease, and declare all in the house unclean Then, after that, the priest shall go to

37　examine the house itself, and enquire into the disease, and if he finds the infection in the walls of the house,— the drains having a greenish-yellow, or purplish, rotting, and there appears

38　decay in their walls, then the priest shall remove the family from the neighbourhood of the house and isolate the house for seven days

39　But the priest shall re-visit it on the seventh day and examine it again, and if the infection has spread in the

40　drains[1] of the house, the priest shall command, and they shall pull away the stones in which the infection is, and remove them to the outside of the town, to the receptacle for refuse,

41　and the house shall be cut off from the houses surrounding it, and they shall pour out the rubbish caused by the cutting it off at the outside of the town, into the receptacle for refuse

42　Then they shall take other stones in the place of these stones, and take other mortar, and repair the house

43　But if the infection returns and spreads in the family after the removal of the stones, and after the destruction of the stones, and after the cutting off of the house, and after

44　its repairing, then the priest shall come and examine it, and if he observes the infection spreading in the house, it is a virulent contagion

45　—the house itself is unclean Therefore he shall break down the house with its stones, and its timber, and all the mortar of the house, and carry it outside the town to the refuse heap

---

[1] Literally "ditch" or "runnings," קִירֹה in root, Heb קָרָה to run towards improperly translated walls in the context of verse F F

And whoever enters that house, all 46 the time that it is isolated, shall be unclean until the evening Whoever 47 rests in that house shall wash his clothes, and whoever eats in that house shall wash his clothing

"But if the priest upon coming to 48 examine observes that the infection is not spreading in that house after the house has been repaired,—then the priest shall pronounce the house clean, for it is cured of the infection Then he shall take, as a sin-offering 49 for the house, two he-goats, and cedar wood, and scarlet wool and hysop, and slay one of the goats into an 50 earthen bowl filled with living water, then prepare the cedar wood, and 51 hysop, and scarlet wool, and the living goat, and dabble them with some blood of the slain goat, and with the living water, and sprinkle the house seven times, and expiate for the house 52 by the blood of the goat, and by living water, and by the living goat, and by the cedar wood, and scarlet wool Afterwards he shall turn the living 53 goat outside the village on the face of the field, and expiate for the house, and declare it clean

"These are the laws about any 54 infectious disease, and its removal, and for infected fabrics or houses, 55 and for ulcerations, and running 56 sores, and for scrofula, with eruptions, 57 —from the day of contagion, until the day of their cure,—these are the laws of infection "

Sanitary Laws for Sexual Diseases.

The EVER-LIVING also spoke to 15 Moses and to Aaron, saying,—

"Speak to the children of Israel 2 and say to them,

"If any one of you has a discharge from their generative organs, they are diseased These then are the 3 diseases in his genitals a discharge from his generative organ, or if the organ ceases from generative power He is then unhealthy Any bed upon 4 which the sufferer from such discharge lies is defiled, and every chair upon which he sits is defiled, and 5 any persons touching his bed shall wash their clothes, and bathe in water, and be unclean until the evening And whoever sits on an article where 6 the sufferer from the discharge has sat, shall wash their clothing, and bathe in water, and be clean until the evening.　　r touches 7 the discharging flesh, shall wash his clothing, and bathe in water, and be

8 unclean until the evening And upon whoever the issue spurts in cleansing it, they also shall wash their clothing, and bathe in water, and be unclean

9 until evening And every carriage upon which the patient rides is un-

10 clean And anyone touching anything that has been under him, shall be unclean until the evening, and whoever carries them shall wash their clothing, and bathe in water, and be

11 unclean until evening And everyone who touches the sufferer from that discharge, with his hand, shall plunge it in water, and wash his clothes, and bathe in water, and be

12 unclean until the evening And an article of pottery that has touched the patient with that discharge, shall be broken , and any article of wood shall be washed with a rush of water

13 " But when he is cured of the discharging, fix for him seven days to purify himself, and to wash his clothing, and to bathe his body in

14 living water, and to cleanse Then upon the eighth day let him prepare two turtle-doves, or two young pigeons, and go to the priest before the EVER-LIVING, at the door of the Hall of

15 Assembly, and the priest shall offer one of them as a sin-offering, and the other as a burnt-offering Thus the priest shall expiate for him before the EVER-LIVING for the discharge

16 " And a man from whom has come the pouring of seed, shall wash the whole of his flesh in water, and be

17 unclean until the evening, and any fabric, or any skin, upon which shall be the pouring of seed, shall also be washed in water, and be unclean until

18 the evening And every woman with whom a man has poured the pouring of seed, shall also wash in water and be unclean until evening

19 " And a woman with whom may be menstruation shall have seven days for the discharge of her body in seclusion, and all touching her shall be

20 unclean until the evening And all that she has upon her during her seclusion is unclean, and all she sits

21 upon is unclean , and all who touch her bed shall wash their clothes and bathe in water, and be unclean until

22 the evening And all touching any article upon which she has sat, shall wash their clothing and bathe in water, and be unclean until the eve-

ing And if anyone lies down with 23 her, or upon any article where she has sat, or touches it, they are unclean until the evening And if any 24 husband copulates with her, when there is menstruation on her, then he shall be unclean for seven days, and any bed upon which he copulated with her is unclean

Law of Sexual Diseases in Women.

" But a woman who has a discharge 25 of blood for many days, which is not her menstruation, or who discharges sap at her menstruation for a long period, beyond the time of her menstrual period, is unclean

" Every bed upon which she lies 26 all the time of her discharge, shall be to her as a bed of menstruation , and every article upon which she sits shall be unclean, as with menstrual uncleanness , and whoever touches 27 her is unclean, and shall wash their clothes and bathe their bodies and be unclean until the evening

" But if she is cured of her dis- 28 charge, appoint seven days for her, and afterwards she shall be clean. Then at the eighth day she shall take 29 two turtle-doves, or two young pigeons, and bring them to the priest at the door of the Hall of Assembly, and 30 the priest shall make of the one a sin-offering, and of the other a burnt-offering, and the priest shall expiate for her before the EVER-LIVING, for the defect of her uncleanness

" In this way the children of Israel 31 shall separate themselves from their sins, and not die in their sins , with the sins of the populations among whom you reside

" These are the laws regulating 32 generative diseases, that come to you from sexual sins "

Laws for the Ministering Priests

The EVER-LIVING also spoke to 16 Moses, after the death of the two sons of Aaron, while offering in the presence of the LORD, when He killed them The EVER-LIVING then said 2 to Moses ,

" Say to Aaron your brother, that he must not come at all times from the sanctuary of the house to within the veil before the expiatories which are over the ark, lest he should die , for I appear in the cloud upon the coverings

This is how Aaron must go to 3

the sanctuary, with a bull, the son of the fold, for a sin-offering, and a
4 ram for a burnt-offering, his body clothed with the sacred robes, and his trousers shall be upon his body, and girt with his waist belt, and turbaned with his turban, and with the sacred robes, and his body and
5 clothing washed in water, and he shall take two goats for a sin-offering, and a ram for a burnt-offering, for the Chiefs of the Children of Israel
6 "And Aaron shall present the bull he has with him for the sin-offering, and expiate for the sins of himself, and the family of his own house,
7 then take the two goats and place them before the FVER-LIVING, at the
8 door of the Hall of Assembly, where Aaron shall cast lots over the two goats,—to allot one to the EVER-LIVING and allot the other as a scape-
9 goat Aaron shall afterwards sacrifice the goat which the lot came upon
10 for the EVER-LIVING, and the goat which the lot came upon for a scape-goat, he shall place alive before the EVER-LIVING, to expiate with it, by sending it as a scapegoat into the field
11 "Aaron shall next sacrifice the bull on account of his own sins, and expiate for himself, and on account of his own house, and slay the bull
12 for his own sins Then he shall take a shovelful of burning coals from off the altar before the EVER-LIVING, and fill his hand with sweet incense powder, and bring it from the house
13 to the veil, and put the incense on to the fire before the EVER-LIVING, and the cloud from the incense shall cover the veil that is over the witnesses,—and he shall not die
14 "Let him next take some of the blood of the bull and sprinkle with his forefinger before the veil towards the east, and before the expiatories he shall sprinkle the blood seven
15 times with his finger, then slay the goat that is for the sins of the nation and bring some of its blood from the house to the veil, and do with that blood as he did with the blood of the bull, and sprinkle some of it upon the veil, and before the veil,
16 and expiate for the sins of the children of Israel, and for their rebellions with all their sins, and do the same to the Hall of Assembly which is erected in the midst of their
17 sins, and no person shall be in the

Hall of Assembly when he goes to expiate in the sanctuary, when he expiates on account of himself, and on account of his house, and for the whole congregation of Israel Then 18 he shall come to the altar that is before the EVER-LIVING and expiate for himself, and take some of the blood of the bull, and some of the blood of the ram, and put upon the horns at the side of the altar, and sprinkle some 19 of the blood with his forefinger seven times, and purify it, and sanctify himself from the sins of the children of Israel When he has 20 finished expiating for the sanctuary, and the Hall of Assembly, and the altar —he shall then present the live goat, and Aaron shall lay his 21 two hands upon the head of the live goat, and confess upon it the whole of the frailties of the children of Israel, and the whole of their faults, and the whole of their sins, and lay them upon the head of the goat, and send it by the hand of a man of My People into the desert, and that goat 22 shall carry upon itself the whole of their frailties to the land of forgetfulness, thus the goat shall be sent to the desert

"Aaron shall next go to the Hall 23 of Assembly, and strip off from himself the robes with which he was clothed at his going to the sanctuary, and leave them there, and bathe his 24 body in water in the Holy Place, then put on his robes, and come and offer the burnt-offering for himself, and the burnt-offering for the nation, and expiate on account of himself and on account of the nation, and 25 burn the fat of the sin-offerings with incense upon the altar

The Scapegoat-man's Duty.

"The man who drove out the 26 scapegoat shall afterwards wash his clothes, and bathe his body in water, and then he may go into the camp

The Priests' Duty continued, and Burning the Sin-offering outside the Camp.

"Next the bull of the sin-offering, 27 and the ram of the sin-offering, some of whose blood was brought for expiating to the sanctuary, shall be brought to the outside of the camp, and burnt with fire,—the skin, and the flesh, and the dung But the 28 person who burns them shall wash his clothes, and bathe his body in water, previous to returning to the camp

The Reason for the Festival.

29 "This shall be a perpetual Institution for you in the seventh month, in the tenth day of the month, that you may humble yourselves, and do no business, either the native, or the 30 foreigner living amongst you, for on that day there is an expiation made for you, to purify you from all your sins before the EVER-LIVING, you 31 must be pure It shall be to you a Rest of Rests, when you shall humble your lives an Institution for ever 32 At that time the priest who has been consecrated, and who has been appointed as priest in the place of his fathers, and has put on himself the 33 sacred robes, shall thus expiate for the Holy of Holies, and the Hall of Assembly, and also expiate for the altar, and for the priests, and expiate for all the people of the congregation 34 And this shall be a perpetual Institution for you, to expiate for the whole of the children of Israel on account of all their sins, once every year "

And it was done as the EVER-LIVING had instructed Moses

The Law of Excommunication for Unauthorized Sacrificing.

17 The EVER-LIVING also spoke to Moses, commanding,—

2 "Speak to Aaron and his sons, with all the children of Israel, and say to them,—

"This is the thing that the EVER-LIVING has commanded to be said,

3 Any man of the house of Israel who slays a bullock, or sheep, or goat, at the altar, or who slays it outside the 4 camp, or at the door of the Hall of Assembly, who comes not to offer a gift to the EVER-LIVING, before the dwelling of the EVER LIVING, blood shall be imputed to that man, blood spilt,—that man shall be excommunicated from association with 5 his People So that, instead of the children of Israel going to their altars that they have in the open fields, they must bring their offerings to the EVER-LIVING at the door of the Hall of Assembly, to the priest, that he may offer for them to the 6 EVER-LIVING, and the priest shall sprinkle the blood upon the altar of

the EVER-LIVING at the door of the Hall of Assembly, and burn the fat with incense, as a delightful breath to the EVER-LIVING

7 "For you shall never sacrifice your sacrifices to demons that you whore after — This is an everlasting command to them, and their posterity

8 "Say also to them, Any man of the House of Israel, or of the foreigners who reside among them, who offers 9 a burnt-offering or sacrifice, and does not cause it to be brought to the door of the Hall of Assembly to offer it to the EVER-LIVING, that man shall be excommunicated from his people 10 And every person of the children of Israel, or of the foreigners who reside amongst them, who eats any blood, or places before Me what he has eaten with the life-blood in it, I will cause him to be excommunicated from association with the nation,— 11 for the life of the body is in its blood, and I have given it to you for the altar, to expiate for your sins,—for the blood with its life expiates 12 Therefore I say to the children of Israel,—No person of you shall eat the blood, and the foreigner that resides among you shall not eat blood

Law for Huntsmen.

13 Any person also from the children of Israel, or from the foreigners who reside among you, who hunts animal or bird, that he may eat it, shall also pour out the blood and cover it with 14 dust, because the life of all flesh is in its blood, as its life Therefore say to the children of Israel you shall not eat the life with the blood of any flesh, for the life of all flesh is in its blood All eating of it, shall be ex- 15 communicated And every person who eats of a dead carcase, or one torn, or mangled, or worried, shall wash his clothes, and bathe in water, and be unclean until the evening— and then clean,—but if he does not wash his body or bathe, he shall bear his sin "

Order to abandon Heathen Customs.

18 The EVER-LIVING also spoke to Moses, commanding,

2 "Speak to the children of Israel and say to them, I am your EVER-LIVING GOD

3 You shall not do as the land of the Mitzeraim where you dwelt there,

And you shall not do as the land of Canan does to which I shall bring you. You shall not continue their 4 customs. You shall practise My Decrees, and observe My Institutions; to walk by them.—I am your EVER- 5 LIVING GOD. And you shall guard My Institutions, and My Decrees, which were made for you, and live in them.—I am the EVER-LIVING.

The Laws of Affinity, and Marriages and Sex.

6 "No person shall approach to a relative of his body to uncover their sexuality; I am the EVER-LIVING.

7 "The sexuality of your father or the sexuality of your mother you shall not uncover. She is your mother. You shall not uncover her sexuality.

8 "You shall not uncover the sexuality of a wife of your father. I am the EVER-LIVING.

9 "The sexuality of your sister, a daughter of your father or a daughter of your mother, born in the house, or born out of it; you shall not uncover the sexuality of them.

10 "You shall not uncover the sexuality of the daughter of your son, or the daughter of your daughter, for that is your own sexuality.

11 "You shall not uncover the sexuality of the daughters of the wives of your father, born to your father. She is your sister.

12 "You shall not uncover the sexuality of the sister of your father, she is of your father's blood.

13 "You shall not uncover the sexuality of the sister of your mother. She is of your mother's blood.

14 "You shall not uncover the sexuality of the wife of the brother of your father. Your love shall not approach to her.

15 "You shall not uncover the sexuality of your daughter-in-law. She is the wife of your son. You shall not uncover her sexuality.

16 "You shall not uncover the sexuality of your brother's wife. She is your brother's wife.

17 "You shall not uncover the sexuality of a woman and her daughter; the daughter of her son; or the daughter of her daughter you shall not take to uncover their sexuality. Copulation with them is wickedness.

18 "And you shall not marry a wife's sister, to grieve her by uncovering her sexuality, whilst she lives.

19 "You shall not approach to a woman unclean by menstruation to uncover her sexuality.

20 "And to the wife of your neighbour you shall not give your copulation for seed, to defile her.

21 "And you shall not give of your seed to pass to Molok; and thus defile the name of your GOD. I am the EVER-LIVING.

22 "And with a man you shall not copulate, with the copulation of a woman. It is abominable.

23 "And to any beast you shall not give your copulation to defile it. And a woman shall not place herself to the face of a beast, to copulate. It is incest.

24 "You shall not defile yourselves with any of these, for with all these the heathen defiled themselves, whom I shall drive out from before you; and they defiled the land. Therefore 25 I punish the sin in it, upon them; and the land spews out its inhabitants.

26 "Therefore you, yourselves, must preserve My Institutions and Decrees, and not practise any of these abominations; either you natives, or 27 foreigners residing among you. For the whole of these abominations the population of the land, whom I shall drive out from before you, practised,— 28 and they defiled the land; if you do so the land will spew you out for your defiling it, as it spewed out the heathen who were before you, for all 29 that they did, with all these abominations. Therefore the people who do them shall be cut off from the boundaries of your people."

The Laws of Moral Duty.

The EVER-LIVING also spoke to 19 Moses, commanding ;—

"Speak to all the chiefs of the 2 children of Israel, and say to them, Be holy: for I your EVER-LIVING GOD am Holy.

"Each of you reverence your 3 mother and father; and keep My Sabbaths; I am the EVER-LIVING GOD.

"You shall not turn to idols; and 4 you shall not make metal gods for yourselves. I am the EVER-LIVING your GOD. And when you offer a 5 thank-offering, you shall offer it to your EVER-LIVING STRENGTH. You 6 shall eat it in the day of sacrifice and the day after; but the remainder to the third day you shall burn with

7 fire. And if anyone eats of it on the third day, it is worthless, and will not

8 be accepted, and the eater of it shall bear his fault, for he profanes the holiness of the EVER-LIVING; so that person shall be excluded from his family.

9 "And when you reap the harvest of your land, you shall not continue cutting to the sides of your field, cutting and gleaning; you shall not cut

10 the gleanings. And you shall not strip your vineyard; nor shall you glean the scatterings of your vineyard. You shall leave them for the poor, and the foreigner. I am your EVER-LIVING GOD.

11 "You shall not rob; and you shall not deceive; and you shall not lie

12 each to his neighbour; and you shall not swear by My Name to a lie; and disgrace the Name of your GOD. I am the EVER-LIVING.

13 "And you shall not oppress; and you shall not plunder; nor retain the wages of a workman with yourself until the morning.

14 "You shall not curse the deaf; and before the blind you shall not place a stumbling-block; but you shall fear your GOD. I am the EVER-LIVING.

15 "You shall not do wrong instead of justice. You shall not despise the face of the lowly, and honour the face of the great. You shall judge your neighbour in righteousness.

16 "You shall not go about slandering your neighbour.
"You shall not lie in wait for the blood of your neighbour. I am the EVER-LIVING."

17 "You shall not hate your brother in your heart.
"You may reprove your neighbour, but not bear ill-will against him.

18 "You shall not take revenge upon the child of your neighbour; but you shall love your neighbour as yourself. I am the EVER-LIVING.

19 "You shall preserve My Institutions.
"You shall not yoke together different kinds of cattle;
"You shall not sow in your field mixed kinds of seed;
"And you shall not put on yourself cloth woven of different materials.

20 "And anyone who lies with a woman in pouring of seed, and she was enslaved as a slave to the man and was not free as a free woman;

or at liberty,—punishment shall not be given to her; she shall not be

21 killed; for she was not free. But she shall bring to the EVER-LIVING to the door of the Hall of Assembly

22 a ram for a sin-offering, and the priest shall expiate for her before the EVER-LIVING with the ram as a sin-offering, for the sin which she has sinned, and the sin which she has sinned shall be forgiven.

23 "When you arrive in the land, and plant any tree for food, you shall consecrate its fruit. It shall remain upon it three years for a consecration.

24 You shall not eat of it. But in the fourth year all its fruits shall be devoted as thanks to the EVER-

25 LIVING. But in the fifth year you may eat its fruit; its produce shall be for yourselves. I am your EVER-LIVING GOD.

26 "You shall not eat anything with its blood.
"You shall not worship serpents.
"You shall not worship clouds.

27 "You shall not cut off the beard on your cheeks; and you shall not destroy the beard of your chin.

28 "You shall not make tattooings on your flesh for spirits, nor put written brands upon yourselves. I am the EVER-LIVING.

29 "You shall not pollute your daughters to whoredom; by causing them to whore, and filling the country with wickedness.

30 "You shall keep My Sabbaths, and you shall reverence My sacred things. I am the EVER-LIVING.

31 "You shall not turn to spirits; or to fortune-tellers, to inquire of them, to sin with them. I am your EVER-LIVING GOD.

32 "You shall rise up before the grey-headed, and pay respect to the presence of a judge, and reverence to your GOD. I am the EVER-LIVING.

33 "And when a foreigner resides in your land you shall not oppress him.

34 As it is with you natives, so it shall be with the foreigners among you; you shall love them as yourselves; for you were foreigners in the land of the Mitzeraim. I am your EVER-LIVING GOD.

35 "You shall not do wrong, in measuring as to length, weight, or measure. You shall have a true

36 scale, true weights, a true bushel, a true gallon. I am your EVER-LIVING GOD Who brought you out of

37 the land of the Mitzeraim, therefore you shall keep the whole of My Institutions, and all My Decrees, and practise them I am the EVER-LIVING "

The Law against Idolatry

20 The EVER-LIVING also spoke to Moses, commanding,

2 " Speak to the children of Israel, to each one of the sons of Israel, and to the foreigners,—the foreigners among Israel Whoever gives their offspring to Molok, they shall be killed ,—the People of the country shall stone

3 them with stones And I will place My face against that person, and will cut him off from his people for giving his offspring to Molok, to defile MY HOLINESS, and to pollute MY HOLY

4 NAME And if, to conceal it, the people of the country cover their eyes from the person who gives his offspring to Molok, to destroy him in

5 death, I, however, will set My face against that person, and destroy him, and cut him off, with all those who whore after him, whoring after Molok , from the midst of their people

Laws of Domestic Morality.

6 " The person also who turns to spirits, and to wizards [1] to whore after them ,—I will put My face against that person, and will excommunicate

7 him from the midst of his people , for you shall make yourselves holy, and be holy, for I am your EVER-LIVING

8 GOD Therefore you shall preserve My Institutions, and practise them I the EVER-LIVING must make you Holy

9 " Whatever person outrages his father or his mother, let him be put to death The blood of the outrager of his father or mother is upon himself

10 " The man who commits adultery with a wife , the man who commits adultery with the wife of his neighbour, shall be killed ,—both the adulterer and adulteress

11 " The man who copulates with a wife of his father, uncovering the sexuality of his father ,—they shall both die ,—then blood is on themselves

12 " The man who copulates with his daughter-in-law ,—both, who have done that villany, shall die Their blood is upon themselves

[1] Heb Fortune-tellers –1 1

13 " And the man who copulates with a male, with the copulation of a woman, commits abomination They shall both die Their blood is on themselves

14 " And the man who takes a woman and her mother It is wickedness They shall burn him in fire with them That wickedness shall not be in the midst of you

15 " And the man who copulates with a beast shall be killed , and the beast shall be slaughtered

16 " And the woman who approaches to a beast, to copulate with it, with the copulation of a woman, both the beast and she shall be killed Then blood is on themselves

17 " And the man who takes his sister, the daughter of his father, or the daughter of his mother, and sees her sexuality, and she sees his sexuality,—they are disgraceful, and shall be excommunicated in the sight of their people He shall bear his sin for uncovering the sexuality of his sister

18 " And a man who copulates with a sick woman, and uncovers the nakedness of her fount upon her,—and uncovers the fount of her blood , both shall be cut off from association with their people

19 " You shall not uncover the sexuality of the sister of your mother, or the sister of your father, for they are his flesh Whoever uncovers them shall bear their sin

20 " The man who copulates with his aunt, uncovering the sexuality of his aunt, they shall each bear their sin They shall be killed openly

21 " And the man who takes the wife of his brother, in uncovering the sexuality of his brother , they shall be exposed

22 " Thus you shall keep all My Institutions, and all My Decrees, and shall practise them, and then the land that I will bring you to as a residence will not spew you out Thus you shall

23 not conduct yourselves according to the customs of the heathen whom I shall drive out from before you, for they practised all these things in their land, therefore I promised you

24 you should inherit their country, and I will give to you the inheritance of that land flowing with milk and honey I am your EVER-LIVING GOD, Who will destroy them from among the nations

25 "You shall also distinguish between the clean animals and the unclean, and between the unclean birds and the clean, and you shall not pollute your lives with animal or bird, or any reptile of the field, which I have

26 pointed out to you as unclean, but you shall be healthy before Me, for I, the EVER-LIVING, am HOLY, and have separated you from the nations, to

27 be for MYSELF Therefore the man or woman who possesses a spirit, or a foreteller, shall be put to death They shall be stoned with stones Their blood is upon themselves "

Laws as to the Mourning of Priests.

21 The EVER-LIVING also spoke to Moses commanding, "Speak to the priests the sons of Aaron, and command them, that they shall not defile

2 themselves for their relatives Not even for a near blood relation of them,— for their mother, or for their father, or for their son, or for their

3 daughter, or for their brother, or for their sister, or their dearest loved daughter who has not been to a man

4 to wed her,—he shall not debase, or degrade himself with grief

5 "They shall not shave strips upon their heads, nor shave off their whiskers, nor cut gashes on their bodies

6 "They are sacred to their GOD, and shall not lower the NAME of their GOD, for they offer bread to the EVER-LIVING their GOD, they offer themselves, and they shall be healthy

Marriage Law of Priests.

7 "They shall not take for a wife a whore, or a loose woman, and they shall not marry a woman who has been divorced, for they are holy to

8 the EVER LIVING And they shall keep themselves holy, as an offering to your GOD He who approaches the Holy must be the same, for I the EVER-LIVING make you holy

9 "And the daughter of a priest who defiles herself with whoredom—she defiles her father You shall burn her with fire

10 "The chief priest, also, over his brothers, upon whose head has been poured the Oil of Consecration and his hand filled by the investiture of the robes, shall not neglect his head,

11 and shall not neglect his robes, and never disorder his person for a death But if it comes to his father,

or his mother,— shall he degrade

12 himself, nor shall he go from the sanctuary, nor shall he wail,—for he has been separated by the Oil of Consecration to his GOD I am the

13 EVER-LIVING Therefore he shall

14 take a maiden for his wife He shall not take a widow, or a divorced woman, or one abandoned to whoredom, any of them, but he shall take a wife only from the virgins of his

15 own people He shall not degrade his race, or his family, for I the EVER-LIVING have sanctified it "

Laws of the High Priestly Succession

16 The EVER-LIVING also spoke to Moses saying,—

17 "Speak to Aaron, and say,—Any man from the offspring of your posterity who may be disfigured shall not approach to offer bread to his

18 GOD For any man in whom there is a defect shall not approach,— anyone blind, or lame, or flat-nosed,

19 or deformed, or a man who has a broken leg, or a broken hand, or

20 humpbacked, or a dwarf, or squint-eyed, or scurvied, or scabbed, or

21 defective in his testicles,—any man of the race of Aaron the priest in whom there may be a defect shall not approach to present offerings to the EVER-LIVING,— because of his defect he shall not approach to present bread to his GOD It is the

22 Bread of GOD for them, Holy of Holies, and the healthy shall eat it

23 He shall also not come within the veil, nor approach to the altar, because of his defect, so as not to profane MY HOLINESS, for I am the EVER-LIVING SANCTIFIER "

24 Moses consequently spoke this to Aaron and his sons, and to all the children of Israel

Domestic Laws for Priests

22 The EVER-LIVING also spoke to Moses, commanding,—

2 "Speak to Aaron and his sons, and separate them, as consecrated, from the children of Israel, so that they may not defile My HOLY NAME by which they are sanctified to Me I am the EVER-LIVING

3 "Say to them, for their posterity, Every man of all your race who approaches to the sanctuary which the children of Israel have sanctified to the EVER-LIVING whilst there is un-

cleanness upon him, that person shall be excommunicated from before Me   I am the EVER-LIVING

4   "Any man from the race of Aaron who has leprosy, or the disease of fornication, shall never eat of what is pure, or if he has a contagion of any disease on his body, or a man who comes from procreative copula,

5   or a man who has touched any reptile that may defile him, or a man that may defile himself by anything that defiles him, a person who defiles him by touch until the evening,

6   he shall not eat of the sacred offerings unless he bathes his body in

7   water   But when the sun sets then he will be clean, and afterwards may eat of the sacred offerings,—for he is clean

8   "Of a dead or torn carcase he shall not eat, to defile himself with it   I am the EVER-LIVING

9   "Thus they shall reverence MY TRUSTS, and not bring sin upon themselves, and die in it, to condemn themselves   I the EVER-LIVING consecrate them

10   "No foreigner shall eat of the sacred offerings   A visitor to the priest, and the hired servant of the family shall not eat of the sacred

11   offerings, but a priest who buys a person, having bought him for money, —that person may eat, and those born in his house may eat of the

12   food   But the daughter of a priest who has a foreign husband may not eat of the Raised-leg of the sacred

13   offerings   But the daughter of a priest who may be a widow, or divorced, and has no offspring for herself, and dwells in the house of her father as in her youth, she may eat of the bread of her father, but any foreigner may not eat it

14   "Any person, however, who unknowingly eats of sacred offerings, shall return five times as much for it, and give it to the priest for the

15   offerings, for the children of Israel shall not profane My sacred offerings, which are lifted up to the EVER-

16   LIVING, and they shall bear the sin of trespass, if they eat of the sacred gifts, for I am the EVER-LIVING Who sanctifies them"

General Laws of Worship.

17   The EVER-LIVING also spoke to Moses and said,

18   "Speak to Aaron and to his sons, and to all the children of Israel, and say to them,

"Any man of the House of Israel, or of the foreigners in Israel, who offers a gift for any of their vows, or for any free-will gift, which they present to the EVER-LIVING for a burnt-offering, that will please, let it 19 be a perfect male from the oxen, or sheep, or goats   Anything that has 20 a defect in it they shall not present, for it will not be pleasing to the EVER-LIVING from them

"And the man who presents a 21 sacrifice of thanks to the EVER-LIVING to fulfil a vow, or a free-will offering, let it be a perfect beautiful sheep,—there must be no defect in it   The blind or torn shall not be 22 presented to the EVER-LIVING, or the sick, or broken-winded, or scurvied, or scabbed   A female also, shall not be offered by them at the altar of the EVER-LIVING   And an 23 ox, or sheep that is deformed or a dwarf,—if you make a vow of them, they will not be accepted   And if 24 castrated, or crushed, or mutilated, or wounded, you shall not present them to the EVER-LIVING—and you shall not so mutilate them in your country

"You shall also not present food to 25 your GOD from any of these, by the hand of a foreigner, for to offer by him would be to desecrate them They would not be accepted from you"

The Laws of Humanity to Animals.

The EVER-LIVING also spoke to 26 Moses commanding,

"When a cow, or a sheep or a 27 goat has young, then you shall let it be for seven days with its mother, but on the seventh day it will be acceptable as a gift of trespass to the EVER-LIVING   But you shall not 28 slay a cow or a sheep and their young upon the same day

"And when you sacrifice a sacrifice 29 of thanksgiving to the EVER-LIVING you should sacrifice it for your delight   Eat it upon the same day, 30 leave nothing of it until the morning

"I am the EVER-LIVING, and you 31 shall keep My Commandments, and practise them,—I am the EVER-LIVING   And you shall not defile My 32 HOLY NAME, for I would be sanctified in the midst of the children of Israel, I am the EVER-LIVING, Who

33 consecrated you. I brought you out from the land of the Mitzæraim to be a GOD to you. I am the EVER-LIVING."[1]

Laws of Festivals.

23 The EVER-LIVING also spoke to Moses commanding :—

2 "Speak to the children of Israel and say to them ;

"These are the festivals of the EVER-LIVING, which you shall proclaim with a Holy Proclamation, as MY FESTIVALS.

3 "You shall do your work for six days, but on the Seventh Day there shall be a rest of rests, with a holy proclamation from all work; you shall do none on the Sabbath. It is for the EVER-LIVING in all your dwelling places.

4 "These are festivals to the EVER-LIVING, with a Holy Proclamation, which you shall proclaim at your festivals.

5 "In the first month, in the fourteenth day of the month, between sunrise and sunset is the Passover

6 of the EVER-LIVING. And on the fifteenth day of that month is the Feast of Unfermented Bread to the EVER-LIVING. For seven days you

7 shall eat unfermented bread. Upon the first day you shall make a holy ploclamation. You shall do no ser-

8 vile work; and you shall offer a trespass-offering to the EVER-LIVING, for seven days. For seven days, by a Holy Proclamation, you shall do no labouring work."

The Law of Harvesting.

9 The EVER-LIVING also spoke to Moses commanding ;

10 "Speak to the children of Israel and say to them ;

"When you come into the country that I will give to you, and reap its harvest, you shall bring the first sheaf of your harvest to the priest,

11 and he shall wave the sheaf before the EVER-LIVING to delight you. The priest shall wave it the day after

12 the Sabbath ; and you shall offer on the day of your waving of the sheaf a perfect lamb, the son of that year, as

a burnt-offering to the EVER-LIVING ;

13 with a food offering of a twelfth of flour mixed with oil as a perfume to the EVER-LIVING, a pleasant breath ; and, as a draught of wine, the quarter of a hin. And you shall not eat in

14 public bread, or oats, or vegetables on that day, until you have brought this gift to your GOD. This is a perpetual Institution for your posterity, in all your dwelling-places.

15 "You shall also count for yourselves from the day after the Sabbath that you bring the Wave-sheaf, seven Sabbaths. They must be complete. Then after the seventh Sabbath, you

16 shall count fifty days, when you shall present a new offering to the EVER-LIVING. You shall bring from your

17 dwellings two wave cakes of two tenths of fine flour. They shall be fermented,— baked in an oven for the EVER-LIVING.

18 "You shall also offer with this bread seven perfect lambs of a year, and a bullock, a son of the fold, and two rams, which shall be a burnt-offering to the EVER-LIVING, with their food-offerings and their drink-offerings, as a gift of sweet-odour to

19 the EVER-LIVING. You shall offer as well one he goat for a sin-offering, and two lambs of a year old for a thank-offering, and the priest shall

20 wave them with the first-made-bread ; he shall wave them before the EVER-LIVING. They shall be sacred to the EVER-LIVING ; with the two lambs for the priest.

21 "Then there shall be made a holy proclamation to the public on that day ; it shall be Holy of Holies to you. You shall not do any labouring work. This is an everlasting Institution, in all your dwellings, for your posterity,

22 that in reaping your harvests, you shall not reap to the edge of your fields in your reaping; and you shall not glean. Leave the gleanings for the poor and the foreigners amongst you. I am your EVER-LIVING GOD."

Laws of the Feast of Remembrance and Forgiveness of Sins.

23 The EVER-LIVING also spoke to Moses saying ;—

24 "Speak to the children of Israel to say :—

"In the seventh month, in the first day of the month, there shall be a Rest for Remembrance of Sins. It is

---

[1] I cannot refrain from remarking that no heathen Code of Law has ever contained laws enforcing humanity to animals. Doing so is the peculiar distinction of GOD'S Revelation to man. Let the reader reflect on it.—F. F.

5 Holy of Holies You shall not do any labouring work, and you shall offer a burnt-offering to the EVER-LIVING "

A Day of Expiation.

6 The EVER-LIVING also spoke to
7 Moses, to say, further, "On the tenth of the seventh month, there shall be a Day of Expiation It shall be Holy of Holies to you, and you shall humble yourselves and offer a burnt-offering to the EVER-LIVING
8 You shall do no labouring work on that day, for it is a Day of Expiation to expiate for you before your EVER-
9 LIVING GOD Therefore every person who does not humble himself publicly on that day shall be cut off from his
10 family, and every person who does any labouring work on that day, I will trouble that person in the midst of
11 his family You shall do no work This is a perpetual Institution for your posterity in all your dwellings
12 It is a Rest of Rests[1] for you, when you shall humble your souls, on the ninth of the month at daybreak, from dawn to evening,—you shall rest to refresh yourselves "

Laws of the Feast of Tabernacles

13 The EVER-LIVING also spoke to Moses,
14 "Speak to the children of Israel and say,—
"On the fifteenth day of the seventh month there shall be the Feast of Tabernacles to the EVER-LIVING for
15 seven days From the first day proclaimed holy, you shall do no
16 labouring work You shall present a burnt-offering to the EVER-LIVING for seven days The eighth day shall be proclaimed Holy for you, and you shall present a burnt-offering to the EVER-LIVING, It shall be a Public Holiday You shall do no labouring work in it

General Festivals.

37 "These are the Assemblies of the EVER-LIVING, which you shall proclaim with a Holy Proclamation, for presenting and offering a burnt-offering to the EVER-LIVING A whole burnt-offering and a food-offering, a sacrifice and fragrance day by day,
38 besides the Sabbaths of the EVER-

---

[1] Sabbath of Sabbaths—L I

LIVING, and besides your gifts, and besides all your vows, and free-wills, which you give to the EVER-LIVING

Feast of the Harvest Home.

39 "Also on the fifteenth day of the seventh month after the reaping of the produce of your land, you shall enjoy the feast of the EVER-LIVING for seven days, from the first day after the Sabbath, until the eighth
40 day after the Sabbath You shall then take for yourselves on the first day handfuls of the finest fruits from the trees, with the palm, and boughs of the bushes, and willow, and enjoy yourselves before your EVER LIVING GOD for seven days Thus you shall
41 feast in this Feast to the EVER-LIVING seven days every year It shall be a perpetual Institution for your descendants You shall hold the festival in
42 the seventh month, living in tents for seven days All the natives of Israel
43 shall live in tents, so that your posterity may know that the sons of Israel dwelt in tents when I brought you out from the land of the Mitzeraim I am your EVER-LIVING GOD "
44 Moses consequently commanded these feasts of the EVER-LIVING to the children of Israel

The Law of the Lamps and Shewbread.

24 The EVER-LIVING also spoke to Moses, commanding,—
2 "Order the children of Israel to bring to you olive oil, pressed pure, for the lamps to raise a clear light
3 outside the Veil of the Witnesses in the Hall of Assembly, which Aaron shall arrange continually from evening till dawn before the EVER-LIVING It shall be an Institution
4 for your posterity for ever, to arrange a pure light before the EVER-LIVING continually
5 "Yourself, also, take flour and bake from it twelve cakes,—these twelve cakes shall be of equal size,
6 and place them in two piles six in a pile, on the pure table before the
7 EVER-LIVING, and place upon the piles pure incense, and they will be the Bread of Remembrance, like a burnt-offering to the EVER-LIVING
8 From a Sabbath Day to a Sabbath Day they shall be always arranged before the EVER-LIVING as in everlasting covenant with the children of

9 Israel. And they shall belong to Aaron and to his sons, and be eaten in the Holy Place, for they are Holy of Holies to them from the offerings to the EVER-LIVING. This is a perpetual Institution."

The Law of Blasphemy.

10 It occurred once that the son of an Israelitish woman, who was also the son of a Mitzerite man, among the sons of Israel, quarrelled in the camp with the son of an Israelitish woman

11 and an Israelite man ; and the son of the Israelitish woman cursed THE NAME, and insulted it. They therefore brought him to Moses. The name of his mother, however, was Shelamith, the daughter of Dibri of

12 the tribe of Dan. So they put him under guard to enquire about him from the EVER-LIVING.

13 The EVER-LIVING consequently spoke to Moses, commanding ;—

14 " Take the blasphemer outside the camp, and let all who heard him lay their hands upon his head, and let

15 all the Assembly kill him. Then you shall command the children of Israel saying ;—Whatever person curses

16 his GOD shall bear his sin, and the blasphemer of the name of the EVER-LIVING shall die. You shall kill him ; all the Assembly shall stone him. All of the population who blasphemes the NAME, whether native or foreigner, shall die.

17 " And whoever strikes off the life of a man, shall die.

18 " And whoever strikes the life of a beast, shall pay life for life.

19 " And a person who inflicts injury upon his neighbour ; as he has done,

20 so you shall do to him. Wound for wound ; eye for eye ; tooth for tooth ; whatever injury he has done to a man, the same shall be done to him.

21 " Thus whoever kills a beast shall compensate for it ; but whoever kills a man shall die.

22 " There shall be equal justice with you for the foreigner, and the native ; —For I am your EVER-LIVING GOD."

23 Moses consequently spoke to the children of Israel, and they brought out the blasphemer from the camp, and killed him with stones. Thus the children of Israel did as the EVER-LIVING commanded to Moses.

Law of the Sabbath of the Land.

The EVER-LIVING also spoke to 25 Moses in Mount Sinai commanding ;

" Speak to the children of Israel 2 and say to them ;—When you arrive in the land that I will give to you, you shall grant the land a rest of rests to the EVER-LIVING.

" You shall sow your fields for six 3 years, and prune your vineyards for six years, and then cease to go to them ; and in the seventh year there 4 shall be a Rest of Rests for the land to the EVER-LIVING. You shall not sow your fields, nor prune your vineyards. You shall not reap the self- 5 grown harvest, nor cut off the bunches from your vine. It is a Rest of Rests for the earth. There shall 6 be a rest of the earth to feed it ; for you, and for your servant, and for your maid servant, and for your hired labourer, and for the foreigners residing with you, and for your cattle 7 and animals that are in your country —who shall all be allowed to eat of it.

The Law of the Jubilee.

" Also reckon for yourselves seven 8 Sabbaths of years,—seven years seven times, and they shall be for you a period of seven sevens of years,— forty-nine years. Then pass a loud 9 sounding trumpet through all the country. It shall be sent out upon the tenth day of the seventh month, on the Day of Expiation, to sanctify the fiftieth year, and proclaim liberty 10 in the country to all its inhabitants. It shall be a JUBILEE to you, when every person shall return to his inheritance, and everyone shall be restored to his family. Every fiftieth 11 year shall be a JUBILEE for you. You shall neither sow nor reap, nor prune the vines ; for it shall be a 12 Holy Jubilee for you. Eat from the field what springs from it. In this 13 Jubilee Year everyone shall return to his inheritance. For what you buy 14 in a sale of your neighbour, or acquire from the hand of your neighbour, does not dispossess your brother of it. According to the 15 number of years after a Jubilee you must purchase from your neighbour, you must buy it according to the number of years to run for yourself. In proportion to the number of years 16 you shall increase the money, and in proportion to the fewness of the years you shall decrease the purchase price Thus from the number to run it shall be purchased for your-

17 self For you shall not dispossess any of your neighbours, but fear your EVER-LIVING GOD, for I am your

18 EVER-LIVING GOD, and you shall practise My Institutions and My Decrees, guarding and observing them, and dwell in the land in

19 safety Then the earth will give her fruits, and you can eat them to your

20 fill, and live securely upon it But if you ask, 'What shall we eat in that seventh year, when we have neither sown nor continued our

21 labours?' I will then send My blessing to you in the sixth year, and make the produce of it for three

22 years But you may sow in the eighth year, and eat the stored produce in the eighth year until the coming in of products in the ninth year—until its produce comes you must eat what was stored

23 "Thus you shall not sell your land for ever, for the land is MINE, and you only foreigners and

24 visitors with Me, and with all the land you purchase, a power of redemption for the inheritance shall be given with the land

Restoration of Land may be Purchased before the Jubilee.

25 "When your brother is reduced to poverty, and sells some of his inheritance, if a relative of his brings the redemption for it, then the purchaser

26 shall restore it to his brother But if the person has not the redemption money, but he acquires it, and obtains possession of the amount for

27 its redemption, then the years from its purchase shall be counted, and the balance paid to the person who purchased it, and his inheritance shall

28 be restored But if he cannot attain possession of enough to pay to the purchaser, it shall remain in his possession until the year of JUBILEE, and when the JUBILEE comes then he shall return to his inheritance

The Law of Real Estate in Walled Towns.

29 "But if a person sells a dwelling-house in a walled town, then the redemption shall be at the end of a

year from its purchase,—that shall be the time of its redemption But 30 if he has not redeemed at the end of the complete year, and the house stands in a town which has walls, he is dispossessed for ever, it shall not return to his posterity at the JUBILEE

"But houses in a court, where 31 there are not fortified walls around, shall return with the land of the farm that belongs to them They shall return with it when the JUBILEE comes

The Law of Real Estate in Levite Cities.

"But the cities of the Levites,— 32 the houses in the cities of the Levites are their inheritance They shall always be redeemable to the Levites, but when redeemed, it shall be by the 33 Levites, and the purchaser shall quit the house, or village he has acquired, at the JUBILEE, for the village homes of the Levites are their inheritance in the midst of the children of Israel But they shall not sell the 34 grazing lands around their villages, for they are a perpetual inheritance for them

The Law of Insolvency

"But if your brother becomes poor, 35 and his hand fails among you, you must help him like a foreigner and settler, and let him live with you Take no usury or increase from him, 36 but fear your GOD, and let your brother live with you You shall not 37 lend your money to him at usury, and you shall not lend him food at increase, for I am your EVER- 38 LIVING GOD Who brought you from the land of the Mitzeraim to give you the land of Canan, to be for you from the EVER-LIVING

"Therefore when your brother be- 39 comes poor with you, and sells himself to you, you shall not work him as slaves work He shall be with you 40 as a hired man, until the year of JUBILEE, to serve you Then he 41 shall go from you, he and his children with him, and return to his family, and to the inheritance of his fathers, for you were slaves in the 42 land of the Mitzeraim when I brought you out You shall not purchase him as you purchase a slave You 43 shall not reduce him to slavery, but shall fear your God

Laws of Slavery.

44 "Your men and women slaves, however, you may buy from the nations that surround you, they shall be

45 your slaves. And you may also buy the children of the foreign residents among you, and from their families who are with you who are born in your country, and they shall be your

46 property. You may also bequeath them to your children after you, to hold them as property for ever, and they shall serve you. But your relatives of the children of Israel are men, and your brothers, you shall not reduce them to slavery.

A Hebrew Slave may Work Himself Free.

47 "When, however, a foreigner or settler among you obtains property in one of your poor brethren, and he is sold to the foreign resident, to be added to the family of the

48 foreigner, he shall be redeemable after he has been sold to him, any one of his relatives may redeem him.

49 His uncle or cousin may redeem him, or any relation by blood of his family may redeem, or he may acquire property and redeem himself,

50 and pay to his purchaser according to the years he bought him for, up to the year of JUBILEE. That shall be the price given to his purchaser—proportionate to the number of years by the scale of wages that

51 might belong to him. If the years are many before them, he shall give back equivalent money to his purchaser,

52 and if few of the years are remaining to the year of JUBILEE, then he shall repay to him proportionate to the space of years, as the

53 redemption fee, according to the wages year by year it shall be. You shall not add a profit for your eyes.

54 But if he is redeemed by none of these, then he shall be freed at the year of JUBILEE, both himself and

55 his children with him. For the children of Israel are MY SERVANTS, whom I brought up out of the land of the Mitzeraim. I am their EVER-LIVING GOD.

Prohibition of Idol-making

26 "You shall not make idols for yourselves, nor shall you set up columns for yourselves, nor shall you erect stone images in your country

for objects of worship,—for I am your EVER-LIVING GOD.

2 "You shall keep My Sabbaths, and you shall reverence My Sanctuary I am the EVER-LIVING.

THE SONG OF BLESSINGS.

Blessings secured by Obedience and Punishment by Revolt.

3 "If you are guided by My Institutions,
And guard My Commandments, and do them,

4 I will then give My rain upon you,
And the earth will give her produce,
And the trees of the field their fruit.

5 And your thrashing shall last till vintage,
And vintage shall overtake seed-time,
And you shall eat to fulness,
And live securely in your land.

6 And I will give the land peace,
And drive savage beasts from the land,
And the sword shall not govern your country,

7 And you shall subdue your foes,
They shall fall before your sword

8 Five of you shall conquer a hundred,
And a hundred defeat ten thousand,
And your foes fall to your sword,

9 And My Presence shall be with you,
And you shall increase and grow,
I will fix My covenant with you,

10 And feed till your rest in quiet,
And sleep and rise refreshed [1]

11 I will fix My Home among you,
And turn not away My soul,

12 But march with you, and be your GOD,
And My PEOPLE you shall be·

13 For I am your LIVING GOD,

---

[1] V. 10 Alternative reading, "And you shall eat the old (or sleeping) store, and bring out the old from the face of the new." But this rendering does not carry the Oriental idea of sleep as the highest blessing, and to my view to translate the word as "old" is a violation of the Hebrew verb Yashen "to sleep," although A.V. and R.V. adopt it.—F. F.

Who brought from the Mitzerites'
land,
To whom you had been enslaved,
And from off you broke their rod,
And in triumph marched you out!

14 But if you refuse to hear Me,
And obey not all My Commandments,

15 And if you despise My Statutes,
And turn your souls from My
Laws,
To neglect to do My Command-
ments,
And break away from My Bonds,—

16 Then I will do this to you,—
Will send you consumption, and
fever,
And wasting of eyes, and a fainting
soul,
And scatter your race to the wind,
And your foes shall devour your-
selves

17 I will set my face against you,
And strike you before your foes,
And those who hate you shall
drive,
And you fly from instead of
pursue,

18 And if for this you will hear Me not,
I will sevenfold punish your sins,

19 And break the pride of your
strength,
And turn your skies into iron,
And make your ground like brass,

20 And send you a choking wind,
And your land not give her growth,
Nor the trees of the land their
fruit

21 And if you load Me perversely,
And will not listen to Me,
I will sevenfold punish your sins,

22 And wild beasts shall destroy your
sons,
And cut off your herds, and reduce,
And haunt you upon your roads

23 If for these you turn not to Me,
But perversely load Me still,

24 Then I will load you with grief,
And heavily strike your sins,

25 And bring cruel slaughter upon
you,
To avenge the broken Law,
And crowd you into your cities,
And there send the plague to you,
And give to the hand of your foe-
men

26 I will then break the staff of bread
And in one oven ten shall bake,

And your bread shall be given by
weighing,
You shall eat, but shall not be filled

27 If for this you will not hearken,
But still recoil upon Me,

28 I then will advance on you fiercely,
And charge on you in My
wrath,—
I, Myself, for your sevenfold sins

29 You shall then eat the flesh of
your sons
And the flesh of your daughters
consume

30 And I will destroy your High
Towers,
And cut off your Sin-gods from
you,
Your carrion fling to your carrion
Idols,

31 And from you My soul turn away

I will turn your cities to deserts,
And your sanctifications reject,
And smell not the smell of your
sweets

32 Your land shall be turned to a
waste,
And o'er it your enemies rule,
And there shall dwell for themselves,

33 While I fling you out to the
heathen,
And after you blow scorching
wind,
And by it your land shall be wasted,
And your skins shall be burnt by
its breath,—

34 Till the ground has enjoyed all its
Sabbaths
By the time that it lies as a waste,
And your haters shall be in the
land,
Whilst it rests, and delights in its
rest

35 It shall rest in its desolate time —
For you gave it not rest in your
rests,
While upon it you rested yourselves

36 Your fragments shall have coward
hearts,
As you crouch in the lands of your
foes,—
Who shall drive you by threatening
voice,
And you fly as men fly from hot
blasts,
And fall down when no one pursues

37 You shall stagger the one on the
other,

As though from the face of such
    blasts,
Though no one pursues,
And never stand up to your foes.

38   You shall wander among every
    nation,
And tramp in the lands of your
    foes,

39   And your remnants shall waste in
    your sins
In the land of your foes as they
    watch,
For the sins of your fathers and
    selves,—
Till confessing the faults of your-
    selves,

40   And the faults that your fathers
    have done ;
And your treacherous revolt against
    Me,
And the fury with which you as-
    sailed !

41   I, therefore, dealt fiercely with you,
And brought to the land of your
    foes.

If your hard hearts, however, there
    bow,
And you purify them from their
    sins,

42   I will think of My Bond made with
    Jacob,
And also with Isaac My Bond,
And with Abraham remember My
    Covenant,—
And also remember the Land.

43   Thus the Land rid of their load,
And freed, shall in quietude rest.
But they shall be gorged with their
    sins,
And gorged by My Judgments
    despised,
And My Statutes their souls had
    abhorred.

44   But tho' thus, in the land of their
    foes,—
I will not reject them, nor loathe,
So far as My Treaty to break,
For I am their STILL-LIVING GOD !

45   I therefore will bring to their minds
My old treaty contracted with them
In the sight of the Heathen
    around,
To be their GOD,— for I am THE
    LIFE ! "

46   These are the Institutions and
Judgments and the Laws which the
EVER-LIVING appointed between
Himself and between the children of

Israel at Mount Sinai, by the hand
of Moses.

The Law of Personal Vows on Mankind.

The EVER-LIVING also spoke to 27
Moses, saying ;—

"Speak to the children of Israel 2
and say to them, When a person
separates himself, for you to value
his life for the EVER-LIVING, you 3
shall value him for a male from twenty
years old to sixty years ; and your
valuation for a male shall be fifty
shekels of silver by the sacred shekel,
but if it is for a female, your valuation 4
shall be thirty shekels. But if from 5
five up to twenty years old, then the
value of a male shall be twenty
shekels, and for a female ten shekels.
But if from a month up to five years 6
old, then the value of a male shall be
five shekels of silver, and for a female
the value three shekels of silver. But
if they are sixty years old or more, if 7
a male, then the value shall be fifteen
shekels, and for a female ten shekels.
But if the redeemable person is de- 8
fective, then he shall be placed before
the priest, and the priest shall estimate what may be the amount of his
value for the vow he is to pay to the
priest.

Vows upon Animals.

"But if it is a beast that they sacri- 9
fice from, that is vowed to the EVER-
LIVING, all that belongs to it shall
be sacred to the EVER-LIVING. They 10
shall not alter or change it good for
bad, or bad for good ; but if it is
changed it shall be changed for a
beast of the same kind, and the exchange shall be sacred. But if of any 11
unclean beast, which they do not
offer as a gift to the EVER-LIVING,
then the beast shall be shown to the
priest, and the priest shall estimate 12
its value between good and bad, and
it shall be redeemed as the priest
decides, but if they redeem it, they 13
shall then add a fifth part to the
valuation.

Vows upon a House.

"But if a man devotes his house as 14
sacred to the EVER-LIVING, then the
priest shall estimate between good
and bad as the priest values it so it

15 shall stand, but if the consecrator redeems his house, he must add one fifth to the money-value above what has been fixed for it

Vows on a Farm.

16 "But if anyone consecrates his inherited farm to the EVER-LIVING it shall then be valued according to its acreage, what takes a khomer of seed
17 at fifty shekels of silver But if he consecrates his farm before the year
18 of Jubilee, the priest shall then calculate for him the money on the basis of the years remaining until the year of Jubilee, and equate the valuation
19 But if he redeems the farm which he had consecrated, he shall then add a fifth above the valuation price, and it
20 shall continue his But if he does not redeem the farm, or if he sells the land to another person afterward,
21 he cannot redeem it for ever, but the farm shall be consecrated to the EVER-LIVING, until the arrival of the Jubilee the estate shall be as a farm
22 for cultivation for the priests But if the farm has been purchased, and was not an entailed estate which he
23 consecrated to the EVER-LIVING, then the priest shall fix a redemption for him by the amount of value according to the year of Jubilee, and decide the value from the day he has consecrated to the EVER-LIVING
24 Then the estate shall return at the year of Jubilee from the person who bought it, to the person to whom it was an
25 entailed land Every valuation shall be by the sacred shekel, twenty ghera are a shekel
26 "However, a first-born that is born

to the EVER-LIVING, no man shall consecrate, whether an ox or a sheep It is the EVER-LIVING'S
27 "But if of an unclean beast, then it shall be valued as an ox, and one fifth of the price above it, and if it is not redeemed, it shall be sold at the valuation
28 "However, anything devoted to destruction, which a person devotes to the EVER-LIVING, of anything he possesses, from man to beast or an estate of inheritance, he shall not sell it, but he shall redeem[1] every devoted thing, it shall be Holy of Holies to the EVER-LIVING Any-
29 thing devoted, which is devoted by a man, which is unredeemable, shall be put to death

What is Tithable

30 "And all tithe of the land, from the grain of the earth, from the fruit of the tree, is sacred to the EVER-LIVING, but if a person redeems it,
31 from tithe, he shall add one fifth to it All tithe of cattle and sheep, all
32 that passes under the measure for tithing, shall be sacred to the EVER-LIVING You shall not distinguish
33 between good and bad, and not change, but if you do change, then the exchange shall be sacred, it shall not be redeemed "
34 These are the commands which the EVER-LIVING commanded by Moses to the children of Israel at Mount Sinai

---

1 V 28 The Hebrew text reads, לֹא יִגָּאֵל, "loygal," ' shall *not* be redeemed,' which is clearly an error of transcription, as it s contrary to the sense - F F

END OF THE BOOK OF LEVITICUS

THE FOURTH BOOK OF MOSES, COMMONLY CALLED

NUMBERS.

(BE MIDBAR = IN THE DESERT.)

Command to Organize an Army

The Census of Israel.

1 THE EVER-LIVING also spoke to Moses in the desert of Sinai, at the Hall of Assembly, in the first month, in the second year of the years after coming from the land of the Mitzeraim, commanding,

2 "Record the names of all the chiefs of the children of Israel by the families of their ancestors in the Register of Names, each man from

3 his own roll, from twenty years old and upwards, all who can go to war of the children of Israel — you and Aaron organize them into their own

4 regiments They must be assigned each to his own tribe,—each to the captain of the house of his ancestors

5 And these are the names of the men you shall appoint over them

"To Reuben, Alizur the son of Shadiaur,

6 "To Simeon, Shemuhal, the son of Tzurishadai,

7 "To Judah, Makshan, the son of Aminadab,

8 "To Issakar, Nakishan the son of Tzoar,

9 "To Zebulon, Aliab, the son of Khilon,

10 "To the sons of Joseph,—To Ephraim, Alishamar, the son of Amihud,

"To Manasseh, Gamahal the son of Phidatzur,

11 "To Benjamin, Abidan the son of Ghidoni,

12 "To Dan, Akhiazer the son of Amishaddai,

13 "To Asher, Phanuel the son of Aknan,

14 "To Gad, Aliashur the son of Rauel,

15 "To Naphthali, Akhira the son of Ainan,

16 "I have nominated these to be chiefs to bear the standards of the tribes of their ancestors. They are the princes of the regiments of Israel"

17 Moses and Aaron therefore took these men who were indicated to them by name, and they summoned all the

18 chiefs of families on the first of the second month, and they produced to them their records of the houses of their fathers, from the Books of Register, from twenty years old and

19 upwards by their records,—as the EVER-LIVING commanded to Moses, and appointed in the desert of Sinai

20 And these were descendants of the sons of Reuben, the oldest son of Israel, according to the registers of their ancestral houses in the records of names on their heads,— all males of twenty years old and upwards, all

21 capable of army-service, regimented under the standard of Reuben, forty-six thousand, five hundred

22 Of the men descended from Simeon, by the register of the house of their fathers, arranged from the records of names on their heads, all males of twenty years old and upwards,—all

23 capable of army-service,—regimented under the standard of Simeon, fifty-nine thousand, and six hundred

24 Of the men descended from Gad, from the registers of their ancestral houses by the record of names, from twenty years old and upwards,—all

25 capable of army-service, — regimented under the standard of Gad, forty-five thousand, six hundred and fifty

26 Of the men descended from Judah, by the register of their ancestral houses, by the record of names, from twenty years old and upwards,—all

27 capable of army-service,—regimented under the standard of Judah, seventy-four thousand, six hundred

28 Of the men descended from Issakar, by the registers of their ancestral houses in the record of names, from twenty years old and upwards,—all 29 capable of army-service,—regimented under the standard of Issakar, fifty thousand, four hundred

30 Of the men descended from Zebulon, by the registers of their ancestral houses in the record of names, from twenty years old and 31 upwards,—all capable of army-service,—regimented under the standard of Zebulon, fifty-seven thousand, four hundred

32 Of the men of Joseph , of the sons descended from Ephraim, by the registers of their ancestral houses, by the record of names, from twenty years old and upwards,—all capable of army-service,—regimented under 33 the standard of Ephraim, forty thousand, five hundred

34 Of the men descended from Manasseh, by the registers of their ancestral houses, by the record of names, from twenty years old and upwards, 35 —all capable of army-service,—regimented under the standard of Manasseh, thirty thousand, two hundred

36 Of the men descended from Benjamin, by the registers of their ancestral houses, by the record of names, from twenty years old and upwards, 37 —all capable of army-service,—regimented under the standard of Benjamin, thirty-five thousand, four hundred

38 Of the men descended from Dan, by the registers of their ancestral houses, by the record of names, from twenty years old and upwards,—all 39 capable of army-service,—regimented under the standard of Dan, sixty-two thousand, seven hundred

40 Of the men descended from Asher, by the registers of their ancestral houses, by the record of names, from twenty years old and upwards, 41 —all capable of army-service,—regimented under the standard of Asher, forty-one thousand, five hundred

42 Of the men descended from Naphthali, by the registers of their ancestral houses, by the record of names, from twenty years old and upwards, 43 —all capable of army-service,—regimented under the standard of Naphthali, fifty-three thousand, four hundred

44 These were the Army Divisions that Moses and Aaron organized , and the generals of Israel were twelve men,—each was appointed from the 45 house of their fathers And the officers of the children of Israel were all from the house of their fathers from twenty years old and upwards, all capable of army-service in Israel , 46 and the total number of all the enrolled was six hundred and thirty thousand, five hundred and fifty 47 The Levites, however, were not enrolled among them

The Appointment of a Priesthood

48 Then the EVER-LIVING spoke to Moses commanding ,

49 ' Regarding the tribe of Levi , you shall not enrol it, so that they may not raise their head in the midst of 50 the sons of Israel However you shall organize the Levites for the sanctuary of the nation, and for all the services, and for all pertaining to them They shall carry the sanctuary and all its furniture, and shall encamp round and guard the sanctuary 51 When the sanctuary is to advance, the Levites shall take it down , and when the sanctuary is to be pitched the Levites shall raise it, and the stranger who approaches shall be 52 killed But the sons of Israel shall attend each to their own camp, and 53 each to the flag of their regiments, whilst the Levites must attend about the sanctuary of the nation, that there may not be anger upon the nation of the sons of Israel , therefore the Levites shall guard the sanctuary of the nation "

54 The children of Israel consequently did all that the EVER-LIVING commanded to Moses They did it

The Orders for Encamping.

2 The EVER-LIVING also spoke to Moses commanding ,

2 " Let each encamp by his flag at the standard of the ancestral house of the sons of Israel Let them begin to encamp around the Hall of Assembly on the east

3 " The encampment on the east, from the sunrising, shall be for the standard of the camp of the army of Judah , and let Nakhshan the son of Amminadab command the sons of 4 Judah, with his organized force of seventy-four thousand, six hundred

5 " And let the tribe of Issakar encamp next them, and the commander of the sons of Issakar be Nathanael

6 the son of Tzoar, with his organized force of fifty thousand, four hundred

7 " Next the tribe of Zebulon Let the commander of the sons of Zebulon be Aliab the son of Khelon,

8 with his organized force of fifty-seven thousand, four hundred

9 " All the regiments in the camp of Judah numbering one hundred and eighty-six thousand, four hundred, this force shall march first

10 " The standard of Reuben shall be on the south with its force, and the commander of the sons of Reuben shall be Aliezar the son of Shadiaur,

11 with his organized force of forty-six thousand, five hundred

12 " And let the tribe of Simeon encamp next them, and the commander of the tribe of Simeon be Shlumiel the son of Tzurishadai,

13 and his organized force be fifty-nine thousand, six hundred

14 " Then the tribe of Gad, and let the commander of the sons of Gad be

15 Ahsaph the son of Rauel, with his organized force of forty-five thou-

16 sand, six hundred and fifty All the organized forces in the camp of Reuben were one hundred and fifty-one thousand, four hundred and fifty And this division shall march second

17 " But the camp of the Hall of Assembly shall march with the Levites between the camps as they encamp,—they shall march each alongside of their flag

18 " Let the standard of the camp of Ephraim with his force be on the west, and the commander of the sons of Ephraim shall be Alishamah the son

19 of Amihud, and his organized force be forty thousand, five hundred

20 " And next to him let there be the tribe of Manasseh, and the commander of the sons of Manasseh shall be Gamaliel the son of

21 Phidatzur, and his organized force be thirty-two thousand, two hundred

22 " Then the tribe of Benjamin, and the commander of the sons of Benjamin shall be Abidan the son

23 of Khidaoni, and his organized force be thirty-five thousand, four hundred

24 " All the enrolments in the camp of Ephraim were one hundred and eight thousand, one hundred, they shall march third with their force

25 " Let the standard of the tribe of Dan be on the north with its force, and the commander of the sons of Dan shall be Arhiazur the son of

Amishadai, and his organized force 26 be sixty-two thousand, seven hundred

" And let the tribe of Asher encamp 27 next them, and the commander of the sons of Asher shall be Phanuel 28 the son of Akran, and his organized force was one and forty thousand, five hundred

" Then the tribe of Naphthah, and 29 let the commander of the sons of Naphthah be Akhira the son of Ainan, and his organized force be 30 fifty-three thousand, four hundred

" All the enrolments in the camp 31 of Dan were one hundred and fifty-seven thousand, six hundred, who marched in the rear after their flags "

These were the divisions of the 32 children of Israel, by their ancestral houses The numbers in the regiments, in the camps of their forces, were six hundred and three thousand, five hundred, and fifty [1] But the 33 Levites were not enrolled among the sons of Israel, as the EVER-LIVING commanded to Moses

The children of Israel did as 34 the EVER-LIVING commanded to Moses They encamped by their regiments, and thus they marched,— each with his family, by the house of their fathers

---

Families of Moses and Aaron

The following were the children of **3** Aaron and Moses at the time the EVER-LIVING spoke with Moses at Mount Sinai

The Sons of Aaron.

And these are the names of the 2 sons of Aaron The eldest Nadab, and Abihu, Aliazar and Aithamar These were the names of the sons of 3 Aaron the consecrated priest, who filled the office of priests But Nadab 4 and Abihu died before the LORD, when they offered strange fire before the EVER-LIVING in the Wilderness of Sinai, and they had no sons, so Aliazar and Aithamar became priests in the presence of Aaron their father.

Confirmation of Levites as Priests.

Then the EVER-LIVING spoke to 5 Moses saying,

" Present the tribe of Levi, and 6 station them before Aaron the priest,

1 Note 5 lit a set f for fives "—F. F

7 and they shall serve with him, and guard what is intrusted to him, and the trusts of all the congregation, in the Hall of Assembly, and perform
8 the services of the sanctuary. They shall also guard all the furniture of the Hall of Assembly, and the trusts of the children of Israel, and perform
9 the services of the sanctuary. Therefore give the Levites to Aaron and his sons. Presenting them to him as an offering for the children of Israel,
10 and instruct Aaron and his sons, that they must preserve the priesthood, and the stranger who approaches it shall die."

Separation of the Tribe of Levi.

11 The EVER-LIVING also spoke to Moses commanding,—
12 "I, also, now, have taken the Levites from among the children of Israel, so the Levites shall be Mine,
13 for all the firstborn were Mine at the time when I cut off all the firstborn in the land of the Mitzeraim. I then dedicated all the firstborn of Israel to Myself, from man and also from beast. They shall be Mine. I am the EVER-LIVING."

The Levites to be Organized

14 The EVER-LIVING also spoke to Moses in the Wilderness of Sinai, commanding,
15 "Organize the sons of Levi by their ancestral houses from their registers,—you must organize every male from a month old and upwards."
16 Moses consequently organized them as the EVER-LIVING commanded, and these were the sons of
17 Levi by their names,—Gershon, and Kahath, and Merari.
18 And these were the names of the sons of Ghershon, by their registers, Libni and Shimai.
19 And the sons of Kahath, by their registers, Amram and Itzar, Khabron and Ouzal.
20 And the sons of Merari by their registers, Makhli, and Mashi.
These are from the registers of the
21 ancestral houses of Levi, from the registers of Ghershon, from the registers of Libni, from the registers of Shimai. These were from the registers of the Ghershonites.
22 They were organized from the books, every male from a month old

and upwards,[1]—then enrolment was seven thousand, five hundred.
"The families of the Ghershonites 23 shall encamp behind the sanctuary, to the westward, and the commander 24 of the house of the Ghershonites shall be Ahasaph the son of Lael. Thus the duties of the sons of Gher- 25 shon shall be in the Hall of Assembly about the sanctuary, and the sacred tabernacle, and the screen before the entrance of the Hall of Assembly, and 26 the curtains of the court, and the screen at the entrance of the court, that is above the sanctuary, and around the altar, and all the instruments for the whole of the services."
And those enrolled from the 27 families of the Amramites, and from the families of the Izeharites, and from the families of the Khabronites, and from the families of the Azrialites, those who were from the families of Kaharites according to the register,— 28 all the males, from a month old and upwards, were eight thousand, six hundred to form the guard of the Holy Place.
"The families of the sons of 29 Kahath shall encamp upon the south side of the sanctuary, and the com- 30 mander of the families of Kahathites shall be Ahzaphan the son of Azial. They shall be entrusted with the ark, 31 and the table, and the lamp, and the altars, and the sacred furniture, which they shall guard, with the screen, and all the appliances of the services. The prince who commands 32 the Levites shall be Ahzazar the son of Aaron, the priest, who shall be appointed to guard the sacred trusts."
But in conjunction with Merari 33 were the families of Makhli, and the family of Mushi. They were with the family of Merari. They were also en- 34 rolled in the register every male from a month old and upwards, six thousand, two hundred,
"And the commander of the 35 ancestral house of Merari shall be Tzurial the son of Abikhail. They shall encamp at the north side of the sanctuary, and the duties of the sons 36 of Merari shall be the guardianship of the planks of the sanctuary, and the cross-bars, and the pillars, and

1 V. 22 N.B. lit. "from the son of a r.... and upwards. I... I... al of the si... h... su... of le... al... al... Com-
p... S... with R... un... F

he bases, and all the appurtenances,

37 as well as the pillars of the surrounding court, and their bases, and the spikes and ropes.

38 "But Moses and Aaron shall encamp before the sanctuary on the east, in front of the Hall of Assembly, and Aaron and his sons shall guard the sacred things confided to them in trust for the children of Israel; and if a stranger approaches he shall be killed."

39 All the enrolments of the Levites that Moses and Aaron organized before the EVER-LIVING from their families, all males from a month old and upwards, were twenty-two thousand.

Census of the Firstborn ordered.

40 The EVER-LIVING also said to Moses, "Take a census of every firstborn male of the children of Israel, from a month old and upwards, and record them in a register by name.

41 But you shall separate the Levites for Myself,—I, the EVER-LIVING—instead of all the firstborn of the children of Israel, and the cattle of the Levites also instead of the firstborn of the cattle of the children of Israel."

42 Moses therefore enumerated as the EVER-LIVING commanded him, every

43 male of the children of Israel, and all the firstborn males were recorded in the register of names, from a month old and upwards, to the number of forty thousand, two hundred and seventy-three.

Separation of the Levites ordered.

44 The EVER-LIVING afterwards spoke to Moses, commanding;—

45 "Separate the Levites instead of the firstborn of the children of Israel, and the cattle of the Levites instead of their cattle. The Levites shall be

46 Mine; I am the EVER-LIVING. And for the redemption of the firstborn of the children of Israel in excess of the

47 number, take five shekels for each head, by the sacred shekel. Let there be twenty grains to a shekel,

48 and give the money to Aaron and his sons to redeem that excess."

49 Moses consequently collected the money for their ransom from the persons in excess of the firstborn

50 who were ransomed, from the children of Israel. The tax by that money produced one thousand three hundred and sixty-five shekels, by the sacred shekel. Moses gave the money 51 of the ransom to Aaron and his sons before the EVER-LIVING:—as the EVER-LIVING commanded to Moses.

The Sons of Kahath appointed Guardians of the Sacred Vessels.

The EVER-LIVING also commanded 4 Moses,

"Enumerate the persons of the 2 sons of Kahath from among the sons of Levi, by the registers of their ancestral house, from the age of 3 thirty years and upwards to fifty years;—all capable of army service,—to conduct the business of the Hall of Assembly. The work of the sons 4 of Kahath shall be in the Hall of Assembly, Holy of Holies. But 5 Aaron and his sons shall proceed to pitch the tabernacle and to take down the veil of the screen and to cover with it the Ark of Witnesses; and 6 they shall put over it the covering of badgers' skins, and spread the beautiful azure cloth over all, and put in the staves. And spread the azure 7 cloth over the Table of the Presence, and place upon it the dishes, and the cups, and the hammers, and the coronal, and the pitcher, and the bread, arranged upon it. Then they 8 shall spread over them the blue-red cloth, and cover it with the covering of badger skin and put the staves into its handles. Then take the 9 azure cloth and cover the lamps of light, and the reflectors, and the snuffers, and their dishes, and collect the whole of the furniture, whose guardianship is with them, and place them, and the whole of the 10 furniture, under the covering of badger skin, and put them on the waggons. They shall also spread 11 the azure cloth over the Golden Altar, and cover it with the covering of badger skin, and put its staves into it.

"They shall also take the whole of 12 the instruments, the custody of which is with them, to the Holy-place, and cover with the azure cloth, and wrap them in the covering of badger skin, and put them on the waggons. They 13 shall also clean the altar and spread over it the purple cloth and place upon it all its instruments whose custody is with them;—the shovels, 14 the rakes, and sprinklers, and the brushes, and all the instruments of the altar, and spread over them a covering of badger skin, and put the 15 staves into the handles. And Aaron and his sons shall complete the covering of the sanctuary, and the whole of the sacred furniture, at the striking of the camp; and afterwards the sons of Kahath shall come to carry them. But they shall not approach the sanctuary for fear of death. The sons of Kahath shall carry them to 16 the Hall of Assembly, and Aliazar, the son of Aaron the priest, shall provide oil for the lamps, and sweet incense, and pure offerings, and Oil of Consecration,—having the care of all the sanctuary, and all that is in it, with the Holy-place, and all its furniture."

17 The EVER-LIVING also commanded Moses and Aaron;

18 "Separate for Me the family of the Kahathites from amongst the Levites, 19 and do this to them, so that they may live and not die. Let Aaron and his sons conduct them up to the Holy of Holies, and set each of them to the work he is to do, and to his labour. 20 But they shall not approach to see, except the covering of the sacred things, for fear of death."

21 The EVER-LIVING also spoke to Moses commanding;—

Organization of the Ghershonites.

22 "Enumerate the individuals of the sons of Ghershon from the registers 23 of their ancestral house, from thirty years old and upwards to fifty years old. Organize all of them capable of army service, to perform the work 24 of the Hall of Assembly. These are the services for the families of the Ghershonites to work and carry out; 25 they shall carry the curtains of the sanctuary and cover the Hall of Assembly with the covering of badger skin that is extended above it, and the screen at the door of the Hall of 26 Assembly, and the curtains of the court that is around the sanctuary, and the altar, and the ropes, and all the furniture of the services, all this 27 is their service. The sons of the Ghershonites shall be under the direction of Aaron and his sons, for any service; for any carrying, and for any labour, and you shall organize them for every labour by their families. 28 This shall be the service of the families of the Ghershonites at the Hall

of Assembly; and also their duties under the order of Aithamar, the son of Aaron the priest.

Organization of the Sons of Merari.

"Organize the sons of Merari from 29 the registers of their ancestral house; from thirty years old up to fifty years 30 old. Organize all capable of army service, to do the work of the Hall of Assembly. And this is their duty to 31 carry in all the appliances of the Hall of Assembly; the planks of the sanctuary, and the cross-bars; and the pillars and their sockets; with the 32 pillars of the court around it, and their sockets, and pegs, and ropes; with all the furniture and all the instruments; and they shall pack up the furniture carefully for carriage.

"This shall be the duty of the 33 family of the sons of Merari in all their service in the Hall of Assembly, under the orders of Aithamar, the son of Aaron the priest."

Moses consequently organized, and 34 Aaron enumerated the family of the sons of Kahathites from the registers of their ancestral house, from the age 35 of thirty years and upwards to fifty years of age, all capable of army service, for work in the Hall of Assembly. And there were organized from the 36 registers, one thousand, seven hundred and fifty. These were enrolled 37 from the registers of the Kahathites, all for service in the Hall of Assembly, as Moses and Aaron were instructed from the presence of the EVER-LIVING, by the hand of Moses.

The sons of Ghershon were thus 38 enrolled from the registers of their ancestral house, from thirty years of 39 age, and upwards, to fifty years old, all capable of army service, to serve in the Hall of Assembly. And there 40 were enrolled from the registers of their ancestral house, one thousand, six hundred and sixty. They were 41 organized from the families of the sons of Ghershon, all for service in the Hall of Assembly, whom Moses and Aaron organized by the command of the EVER-LIVING.

There were also enrolled from the 42 families of the sons of Merari from the registers of their ancestral house, from thirty years of age upwards to 43 fifty years old, all capable of army service, for the service of the Hall of

44 Assembly, and their number was by the registers, three thousand, two

45 hundred. These were enrolled from the registers of the sons of Merari whom Moses and Aaron appointed by an order from the EVER-LIVING, by the hand of Moses.

46 Moses and Aaron, and the Princes of Israel, with the Levites, appointed all those enrolled from the registers

47 of their ancestral houses, from thirty years of age, and upwards, to fifty years old, who were all to execute the duties of the service, and do the carrying in the Hall of Assembly;

48 and their number was nine thousand,

49 five hundred and eighty. They were appointed by order of the EVER-LIVING, by the hand of Moses, every one to his duty, and to his office, and appointment; as the EVER-LIVING commanded to Moses.

Command to expel Prostitutes and Profligates from the Camp.

5 The EVER-LIVING also spoke to Moses commanding;—

2 " Command the children of Israel that they must send out of the camp all afflicted by contagious disease, and all with venereal diseases, and all

3 of foul life; whether male or female, so that they may not infect the camp, in the midst of which I dwell."

4 The children of Israel accordingly did so, and sent them to the outside of the camp, as the EVER-LIVING had commanded to Moses. The children of Israel did it.

The Law of Forgiveness of Sin.

5 Then the EVER-LIVING commanded to Moses saying;—

6 " Say to the children of Israel, The man or woman who perversely commits any human sin against the EVER-

7 LIVING; that person is guilty. But if they make confession of the sin which they have committed, and would remedy the wrong they have done, and remove it from them, let them add a fifth part to it, and give to him

8 who has been wronged. But if the man does not possess the means of restoration for the wrong he has done, the culprit shall return to the EVER-LIVING, by the priest, in place of it, a ram as an expiation which shall expiate for him as to the wrong.

9 " And every such addition consecrated by the Children of Israel which

they offer through the priest, shall be the priest's. But whatever a person 10 devotes must be his own property; and what a man gives to the priest shall be the priest's property." [1]

Law of Suspicion of Adultery.

The EVER-LIVING also spoke to 11 Moses commanding;—

" Speak to the children of Israel 12 and say to them; If a man suspects his wife of having gone astray, and of a man having had sinful intercourse with her; and that his wife has hidden 13 from his sight that she has been defiled; but he has no witness of it, and she has not been divorced; yet 14 the breath of suspicion has passed over her, and he suspects his wife, that she has been defiled, or that a breath of suspicion has passed over her, and he suspects his wife although she may not have been defiled; then 15 the man shall bring his wife to the priest, and shall bring as a gift for her with her the twelfth of an epha of barley meal, without any oil poured upon it; nor shall he put incense with it,—for it is an offering of jealousy;— an offering of remembrance, for reminding of frailty.

" Then the priest shall make her 16 advance, and place her before the EVER-LIVING, when the priest shall 17 take holy water in an earthenware cup, and some dust that is on the floor of the sanctuary, and put it into the water. The priest shall then 18 station the woman before the EVER-LIVING, and uncover the woman's head, and place in her hands the Gift of Remembrance,—the Gift of Jealousy,—and the bitter water of cursing shall be in the hand of the priest. The priest shall also ad- 19 minister an oath to her, and say to the woman;

" ' If a man has not had connection with you, and if you have not turned to a seducer instead of your husband, be free from the water of this bitter curse; but if you have 20 turned to another than your husband, with whom you have been sinning, and that a man has been to you instead of your husband '—(here the 21 priest shall swear the woman with this oath, and the priest shall say to

---

[1] V. 10. This verse is very obscure in the Hebrew but the version above given seems to be its meaning.— F. F.

the woman)—'then may the EVER-LIVING make you a curse and imprecation among your relatives! May the EVER-LIVING make your thigh to
22 rot and your belly to swell, and may this water of cursing become in your bowels as rottenness to the bowels, and as swelling to your thigh!'

"(Then the woman shall say) 'So let it be! So let it be!'

23 "The priest shall afterwards write these curses on a tablet, and wash
24 them off with the bitter water, and the woman shall drink the water of the bitter curses, and swallow the water of the bitter curses.

25 "Then the priest shall take from the hand of the woman the Gift of Jealousy, and wave the Gift before the EVER-LIVING, and offer it upon
26 the altar. The priest shall also take a handful from the remembrance, and cause it to be burnt at the altar, and after that the woman shall drink
27 the water, and the water drunk shall —if she has been corrupted, and has dishonoured her husband—then become a bitter curse, and swell her belly, and rot her thigh, and the woman shall be a curse in the circle of her relatives.

28 "But if the woman has not defiled herself, and is pure, then she shall be free from them, and be conceiving children.

29 "These are the laws about the suspicion that a woman has turned from her husband and degraded herself;
30 or for a man when there passes over him the breath of suspicion, and he suspects his wife, and brings her before the EVER-LIVING. The priest shall proceed towards them according
31 to this enactment, and free the husband from his passion, and thus continue the woman's marriage rights."

Law of Nazarite Vows.

6 The EVER-LIVING also spoke to Moses commanding;—
2 "Speak to the children of Israel and say to them, The man, or woman who dedicates himself by a vow of separation, as a Nazarite, to the
3 EVER-LIVING, shall abstain from wine and strong drink; he shall not drink of fermented wine, or fermented drink, nor drink any product of grapes, nor
4 eat of fresh or dried grapes. He may not eat during all the period of his dedication of anything made from the vine, either wine or vinegar, or even

grape skins. Nor during the period 5 of his dedication shall a razor be passed over his head, until he has completed the time for which he dedicated himself to the EVER-LIVING. The flowing locks of the hair of his head shall be sacred to the EVER-LIVING. Nor shall he, during 6 the whole period of his dedication to the EVER-LIVING, approach to a dead body; nor defile himself for his father 7 or his mother, or his brother, or his sister, if they die; for the dedication to his GOD is upon his head. All the 8 period of his dedication he is sacred to the EVER-LIVING. Even if anyone 9 shall die near him suddenly, that incident will defile the dedication of his head. To purify himself he shall shave his head on the same day, and it shall be shaven again on the seventh day; and on the eighth day he shall 10 bring two turtle-doves or two young pigeons to the priest, at the door of the Hall of Assembly, and the priest shall 11 use one of them for a sin-offering, and the other for a burnt-offering, and expiate for him about the defilement of his body, and his head shall be sanctified in that day. But he shall 12 separate himself anew for his dedication to the EVER-LIVING, and bring a he lamb of one year as a trespass-offering, for the previous period has failed by a defect in his separation.

Law of Release from Nazaritehood.

"And these are the rules for the 13 Nazarite, at the day when he completes the period of his separation—he shall come to the door of the Hall of Assembly, and present as his gift 14 to the EVER-LIVING a perfect he lamb of the year for a burnt-offering; and a perfect ewe lamb of the year for a trespass-offering; and a perfect ram for a peace-offering; and a basket of 15 cakes of flour mixed with oil; with their food and drink offerings, and 16 the priest shall offer them before the EVER-LIVING, and make the sin-offering, and the burnt-offering. But 17 of the ram he shall make a sacrifice of thanks to the EVER-LIVING with the basket of cakes, and the priest shall also offer the food-offering, and the drink-offering.

"He shall then shave the Nazarite 18 at the door of the Hall of Assembly, at the end of his dedication, and take the hair of his head that he had dedicated, and put it upon the fire which is under the sacrifice of thanks.

19 Then the priest shall take the boiled shoulder of the ram, and one of the unfermented cakes from the basket, and one of the thin cakes, and put them into one of the hands of the Nazarite, who is being released from

20 his dedication. Then the priest shall wave them before the EVER-LIVING, they shall be sacred to the priest, as well as the raised breast, and the raised leg;—and the Nazarite may afterwards drink wine.

21 "These are the laws of separation when anyone vows to give himself to the EVER-LIVING. He shall not dedicate himself, unless he knows he is able to perform what his mouth has vowed. When he has vowed he shall perform it, by this law of separation."

The Priestly Blessing.

22 The EVER-LIVING also spoke to Moses, commanding ;—

23 "Speak to Aaron and to his sons, You shall bless the children of Israel in this way, saying ;—

24 "'The LORD bless you and guard you.

25 The LORD spread His canopy over you,
And be gracious to you.

26 The LORD make His face beam upon you,
And give you peace !'

27 "Then I will place My Name upon the children of Israel and bless them."

The Consecration of the Sanctuary.

7 And when the time came that the sanctuary was finished, Moses erected, and consecrated, and sanctified it, with all its furniture ; and the altar and all its instruments ; and

2 sanctified them. Then the Princes of Israel, the heads of their ancestral houses, the Princes of the tribes and the commanders of regiments,

3 approached, and brought as their gifts to present to the EVER-LIVING six covered waggons and twelve bullocks; a waggon for two princes, and a bullock for each, and presented them before the sanctuary.

4 Then the EVER-LIVING spoke to Moses, commanding ;—

5 "Receive them, and they shall be to perform the work of the Hall of Assembly. Therefore give them to

the Levites, each according to the amount of their work."

6 Moses consequently accepted the waggons, and the bullocks, and gave

7 them to the Levites ;—he allotted two waggons and four of the bullocks to the sons of Ghershon, for their work.

8 And four of the waggons and eight of the bullocks he allotted to the sons of Merari for their work, under the control of Aithamar, the son of Aaron, the priest.

9 But to the sons of Kahath he gave none, for the sacred work they did was laid upon their shoulders.

Consecration of the Altar.

10 The princes also came forward at the dedication of the altar, on the day of its consecration, and the princes presented their gifts before the altar.

Gifts from the Princes.

11 But the EVER-LIVING said to Moses, "Let them offer their gifts at the dedication of the altar, one prince a day, then another prince a day."

12 So Nakhshon the son of Aminadab of the tribe of Judah, presented his

13 gift the first day ; and his gift was a silver dish of a hundred and thirty shekels, a silver watering-can, of seventy shekels, by the sacred weights, both filled with fine flour mixed with oil as a food-offering.

14 One cup made of gold, full of incense.

15 A bullock from the fold ; a ram ; a sheep of the year, for a burnt-offer-

16 ing, one he-goat for a sin-offering and

17 two bullocks for a sacrifice of thanks, with five rams, five he-goats, five sheep of a year old ;—these were the gift of Nakhshon the son of Aminadab.

18 On the second day Nathaniel the son of Tzoar, prince of Issakar, came

19 forward. He offered as his gift a silver dish of one hundred and thirty shekels, a silver watering-pot of seventy shekels, by the sacred weight, both of them full of fine flour mixed

20 with oil, as a food-offering. A cup

21 made of gold, full of incense; a bullock from the fold, a ram, a sheep

22 of the year for a burnt-offering, a he-

23 goat for a sin-offering, and as a sacrifice of thanks, two bullocks, five rams, five he-goats, five sheep of a year old ;

this was the offering of Nathaniel the son of Tzoar.

24 On the third day, the prince of the sons of Zebulon, Ahab, the son of
25 Khelon, presented a silver dish of a hundred and thirty shekels, a silver watering-can of seventy shekels, by the sacred weights, both full of fine flour mixed with oil for a food-offer-
26 ing, a cup made of gold, full of
27 incense, a bullock from the fold, a ram, a sheep of the year, for a burnt-
28 offering, a he-goat for a sin-offering,
29 and for a sacrifice of thanks two bullocks, five rams, five he-goats, five year old sheep—these were the gift of Ahab the son of Khelon

30 On the fourth day, the prince of the sons of Reuben, Aliazer the son
31 of Shadiaur, presented a silver dish of one hundred and thirty shekels, a silver watering-can of seventy shekels, by the sacred weights, both full of fine flour mixed with oil, for a food-
32 offering, a cup made of gold, full of
33 incense, a bull from the fold, a ram, a lamb of the year for a burnt-offer-
34 ing, a he-goat for a sin-offering, and
35 for a sacrifice of thanks, two bullocks, five rams, five he-goats, five year old sheep—these were the gift of Aliazar the son of Shadiaui

36 On the fifth day the prince of the sons of Simeon, Shelumial the son
37 of Tzorishadai, presented a silver dish of one hundred and thirty shekels, by the sacred weight, a silver water-ing-can of seventy shekels, by the sacred shekel, both full of fine flour mixed with oil for a food-offering,
38 a cup made of gold, full of incense,
39 a bull from the fold, a ram, a year
40 old lamb for a burnt-offering, a he-
41 goat for a sin-offering, and for a sacrifice of thanks, two bullocks, five rams, five he-goats, five year old sheep—these were the gift of Shelu-mial the son of Tzorishadai

42 On the sixth day the prince of the sons of Gad, Aliasaf the son of Rauel
43 presented a silver dish of one hundred and thirty shekels, by the sacred weight, a watering-can of seventy shekels, by the sacred weight, both full of fine flour mixed with oil for a
44 food-offering, a cup made of gold,
45 full of incense, a bull from the stall, a ram, a lamb of one year old for a
46 burnt-offering, and for a sacrifice of
47 thanks, two bullocks, five rams, five he-goats, five year old sheep—these were the gift of Aliasaf the son of Rauel

48 On the seventh day the prince of the sons of Ephraim, Alishamah the son of Amihud, presented a silver
49 dish of one hundred and thirty shekels, a silver watering-can of seventy shekels, by the sacred weights, both full of fine flour mixed
50 with oil for a food-offering, a cup
51 made of gold, full of incense, a bull from the fold, a ram, a sheep of a year
52 old for a burnt-offering, a he-goat
53 for a sin-offering, and for a sacrifice of thanks two bullocks, five rams, five he-goats, five year old sheep—these were the gift of Alishamah the son of Amihud

54 On the eighth day the prince of the sons of Manasseh, Gamalial the son
55 of Phidhatzur, presented a silver dish of one hundred and thirty shekels, a silver watering-can of seventy shekels, by the sacred weights, both full of fine flour mixed with oil, for
56 a food-offering, a cup made of gold,
57 full of incense, a bull from the fold, a ram, a year old sheep, for a burnt-
58 offering, a he-goat for a sin-offering,
59 and for a sacrifice of thanks, two bullocks, five rams, five sheep of a year old   These were the gift of Gamalial the son of Phidhatzur

60 On the ninth day the prince of the sons of Benjamin, Abidan, the son
61 of Gadoni, presented a silver dish of one hundred and thirty shekels, a silver watering-can of seventy shekels, by the sacred weights, both full of fine flour mixed with oil, as a food-
62 offering, a cup made of gold, full of
63 incense, a bull from the fold, a ram, a sheep of a year old, for a burnt-
64 offering, and for a sacrifice of thanks,
65 two bullocks, five rams, five year old sheep   These were the gift of Abidan the son of Gadoni

66 On the tenth day the prince of the sons of Dan, Akhiazar the son of
67 Amishadai, presented a silver dish of one hundred and thirty shekels, a silver watering-can, of seventy shekels, by the sacred weights, both full of fine flour mixed with oil, as a food-
68 offering, a cup made of gold, full of
69 incense, a bull from the fold, a ram, a year old sheep for a burnt-offering,
70 a he-goat for a sin-offering, and as a
71 sacrifice of thanks, two bullocks, five rams, five he-goats, five year old sheep   These were the gift of Akhiazar the son of Amishadai.

72 On the eleventh day the prince of the sons of Asher Phinuel the son of
73 Akran presented a silver dish of one

hundred and thirty shekels, a silver watering-can of seventy shekels, by the sacred weights, both full of fine flour mixed with oil, as a food-offer-

74 ing, a cup made of gold, full of

75 incense, a bull from the fold, a ram, a sheep of a year old, for a burnt-

76 offering; a he-goat for a sin-offering,

77 and for an offering of thanks, two bullocks, five rams, five goats, five year old sheep.   These were the gift of Phanuel the son of Akran.

78   On the twelfth day the prince of the sons of Naphthali, Akhaira the

79 son of Ainan, presented a silver dish of one hundred and thirty shekels, a silver watering-can of seventy shekels, by the sacred weights, both full of fine flour mixed with oil, for a food-

80 offering, a cup made of gold full of

81 incense, a bull from the fold, a ram, a lamb of a year old, for a burnt-

82 offering, a he-goat for a sin-offering,

83 and as a sacrifice of thanks, two bullocks, five rams, five he-goats, five sheep of a year old.   These were the gift of Akhaira the son of Ainan.

84   These were dedicated on the altar at the time it was consecrated, by the Princes of Israel:—twelve silver dishes; twelve silver watering-cans,

85 twelve cups made of gold.   Each of the silver dishes was one hundred and thirty, and each of the watering-cans seventy; all the silver vessels were one thousand four hundred, by the sacred shekel.

86   The cups of gold full of incense were twelve; ten to a cup, by the sacred shekel; all the gold was one hundred and twenty.

87   All the bullocks for burnt-offerings were twelve, the bulls and rams, twelve, the lambs of a year old, twelve, with their food-offerings, and the he-goats were twelve for sin-offerings.

88   And all the cattle for the sacrifices of thanks, twenty-four bulls, sixty rams, sixty he-goats, sixty sheep of a year old.   Thus the altar was dedicated after its consecration.

God speaks to Moses at the Dedication of the Altar.

89   Then Moses went into the Hall of Assembly to speak to HIM, and heard the VOICE speaking to him from the Mercy seat, which is upon the Ark of the Witnesses, from between the two Kerubim, there HE spoke to him

Consecration of the Lamps.

And the EVER-LIVING spoke to 8 Moses commanding;—

" Speak to Aaron, and say to him; 2 When you set up the lamps opposite the reflectors, light the seven lamps."

Aaron consequently did so, erecting 3 the lamps opposite the reflectors, as the EVER-LIVING commanded to Moses.   And this was the form of the 4 reflectors, concaves of gold on stalks at the cups.   They were concave that they might reflect the light, as the EVER-LIVING showed Moses, so he made the reflectors.

The Levites consecrated to God.

The EVER-LIVING also spoke to 5 Moses commanding:—

" Take the Levites from among the 6 children of Israel and purify them. Purify them in this manner; pour 7 water for sin over them, and let them pass it naked over all their body, and wash their clothing and purify themselves.

"Then take a bull from the fold, 8 with its food-offering of fine flour mixed with oil, and a second bull from the fold take for a sin-offering, and present the Levites before the 9 Hall of Assembly, and collect all the chiefs of the children of Israel.   And 10 when you have presented the Levites before the EVER-LIVING, then the children of Israel shall lay their hands upon the Levites, and Aaron 11 shall wave the Levites before the EVER-LIVING, for the children of Israel, and they shall be appointed to perform the services of the EVER-LIVING.

" Then the Levites shall lay their 12 hands upon the head of the bulls, and Aaron shall make of the first a sin-offering, and of the other a burnt-offering to the EVER-LIVING, to expiate for the Levites.

"Afterwards station the Levites 13 before Aaron, and before his sons, and wave them to the EVER-LIVING, and separate the Levites from the 14 midst of the children of Israel, and the Levites shall be Mine.   And after 15 that you shall bring the Levites to serve in the Hall of Assembly, but you must purify them and wave them; for they are a Gift, given to Me, from 16 out of the children of Israel.   I have taken them to Myself instead of the first-born product of the womb of all

17 the children of Israel For all the first-born of the children of Israel were Mine, of man or of beast, from the day when I cut off all the first-born in the land of the Mitzeraim I

18 sanctified them to Myself Therefore I take the Levites instead of all the first-born of the children of Israel,

19 and I give the Levites to Aaron and to his sons from among the children of Israel to perform the duties of the children of Israel in the Hall of Assembly, and to expiate for the children of Israel, and that the children of Israel may not be struck when the children of Israel approach to the sanctuary "

20 Moses and Aaron consequently did in conjunction with all the chiefs of the families of the children of Israel to the Levites, according to all that the EVER-LIVING commanded to Moses, regarding the Levites The children of Israel did it to them

21 They also offered sin-offerings for the Levites, and they washed their clothing, and Aaron waved them before the EVER-LIVING, and Aaron expiated

22 for them, and purified them, and after that the Levites went to perform their duties in the Hall of Assembly before the EVER-LIVING, as JEHOVAH commanded to Moses about the Levites, so they did

The Duties of the Levites.

23 The EVER-LIVING also spoke to Moses commanding,—

24 "The Levites shall do this—from the age of twenty-five and upwards they must serve in the duties of the

25 Hall of Assembly, but at the age of fifty they shall retire from service in those duties, and not serve further,

26 except to superintend their brothers in the Hall of Assembly, to keep guard, but not perform the services This is how you shall arrange for the Levites who superintend "

The Passover instituted

9 The EVER-LIVING also spoke to Moses in the Wilderness of Sinai, in the second year after coming out from the land of the Mitzeraim, in the first month, commanding,—

2 "Let the children of Israel make

3 the Passover in their Assembly, offering it upon the fourteenth day of this month, between morning and evening You shall sacrifice it in the

Assembly with all its ordinances, and all its rites "

4 Moses consequently spoke to the children of Israel to sacrifice the Pass-

5 over Therefore they offered the first Passover on the fourteenth day of the month between morning and evening, in the Wilderness of Sinai The children of Israel did all that the EVER-LIVING commanded to Moses

6 But there were men who were unclean from a human corpse, so that they were not able to eat of the Passover or to sacrifice the Passover on that day, so they approached the presence of Moses and the presence

7 of Aaron upon that day, and those men said, "There is a defilement upon us from a human corpse, by which we are prevented from offering the Gift to the EVER-LIVING in the Assembly together with the children of Israel "

8 When Moses replied, "Stay, and I will hear what the EVER-LIVING commands about you "

9 Then the EVER-LIVING spoke to Moses commanding,—

The Unclean to eat the Passover as well as the Clean

10 "Speak to the children of Israel saying, Any one of you who may be unclean from a human corpse, or away upon a journey, or in your families, still let him sacrifice the

11 Passover to the EVER-LIVING, in the second month, he shall offer it It shall be eaten with unfermented

12 bread and bitter herbs None of it shall remain with you until the morning, and you shall not break a bone of it, but sacrifice it with all the

13 ordinances of the Passover And whoever may be clean, and has not been on a journey, and fails to sacrifice the Passover,—that person shall be excommunicated from his relatives, for not offering the gift to the EVER-LIVING with the Assembly That

14 person is guilty for his sin And if a foreigner resides with you and sacrifices the Passover to the EVER-LIVING it must be with the ordinances of the Passover and its rites It must be offered with the same ordinances by you, both for the foreigner and the native of the country "

The Erection of the Sanctuary.

15 On the day of the erection of the sanctuary the cloud covered the

Tabernacle of the Hall of Witnesses, and in the evening there was over the Tabernacle like the light of fire

16 until morning. So it was always—the cloud covered by day, and the

17 light of fire at night. And when the cloud arose from off the Hall, then the children of Israel marched, and at the place where the cloud settled the children of Israel encamped

18 The children of Israel marched at the command of the EVER-LIVING, and they encamped at the command of the EVER-LIVING every day —they encamped where the cloud rested

19 upon the Tabernacle. But when the cloud rested upon the Tabernacle many days, then the children of Israel watched the EVER-LIVING and did

20 not march. And if the cloud remained a number of days upon the Tabernacle by command of the EVER-LIVING they encamped, and at the command of the EVER-LIVING

21 they marched. But if the cloud remained from evening to morning, and the cloud went up at the morning, then they marched, whether day or night, thus when the cloud

22 went up they marched; but whenever for days, or a month, or long periods, the cloud rested upon the Tabernacle the Children of Israel encamped, and did not march, but

23 on it going up they marched. By command of the EVER-LIVING they marched. They waited the order of the EVER-LIVING by the hand of Moses

The Order to make Gongs

10 The EVER-LIVING also spoke to Moses commanding,—

2 " Make two silver gongs for yourself. Make them concave, and use them to call the Parliament, and to prepare

3 the camp for marching, so that when you beat them all the Parliament will know how to come to you at the door

4 of the Hall of Assembly. And if you beat one of them the generals and colonels of the regiments of Israel,

5 will know to come to you. When you beat an Arise, then the divisions of the camp on the east shall march

6 " When you beat the Arise, a second time, the divisions of the camp on the south shall march. They shall prepare to march at the Arise

7 " But when the call to a Meeting you shall blow a trumpet not sound

an Arise. The sons of Aaron, the 8 priest, shall beat the gongs, and this shall be a perpetual institution for your posterity

" And when you go to war in your 9 land, to distress those who distress you, terrify them with the gongs, and remember the presence of your EVER-LIVING GOD, and He will encourage you against your enemies

" Also in the days of your festivals, 10 and in your assemblies, and on the first of the months beat the gongs with your burnt-offerings, and with your thank-offerings, and they shall be reminders for you before your GOD, I am the EVER-LIVING GOD "

The First March from Sinai in Martial Array.

It occurred in the second year, in 11 the twelfth month, that the cloud arose from off the Tent of Witnesses, so the children of Israel marched 12 from the Wilderness of Sinai, and the cloud settled on the Wilderness of Paran. They also marched in divisions 13 by the order of the EVER-LIVING, under the control of Moses

The standard of the sons of Judah 14 marched in divisions as an army, and Nakhshon the son of Aminadab was over that army

And Nathaniel the son of Tzoar 15 was over the army of the tribe of the sons of Issakar,

And Aliab the son of Khelon 16 was over the army of the sons of Zebulon,

Then the sons of Ghershon and the 17 sons of Merari having taken down the Tabernacle marched, carrying the Tabernacle

Then the standard of the tribe of 18 Reuben marched with their army, and Aliazer the son of Shadiaur was over it

And Shelumial the son of Tzori- 19 shadai was over the army of the tribe of Simeon

And Aliasaf the son of Daual was 20 over the army of the tribe of the sons of Gad

Then the Kahathites marched carry- 21 ing the sanctuary, and they erected the Tabernacle after the advance

Then the standard of the camp of 22 the sons of Ephraim marched with their army, and Alishamiah the son of Amniad was over the army

And Gamaliel the son of Phidatzhur 23

was over the army of the tribe of the sons of Manasseh

24 And over the army of the tribe of the sons of Benjamin was Abidan the son of Gidoni

25 Then marched the standard of the camp of the sons of Dan, by regiments, with all the troops of their army, and Akhazer the son of Amishaddi was over that army

26 And Phanuel the son of Akhan was over the army of the tribe of Asher

27 And Akhira the son of Ainan was over the army of the sons of Naphthali

28 Thus the children of Israel marched,—they marched by their armies

Moses invites his Father-in-Law to join Israel.

29 Moses, however, spoke to Rauel the Midianite, the father-in-law of Moses, "March with us to the place that the EVER-LIVING said to us, I will give it to you. March with us, and we will benefit you, for the EVER-LIVING has promised good to Israel"

30 But he replied to him, "I will not go from my country and from my children, with you"

31 But he answered, "Do not now forsake us, for you know the routes of the desert, and you can be eyes for

32 us. And it shall be that if you will go with us then when we receive the success the EVER-LIVING will obtain for us, we will reward you"

33 So they marched from the Mount of the EVER-LIVING three days' journey, and the Ark of the Covenant of the EVER-LIVING marched before them, three days' journey, to guide

34 them to a halting place, and the cloud of the EVER-LIVING was over them by day, in their march from

35 the camp. And when they began their march, Moses stood up and said, "The EVER-LIVING deliver you from your enemies, and march before

36 your face supporting you." But when they encamped, Moses said, "JEHOVAH bring home the many regiments of Israel"

11 But bad people murmured in the ears of the EVER-LIVING,—and the LORD heard it, and was displeased, so the LORD caused a fire to break out amongst them, and it consumed

2 the rear of the camp, so the people called upon Moses, and Moses prayed

to the EVER-LIVING,—and quenched the fire. He therefore called the 3 name of that spot "The Burnings,"[1] because the LORD there burnt them with fire

A Mutiny in the Camp.

But the mixed people who were 4 amongst them, longed, and desired, and wept. Some of the children of Israel also did the same and said,

"When shall we eat flesh? We 5 remember the fish that we ate in Mitzer for nothing, with the cucumbers, and the melons, and the lettuces, and the onions, and the garlic! But 6 now our souls are sick! There is nothing but this manna to look at!"[2]

Moses, however, heard the people 10 weeping, each family at the door of their tent, and the LORD was very angry, and in the eyes of Moses it was bad. Therefore Moses said to 11 the EVER-LIVING, "Why have You brought evil upon Your servant? And why have I not found favour in Your eyes for You to remove the weight of all this people from off me? Have I 12 begotten all these people? or have I brought them forth, that You should say to me carry them in your lap, as a mother carries in her lap, because as a woman I have sworn to feed them? I have no flesh to give to all 13 this nation! who cry to me saying, 'Give us flesh that we may eat!' I cannot feed them! I cannot carry all 14 this nation! They are too heavy for me, and therefore do this to me,— kill me, now, kill me, if I have found 15 favour in Your eyes!—that I may not see myself torn to pieces!"

But the EVER-LIVING answered 16 Moses, "Add to yourself the seventy men from the rulers of Israel whom you know to be able to rule the people and to control them, and take them with you to the Hall of Assembly, and present them there with yourself, and I will descend and speak 17

---

1 Thabarah —F F

2 Verses 7 to 9 are evidently the note of an old transcriber, so I place them at the foot, as not being part of the original text.—F F

And the manna was like coriander seed, 7 and the look of it was like the appearance of gum! The people despised it, but they 8 gathered it and ground it in mills or beat it in mortars, and boiled it in pans, and made their cakes of it, and its taste was like butter of cakes. When the dew 9 fell in the camp at night the manna came down with it.

with you there, and will support you with the spirit that is upon you, and I will put it upon them, and they shall carry, along with yourself, the load of this nation, and you shall not carry it alone.

18 "But as for this People, order them to sanctify themselves for to-morrow, and they shall eat flesh, for the EVER-LIVING has heard their weeping, saying, 'Would that we could eat meat, such as we enjoyed among the Mitzeraim.' Therefore the EVER-LIVING will give them flesh, and they can eat it.

19 They shall not eat it for one day only, or for two days, or for five days, or for ten days, or for twenty

20 days; but for a month's time,—until it is ejected from their mouth, and the greedy loathe it,—because they have turned away from the EVER-LIVING, Who is in the midst of them, and wept before Me saying, 'Why has He brought us from the Mitzeraim?'"

21 But Moses replied, "There are six hundred thousand of marching men in the nation I am surrounded by,—and you say supply them with flesh meat, and let them eat it for a

22 month. If the sheep and cattle are slaughtered for them, could they obtain it? If all the fish in this sea were added to them,—could they obtain it?"

23 The EVER-LIVING, however, answered Moses, "Is the hand of JEHOVAH cut off? Now you shall see whether My Word is honoured or not!"

24 Then Moses went out, and related to the People all the words of the EVER-LIVING, and he selected seventy from the rulers of the People, and

25 stationed them around the Hall, and the EVER-LIVING descended in the cloud, and spoke with him and strengthened him with the spirit that was over him, and placed it upon each of the seventy rulers, and the spirit rested upon them and they addressed the audience, and did not

26 fail. But two men separated themselves in the camp;—the name of one was Aldad, and the name of the other was Midad;—but the spirit fell upon them, for they were enrolled, although they did not go to the Assembly, and they addressed the

27 people in the camp. Therefore a youth ran and reported it to Moses

and said, "Aldad and Midad are addressing a meeting in the Camp!"

28 So Joshua the son of Nun, the lieutenant of Moses, went to enquire, and then said "My Lord Moses, restrain them."

29 Moses, however, replied to him, "You displease me! for I wish the EVER-LIVING would make all the People orators. I wish the EVER-LIVING would lay His spirit upon them."

30 So Moses and the rulers of Israel remained in camp, and a wind came

31 from the EVER-LIVING and brought up quails from the sea, and they were scattered over the camp for a day's journey on this side, as far as a day's journey on the other side, all round the camp, and were heaped on the surface of the ground.

32 Then the people arose all that day and all that night, and all the next day to collect the quails, and the smallest collection was ten bags, and they spread them all about the camp.

33 The flesh was still between their teeth unconsumed when the anger of the LORD burnt against the People, and the LORD struck them with a

34 very great stroke, so they called the name of that spot the "Graves of Greed"[1] for they buried there the

35 people who were greedy. Then the people marched from the Graves of Greed to the Greenfields, and stayed at those fields.[2]

Miriam and Aaron quarrel with Moses over his Marriage.

12 Then Miriam and Aaron quarrelled with Moses about the Kushite woman whom he had taken, for Moses had

2 married a Kushite, so they asked "Has the EVER-LIVING spoken only with Moses? Has He not also spoken to us?" And the EVER-

3 LIVING heard it. But the man Moses was very gentle, more so than any man on the face of the earth.

4 Then the EVER-LIVING spoke suddenly to Moses, and to Aaron, and to Miriam, "Go all three of you to the Hall of Assembly."

5 So all three went, and JEHOVAH descended in the form of the cloud and stood at the door of the Hall, and called Aaron and Miriam. Both

6 of them accordingly went. When He

[1] Kibroth Hattaavah.—F. F.
[2] Hazeroth, in Hebrew.—F. F.

said to them, "Listen now to My words If you are prophets of the EVER-LIVING look at ME When I speak to you, it is a revelation in

7 your dreams It is not the same as with My servant Moses,—he is faith-

8 ful in all My House I speak face to face with him, and in visions, and he has not to seek the EVER-LIVING in enigmas and parables Then why have you not regarded the message

9 of My servant Moses?" And the anger of the EVER-LIVING burnt at them, and He departed

10 Then the cloud turned from above the Hall, and Miriam had become a leper as white as snow, and Aaron recoiled from Miriam now she was a

11 leper, and Aaron said to Moses, "Pray to the ALMIGHTY so that HE may not lay upon us the sin which we attempted, and that we have com-

12 mitted Let her not be like what comes dead from its mother's womb, —with half of its flesh consumed !"

13 Therefore Moses cried to the EVER-LIVING, saying, "I pray GOD to cure her now"

14 And the EVER-LIVING replied, "If her father had spit in her face would she not be disgraced for seven days? Let her be isolated for seven days outside the camp, and after-wards she may return"

15 Miriam was therefore isolated out-side the camp for seven days, and the people did not march until the

16 return of Miriam, but the people marched afterwards, from the Green-fields,[1] and encamped in the Wilder-ness of Paran

A Survey of Canan ordered

13 Then the EVER-LIVING spoke to Moses, commanding,

2 "Send men and let them survey the land of Canan, which I will give to the children of Israel You shall send a man from each tribe of their fathers,—all of them nobles"

3 Moses consequently sent them from the Wilderness of Paran by command of the EVER-LIVING All were nobles, chiefs of the children of

4 Israel, and their names were these — Of the tribe of Reuben, Shamna the son of Yikri,

5 Of the tribe of Simeon, Shafat the son of Khori,

Of the tribe of Judah, Kaleb the 6 son of Jephunah,

Of the tribe of Issakar, Izal the 7 son of Joseph,

Of the tribe of Ephraim, Hoshea 8 the son of Nun,

Of the tribe of Benjamin, Phalat 9 the son of Rafna,

Of the tribe of Zebulon, Gadial the 10 son of Sodi,

Of the tribe of Joseph—the tribe of 11 Manasseh, Gadi the son of Susi,

Of the tribe of Dan, Amiel the son 12 of Gamali,

Of the tribe of Assher, Sethor the 13 son of Mikal,

Of the tribe of Naphthali, Nahbi 14 the son of Wafsi,

Of the tribe of Gad, Ganal the son 15 of Makri,

, These were the names of the nobles 16 whom Moses sent to survey the land, and Moses surnamed Hoshea the son of Nun, Joshua [1]

Instructions to the Spies.

Moses then sent them to survey 17 the land of Canan, and instructed them, "Go up from the south, and ascend to the hills and examine the 18 land, what it is, and what its people are who inhabit it Their strength, their weakness,—if they are few or many And what kind of country it 19 is they live in, whether it is good or bad, and what kind of cities they inhabit, with their camps and fort-resses Also examine the fertility of 20 the land, if it is watered, if there are trees in it or not, and then size, you must also collect some of the fruit of the country, for it is the time of grape harvest"

They therefore went up, to survey 21 the country from the Wilderness of Tzin to the plain that extends to Khamath

Thus they ascended from the south 22 as far as Hebron, where resided Akhi-man, Shashai, and Thalmai, three children of Anak [2] So they only 23 went as far as the brook Eshkol, and decided to cut off a single branch of grapes from there, and carried it on a yoke between two

[1] The Saviour or Victor —F F
[2] The parenthesis, v 22, is apparently an editorial note, not part of the text of Moses —F F

(Hebron was built seven years before Zoan in Mitzai— F F

[1] Katzeroth in Hebrew.—F F

They also took pomegranates, and
24 figs; therefore they named that spot
the Brook of Grapes on account
of the grapes which they cut from
there for the sons of Israel.

25 There they turned back from sur-
veying the country at the end of forty
26 days, and marched and came to Moses
and Aaron, and all the chiefs of the
children of Israel, in the Wilderness of
Paran, at Kadish, and reported the
matter to them and all the Council,
and showed the fruit of the country,
27 and continued, and said ;—

Report of the Spies.

"We have been to the country to
which you sent us, and it is indeed
flowing with milk and honey, and
28 this is its produce; however, the
people who inhabit the country are
strong, and their cities are very great
fortresses, and we saw the sons of
29 Anak there! Amalek inhabits the
south country, and the Hitites, and
the Jebusites, and the Amorites inhabit the hills, and the Cananites
inhabit along the sea, and alongside
the Jordan."

30 But Kaleb had been silent before
the people and Moses. Now he said ;
"Ascending let us go up and conquer
them, for we are able to do it!"

31 But the princes who went up with
him replied; "We are not able to
overpower those people, for they are
32 stronger than us!" And they brought
reports to the Children of Israel
about the country they had surveyed,
saying; "The country that we
travelled over to examine it, is a
country that devours its inhabitants;
and all the people whom we saw were
33 tall men; and we saw the Nephilim
there, sons of Anak, more than
giants, and we were in our own eyes
like locusts,—and we were like gnats
in theirs!"

14 Then all the Council arose and
gave out their votes. The people
also wept in that night; and
2 all the children of Israel complained against Moses and against
Aaron. And all the Council asked;
"Which was better for us? to die in
the land of the Mitzeraim, or for us
3 to die here in this desert? And why
did the EVER-LIVING bring us to this
country to fall by the sword? Our
wives and our children will be
plunder. Is it not better for us to
return to Mitzer?

Then every man said to his brother, 4
"Let us choose a leader and return
to the Mitzeraim."

But Moses and Aaron fell on their 5
faces before all the chiefs of the
children of Israel, and Joshua the 6
son of Nun, and Kaleb the son of
Jephunah, who had surveyed the
country tore their garments, and 7
addressed all the chiefs of the children of Israel and said ;—

"The country that we travelled
over to survey it, is a very, very good
land. If the EVER-LIVING is pleased 8
with us, and goes with us to this
country, He can give us this land
which flows with milk and honey.
Rebel not against the EVER-LIV- 9
ING! and fear not the people of the
country, for we can devour them,
throwing a shadow over them. Since
the LORD is with us, fear them not!"

All the Council threatened, how- 10
ever, to murder them with stones;
but the Glory of the EVER-LIVING
appeared in the Hall of Assembly to
all the children of Israel.

Then JEHOVAH said to Moses, 11
"How long shall I be despised by
this people? How long will they not
trust to Me, in spite of all the wonders I have effected for them? I 12
could strike them with a word and
destroy them, and could make from
yourself a nation mightier than they."

Moses, however, said to the EVER- 13
LIVING, "But when the Mitzerites
hear of it, from the midst of whom
You brought up this people by Your
Might, and the inhabitants of this 14
country hear, who have heard that
JEHOVAH is in the midst of this
People,—who eye to eye have seen
You are the EVER-LIVING, — and
Your cloud has stood over them,—
and with a perpetual cloud You have
marched before them by day, and
with a perpetual fire by night,—that 15
You have killed this People as a
single man,—then the heathen, who
have heard this report of You, will
say; 'Because JEHOVAH was not able 16
to bring this People to the country
that He swore to them, He has slain
them in the desert!' Consequently, 17
now, O! EVER-LIVING, increase
Your mercy, as You promised, saying, 'I am the EVER-LIVING, slow 18
to anger, and of great mercy; for-
bearing towards passion and sin;
and not destroying the helpless;
punishing the fault of the fathers

upon their children to the third and
19 the fourth generation ' Forgive,
now, the passion of this people ,—for
Your Mercy is great, and as You have
endured these people from Mitzer
until now "

20 Then the EVER-LIVING replied,
" I will forgive, as you request ,—for
21 I LIVE FOR EVER, and the Majesty
of the EVER-LIVING will fill the
22 whole earth However all the men
who have seen My Majesty, and the
wonders that I effected amongst the
Mitzeraim, and in the Wilderness,—
yet have revolted from Me these ten
times and not listened to My Voice,
23 —they shall not see the land which I
promised to their fathers,—that is,
all who despised Me, shall not see
24 it. But I except My servant Kaleb
His spirit was steadfast in him, and
he was perfect after Me, therefore he
shall arrive at the country where he
went and his posterity shall inherit it "

The Israelites Retreat.

25 However, as the Amalekites and
the Cananites occupied the valley,
on the next day they turned face and
retreated from them towards the
Wilderness leading to the Sea of Suf [1]

Punishment for the Revolt Denounced.

26 There JEHOVAH spoke to Moses
and Aaron, saying,—
27 " For how long shall I hear the
complaints of this vile mob complaining against Me ? These complaints of the children of Israel that
28 they murmur against Me ? Say to
them, 'As I live, says JEHOVAH,
according to their demand to My
29 ears, I will do to them ! In this
desert their corpses shall fall with
all their officers and rulers, from the
age of twenty years and upwards,
30 who complained against Me They
shall not arrive at the country that I
raised My hand to lead them into,—
except Kaleb the son of Jephunah,
31 and Joshua the son of Nun But
their children which they said would
be enslaved, I will bring in, and
they shall see the country which you
32 despised , but your corpses shall fall
33 in this desert, and your sons shall be

scattered in the desert forty years, for
you shall carry your whoredom until
your bodies sink in the desert By 34
the number of the days when you
should have been examining the
country,—forty days,—a year for a
day, a year for a day, you shall carry
your crimes,—forty years Thus shall
you recognize your rebellion I, the 35
EVER-LIVING, have declared I will do
this, to all this vile mob, who revolted
against Me in this desert —They shall
perish there —They shall die ! And 36
the men whom Moses sent to spy
the country, and who returned and
complained about it, the whole of that
band shall become dung upon the
earth ! Those men shall die who 37
reported bad of the land, to fight
against the EVER-LIVING Yet Joshua 38
the son of Nun, and Kaleb the son of
Jephunah, shall live from among those
who went to survey the country '"

The Israelites Demand a Battle but the Amalekites Defeat Israel.

And Moses repeated these words 39
to all the children of Israel, and the
People mourned greatly At the 40
morning, however, they arose to go
up to the top of the hill, crying,
" Here we are ! Let us go up to the
place which the EVER-LIVING said,
—for we have sinned "

But Moses replied, " What is this ? 41
You transgress the command of
JEHOVAH,—and He is not pleased
You shall not go up,- for the EVER- 42
LIVING is not with you, so you will
be defeated before your enemies, for 43
the Amalekites and Cananites are
before you, and they will defeat you
by the sword, because you have
deserted from the EVER-LIVING, and
JEHOVAH is not with you "

They, however, arrogantly ascended 44
to the top of the hill , but the Ark of
the Covenant of the EVER-LIVING
and Moses did not move from the
camp —So the Amalekites and the 45
Cananites who were encamped upon
the hill, charged down and repulsed
them, and pursued them as far as the
valley

The Laws of Sacrifices and Offerings

Afterwards the EVER-LIVING spoke 15
to Moses commanding,—
" Speak to the children of Israel 2
and say to them,

---

[1] Red Sea literally " The Sea of Weeds "
Not the main sea, but only the shallows at
the head of the Gulf of Suez as the whole
history seems to indicate —F F

"'When you come to your permanent country which I will give to you,

3 and you make a gift to the EVER-LIVING,—a burnt-offering, or a sacrifice to fulfil a vow, or a free-will offering, or in your festivals to make a pleasant breath to the EVER-LIVING

4 with an ox or a sheep, then approaching, present as your gift to the EVER-LIVING as a food-offering, a tenth of fine flour mixed with the fourth of a hin

5 of oil, and of wine for a drink-offering you shall offer the fourth of a hin, with the burnt-offering, or the sacri-

6 fice of a single lamb. Or with a ram, you shall offer as a food-offering a twelfth of fine flour mixed with the

7 third of a hin of oil, and the third part of a hin of wine for a drink-offering, presented as a pleasing breath to the LORD.

8 "'And when you offer a bullock as a burnt-offering, or a sacrifice to fulfil a vow, or as a thank-offering to

9 the EVER-LIVING, you shall offer with the bullock, as a food-offering, three tenths of fine flour mixed with

10 half a hin of oil; and as a drink offering, present half a hin of wine as a gift of pleasant breath to JEHOVAH.

11 "'And the same shall be done with each ox, each ram, each lamb

12 of the sheep, or goats. According to the number which are offered, this shall be done, with each one of the

13 number. Make every presentation in the same way as these, to offer a pleasing breath to the EVER-LIVING.

14 And whatever stranger resides with you, or is settled among your posterity, when he makes an offering of a pleasing breath to the EVER-LIVING,

15 he shall do the same as you do. It is a common Institution alike for you and the foreigner who resides with you. It is a perpetual Institution for your posterity, both for you and the

16 foreigner before JEHOVAH. There shall be one law, and one rule for yourselves and for the foreigners residing with you.'"

Law of Harvest-home Offerings.

17 The EVER-LIVING also spoke to Moses commanding ;—

18 "Speak to the children of Israel and say to them ; 'When you arrive at the country where I will bring you,

19 and eat of the bread of the land, you shall lift it up before the EVER-

20 LIVING. You shall lift up the first cake from the dough the same as you hold up of your grain ;—so shall you hold it up. You must give the first 21 of your grindings to the EVER-LIVING as a lift-offering from your produce.

Offerings for National Sins.

"'But if you wander from, and do 22 not practise all these commands which JEHOVAH has dictated to Moses; all that the EVER-LIVING 23 has commanded to you by the medium of Moses, from the day when the LORD commanded them, to your furthest posterity ; or if your Parlia- 24 ment should inadvertently commit an error, then all your Parliament shall offer a bull from the herd as a burnt-offering, for a pleasant breath to the EVER-LIVING ; with its food-offering and drink-offering, as decreed, and a ram of the goats for a sin-offering ; and the priest shall expiate 25 for all the Parliament of the children of Israel, and forgive them their fault, when they bring the offering to present to JEHOVAH, and make a sin-offering for their fault. 26

Offerings for Personal Faults.

"'But if an individual commits a 27 fault, then he shall present a she-goat of a year old as a sin-offering; and the priest shall expiate for that 28 person for the fault he has inadvertently committed, before the EVER-LIVING. He shall expiate for it, and shall pardon him for it. There is 29 one law for the native of the children of Israel, and for the foreigners among them, for you to observe regarding faultiness. But the person 30 who acts with a wicked hand, whether a native or a foreigner, in contempt of the EVER-LIVING,—that person shall be excommunicated from among his people. For he has despised the 31 command of the LORD and broken His decree, by his sin.'"

The Law of Sabbath-breaking.

While the children of Israel were 32 in the Wilderness, they found a man collecting sticks on the Sabbath day, and those who found him gathering 33 sticks presented him to Moses and Aaron and to all the Parliament, who 34 put him under guard, for they could not decide what to do with him. But 35 the EVER-LIVING said to Moses ;—

"The man must die! Let all the

Assembly kill him with stones outside the camp "

36　The whole Assembly, therefore, took
him outside the camp and killed him
with stones,—so he died as the EVER-
LIVING had commanded to Moses

Israel ordered to make Fringes.

37　The EVER-LIVING also spoke to
Moses, commanding,—

38　"Speak to the children of Israel
and say to them, Make fringes upon
the borders of your clothing always,
and place above the fringes cords of

39　purple, so that the fringes may be
like flowers for you to remember the
commands of the EVER-LIVING by,
and to practise them, and that you
may not wander after your hearts,
and after your eyes, as you have wan-

40　dered after them, but, instead, that
you may remember and practise all
My commands, and live holily to your

41　GOD　I am your EVER-LIVING GOD,
Who brought you from the land of the
Mitzeraim to be your GOD　I am the
EVER-LIVING GOD "

The Revolt of Korah

16　Korah, the son of Itzhar, the son of
Kahath, the descendant of Levi, and
Dathan and Abiram, sons of Ahab, and
Ann, the son of Pelath, the son of

2　Reuben, conspired and stood up to
resist Moses, with a hundred and
fifty others of the princes of the
Parliament of the children of Israel,

3　titled nobles of the nation, and they
addressed Moses and Aaron and said
to them,

"You assume too much to yourselves,—for all the Parliament, all
of them, are sacred, and the EVER-
LIVING is among them "

4　When Moses heard it, he bowed his

5　head, and spoke to Korah and all his
band, saying,

"In the morning JEHOVAH will
make known who are His and sacred,
and who are to approach to Him, and
whom He has chosen to approach to

6　Himself　Let Korah and all his band

7　take bowls for themselves, and put
fire and sweet incense into them, and
the men whom JEHOVAH chooses
shall be the Sacred　You are pre-

8　sumptuous, sons of Levi " And Moses
continued to Korah, "Listen, now,

9　sons of Levi　Was it too little for
you that the GOD of Israel appointed
you from among the families of Israel,
to approach to Him, to perform the

services of the sanctuary of the EVER-
LIVING, and to stand before the
congregation to minister, and in-　10
cluded you and all your brothers with
you,—but would you demand the
Priesthood also? However, you, and　11
all your associates, station yourselves
before the EVER-LIVING together
with Aaron —What is he that you
should murmur against him? "

Then Moses sent to summons　12
Dathan and Abiram, the sons of
Ahab, but they would not come, but
replied—

"We will not come ! Is it nothing　13
that you have brought us up out of a
land flowing with milk and honey to
kill us in this desert,—that you would
dominate over us as a tyrant? You　14
have brought us to no land flowing
with milk and honey ! nor given us
farms and vineyards to possess !
Would you dig out the eyes of these
men ?　We will not come ! "

Moses was very angry at this and　15
said to JEHOVAH, " I have not taken
as a gift even an ass from them, and
I have not wronged one of them "

Then Moses said to Korah, " Let　16
you and all your associates come
before the EVER-LIVING,—you, and
they, and Aaron to-morrow, and let　17
each take a censer and put on it
incense, and present it before the
EVER-LIVING,—each of the hundred
and fifty, a censer, and you and
Aaron, each a censer "

So each took his censer, and they　18
put fire in their censers, and offered
incense upon it, and stationed themselves at the door of the Hall of
Assembly, with Moses and Aaron
Korah also collected all his asso-　19
ciates with himself at the door of the
Hall of Assembly, and the Glory of
the EVER-LIVING appeared to all the
congregation

But the EVER-LIVING spoke to　20
Moses and to Aaron saying, " You
shall be magnified in the midst of this
Assembly,—but I will consume them　21
with might ! ' "

They however fell upon their faces　22
and said, " GOD, the GOD giving life
to all flesh ! one man only has sinned,
—and will you be angry with all the
Parliament ? "

Destruction of Korah, Dathan and Abiram.

Then the EVER-LIVING spoke　23
to Moses saying, " Speak to the　24

Parliament and command them to run out from around the tents of Korah, Dathan, and Abiram."

25 Moses therefore arose, and went to Dathan and Abiram, and the Judges 26 of Israel went after him, and they spoke to the Parliament saying, "Remove from the halls of these depraved men, and touch nothing belonging to them, for fear you should 27 share in their sin." Consequently they came away from the tents of Dathan and Abiram, but Dathan and Abiram came and stood at the opening of their tents, with their wives and 28 children, and infants. Then Moses spoke and said,—

"You shall learn by this whether JEHOVAH has sent me to do all these things, for I have not done them by 29 myself,—if these die as all men die, and the fate of all men falls upon them then the EVER-LIVING has not 30 sent me. But if JEHOVAH prepares it, and the earth opens her mouth and swallows them, and all who are with them, and they go down alive to the grave,—then you will know that the EVER-LIVING has rejected these men."

31 And it occurred that as he finished speaking these words, the ground 32 split under them, and the earth opened her mouth and swallowed them and their homes, and all the men who were with Korah, and all 33 their wealth, and they, and all who were with them, rushed down alive into the grave, and the earth closed over them, and they perished in the 34 midst of the public. Then all Israel who were around them fled with a shriek, for they said, "The earth 35 may swallow us also." Fire also came out from JEHOVAH and consumed the hundred and fifty men as they offered incense.

17 The EVER-LIVING then spoke to 2 Moses saying, "Command Aliazar the son of Aaron the priest, to collect the censers from among the burnt people, and the fire, for they are sacred.

3 "The censers of these sinners are for their lives, and you shall make of them thin spread plates for the altar, for they have been presented before the EVER-LIVING and are sacred, and they shall be warnings to the children 4 of Israel." Aliazar the priest subsequ.... t .. .. which h. burnt p...... ....

and made plates of them for the altar)" "And the children of Israel 5 shall remember the reason why a strange man, who is not of the family of Aaron, may not approach to offer incense before the EVER-LIVING, so that he may not be like Korah, and that they may know that JEHOVAH has spoken by the medium of Moses."

The Parliament and the Crowd Mutiny.

But all the Parliament of the chil- 6 dren of Israel murmured against Moses and Aaron next day, exclaiming,—"You have killed the People of the EVER-LIVING!"

But when the Parliament collected 7 against Moses and Aaron, they retreated to the Hall of Assembly, and then the cloud descended, and the Glory of the EVER-LIVING appeared, so Moses and Aaron came into the 8 front of the Hall of Assembly, and 9 JEHOVAH spoke to Moses, saying,—

"Rise up from the midst of this 10 crowd and I will consume them with might!"

But they fell on their faces and 11 Moses said to Aaron, "Take you a censer and put fire into it from off the altar, and place incense, and go quickly and make an expiation for them, because anger is coming from the EVER-LIVING to strike the profane."

So Aaron did as Moses commanded, 12 and rushed into the midst of the meeting, where the stroke of destruction was on the People, and offered incense and expiated for the nation, and stood between the living and the 13 dead,—and the stroke was arrested. But the dead from the stroke were 14 fourteen thousand seven hundred, besides those who died over the affair of Korah. Then Aaron returned to 15 Moses to the opening of the Hall of Assembly, and the stroke was arrested.

Tribal Staves ordered to be taken away.

The EVER-LIVING also spoke to 16 Moses, commanding,—

"Speak to the children of Israel 17 and take the staves from each of their tribes. The staff from each ancestral house, from each chief of an ancestral house.—Twelve staves, ..d rec rd the ... me of each upon his sta." And record the name of 18

Aaron upon the staff of the tribe of Levi. Thus there shall be a staff from the head of each ancestral

19 house, and place them in the Hall of Assembly with the Witnesses as

20 an evidence for them there. And the staff of the man I may choose shall blossom. Thus I will exclude the complaints of the children of Israel from Me."

21 Moses accordingly spoke to the children of Israel, and each of the princes gave him their staff,—each prince a staff,—each prince of an ancestral house of the twelve tribes. But the staff of Aaron was placed in the middle of the other staves.

22 Afterwards Moses presented the staves before the presence of the EVER-LIVING in the Hall of Assembly.

23 And when Moses came next day to the Tabernacle of the Witnesses, the staff of Aaron had budded and blossomed for the House of Levi! Buds had also come out, and borne flowers,

24 and ripened into almonds. Moses therefore brought out all the staves from the presence of the EVER-LIVING to all the children of Israel, and they examined them, each man taking his own staff!

25 Then the EVER-LIVING said to Moses, "Return the staff of Aaron to the presence of the Witnesses, to keep it as an evidence to the Sons of Disobedience, and let them stop their complaints against Me, that they may not die."

26 Moses consequently did as the EVER-LIVING commanded him. He did it.

The People decree Death to all who attempt to enter the Sanctuary.

27 The children of Israel after that spoke to Moses saying,—"We perceive that we shall expire, we shall perish, all of us will perish. Let all who approach to the sanctuary of the EVER-LIVING be killed, so that we may not all expire."

18 Then the EVER-LIVING commanded Aaron "You and your sons, and the house of your father with you, shall carry the spirit of consecration, and you and your sons with you shall carry the spirit of the

2 priesthood, and your brothers of the tribe of Levi, of the standard of your father, shall also approach with you and attend upon you, and guard you, and your sons with you, before the Tabernacle of the Witnesses. And

3 they shall guard you, and guard all the Hall, together with the sacred furniture. But they shall not approach to the altar, for fear they, as well as you, should die, but they

4 shall attend upon you and guard in watches the Hall of Assembly and all the services of the Hall, and a foreigner shall not approach with them. By them also the holy things

5 shall be guarded, and the altar be guarded so that anger may never come upon the children of Israel. For I have taken to Myself your

6 brothers of Levi from among the children of Israel, to give them as gifts to the EVER-LIVING, to perform the services of the Hall of Assembly. But you and your sons with you

7 shall guard the priesthood, and all the matters of the altar, and of the House of the Veils, and perform the services prescribed for the priesthood. And the stranger who approaches shall die."

Confirmation of Endowments for the Priesthood

8 The EVER-LIVING also said to Aaron "And I, see, I have given to you the guardianship of My High Things, and of all the sacred things of the children of Israel,—I have given them to you and to your sons to consecrate, and to preserve for ever.

9 "These shall be yours from the sacred offerings,—all the gifts offered by fire, all food-offerings, and sin-offerings, and all the presents which they make to Me. They are consecrated strictly to you, and to your

10 sons. You shall eat them in the sanctuary. Every male may eat of them with you. They shall be sacred to you. You shall also take some-

11 thing from all the wave-offerings of the children of Israel for yourself and your sons, and for your daughters with you, as a perpetual Institution. All the clean in your house may eat of them.

12 "All the melted fat, and the best of the vintage, and the first of the corn which they present to the EVER-LIVING are given to you. The first

13 fruits of all that their land produces which they bring to the EVER-LIVING, shall be yours. All who are clean in

14 your houses may eat of them. Every convict in Israel shall be yours.

15 Every thing bursting the womb of any species which they offer to the EVER-LIVING, whether of man or beast, shall be yours; but you must set free for a ransom the firstborn of man, and the firstborn of cattle you

16 shall free for a sin-offering; and they shall be ransomed at a month old, at a valuation of five shekels of silver by the sacred shekel.[1]

17 "You shall not, however, ransom the firstborn of a cow, or the firstborn of a sheep, or the firstborn of a goat, they are sacred; their blood is to be poured out on the altar, and their fat is to be burnt as an offering of pleasant perfume to the EVER-

18 LIVING. But of their flesh, the breast shall be yours, for waving it,

19 and the right leg shall be yours. All the exalted offerings of the sanctuaries, which the children of Israel lift up to the EVER-LIVING, I give to you, and to your sons with you, as a perpetual Institution. It is a covenant of salt for ever before the EVER-LIVING for you and your posterity after you."

Endowments of the National Church.

20 The EVER-LIVING also said to Aaron, "You shall have no possession in the land, and there shall be no portion for you in it. I am your portion and inheritance among the children of Israel.

21 "But to the sons of Levi I give all the tithe of Israel for an inheritance, in payment for the work they perform in the services of the Hall of As-

22 sembly, and if ever the children of Israel offer a sacrifice in the Hall of Assembly, they shall bear the sin to

23 death; because the work of Levi is in the Hall of Assembly, and they shall bear its burden, as a perpetual Institution, for your posterity. Therefore they have no inheritance among

24 the children of Israel, for the tithes of the children of Israel which they bring to lift up and present to the EVER-LIVING I give to the Levites as an inheritance; therefore I have said to them, you shall hold no inheritance among the children of Israel."

The Duties of the Levites.

25 The EVER-LIVING also spoke to Moses, commanding;—

"Speak to the Levites and say to them,

26 "Since I have taken you from the children of Israel, the tithe which I have given to you from them as your inheritance,—you shall present from it as a present to the EVER-LIVING,

27 —a tenth of the tithe with which they are tithed, for your account. You shall also lift up some of the grain from the corn, and a portion

28 from the grapes. Thus you shall present presentations to the EVER-LIVING, from all the tithes which are taken from the children of Israel;

29 and give a part of those presentations to the EVER-LIVING, to Aaron the Priest. From all the presentations presented to the EVER-LIVING, present a part of all the best that is consecrated for you.

30 "You shall therefore command them,[1] when presenting the fat, to account some of it as for the Levites, like the offerings of corn, and the

31 offerings of grapes; and they may eat them in any of their villages, and houses, as their wages on account of their work in the Hall of Assembly,

32 and they will not be committing sin by taking away the fat, and the offerings of the children of Israel. They do no wrong, and they shall not die."

The National Sacrifice for Sin.

19 The EVER-LIVING also spoke to Moses, commanding;—

2 "The following is a constitutional law which JEHOVAH commands, saying;—Command the children of Israel to select for you a red heifer, perfect, and who has not a spot upon her, which has never been under a yoke. Let them

3 bring it to Aliazar the priest, and he shall take her outside the camp and slay her in their presence. Then

4 Aliazar the priest shall take some of her blood on his finger, and sprinkle the front of the Hall of Assembly

5 seven times with the blood, and burn the heifer in their sight with its skin, and flesh, and its dung. He shall

6 burn it to dissolution. Then the priest shall take cedar and hyssop

---

1 V. 16. "It is ten grains" is an ancient editor's note.—F. F

"(It is ten grains)

---

1 V. 30. The "them" here clearly refers to the Nation or Offerers, not to the Levites. If this is not borne in mind the passage seems contradictory.—F. F.

wood, and scarlet wool, and ashes from among the cinders of the heifer

7 "The priest shall then change his clothing, and wash his body with water, and afterwards return into the camp But the priest shall be

8 unclean until the evening Those who burnt her also shall change their clothes, and wash their bodies in water, and be unclean until the evening

9 "Afterwards a clean man shall remove the ashes of the heifer and place them outside the camp in a clean place, and they shall be as a witness to the children of Israel to keep themselves from the impurity of sin

10 "Then the remover of the ashes of the heifer shall strip off his clothes, and be unclean until the evening

The Law against Contagion by a Corpse.

"This also shall be a perpetual Institution to the children of Israel, and to the foreigners who reside

11 among them, that whoever touches the corpse of a man shall be unclean

12 for seven days If he offers a sin-offering on the third day, then he shall be clean on the seventh day but if he does not offer a sin-offering on the third day he shall not be clean on the seventh

13 "Whoever touches a corpse,—the body of a man who died,—and does not make a sin-offering at the sanctuary of the EVER-LIVING, is defiled, and that person shall be excommunicated from Israel, because he has not washed the filth from off himself with water, he shall be unclean while the impurity is on him

Sanitary Laws about Deaths.

14 "These are the laws about persons who have died in a dwelling All who come to the dwelling, and all who are in the dwelling are unclean for

15 seven days Every vessel, also, which is open, unless there is a lid upon the

16 opening, is defiled And whoever touches a man killed in fight, or the bones of a man, or killed accidentally,

17 shall be defiled for seven days You shall consequently take to the defiled person some of the ashes of the fires of sin-offerings, and put them on

18 living water, in a cup and take hyssop and dabble with the water the

man who is to be purified, and sprinkle it upon the dwelling and over all the furniture, and over all the persons who may be there, and over the man who has touched the bones, or the slain, or the dead by accident, and 19 sprinkle the purification upon the defiled at the third day, and upon the seventh day, and make a sin-offering for him upon the seventh day, and he shall change his clothes and bathe in water, when he shall be purified at evening But the man who is 20 defiled, and does not offer a sin-offering, that person shall be excluded from the entry into the Holy Assembly of the EVER-LIVING The defiled not having washed his filth from off him, is unclean Therefore this shall 21 be a perpetual Institution to you, and for this reason the filthy shall change their clothes, and who touches anything filthy shall be unclean until the evening, and all that touches 22 him who is unclean, shall be unclean, and the person he touches shall be unclean until the evening"

March to the Wilderness of Tzin.

All the congregation of the children 20 of Israel afterwards marched to the Wilderness of Tzin, in the first month, and settled in Kadesh Now Miriam died there, and they buried her there However water was deficient for the 2 nation, so they appealed to Moses 3 and Aaron, and the people disputed with Moses, and, complaining, they said,—"Oh that expiring we could die before the LORD' And why has 4 the LORD brought the congregation to this Wilderness,—we and our cattle? And why did He bring us up 5 from Mitzer to conduct us to this vile place? It is not a place of vegetables, and figs, and cucumbers, and pomegranates' and there is no water to drink'"

Moses and Aaron therefore went 6 before the crowd at the opening of the Hall of Assembly, and fell on their faces, and the Majesty of the EVER-LIVING appeared over them

The Waters of Strife. Water brought from the Rock.

Then the EVER-LIVING spoke to 7 Moses, commanding,—

"Take your staff, and convoke the 8 Parliament,—you and your brother Aaron,—and command the rock in their sight, and it will give them water and bring out water for them from the rock, and quench the thirst of the people and their cattle "

9   Moses therefore took his staff from the presence of the EVER-LIVING, as

10   he was commanded, and Moses and Aaron addressed the crowd before the rock, and said to them,

"Listen now you rebels! out of this very rock water shall come for you "

11   Then Moses raised his hand, and struck the rock with his staff twice, and a rush of water came out, and quenched the thirst of the people and of their cattle

12   But the EVER-LIVING said to Moses and Aaron,—" Because you have not been true to Me, to consecrate Me in the sight of the children of Israel,— you shall not bring this People into the land which I will give them '

13   These were the Waters of Strife,[1] —where the children of Israel strove with the EVER-LIVING But He was sanctified at them

The King of Edom asked to Allow Israel to Pass.

14   Moses afterwards sent messengers from Kadesh to the Commander of Edom, to say,—

" Thus says your brother Israel, you know all the labours that we have

15   met How our fathers went down to the Mitzeraim and resided in Mitzer many days, and how the Mitzerites

16   ill-treated our fathers But we appealed to the EVER-LIVING and He heard our voice, and sent a messenger, and brought us from among the Mitzerites, and now we are at Kadesh a village at the edge of your borders

17   Let us now pass through your country We will not pass through farms and vineyards We will not drink of water from the wells, but travel upon the Travelling Highway We will not delay in our march nor extend to the right or the left when we cross your boundaries

18   But Edom replied to him, " You shall not pass through me,—or I will advance with the sword, and fight you "

19   Then Israel answered,—" I will go up by the mountain road, and if I

drink water I will buy it, and I will give a price for biscuits Nothing shall stick to my feet as I pass over "

20   But he replied, " You shall not pass through ! " And Edom came out to fight with the People grievously,

21   and with a strong hand Thus Edom refused to give Israel a passage through his boundaries So Israel turned away from them

March to the Highlands.

22   Then the children of Israel marched, all the nation, to the peak of the Highlands, where the EVER-LIVING

23   said to Moses and Aaron in the Highlands, on the borders of the land of Edom,—

Death of Aaron.

24   " Aaron shall be added to his people, because he shall not arrive at the land which I will give to the children of Israel, because you did not exalt My Presence at the Waters of Strife

25   Take Aaron and his son Ahazar, and ascend with them the Peak of the

26   Highlands, where Aaron shall take off his robes, and you shall put them upon Ahazar his son And afterwards Aaron shall die there '

27   Moses consequently did as the EVER-LIVING commanded, and ascended the Peak of the Highlands, in the sight of all the People Then

28   Moses stripped Aaron of his robes, and clothed Ahazar his son with them, and Aaron died there on the top of the Peak Then Moses and Ahazar came down from the Peak

29   And all the People saw the death of Aaron, all the house of Israel, so they wept for Aaron thirty days

The Cananites of Arad attack Israel.

21   When the Cananites of the kingdom of Arad, who occupied the south, heard that Israel was coming by the road of the Atharim, they fought with Israel, and took some of them prison-

2   ers Then Israel waved a vow to the EVER-LIVING, and said,—

" If you will give this people to my hand, then I will destroy their towns '

3   And the EVER-LIVING listened to the voice of Israel, and gave them the Cananites, so they destroyed them and their towns, and named the district Destruction

---

1 V 13 V Meribah Waters of Strife —F F

Retreat towards the Sea of Weeds.

4 Then they marched from the Peak of the Highlands towards the Sea of Weeds, and skirted the land of Edom, but the retreat depressed the spirit
5 of the People. so the People spoke against GOD, and against Moses,— " Why have you brought us up from the Mitzeraim to die in a desert, where there is neither bread, nor water, and our spirits depressed by
6 this vile food ? " The LORD therefore sent to the People inflammatory serpents, who stung the People, and a great number of the people of Israel died
7 Then the People came to Moses and said, " We have sinned, because we have spoken against the EVER-LIVING and against you Pray to JEHOVAH that He may send the serpents away from us "
So Moses prayed on account of the
8 People Then the EVER-LIVING said to Moses, " Make for yourself a fiery Serpent, and put it up as a standard, —and it shall be that when anyone is stung, he can look upon it and live "

The Brazen Serpent made.

9 Then Moses made a serpent of brass, and set it up as a standard, and when anyone was stung by a serpent and looked upon that serpent of brass, he lived

The March to Aboth and Ain.

10 The children of Israel afterwards marched, and encamped in Aboth
11 Then they marched to Ain-on-the-fords, in the desert that is opposite to Moab from the rising of the sun
12 From there they marched and en-
13 camped at the brook of Arad From there they marched and encamped at the ford of Arnon which is in the desert that extends as a boundary for the Amorites, for the Arnon is the boundary between Moab and the
14 Amorites As it is said in " The Book of the Wars of the Lord "
" He helped them from Soof to the banks of the Arnon,
15 And the source of the brooks near the dwellings of Ar,
Which slope to the boundary of Moab
16 And from there to the Well

This is the Well where the EVER-LIVING said to Moses, " Let the people rest, and provide them water "
Then Israel sang this song,   17

Song of the Well

" Spring up Well to refresh us ,—
Dug by rejoicing princes ,   18
By the People's Chiefs and Ruler ,—
A refreshing gift in the Desert !
And a gift from the rivers of GOD, 19
From the rivers of GOD in the hills

From the heights it passed to the 20
valley ,
To Moab's plain from the Peak of Pisgah,
And clothed the face of the waste ! " [1]

Ambassadors sent to Sihon.

Then Israel sent ambassadors to 21
Sihon, king of the Amorites, saying,—

Request to March through Ammon.

" I wish to pass through your 22
country I will not extend into the farms and vineyards I will not drink water from the wells, and I will march on the Traveller's Highway

---

[1] Note upon verses 18—20 Part of v 18 and all verses 19, 20 are in A V , and R V , translated as a description of marches, not as I do, as a part of the " Song at the Well " But to take those verses as geographical names is a clear contradiction to the context, which states that the Israelite army was on the borders of Moab and the Amorites, waiting for permission to pass over, not five marches —100 miles—from there , as five marches in Oriental reckoning would have been" Therefore I read them as a part of the song of thanksgiving for finding the well after the long waterless marches

However I here add the usual version of the verses as translated in a jargon of Hebrew and English, for those who prefer it

A V Ch xxi , v 18 (part of) to 20 ' And from the Wilderness they went to Mattanah and from Mattanah to Nahaliel and from Nahaliel to Bamoth and from Bamoth in the valley, that is in the country of Moab, to the top of Pisgah, which looketh towards Jeshimon "

To further prove that verses 18 to 20 are a part of the Song of the Well, and not a series of geographical names, consult Ch xxxiii , vv 47—50, where in the Way-book of the Marchings no mention is made of any such places or journeys, as all former trans-
it 's tru   t   r d   - em to be
- 1 1

only, until I have passed over your boundaries."

Sihon Refuses and the Amorites are Defeated.

23 But Sihon would not allow Israel to pass over his borders; so Sihon collected all his forces and advanced to attack Israel in the desert. When he arrived at Yatz, he fought with

24 Israel, but Israel defeated him by the sword, and seized the country from the Arnon as far as the Jabok, from the sons of Ammon,—for that is the

25 boundary of the Amorites. The Israelites also captured all the cities —Israel occupied all the villages of the Amorites,—with Heshbon and all its villages; for Heshbon was the

26 capital of Sihon, the king of the Amorites, for formerly he had a war with the king of Moab, and took the whole of his country from his posses-

27 sion as far as the Arnon. Therefore the poets say ;—

"Bring straw to Heshbon,
And build a city for Sihon,

28 For a fire coming to Heshbon,
A flame from the palace of Sihon,
Shall burn up Ar of Moab,
Going up to the cliffs of Arnon!

29 Alas! for you, Moab, the people of Kemosh!
Your sons are given to flight,
And your girls as slaves to Sihon the Amorite king;

30 And the archers destroy from Heshbon to Dibon,
And waste from Noph as far as to Midba!"

31 Thus Israel occupied the country of the Amorites.

Jazer Captured.

32 Moses then sent infantry to Jazer, who captured it and its villages, and they drove out the Amorites who were

33 there. Then they turned and ascended by the road from Heshbon, when Og, king of Bashan advanced to attack them, he and all his forces, in the battle of Adrai.

34 But the EVER-LIVING said to Moses; —"Fear him not! For I will give him into your hand,—him and all his People, and his country; and you shall do to him as you did to Sihon, king of the Amorites, who resided in

35 Heshbon." They consequently defeated him, and his sons, and all his

forces, until there was not a detachment left to him, and they seized his country.

22 Then the children of Israel marched and encamped again at the fords of Moab, at the ford of the Torrent, opposite Jerikho.

Balak sends for Balaam.

2 When Balak the son of Tzifor saw all that Israel had done to the Amorites,
3 Moab was greatly terrified at the presence of the People,— for they were many,—and Moab was startled at the sight of the children of Israel.
4 Therefore Moab said to the judges of Midian, "Now this Crowd is licking up all round about us, like a bullock licks up the grass of the field!" So Balak the son of Tzifor, the king of Moab, was terrified. Consequently
5 he sent ambassadors to Balaam the son of Beor, of Pethor, which is by the river of the land of the sons of Amo, to invite him, saying ;—

The Letter to Balaam.

"A nation has come out from the Mitzeraim and covers the face of the country, and it occupies my borders.
6 So, now, I pray you to come and curse this People for me, for it is stronger than mine, so that I may be able to defeat and drive it from the country; for I know that whoever you bless is lucky, and whoever you curse is unfortunate!"

7 The princes of Moab consequently went, with the princes of Midian, with presents in their hands, and came to Balaam, and gave him the
8 message of Balak, and he replied, "Stay here to-night, and I will return to you the answer that the EVER-LIVING dictates to me." So the princes of Moab stayed with Balaam.

9 But a Divine Messenger came to Balaam and asked, "Who are these men with you?"

10 And Balaam replied, "Balak the son of Tzifor, king of Moab, has sent
11 to me, 'There is a People that has come from Mitzer and it covers the face of the country. Now come, curse it for me, so that I may be able to fight with, and drive it away!'"

12 Then the Messenger replied to Balaam, "You must not go with them, nor curse this People—for it is blessed."

13 Balaam therefore arose in the morning, and said to the princes of Balak, "Return to your own country, for the EVER-LIVING refuses to allow me to

14 go with you!" So the princes of Moab arose and went to Balak, and said, "Balaam refused to come with us!"

15 However Balak proceeded to send again more princes, and of higher

16 rank than the former, and they came to Balaam and said to him, "Balak the son of Tzifor says thus,—'Do not

17 refuse, I pray you, to come to me, for I will honour you very greatly, and whatever you demand of me I will do, only come, I entreat you, to curse this People for me!'"

18 But Balaam replied and said, 'If Balak would give to me his palace full of silver and gold, I should not be able to pass beyond the command of the EVER-LIVING GOD, to do little

19 or much But yet rest yourselves, I beg, here to-night, and I will learn what the EVER-LIVING may say again to me"

20 A Divine Messenger then came to Balaam at night and said to him, "If these men invite you, arise, go with them But you shall execute the command that I shall command you!"

21 Therefore Balaam arose at daybreak, and saddled his ass, and went

22 with the princes of Moab But GOD was angry because he went, and placed a Messenger of the EVER-LIVING in the path to oppose him as he rode on his ass, and the two youths

23 with him, and the ass saw the Messenger of JEHOVAH stationed in the path with a drawn sword in his hand, so the ass turned out of the path and went on to the field But Balaam struck the ass to turn her into the

24 path Then the Messenger of JEHOVAH placed himself in the hollow path of a vineyard, with a wall on

25 both sides But the ass saw the Messenger of JEHOVAH and she pressed against the wall, and squeezed the leg of Balaam against the wall, and

26 refused to go forward Then the Messenger of JEHOVAH passed on, and stationed himself in a narrow place where there was no room to turn to

27 the right or to the left But the ass saw the Messenger of JEHOVAH, and crouched down under Balaam And Balaam was furious, and struck the

28 ass with his stick Then the EVER-LIVING opened the mouth of the ass, and she said to Balaam "What have I done to you, that you have struck me these three times?"

29 But Balaam answered the ass,— "Because you have vexed me! I wish there were a sword handy to me, that I might kill you on the spot!"

30 The ass, however, replied to Balaam, "Am I not your own ass, upon whom you have ridden from the day I was yours? Have I been accustomed to do this to you?" And he answered "No"

31 Then JEHOVAH opened the eyes of Balaam, and he also saw the Messenger of the EVER-LIVING standing in the path, with a drawn sword in his hand And he bowed and made reverence before him

32 But the Messenger of the EVER-LIVING said to him, "Why have you struck your ass these three times?

33 I was sent to oppose you, for your conduct is perverse before me, and the ass saw me, and turned from my face these three times If she had not turned away from me, I should most certainly have struck and slain you but yet preserved her alive"

34 Then Balaam said to the Messenger of JEHOVAH, 'I have sinned! But I did not know that you stood to meet me in the path Yet now if I am wrong in your sight I will return home?"

35 The Messenger of the EVER-LIVING, however, replied to Balaam, "Go with these men,—but except the words that I shall command you, utter nothing" So Balaam went with the princes of Balak

36 When Balak heard that Balaam was coming, he went out to meet him to Ar of Moab, which is on the banks of the Arnon where his border

37 ends, and Balak said to Balaam, "Did I not send to you to invite you? Why did you not come to me? Am I not quite able to honour you?"

38 But Balaam answered Balak,— "Although I have come to you, I am not now able to speak a word except what the EVER-LIVING puts into my mouth! That I must utter!"

The First Sacrifice of Balak and Balaam.

Then Balaam walked with Balak, and they went into the Palace

39 gardens where Balak sacrificed an ox and a sheep, and sent them to Balaam, and to the princes who were with him. But in the morning Balak took Balaam, and ascended the tower of Bal, and showed from there the whole mass of the People.

23 Then Balaam said to Balak, " Build for me here seven altars, and prepare for me here seven bullocks and seven rams."

2 Balak accordingly did as Balaam said, and Balak and Balaam offered up a bullock and a ram on each altar.

3 Then Balaam said to Balak, ' Stand here by your offerings, and I will go yonder to meet the EVER-LIVING to inquire, and whatever He may show me I will report to you."

4 So he went to a cliff, where Balaam met GOD and said to Him, " I have built seven altars, and offered a bullock and a ram on each altar."

5 The EVER-LIVING then put a speech into the mouth of Balaam, and said,—" Return to Balak and say thus,—"

6 So he returned to Balak, who stood by his offerings,—he, and all

7 the Princes of Moab, and he there began his poem and said,—

Balaam's Prophecy.

BALAAM "From Aram, Balak, Moab's king brought me,—
From the hills of the East I have come."

BALAK "Curse for me Jacob, insult for me Israel!"

BALAAM "How can I curse, whom GOD has not cursed?

8 How can I insult, whom JEHOVAH insults not?

9 Whom I see from the top of the rocks,
And from the hills I survey him—
A People dwelling alone,
And not mixed up with the nations!—

10 Who can number the dust of Jacob?
Who can count Israel's increase?
Let my life die the death of the righteous!
Let my last days be like to his!'"

11 Then Balak exclaimed to Balaam, "What have you done for me? I instructed you to curse my enemies! And yet you have blessed them."

But he answered and said, "Was 12 it not what the EVER-LIVING put into my mouth?—I was obliged to speak it!'"

Balak, however, answered him, 13 "Come, then, with me to another place, where you can look and only see a part of the encampment, and not survey the whole,—and curse them from there!"

The Second Sacrifice of Balak and Balaam

So he took him to the Field of 14 Towers, at the top of Pisgah, and built seven altars, and offered a bullock and a ram on each altar. Then he said to Balak, " Stand here 15 by the offerings and I will go yonder." And the EVER-LIVING met Balaam 16 and put a speech in his mouth, and said, " Return to Balak and say thus,—" So he went to him, 17 and found him standing by his offerings, and the princes of Moab with him, and Balak asked him, "What does the EVER-LIVING command?" Then he began his 18 poem and said,—

The Second Prophecy of Balaam

"Stand up, Balak, and hear!
Listen intently, son of Tzifor!
GOD is not a man to lie,—   19
Or a son of man to change his purpose!
HE has said!—and will HE not do?
And spoken!—will HE not perform?
Blessing, HE ordered me to 20 bless,—
And I cannot reverse it!
He perceived no fault in Jacob, 21
And saw not in Israel wrong!
The LIVING GOD is with him,
And a Kingly Cheer is his!
GOD brought him up from Mitzer, 22
He is like to a mighty bull!
There is no chain for Jacob,— 23
For Israel no subjector!
In time they will say of Jacob and Israel,
What wonders GOD has done!
See the People! how it 24 advances!—
Like a lion it rears and stands!
It lies not down till the prey is devoured,
And its thirst is quenched in blood!"

25 Balak then exclaimed to Balaam, "Alas! cursing, you have not cursed! but blessing you have blessed!"

26 But Balaam responded, and said to Balak, "Did I not tell you this, saying—All that the EVER-LIVING commands to me I must do?"

The Third Sacrifice of Balak and Balaam.

27 And Balak answered to Balaam, "Come now,—I will take you to another place. Perhaps it may be right in the eyes of the Gods, and they may curse for me from there."

28 So Balak took Balaam to the top of the Gorge of Paur,—to the cliff opposite the desert.

29 There Balaam said to Balak, "Build for me here seven altars and prepare for me seven bullocks and

30 seven rams." And Balak did as Balaam told him and offered a bullock and a ram on each altar.

24 But Balaam saw that it was good in the eyes of the EVER-LIVING to bless Israel, therefore he went not, as at the other times, to call upon snakes, but turned his face towards the

2 Wilderness, and seeing Israel encamped by tribes, and seeing the spirit of the EVER-LIVING

3 above them, he began his poem and said,—

The Third Prophecy of Balaam

FIRST STANZA

" Balaam the son of Beor, says,—
And the man with opened eyes declares,—

4 Who heard the speaking GOD dictate,
Who saw the ALMIGHTY Life,
Entranced, but yet with opened eyes!—

5 How lovely, Jacob, are your halls,
What tents are yours, O Israel!

6 They wave like rivers!
Like watered gardens,
Like groves the LORD has planted!
Like cedars beside the brooks!

7 Dew-drops hang from his leaves,
And his seed has plenty of water —
His king shall be greater than Agag
And his dominions exalted

SECOND STANZA

"GOD brought him from Mitzer! 8
What a mighty bull he is!
He devours opposing nations,
Grinds their bones, and crushes the splinters!
He shall couch his paws like a 9 lion,—
Like a tiger—who dare arouse him?
Who blesses you, myself will bless,
And I will curse your curser!"

Balak then became furious with 10 Balaam, and struck his hands together, and Balak exclaimed at Balaam,

"I invited you to curse my enemy, and yet you have blessed him these three times! So now be off, by 11 yourself, to your own country! I said I would ennoble you,—but, however, the LORD keeps you from honours."

Balaam, however, replied to Balak, 12 "Did I not also inform the ambassadors whom you sent to me, that if 13 Balak should give me his palace full of silver and gold, I should not be able to pass beyond the command of the EVER-LIVING to do good or bad? Whatever the EVER-LIVING commands me, I must speak! And as I 14 am going to my country, I will inform you what this people will do to your people hereafter." Then he began 15 his poem and said,

The Doom of Moab.

" Balaam the son of Beor says,—
And the man with opened eyes declares,—
Who heard the speaking GOD, 16 proclaims,
Who knows the intention of the Highest!
Who saw the Almighty in a trance,—
Who fell,—when his eyes were opened!
I shall see Him,—but not now! 17
I behold Him, but not near!
He brings a Star from Jacob!
And from Israel wields a Staff,
That breaks the sides of Moab,
And destroys his warlike sons
And he will seize upon Edom, 18
And possess his enemy Seir,—
For Israel forms his Host, 19
And Jacob's son comes down,
And cuts off those left from the Fort

20 Then he turned towards Amalek and continued his poem and said;

The Doom of Amalek.

"Amalek was the first of the nations,
But his posterity shall be destroyed."

21 Next he looked towards the Keni and continued his poem and said;—

The Doom of the Keni.

22 "You place and fix your house in the rock,
Yet the flame shall rage on the wall of your home!"

23 And concluding his poem he exclaimed,

"Alas! who can stand against God?
24 For He strikes with a crushing hand!
Then woe to Ashur, and woe to Heber,—
For they also at last shall fail!"

25 Then Balaam arose and went and returned to his own country; and Balak also went away.

Israel seduced by Moab's Girls.

25 But Israel remained at The Acacia Woods,[1] and the people polluted themselves by fornication with the 2 women of Moab, who invited the people to the sacrifices of their gods. So the people ate, and worshipped 3 their gods, and Israel joined itself to Bal-peor. Therefore the EVER-LIVING was angry with Israel, and 4 the LORD said to Moses, "Seize the whole of the chiefs of the People, and hang them before the EVER-LIVING in open sunlight, so that the burning anger of the LORD may be turned from Israel."

5 Consequently Moses said to the rulers of Israel, "Each of you slay the men who have joined themselves to Bal-peor."

6 But a prince of the children of Israel went and brought to his brothers a Midianitess in the sight of Moses, and in the sight of all the Parliament of the children of Israel, while they were weeping at the door of the Hall of Assembly.

7 When Phinehas the son of Aliazer, the son of Aaron, the priest, saw it, he arose from among the Parliament, and took a javelin in his hand, and 8 went after the Israelite to his tent, and stabbed both the man of Israel and the woman through their bodies, and arrested the plague upon the children of Israel. But those who 9 died from the plague were twenty-four thousand.

Promise to Phinehas for Zeal.

Then the EVER-LIVING spoke to 10 Moses, commanding;—

"Phinehas the son of Aliazer, the 11 son of Aaron the priest, has turned death away from the children of Israel, by the zeal with which he was zealous for Me among them. There- 12 fore I command to give to him the bond of peace; and he and his heirs 13 after him shall have an enduring priesthood, because he was zealous for his God; therefore he shall expiate for the children of Israel."

But the name of the Israelite who 14 was killed when the Midianitess was killed, was Zimri, the son of Salwa, an ancestral prince of the house of Simeon; and the name of the 15 Midianitess was Kosbi, the daughter of Tzur, chief of a tribe of an ancestral house of Midian.

Order to attack Midian.

The EVER-LIVING spoke to Moses, 16 commanding;—

"Assail the Midianites, and cut 17 them off from you, for they troubled 18 you by their plots, which they contrived against you in the affair of Kosbi the daughter of a prince of Midian, their sister, who was slain at the time of the plague, about the Peor matter; when the plague 19 was ended."

A Fresh Census ordered.

The EVER-LIVING afterwards also 26 commanded to Moses, and to Aliazer the son of Aaron the priest, saying; "Take a census of all the families 2 of the children of Israel, from the age of twenty years and upwards by the houses of their ancestors, all in Israel capable of army service."

Consequently Moses commanded 3 Aliazer the priest, while they were at the fords of Moab, by the Torrent near Jeriko, saying;

[1] "Shittim" in Hebrew

4   " From the age of twenty years and upwards, as the EVER-LIVING commanded to Moses, when the children of Israel were brought up from the land of Mitzer "

Census of the Hereditary Nobles of Israel.

5   Reuben was firstborn son of Israel, of Reuben, Khanok, from him were the families of the Khanokites,

From Philua, the families of the Philuaites,

6   From Hezron, the families of the Hezronites,

From Karmi, the families of the Karmites,

7   These were the families of the Reubenites, and there were enrolled forty-three thousand, seven hundred and thirty

8   And the son of Philua was Eliab,

9   And the sons of Eliab Nemuell, and Dathan, and Abiram,—from him came Dathan and Abiram who excited the Parliament that revolted against Moses and Aaron, in the revolt of Korah, when they rebelled against

10   the EVER-LIVING, but the earth opened her mouth and swallowed them and Korah into death, with all those persons to the number of one hundred and fifty men, who had

11   joined them But the son of Korah did not die

12   The sons of Simeon by their families were,—

From Namuel, the families of the Namuelites,

From Jamin, the families of the Jaminites,

From Jakin, the families of the Jakinites,

13   From Zarakh, the families of the Zarakhites,

From Shaul, the families of the Shaulites,

14   These were the families of the Simeonites,—twenty-two thousand, two hundred

15   The sons of Gad by their families were,—

From Tziphon, the families of the Tziphonites,

From Khaghi, the families of the Khaghites,

From Shuni, the families of the Shunites,

16   From Azni, the families of the Aznites,

From Ari, the families of the Arites,

From Arod, the families of the 17 Arodites,

From Arah, the families of the Aralites,

These were the families of the sons 18 of Gad, there were enrolled of them forty thousand, five hundred

The sons of Judah, Ar, and Onnan, 19 but Ar and Onnan died in the land of Canan

These, however, were the sons of 20 Judah by their families,

From Shelah, the families of the Shelaites,

From Pheretz, the families of the Pheretzites,

From Zerakh, the families of the Zerakhites,

And there were of the sons of 21 Pheretz,

From Khatzran, the families of the Khatzranites,

From Khamal the families of the Khamalites,

These were the families of Judah 22 who were enrolled, seventy-six thousand, five hundred

The sons of Issakar by their families 23 were,—

From Thola, the families of the Tholites,

From Phuwah, the families of the Phuites,

From Yashub, the families of the 24 Yashubites,

From Shimron, the families of the Shimronites,

These were the families of Issakar, 25 with an enrolment of sixty-four thousand, three hundred

The sons of Zebulon by their 26 families were,—

From Sored, the families of the Soredites,

From Alan, the families of the Alanites,

From Yakhlal, the families of the Yakhlalites.

These were the families of the 27 Zebulonites, with an enrolment of sixty thousand, five hundred

The sons of Joseph, by the families 28 of Manasseh and Ephraim were,—

The sons of Manasseh,   29

From Makir, the families of the Makirites,

But Makir begot Gilad—from Gilad were the families of the Giladites,

These were the sons of Gilad,   30

From Aiazar the families of the Aiazarites,

From Khelag, the families of the Khelagites,

31 From Asrial the families of the Asrialites,

From Shekem the families of the Shekemites,

32 From Shemida, the families of the Shemidaites,

From Khefer, the families of the Kheferites,

33 From Tzilafkad, the son of Khifir, there were no sons, but only daughters, and the names of the daughters of Tzilafkad were Makhlah, and Noah, Khaglah, Milkar and Thirtzah

34 These were the families of Manasseh enrolled, fifty-two thousand and seven hundred

35 These were the sons of Ephraim by their families,

From Shuthlakh were the families of the Shuthlakhites,

From Beker, the families of the Bekerites,

From Thakhan, the families of the Thakhanites,

36 And these were the sons of Shuthlakh,

From Aran, the families of the Aranites,

37 These were the families of the sons of Ephraim, by enrolment, thirty-two thousand, five hundred These were the sons of Joseph by their families

38 The sons of Benjamin by their families were,—

From Bola, the families of the Bolites,

From Ashbel, the families of the Ashbelites,

From Akhim, the families of the Akhirmites,

39 From Shifafam, the families of the Shifafamites,

From Khofam, the families of the Khofamites,

40 And there were sons of Bola, Arad, and Naman,

From Arad, the families of the Aradites,

From Naman, the families of the Namanites,

41 These were the sons of Benjamin by their families, by enrolment, forty-five thousand, six hundred

42 These were the sons of Dan by their families,

From Shukham, the families of the Shukhamites,

These were the families of Dan by 43 their families, all the families of the

Shukhamites, by enrolment, were sixty-four thousand, four hundred,

The sons of Asher by their families 44 were,

From Imna, the families of the Imnites,

From Ishua, the families of the Ishuites,

From Beriah, the families of the Beriahites,

From the sons of Beriah,   45

From Kheber, the families of the Kheberites,

From Malkiel, the families of the Malkielites,—and the name of the daughter of Asher was Sarakh

These were the families of the sons 46 of Asher, by enrolment, fifty thou- 47 sand, four hundred

The sons of Naphthali, by their 48 families, were,

From Yakhzal, the families of the Yakhzalites,

From Guni, the families of the Gunites,

From Itzri, the families of the 49 Itzrites,

From Shilam, the families of the Shilamites,

These were the families of Naph- 50 thali, by their families, by enrolment, forty-five thousand, four hundred

These were enrolled of the sons 51 of Israel, six hundred and one thousand, seven hundred and thirty (601,730)

Division of the Land ordered.

The EVER-LIVING afterwards 52 spoke to Moses and said,

" You shall divide the country into 53 estates for them according to the number of the names To the more 54 numerous you shall increase the portions, and to the lesser lessen the portions, each according to the enrolment shall be given their possessions You shall distribute the 55 portions of land by lots They shall 56 inherit by the names of the tribes of their fathers "

The Noble Families of Levi.

These, also, were the chiefs of 57 Levi, by their families,

From Ghershon, the families of the Ghershonites,

From Kahath, the families of the Kahathites,

From Merari, the families of the Merarites,

58   These are the families of the Levites,

The family of Libni, the family of Khabani, the family of Makhli, the family of Mushi, the family of Kharaki, and Kahath begot Amram,

59   and the name of Amram's wife was Yokabed, a descendant of Levi, who was born to Levi in Mitzer,[1] and she bore to Amram, Aaron, and Moses,

60   and Miriam their sister. And there were born to Aaron, Nadab and Abihua, and Aliazer, and Aithamar.

61   But Nadab and Abihua died in presenting strange fire in the presence of the EVER-LIVING.

62   Their enrolment was twenty-three thousand, all males from a month old and upwards. But they were not numbered among the children of Israel, for no portion was given to them among the children of Israel.

63   This was the census taken by Moses and Aliazer the priest, when they enumerated the sons of Israel at the Fords of Moab near the

64   Torrent, by Jeriko. But among these there was not one who had been enrolled by Moses and Aaron the priest when they enumerated the children of Israel in the desert of

65   Sinai, for the EVER-LIVING had said, "They should die in the desert and there should not remain a man of them, except Kaleb, the son of Jephanah, and Joshua, the son of Nun."

The Law of Heiresses

27   On one occasion the daughters of Tzilafkad, the son of Khafer, the son of Makir, the son of Manasseh, the son of Joseph,—(and the names of these girls were Makhlah, Noah, and Khaglah and Mikah, and Thirt-

2   zah,)—approached, and placed themselves before Moses, and Aliazer the priest, and the Princes, and all the Parliament at the opening of the Hall of Assembly, saying,—

3   "Our father died in the desert, for he was among the confederacy who revolted against the EVER-LIVING with the associates of Korah, and he died for his sin, and he had no

4   sons. Why should the name of our

father be taken from among his family because he had not a son? Give us an inheritance among the brothers of our father."

Moses therefore presented it for 5 decision before the EVER-LIVING, and JEHOVAH commanded Moses 6 saying,—

"What the daughters of Tzilafkad 7 have asked of you grant—Give them a share to inherit amongst the brothers of their father, and assign the inheritance of their father to them. You shall also command the 8 children of Israel, that, when a man dies and has not a son, you shall assign his estate to his daughters. But if he has no daughter you shall 9 assign his estate to his brother. But if he has no brother then you 10 shall give his estate to his father, or 11 to his next of kin of his own family, and he shall possess it, and this shall be an institution of justice, which the EVER-LIVING commands to Moses."

The Death of Moses fixed

Then the EVER-LIVING said to 12 Moses, "Ascend this hill by the fords, and survey the country which I have given to the children of Israel. When 13 you have seen it, you shall be added to your fathers, yourself, as Aaron your brother was added, because you 14 rebelled openly in the Wilderness of Tzin, when the Parliament rebelled, in not sanctifying Me at the Waters, in their sight, at the Waters of Strife in the Wilderness of Tzin."

And Moses replied to the EVER- 15 LIVING and said, "Appoint a man, 16 LIVING GOD of the breath of all flesh, over the Assembly, who may 17 go out before them and come in before them, and who can lead them out and bring them back, so that the Assembly of the EVER-LIVING may not be like sheep without a shepherd."

Joshua appointed to succeed Moses.

The EVER-LIVING replied to 18 Moses "Take to yourself Joshua the son of Nun, a man who has spirit in him, and strike your hand upon him, and place him before Aliazer the 19 priest, and before all the Parliament, and appoint him in their sight, and 20 put your Majesty upon him, so that all the representatives of the children of Israel may listen to him. Thus 21

---

1 V. 59 "Born to Levi in Mitzer," in the Hebrew idiom of language, does not mean to Levi personally, but simply a descendant of the Tribe. The length of time makes it impossible for him to have been Levi's personal child.— F. F.

let him stand in the presence of
Aliazer the priest, who shall enquire
for him by the decision of the Urim
in the presence of JEHOVAH. At his
command they shall come in, and at
his command they shall go out, and
all the children of Israel with him,
and all their Parliament."

22   Moses therefore did as the EVER-
LIVING ordered him, and took Joshua,
and stationed him before Aliazer the
23 priest, and before the Parliament, and
struck his hand upon him, and he
was appointed as the LORD commanded to Moses.

The Shewbread ordered, and Daily Offerings.

28   Then the EVER-LIVING spoke to
Moses and said;

2   "Command the children of Israel
and say to them; You shall take
care to present to Me the Shewbread, as an acceptable offering, at
3 the proper times. Also give them
this order about the offering which
they are to make to the EVER-LIVING
of the two perfect lambs of a year old
daily, as a perpetual burnt-offering.
4 They shall offer one lamb at daybreak, and offer the second in the
5 afternoon; with the tenth of an
ephah of fine flour mixed with a
6 quarter of a hin of beaten oil; sacrifices such as were made constantly
at Mount Sinai, for a delightful offer-
7 ing to the EVER-LIVING. With a
drink-offering of a quarter of a hin
for each lamb to pour as a drink-
8 offering to JEHOVAH. And sacrifice
the second lamb in the afternoon as
a grateful, pleasant perfume to the
EVER-LIVING.

9   "But upon the Sabbath day two
perfect lambs of a year old, with two
tenths of fine flour mixed with the
10 oil and the drink-offering. That shall
be the burnt-offering for the Sabbath, as well as the perpetual burnt-
offerings with their drink-offerings.

11   "And on the first of the month you
shall present as a burnt-offering to
the EVER-LIVING, two bullocks from
the fold, and one ram, with seven
12 perfect he-lambs of a year old, and
three tenths of fine flour mixed with
oil as a food-offering for a bullock;
and two tenths of fine flour mixed
with oil as a food-offering with a
13 single ram, and a tenth of an asheran
of fine flour mixed with oil to one

lamb, as a sacrifice of pleasant scent
to the EVER-LIVING, and their drink- 14
offerings shall be half a hin for a
bullock, and the third of a hin of
wine for the ram, and a quarter of a
hin of wine for a lamb. This shall
be the burnt-offering month by
month for every month of the year;
with one ram of the goats for a sin- 15
offering to the EVER-LIVING. It
shall be offered along with the perpetual burnt-offering and the drink-
offering.

"In the first month also,—on the 16
fourteenth day of the month,—is the
Passover of the EVER-LIVING; and 17
on the fifteenth day of this month
shall be a festival of seven days,
when biscuits shall be eaten. On the 18
first day proclaim a holy rest. You
shall do no labouring work, but present 19
as a sweet burnt-offering to the EVER-
LIVING, two bullocks from the herd,
and a ram, and seven lambs of a year
old. Perfect ones shall be chosen;
with a food-offering of three tenths 20
of fine flour mixed with oil, for each
bullock, and two tenths offered with
the ram. A single tenth shall be 21
offered with each lamb of the seven
lambs. One he-goat also for a sin- 22
offering, to expiate for you; you 23
shall offer these beside the sacrifice
at daybreak, which is offered continually. Do the same daily for 24
seven days offering bread as a sweet,
delightful perfume to the EVER-
LIVING. It must be offered besides
the perpetual burnt offering, and
drink-offering. Proclaim also that 25
the seventh day shall be holy to
you. You shall do no labouring work
in it.

"And upon the Day of First-fruits 26
you shall present a bread-offering
from the land to the EVER-LIVING,
when a holiday shall be proclaimed
as a rest for you. You shall not do
any labouring work in it; but present, 27
as a burnt-offering, delightful to the
EVER-LIVING, two bullocks from the
herd and a ram with seven lambs of
a year old, and as a bread-offering, 28
three tenths of fine flour mixed with
oil for each bullock, and two tenths
with a ram, with a tenth of an 29
asheran for each lamb, of the seven
lambs; and a he-goat to expiate for 30
you; beside perpetual sacrifices and 31
the bread-offerings you offer daily,
there shall be these with their drink-
offerings

29 "And in the seventh month you shall proclaim the first of the month holy to the EVER-LIVING You shall do no servile work Make it your
2 day of rejoicing to the LORD, and offer as a burnt-offering delightful to the EVER-LIVING a bullock from the fold, a ram, and seven perfect lambs
3 of a year old, and as a bread-offering three tenths of fine flour mixed with oil for the bullock,—two tenths with
4 the ram, and one tenth with each one
5 of the seven lambs, and a ram of the goats as a sin-offering to expiate for
6 you, beside the burnt-offerings of the month, and the food-offerings, and their bread-offerings, and drink-offerings as decreed, for a pleasant scent to the EVER-LIVING
7 "And you shall proclaim the tenth of the seventh month holy to the EVER-LIVING, when you shall lower
8 your lives, and do no work, but offer in burnt-offerings to the EVER-LIVING as a sweet perfume, a bullock from the herd, a ram, seven perfect
9 lambs of a year old, and as a bread-offering three tenths of fine flour mixed with oil for the bullock, two
10 tenths for the ram, the tenth of an asheran for each one of the seven
11 lambs, with a ram of the goats as a sin-offering, beside the sin-offerings of expiation, and the perpetual sacrifices, and the food-offerings and drink-offerings
12 "And you shall also proclaim the fifteenth day of the seventh month holy to you You shall not do any labouring work in it, but feast a festival to the
13 EVER-LIVING for seven days Then you shall present as a burnt-offering of delightful scent to JEHOVAH, thirteen bullocks, two rams, fourteen he-lambs for a year old They
14 shall be perfect, with their food-offerings of three tenths of fine flour mixed with oil, to each bullock, of the thirteen bullocks, two tenths to
15 each ram of the two rams, and a tenth of an asheran to each of the
16 lambs, of the fourteen lambs, with a he-goat as a sin-offering, beside the perpetual food-offerings and drink-offerings
17 "And upon the second day, twelve perfect bullocks from the herd, two rams, fourteen lambs of a year old,
18 with bread-offerings and drink-offerings for the bullocks for the rams and for the goats, as the rule as

decreed, with a ram of the goats as 19 a sin-offering, beside the perpetual sacrifices with their bread and drink offerings
"And upon the third day, twelve 20 perfect bullocks, two rams, fourteen lambs of a year old, with bread and 21 drink offerings with the bullocks, rams, and lambs, according to the rule decreed, and a goat for a sin- 22 offering, beside the perpetual sacrifices, and their bread and drink offerings
"And upon the fourth day, ten 23 perfect bullocks, two rams, fourteen lambs of a year old, with bread and 24 drink offerings according to the rule decreed, and a he-goat for a sin- 25 offering, beside the perpetual sacrifices with their bread and drink offerings
"And upon the fifth day,—nine 26 perfect bullocks, two rams, fourteen lambs of a year old, with bread and 27 drink offerings for the bullocks, for the rams, and for the lambs according to the rule decreed, and a he- 28 goat for a sin-offering, beside the perpetual sacrifices, with their bread and drink offerings
"And upon the sixth day,—eight 29 perfect bullocks, two rams, fourteen lambs of a year old, with bread and 30 drink offerings for the bullocks, for the rams, and for the lambs, according to the rule decreed, with a he- 31 goat for a sin-offering, beside the perpetual sacrifices, with their bread and drink offerings
"And upon the seventh day,— 32 seven perfect bullocks, two rams, fourteen lambs of a year old with 33 bread and drink offerings for the bullocks, the rams, and lambs, according to the rule decreed, and a 34 he-goat for a sin-offering, beside the perpetual sacrifices, with their bread and drink offerings
"And upon the eighth day you 35 shall have a Festival You shall do no servile work, but present as a 36 sacrifice of delightful scent to the EVER-LIVING a perfect bullock, a ram, and seven lambs of a year old, with bread and drink offerings for 37 the bullock, for the ram, and for the lambs, according to the rule decreed, with a he-goat for a sin-offering, 38 beside the perpetual sacrifices with their bread and drink offerings You 39 shall sacrifice these to the EVER-LIVING in your Festivals your

vows, and free-will offerings, with your sacrifices, and your bread and drink offerings, and your thank-offering "

30 Moses consequently reported to the children of Israel all that the EVER-LIVING commanded to Moses

The Law of Vows to God.

2 Then Moses addressed the chiefs of the tribes of the children of Israel, saying ,

"This is the thing that the EVER-LIVING commands,

3 "A person who vows a vow to JEHOVAH, or swears an oath to bind his soul, shall not repudiate his word, but perform all that has come out of his mouth

Law of Vows by Women

4 "And a woman who has vowed a vow to the EVER-LIVING, but who is yet in the house of her father in her

5 youth, when her father hears of her vow, and the bond with which she has bound her soul, and her father is silent upon it, then every vow shall stand, and every bond shall stand, with which she has bound her soul

6 But if her father comes to forbid her at the time he hears of any vow or bond with which she has bound her soul, it shall not stand , and JEHOVAH will release her, because her father forbids it

7 "But if she has a husband, and she takes a vow upon her, or rashly utters from her lips what might bind

8 her soul , when her husband hears of it, if he keeps silent to her at the time he hears, then the vow and bond with which she has bound her

9 soul shall stand , but if at the time her husband hears of it, he prohibits it , then the vow which she has vowed upon herself, and the rash utterance of her lips by which she has bound her soul, shall be annulled, and the EVER-LIVING will release it

10 "But the vow of a widow, or a divorced woman,—all that they bind upon their souls shall stand upon them

11 "Yet if the mistress of a house binds a bond upon her soul with an

12 oath , if when her husband hears of it he keeps silent to her, not forbidding it, then every vow and every bond which she has bound upon her

soul shall stand But if at the time 13 her husband hears it he annuls them, all that came out of her lips as a vow, or a bond upon her soul, shall not stand Her husband has annulled it, and the EVER-LIVING will release it Every vow and every oath bind- 14 ing to afflict the soul, her husband may confirm and her husband may annul , but if her husband keeps 15 silent to her from day to day, then he confirms them , for he was silent to her at the time he heard But if 16 he annuls them, after having heard of them, then he takes away any blame "

These are the laws that the EVER- 17 LIVING commanded to Moses about husband and wife , and about father and young girl in the house of her father

War with Midian commanded.

The EVER-LIVING spoke to Moses 31 and said ,—

"Arouse the children of Israel 2 against the Midianites after you have enumerated your people "

Moses therefore spoke to the People 3 saying ,—

"Select from yourselves officers for a war with the Midianites, for the LORD has ordered an advance against Midian, of a thousand from each 4 tribe, from all the tribes of Israel, to go upon an expedition " So they 5 massed from the tribes of Israel, by a thousand from each tribe, twelve thousand chosen for the war, and 6 Moses sent the thousand from each tribe to the war, with Phinehas the son of Ahazer the priest, and the sacred furniture, and the gongs in his possession to encourage them These made war against Midian as 7 the EVER-LIVING commanded Moses, and slew every leader They also 8 slew the kings of Midian in the slaughter, Air, and Rekem, and Tzur, and Khur, and Raba, the five kings of Midian, and also slew Balaam the son of Beor with the sword

Then the children of Israel took 9 possession of the women of Midian, with their children, and all the cattle, and all their property, and all their people, as booty, with all the villages which they inhabited, and burnt all 10 their furniture with fire, and carried off 11 all the plunder, and all the spoil from the field and from the person Then 12 they brought the captives to Moses, and Aliazer the priest, and to the Parliament of the children of Israel, along with the plunder, and the booty, to the camp at the Fords of Moab, which was beside the Torrent near Jeriko.

13 Then Moses and Aliazer the priest, with all the princes of the Parliament went out to meet them outside the

14 camp. But Moses was angry with the officers of the army, the colonels of regiments, and captains of companies, who returned with the army

15 from the war, and Moses asked them ;

"Why have you kept the women alive ? What were they to the children of Israel under the advice of

16 Balaam ?—They seduced them to desert the EVER-LIVING in the affair of Peor, and they brought a pestilence upon the congregation of JEHOVAH.

17 Now, therefore, kill every male child, and every woman who has known

18 man sexually,—kill ! But let every young girl who has not known a man

19 sexually live for yourselves. Also pitch your tents outside the camp for seven days, all who have killed a person, or been wounded in battle. You must be cleansed from defilement at the sixth day, and on the seventh day, you and your prisoners,

20 and all your clothing and every article of leather, and all fabrics of hair, and every article of wood, shall be cleansed."

The Law of Prize in War, and its Purification.

21 Then Aliazer the priest said to the commanders of the army who came from the war, "This is the Constitutional Law which the EVER-LIVING

22 has commanded to Moses. All the gold and the silver, and the brass, and the iron, the tin, and the lead,

23 all things which can resist fire, you shall put through the fire to purify them ; but everything that is not able to endure fire shall be cleansed by passing through water, by washing

24 in water. You shall also wash your clothes on the seventh day, and purify yourselves, and afterwards you may enter the camp."

Law of Dividing Booty of War.

25 The EVER-LIVING also spoke to Moses and said :

26 "You, and Aliazer, and the princes of the fathers of the Parliament, take an account of the booty of the prisoners ; both of the men and of the

27 cattle, and divide the booty among the captors of the brigade who brought it from the campaign, and among all

28 their people. But take off a tax from them for the EVER-LIVING from the soldiers who actually went into battle, one head from five hundred of the men, and of the cattle, and of the asses,

29 and of the sheep. You shall take it from their share, and give it to Aliazer the priest, as a tax for the

30 EVER-LIVING. But from the share for the children of Israel you shall take one from every fifty of the men, of the cattle, and of the asses, and of the sheep, and from all the animals, and give them to the Levites who form the guard of the sanctuary of the EVER-LIVING."

31 Moses and Aliazer therefore did as

32 JEHOVAH commanded to Moses ; and the prize, beside the plunder that the People plundered in the army,—was of sheep six hundred and seventy-

33 five thousand, and of cattle seventy-

34 two thousand ; and of asses sixty-one

35 thousand, and of persons, with the girls who had not known man sexually, all the human individuals were thirty-two thousand.

36 But the half of the booty that came to the army was ;—from the number of sheep three hundred and thirty-seven thousand, and five hundred.

37 And the tax of the LORD from the sheep was six hundred and seventy-

38 five ; and of cattle thirty-six thousand ; and the tax to the LORD seventy-two.

39 And of asses thirty thousand and five hundred ; and the tax for the

40 LORD was sixty-one. And of human beings, sixteen thousand ; and the tax for the EVER-LIVING thirty-two persons.

41 And Moses gave the taxes which were the LORD'S, as a raised offering, to Aliazer the priest, as the EVER-LIVING commanded to Moses.

42 But the portion of the children of Israel, which Moses took from the

43 soldiers, and which was the share of the Parliament,—was of sheep three hundred and thirty-seven thousand,

44 and five hundred ; and of cattle,

45 thirty-six thousand, and of asses

46 thirty thousand, five hundred ; and of

47 human beings sixteen thousand. Moses also took from this share of the children of Israel one from every

fifty, both of the men, and of the beasts, and gave them to the Levites of the guard who guarded the sanctuary of the EVER-LIVING, as the LORD commanded to Moses

The Army Officers offer a Free Gift.

48 Then the officers of the regiments of the army—the colonels of regiments, and the captains of companies,

49 presented themselves to Moses, and said to Moses,—

"Your servants were promoted to be the chief commanders in the campaign which is in our hand, and not

50 a man of us is missing, therefore we present this gift to the EVER-LIVING, each from what he has found of articles of gold, anklets, and bracelets, seals, earrings, and beads, to expiate for our persons before the EVER-LIVING, for our lives"

51 Moses and Ahazer the priest, therefore, accepted from them all these

52 articles made of gold And the weight of the gold presented to the EVER-LIVING by the colonels of the regiments, and the captains of companies, was sixteen thousand, seven hundred

53 and fifty shekels, for the commanders in the army had each plundered for

54 themselves, so Moses and Ahazer the priest accepted the gold from the commanders of regiments and companies, and brought it into the Hall of Assembly, as a remembrance from the children of Israel before JEHOVAH

The Reubenites and Gadites ask for Yazer and Gilad.

32 But the number of cattle belonging to the sons of Reuben, and the sons of Gad was very numerous, and they saw that the district of Yazer, and the district of Gilad were places for

2 cattle So the sons of Gad and the sons of Reuben came to Moses and Ahazer the priest, and the princes of the Parliament, to say,

3 "Ataroth, and Diban, and Nimrah, and Kheshbon, and Alalah, and

4 Shibma, and Nebo, and Ban,—the country that the EVER-LIVING has conquered before the Commonwealth of Israel,—is a place for cattle, and

5 your servants possess cattle And," they continued, "if then your servants have found favour in your eyes, give this district to your servants to poss......"......... the J......

But Moses said to the sons of Gad, 6 and to the sons of Reuben,—

"Your brothers are going over the Jordan, and would you stay here? Why should you discourage the hearts 7 of the children of Israel from passing to the country which the EVER-LIVING has given to them? Your fathers 8 did the same, when I sent them from Kadesh-Barnea to survey the country, when they proceeded to the brook of 9 Ashkol, and examined the country, and discouraged the hearts of the children of Israel, so that they would not go to the land which the EVER-LIVING had given them, and the 10 anger of JEHOVAH burnt at that time, 11 and He declared, saying,—'The men who come up out of the Mitzeraim, from twenty years old and upwards, shall not see the country which I promised to Abraham, to Isaac, and to Jacob, – for they are not sincerely following Me,—except Kaleb the son 12 of Jephunah, the Kenezite, and Joshua the son of Nun, who sincerely followed the EVER-LIVING' The anger 13 of JEHOVAH consequently burnt against Israel, and they wandered forty years in the Wilderness, until all that generation who had done wrong in the sight of the EVER-LIVING had died And now you arise 14 in the place of your fathers to continue the burning anger of the LORD against Israel, for you are turning 15 back from Him, and will cause Him to retain them in the Wilderness and consume all this people!'"

But they pressed upon him and 16 said,—

"We will build folds to guard our sheep, and cities for our children, but 17 we ourselves are ready for action, and will advance ardently before the children of Israel to their districts wherever they may go But our children can rest in the fortified towns, guarded from the inhabitants of the country We will not return to our 18 homes until the children of Israel have each been put into possession of his estate And we will not inherit 19 over the Jordan, nor westward, but our possessions shall be to the east of the fords of the Jordan"

Then Moses replied to them, 20

"If you will do this,—if you will be ready for action before the EVER-LIVING in the war, and pass fully 21 .... the Jordan before the EVER-LIVING until His enemies are

22 driven from before Him, then, when the country is subdued to JEHOVAH, you may return, and this district shall be given you from the EVER-LIVING, and from Israel, and this country shall be yours to possess it

23 in the presence of the LORD But if you will not do so, then you will sin against the EVER-LIVING,—and you know the punishment for sin that will

24 meet you You can build towns for your children, and folds for your flocks,—and return when you have done so "

25 The sons of Gad and the sons of Reuben replied to Moses saying,— "Your servants will do as Our Lord

26 commands Our children, wives and cattle shall be here in the cities of

27 Gilad, but your servants will pass over fully equipped for war with the army of the EVER-LIVING, as your Lordship has said "

The Parliament called to sanction the Proposals of Reuben and Gad.

28 Then Moses convoked Ahazer the priest, and Joshua the son of Nun, and the chief fathers of the tribes of

29 the children of Israel,—and Moses said to them, " If the sons of Gad and the sons of Reuben pass over the Jordan fully equipped for the war of the EVER-LIVING, and subdue the country before you, then you shall give them the land of Gilad for a

30 possession But if they do not go over ready for action, then they shall only inherit in the land of Canan "

31 The sons of Gad, and the sons of Reuben answered, saying,— "Your servants will do what the

32 EVER-LIVING has said We will pass over fully equipped before the EVER-LIVING to the land of Canan, and we will possess our inheritance on this side of the Jordan "

33 So Moses gave to the sons of Gad and the sons of Reuben, and the half tribe of Manasseh, the son of Joseph, the kingdoms of Sihon, king of the Amorites, and the kingdoms of Og, king of Bashan The land and its towns, with the surrounding country of the villages

34 So the sons of Gad built Diban, and

35 Ataroth, and Arar, and Ataroth-Shufan, and Jazer, and Igbakhah,

36 and Beth-minrah, and Beth-horon,—fortified towns, with folds for sheep

37 And the sons of Reuben built Kheshbon, and Aldeh, Kiriathaim,

and Athbano and Athbal-maon, 38 changing its name, and Sibma, and they called Bethmoth, Shemoth These were the towns they built

Then the sons of Makir, the son 39 of Manasseh, marched to Gilad and captured it, and drove out the Amorites who were in it, so Moses gave 40 Gilad to Makir, the descendant of Manasseh, and he occupied it

Then Yair the son of Manasseh 41 marched and captured some forts, and called them the forts of Yair

Then Nobakh marched and cap- 42 tured Kaneth, and its villages, and named it Nobakh, after his own name

Record of Israel's Marches from Egypt to the Jordan.

These are the marches of the 33 children of Israel who came under the direction of Moses and Aaron from the land of the Mitzeraim by their armies (For Moses registered 2 their advance by marches, by instructions from the EVER-LIVING, and these are the marches they advanced by [1])

They marched first from Ramases, 3 in the first month, upon the fifteenth day of the first month,—

After the morning of the Passover, the children of Israel advanced with a high hand in the sight of all Mitzeraim, whilst the Mitzerites 4 were burying those whom JEHOVAH had killed among them,—all their firstborn And JEHOVAH also executed justice upon their gods

So the children of Israel marched 5 from Ramases, and pitched their tents at Skuth Then they marched 6 from Skuth and pitched at Atham, which is on the border of the desert Then they marched from Atham, and 7 pitched and occupied the Pass of Hakhiroth [2] which is opposite Balzefon, and pitched before the fortress Then they marched from Hakhiroth 8 and passed over through the sea to the desert, and advanced in that direction three days to the Desert of Atham, and pitched at Marah Then 9 they marched from Marah and came to Ailam, and there were at Ailam

---

[1] V 2 is an ancient editor's note, introducing the record of Moses, not part of his text apparently, as the change of person shows —F F

[2] Hakhiroth 'De C it, ot Caves.'
-f f

twelve springs of water, and seventy palm trees, so they pitched there.

10 Then they marched from Ailam and
11 pitched at the Sea of Suf.[1] Then they marched from the Sea of Suf, and
12 pitched in the desert of Zin. Then they marched from the Desert of
13 Zin, and pitched in Dafakah. Then they marched from Dafakah, and
14 pitched in Alush. Then they marched from Alush, and pitched in Rephidim ; but there was no water
15 there for the people to drink. Then they marched from Rephidim, and
16 pitched in the Desert of Sinai. Then they marched from the Desert of Sinai, and pitched in Kiboth Hatha-
17 vah. Then they marched from Kibroth Hathavah, and pitched in Khatzeroth.
18 Then they marched from Khatzeroth,
19 and pitched in Rithmah. Then they
20 marched from Rithmah, and pitched in Rimon-fartz. Then they marched from Rimon-fartz, and pitched in
21 Libnah. Then they marched from
22 Libnah, and pitched in Risah. Then they marched from Risah, and pitched
23 in Kahlatha. Then they marched from Kahlatha, and pitched at Mount
24 Shafir. Then they marched from Mount Shafir, and pitched in Kha-
25 radah. Then they marched from Kharadah, and pitched in Makhloth.
26 Then they marched from Makhloth,
27 and pitched in Thakhath. Then they marched from Thakhath, and pitched
28 in Tharakh. Then they marched from Tharakh, and pitched in Mit-
29 haka. Then they marched from Mithaka, and pitched in Khashmona.
30 Then they marched from Khashmona, and pitched in Moseroth. Then they
31 marched from Moseroth, and pitched
32 in among the Beni Yakan. Then they marched from the Beni Yakan, and pitched in the vale of Gadgad.
33 Then they marched from the vale of Gadgad, and encamped in Yatbatha.
34 Then they marched from Yatbatha,
35 and encamped in Aberona. Then they marched from Aberona, and
36 encamped in Atzin-gaber. Then they marched from Atzin-gaber, and encamped in the desert of Tzin.[2]
37 Then they marched from Kadesh, and encamped at the Peak-hill, on

the borders of the land of Moab, and Aaron the priest ascended the 38 Peak-hill[1] by the order of the EVER-LIVING, and died there, in the fortieth year from the coming of the children of Israel out of Mitzer, on the first of the fifth month. And 39 Aaron was a hundred and twenty-three years old at his death on the Peak-hill.

The Cananites of Arad oppose Israel.

When the Cananite king of Arad 40 heard that the children of Israel were advancing by the south country, he occupied the Peak-hill.

So they marched from the Peak- 41 hill, and encamped at Tzalmonah. Then they marched from Tzalmonah, 42 and encamped at Fonan. Then they 43 marched from Fonan, and encamped at Aboth. Then they marched from 44 Aboth, and encamped at Avi, at the Passes, on the border of Moab. Then 45 they marched from Avi, and encamped at Diban-Gad. Then they marched 46 from Diban-Gad, and encamped at Alman. Then they marched from 47 Alman by Diblathim, and encamped at the Hills of the Passes, opposite to Nebo. Then they marched from the 48 Hills of the Passes, and encamped at the Fords of Moab, on the Jordan. Then they extended along the 49 Jordan from Beth-Yeshimoth to the Acacia Meadows[2] upon the Fords of Moab.

There the EVER-LIVING spoke to 50 Moses at the Fords of Moab,[2] opposite Jeriko, commanding ;—

Commands on the Invasion of Canan.

"Speak to the children of Israel, 51 and say to them ;

"Now you are about to pass over the Jordan to the land of Canan, you 52 shall drive out all the possessors of that country before you, and destroy them, and their towers, and destroy all those bronze idols, and destroy all their High-places, and seize the 53 country ; for I have given the land to you to possess. But you shall divide 54 the land by lots to your families. To

---

[1] Sea of Weeds.—F. F.

[2] (" Which is Kadesh.") The words in the parentheses are a note of an ancient editor to explain the text not part of the Mosaic record.—F. F.

---

[1] Ar-Ahar.—F. F.

[2] The Acacia Meadows, in Hebrew "Abal-shittim.

the large you shall increase the portions, and to the small you shall lessen the portions Whatever lot falls to any one shall be his, and apportioned to him in the tribe of his fathers

55 But if you do not drive out the inhabitants of the land who occupy it, the remainder of them will be pricks in your eyes, and thorns in your sides, and a torment to you in the land where you reside And I will do to you as I intended to do to them "

The Bounds of the Promised Land.

34 The EVER-LIVING also spoke to Moses to say,—

2 " Command the children of Israel and say to them,

" Now you are come to the land of Canan,—the land which has fallen to you to inherit,—the land of Canan

3 with her surroundings And they shall be yours on the south side from the Wilderness of Tzin, on the borders of Edom

" These are your borders south, from the end of the Salt Sea eastward,

4 and along from there your boundary towards the south shall be from the ascent of Akrabim, and across to Tzin, then turn up from the south to Kadesh Barnea, and proceed to the Castle of Adar, and pass over to

5 Atzinar Then the boundary turning from Atzmon towards the River of

6 Mitzer shall proceed to the west, and your boundary shall be the sea, The Great Sea,—that shall be your boundary on the west

7 " And this shall be your boundary on the north, you shall mark out from the Great Sea, at the Hill of

8 Hills ! From the Hill of Hills you shall mark out to the Pass of Khamath, and take a line to the borders of

9 Tzadda Thence your northern boundary shall start and proceed to Khatzar-ainan, that shall be your border to the north

10 " Then you shall mark your eastern boundary from Khatzar-ainan to Shaf-

11 nah, and the frontier shall run from Shafnah with Riblah on the east, to Ain, where the line shall descend and extend to the eastern shoulder of

12 the Lake of Kineroth Thence the frontier shall run by the Jordan and extend to the Salt Sea This shall be your country with its surrounding bounds "

---

1 Lebanon.—I I

The Allotment of Palestine to the Nine and a Half Tribes.

Therefore Moses commanded the 13 children of Israel, saying,—

" This is the country which you shall divide by lot, which the EVER-LIVING has commanded to give to the nine and a half tribes, because the 14 tribe of Reuben have taken for their ancestors' house, and the tribe of the sons of Gad for their ancestors' house, with the house of Ephraim and the half tribe of Manasseh, have taken their share,—these two tribes and 15 the half tribe, have taken their shares before the Jordan, opposite Jeriko [1]

The EVER-LIVING also spoke to 16 Moses, commanding,—

" These two men shall divide the 17 land for you,—Aliazer the priest, and Joshua the son of Nun, with one prince from each of the tribes who shall superintend the division of the land, and these are the names of the 18 men,

" From the tribe of Judah, Kaleb 19 the son of Jefunah,

" From the tribe of the sons of 20 Simeon, Shamuel the son of Amihud,

" From the tribe of Benjamin, 21 Ahdad the son of Kislon,

" From the tribe of the sons of Dan, 22 Prince Buki, the son of Igh,

" From the sons of Joseph,—From 23 the tribe of the sons of Manasseh, Prince Khanial the son of Afod,

" From the tribe of the sons of 24 Ephraim, Prince Kamual, the son of Shiftan,

" From the tribe of the sons of 25 Zebulon, Prince Alizafan, the son of Padnak,

" From the tribe of the sons of 26 Issakar, Prince Faltiel, the son of Azan,

" From the tribe of the sons of 27 Asher, Akhihud, the son of Shalmi,

" From the tribe of the sons of 28 Naphthali, Prince Fidahl, the son of Amihud,

" The EVER-LIVING commands 29 these to divide the land of Canan to the children of Israel "

---

1 V 15 " Before the Jordan, opposite Jeriko," is evidence that in this allotment we have the actual words of Moses, who wrote his narrative on the eastern side of Jordan,—(" on the east towards the sunrise ") is a Jerusalem editor's note, written as an explanation for readers on the West of Jordan, centuries after the death of Moses.—F F

Cities ordered for the Levites.

35 The EVER-LIVING spoke to Moses at the Fords of Moab by the Jordan opposite Jeriko, saying ;

2 " Command the children of Israel, that they must give to the Levites, as a heritable portion, towns for residence, with pastures around those

3 towns, for the Levites. And the towns shall be for their residence, and the pastures for their cattle and

4 their animals. The pastures which you are to give to the Levites outside the walls of the towns shall be a space

5 of two thousand cubits. You shall thus measure from the outside wall of the towns, on the eastern side, two thousand cubits, and on the south side two thousand cubits, and on the west side two thousand cubits, and on the north side, two thousand cubits ; with the town in the centre. These shall be the pasture lands of those towns.

6 " You shall also assign to the Levites these towns ;—six cities of refuge to be provided for man-slayers. And beside them provide forty-two

7 cities—a total of forty-eight. All these towns shall be assigned to the Levites, being for them, and their pasturage.

8 But the towns that you assign from the children of Israel shall be according to their numbers, large, and according to their fewness, small,—each according to the extent of the district which they inherit shall give towns to the Levites. According to their shares, they shall assign equivalent towns to the Levites."

Cities of Refuge ordered.

9 The EVER-LIVING also spoke to Moses, commanding ;—

10 " Speak to the children of Israel and say to them ;

" You are now about to pass over the Jordan to the land of Canan.

11 Therefore appoint for yourselves Cities of Refuge, that man-slayers, who have cut off a life by accident,

12 may fly to them. And they shall be your Cities of Refuge from the Avenger, so that the fugitive may not be killed, until he has stood in the presence of

13 a jury for trial. Therefore shall you appoint six Cities of Refuge for your-

14 selves. You shall appoint three of the Cities on this side the Jordan, and three Cities in the land of Canan,

15 to be Cities of Refuge, for the children

of Israel and for foreigners residing among you. These three cities shall be Cities of Refuge for everyone who has cut off a life by accident. Thus 16 if he strikes any with an instrument of iron, and he dies, he is a man-slayer ; the man-slayer would be killed ; or if he throws a stone which 17 wounds mortally, and the wounded dies, he is a man-slayer ; the man-slayer would be killed ; or strikes 18 with an instrument of wood a deadly blow, and the wounded dies from it, he is a man-slayer ; the man-slayer would be killed. The Avenger 19 would kill the wounder ; he would kill the wounder when found. He would kill him.

20 " But if from hatred he stabs or shoots at one from a hiding place, and kills, or from hatred strikes with 21 his hand, and kills ; he shall be killed who has struck the wound ; The Avenger of Blood shall kill the wounder when he finds him.

22 " But if undesignedly, not from enmity, one stabs or shoots another with any instrument, not treacherously, or kills with a stone, not having 23 seen ;—or it falls upon a person who dies,—whom he did not hate, and did not seek to injure,—then the jury 24 shall judge between the accused and the Avenger, according to these rules ; and the jury shall deliver the accused 25 from the hand of the Avenger. But the jury shall assign him to the City of Refuge to which he shall go, and stay there until the death of the High Priest who has been consecrated with the Oil of Consecration.

26 " But if the man-slayer goes beyond the boundaries of the City of Refuge to which he has fled ; and the Avenger 27 of Blood meets him outside the bounds of the City of Refuge, then the Avenger of Blood may kill the slayer, without blood being upon himself ; for he ought to have remained in the 28 City of Refuge until the death of the High Priest. But after the death of the High Priest the man-slayer may reside in his own district.

The Constitutional Law of Murder.

29 " These shall be Constitutional Laws to your descendants, in all your residences :—

30 " Whoever cuts off a life, the slayer shall be slain on the evidence of two witnesses ; but upon the evidence of one you shall not condemn a person

31 to death And you shall not take any ransom for a life , the man-slayer who mortally injures, shall die a death

32 You shall also not accept a ransom from the refugee to a City of Refuge, to return to rest in the country, until

33 the death of the priest, so that you may not corrupt the land you reside in , for blood pollutes the land, and the land will not cover the blood that is shed upon it , for the life is in the

34 blood , consequently you shall not defile the land you dwell in,—amidst which I encamp,—for I, the EVER-LIVING, encamp in the midst of the children of Israel "

The Law of the Marriage of Heiresses.

36 The ancestral chiefs of the family of the sons of Gilad, the son of Makir, the son of Manasseh of the family of the son of Joseph, came before Moses and the presence of the Princes, the ancestral chiefs of the

2 children of Israel, and said ,

"The EVER-LIVING commanded Our Prince to apportion the land by lot to the children of Israel, and the Prince was commanded by the EVER-LIVING to give the share of Tzilafad,

3 our brother, to his daughters But they may take any one of the sons of the tribes of Israel for a husband, and carry away their shares from the shares of our families, and thus lessen the portions of the tribe to which they belong, and take away from our

4 allotted share And when the Jubilee comes to the children of Israel, then that portion will be added to the portion of the tribe to which they have gone, and the share of the tribe of their fathers will lose their shares ? "

Consequently Moses commanded 5 the children of Israel by instruction from the EVER-LIVING, saying ,—

"The argument of the sons of the tribe of Joseph is fair This is the 6 order of the EVER-LIVING to the daughters of Tzilafad —They may decide to be wives to anyone who is good in their eyes , but their husband shall be only from a family of their father's tribe, so that the portions of 7 the children of Israel may not be removed from tribe to tribe, for all the portions of the ancestral houses of the children of Israel shall be kept together Therefore any daughter 8 inheriting an estate in any of the tribes of the children of Israel, shall become the wife of one from her father's tribe, so that the children of Israel may each inherit the share of his father , for no estate shall 9 change from tribe to tribe After each portion has been allotted, it shall be kept in the same tribe of the children of Israel "

The daughters of Tzilafad accord- 10 ingly did as the EVER-LIVING commanded to Moses And the daughters 11 of Tzilafad, Makhla, Thirza, Khagla, and Milka, and Noah, were given as wives to the sons of their uncles, of 12 the family of the sons of Manasseh, the son of Joseph, they were their wives Thus their portions remained in the tribe of Manasseh their father These were the commands, and the 13 institutions which the EVER-LIVING ordained through the medium of Moses, to the children of Israel, at the Fords of Moab, by the Jordan, beyond Jeriko

END OF THE BOOK OF NUMBERS

THE FIFTH BOOK OF MOSES, COMMONLY CALLED

DEUTERONOMY.

(ALEH HE DIBARIM MOSHEH.)

THE SPEECHES OF MOSES.

INTRODUCTION.[1]

1   The following are the Speeches
which Moses addressed to all the
Children of Israel, before the passage
over the Jordan, in the desert, extending from Suf, between Paran,
and Thofel, and Laban, and Khatzroth
and Yahb.[2]

3   It was during the fortieth year, in
the eleventh month, upon the first of
the month, Moses related to the
children of Israel all that the EVER-
LIVING had commanded him for
them; after he had defeated Sihon, 4
King of the Amorites, who lived in
Heshbon, and Og King of Bashan,
who lived at Ashtaroth, in Adarai, on 5
this side[1] of the ford of the Jordan, in
the land of Moab, Moses began to
publish the law, and said ;—

1 This Introduction was probably written
by Aliazer, the High Priest, for the Sacred
Copy kept in the Ark of the Covenant.—F. F.

2 V. 2, in parentheses, is an explanatory
note of an old Hebrew editor.—F. F.

2   (It is eleven days' journey from Horeb,
when marching by the way of Mount Sair
to Kadesh Barnea.)

1 *That is the eastern side.* This geographical description proves this Introduction to
have been written before Joshua invaded
Palestine, and shows the age of the Orations,
and is an internal proof that we have them
now as Moses wrote and spoke, except for
a few inserted explanatory notes which I
shall indicate as my version proceeds.—F. F.

SPEECH I.

History of the Exodus.

6 Our EVER-LIVING GOD spoke to us in Horeb, saying,—You have remained
7 long enough on this mountain Turn and march, and proceed with all your camps to the highlands of the Amorites, and all their neighbours in the dry lands of the hills, and thence to the plains and desert along the shore of the sea of the land of Canan, and from Lebanon, as far as the great river Frath [1]
8 Attend! I have opened the country to you! Go and seize the land which the EVER-LIVING promised to give to your fathers, to Abraham, to Isaac, and to Jacob,—to give it to them and to their posterity after them
9 But I told you all at that time, I myself could not support you alone!
10 And now your EVER-LIVING GOD has increased you, and, see! you are to-day like the stars of the sky in number!
11 And the EVER-LIVING the GOD of your fathers will add to you, beyond this, a thousand times, and will
12 bless you, as He promised —How can I alone bear your troubling?
13 and carry your contentions? Go! Choose for yourselves skilful, clear-sighted, and educated men to control you, and I will appoint them your chiefs
14 When you answered me, "What you have said is good, what you have said, do it!"
15 I therefore chose as the chiefs of your tribes, skilful and educated men, and gave them to you as your chiefs, colonels of regiments, and captains of companies, and captains of fifties, and captains of tens, with magistrates
16 for your tribes I also ordered your judges at that time saying,—
"Listen between your brothers, and decide just judgments between a man and his brother, and the foreigners
17 among you Do not regard social station in deciding, whether low or high Listen not in fear of the station of a man, for justice belongs to GOD HIMSELF But any matter that is too difficult for you, bring to me, and I will hear it "

I instructed you also at that time 18 as to what things you ought to do
19 Then we marched from Horeb and proceeded through all that great and terrible desert, which you saw on the way to the Hills of the Amorites, when our EVER-LIVING GOD commanded us to advance to Kadesh-Barnea, where I said, "You are now 20 arrived at the Hills of the Amorites, which our EVER-LIVING GOD has given us Look! your EVER-LIVING 21 GOD has provided the country before you to possess Go up, seize it as the EVER-LIVING GOD of your fathers commands you,—fear not nor be terrified " But all of you approached 22 me, asking to send men before you to examine the country, and to report to you about the road by which you could go up to it, and about the cities that you were to go to And 23 the request seemed good in my opinion, and I appointed twelve princes,—one from each tribe,—and 24 they turned and went up to the hills, and descended to the vale of Eshkol, and slandered it But they took into 25 their hands some of the produce of the country and came back to us, and reported the matter, saying, "It is a beautiful country that our EVER-LIVING GOD has given us " But you 26 were not willing to go up, and rebelled against the order of your EVER-LIVING GOD, and murmured 27 in your tents and exclaimed, "Because the EVER-LIVING hated us He brought us out of the land of the Mitzeraim, and would give us into the hands of the Amorites to destroy us '—Alas for 28 our advance! Our brothers have depressed our hearts, by saying they are a people finer and taller than us! Their cities are large and fortified up to the skies, and we also saw the sons of Anak there!'"
But I replied to you, "Be not terri- 29 fied nor fear them Your EVER-LIV- 30 ING GOD Who goes before you, He will fight for you, in the way He did in your sight among the Mitzeraim, and 31 in the desert where you saw how the EVER-LIVING carried you as a woman carries her child, along all the way that you went until He brought you to this spot but on that occasion 32

you were not relying upon your
33 EVER-LIVING GOD, Who marched
before you in the journey to choose
your encampments, as a fire at night,
to show the way you should go, and
34 as a cloud by day. And the EVER-
LIVING heard the sound of your
words and was angry, and swore,
35 saying; "This vile generation shall
never see the beautiful land which I
promised to give to their fathers;
36 only Caleb the son of Jefunah shall
see it; and I will give to him and
his sons the country which he
travelled through, for he went up
confidently, following the EVER-
37 LIVING." The EVER-LIVING was also
angry with me on account of you,
and said, "You shall not go there!
38 Joshua the son of Nun, your lieutenant, shall go. Encourage him, for he
39 shall put Israel into possession. But
your infants whom you said would
be captured; and your sons who
to-day know neither good nor evil,—
they shall go there and I will give it
to them, and they shall possess it.
40 But you, turn back and march to the
desert, towards the sea of Suf!"
41 Then you were grieved and replied;
" We have sinned against the EVER-
LIVING !—We will now go up and
conquer, according to all that the
EVER-LIVING GOD commanded!"
And each one of you put on arms,
42 and went up to the hill. But the
EVER-LIVING said to me, "Order
them, Go not up, and fight not, for I
am not with you;—therefore you will
fly before your enemies."
43 So I spoke to you, but you would
not hear, and you rebelled against
the order of the EVER-LIVING, and
were insolent, and went up to the
44 Hill,—and the Amorites who occupied
the Hill advanced against you, and
drove you, like bees would do, and
routed you like a tempest to the
45 valley. So you returned, and wept
before the EVER-LIVING. But the
EVER-LIVING would not hear your
46 voice, nor listened. Consequently
you were detained at Kadesh for
many days. You remained there a
2 long time; until you turned back
and marched to the desert towards
the Sea of Suf, as the EVER-LIVING
commanded me, and wandered about
the hills of Sair a long time.
2 At last the EVER-LIVING said to
3 me; "You have wandered about
this hill enough. Turn to the north,

and command the People saying to 4
them, 'Pass over the borders of your
brothers, the sons of Esau, who dwell
in Sair. But they will be afraid of
you, so carefully guard yourselves.
And injure them not; for I will not 5
give you a foot's space of their country,
because I have given Mount Sair to
Esau as a possession. You must 6
buy food from them with money, and
eat it; and also purchase water from
them for money, and drink it; for 7
your EVER-LIVING GOD has blessed
you in every work of your hand,
whilst you travelled this great desert
these forty years; your EVER-LIVING
GOD has been with you, and you
have wanted for nothing.'" You 8
consequently passed by your brothers
the sons of Esau, who occupy Sair,
by the road of the Arabah, to Ailath,
and Atzian-gaber, where you turned
off and traversed the road of the
desert of Moab.

There the EVER-LIVING said to 9
me, " Do not trouble Moab, but keep
yourselves from fighting. Turn, for
I have not granted you his country,
because I have given Ar to the sons
of Lot as a possession." [1]

Then you arose and passed the 13
Vale of Yared, and at the passage of
the Vale of Yared, including the 14
period of the march from Kadesh-
Barnea, until the time you crossed
the Vale of Yared, was thirty-eight
years, until all the generation of
fighting men belonging to the camp
were dead, as the EVER-LIVING
threatened them. For the hand of 15
the EVER-LIVING was against them
to destroy them out of the camp until
they perished. And when all the 16
fighting men had died from among
the People, then the EVER-LIVING 17
spoke to me, and said, " Now cross 18

1 Vv. 10 to 13 are an ancient editor's note,
not a part of the text of Moses. It was probably added by Ezra, when he edited the
Pentateuch, after the return from Babylon,
as all the other notes which I consequently
transfer to the foot of the pages.—F. F.

(The Amim formerly occupied it, a 10
great and numerous nation, and tall, like
Anakim; they considered themselves also 11
to be Rephaim like the Anakim,—but the
Moabites called them Amim And the 12
Khorites dwelt in Sair before them, but
the sons of Esau expelled them, and drove
them from the place, and occupied it in
their stead, as the children of Israel did
in the country they ꞏꞏꞏꞏꞏ had which the
ꞏꞏꞏ ꞏꞏꞏꞏ ꞏꞏꞏꞏꞏꞏ

over to-day the boundaries of Moab
19 at Ar   But when you approach the
sons of Amon, neither distress nor
hurt them, for I will not give the
country of the sons of Amon to you
to possess, for I have given it to the
sons of Lot as a possession [1]

24   " Rise ! march ! and cross the River
Arnon ! See ! I have given you Sihon,
King of Heshbon, the Amorite, and
his country to break, assail, and

25 defeat it in war ! I have broken him
this day,—putting the dread and fear
of you upon the face of the nations,
under every sky, who may hear the
reports about you   They tremble
and faint before you ! "

26   Then I sent ambassadors from
the desert of the East to Sihon,
King of Heshbon with proposals of
peace, and said ,—

27   " I wish to pass across your country
by the king's highway, I will not

28 march many days, or deviate   You
shall sell food for money, and I will
eat it , and pay money for the water
you give and I drink it   I only

29 wish to pass over on my feet   Do to
me as the sons of Esau did who dwell
in Sair, and the Moabites who inhabit
Ar, until I have crossed the Jordan,
to the land which our EVER-LIVING
GOD has given us "

30   But Sihon, king of Heshbon was
not willing you should cross over
him, for your EVER-LIVING GOD had
stupefied his mind, and emboldened
his heart, that by it He might give
him into your hand, as He has now
done

31   The EVER-LIVING GOD also said ,
" See ! I have begun to give up Sihon
and his country before you , seize it !
take his land for a possession ! "

---

[1] Vv 20 to end of 23 are a note of an ancient
editor, probably Ezra, not part of the original
text of Moses —F F.

20   (This also was considered a country
of the Rephaim, because the Rephaim
resided there formerly, but the Amorites

21 called them Yim-yimim   They were a
great and numerous people, like the
Anakim, but the EVER-LIVING destroyed
them before those, who drove them out,

22 and inhabited in their place , as He did
for the sons of Esau who occupy Mount
Sair, who expelled the Khorites formerly,
and drove them out, and dwell in their

23 place until this day   The Avites also
resided in the fortresses until the powerful Kaphtorites came from Kaphtor and
defeated them and they reside after
them.)

Then Sihon advanced to meet us, 32
he and all his force to fight at Jahaz
But our EVER-LIVING GOD delivered 33
him to us , and struck him and his
son and all his forces , and at that 34
time we captured all his towns, and
devoted all his cities, nor allowed the
men, women or children to escape
Beside the cattle we seized for our- 35
selves, and the plunder of the cities
which we captured , from Aroar on 36
the banks of the Arnon, and the
towns in the valley, and as far as
Gilad—there was not a city that was
too strong for us,—our EVER-LIVING
GOD delivered the whole to our
approach ! The whole extent of the 37
country of the Ammonites, all along
the vale of Jabbok, with the towns of
the Highlands, and all that our EVER-
LIVING GOD commanded

Then we turned and went up to- 3
wards Bashan, and Og, king of
Bashan advanced to meet us with all
his forces, to fight at Adarai

Then the EVER-LIVING said to me, 2
—" Fear him not, for I have given
him into your power, with all his
forces, and his country , and you
shall do to him as you did to Sihon,
king of the Amorites, who lived in
Heshbon "

So our EVER-LIVING GOD also 3
subjected to us Og, king of Bashan
and all his forces, until not a remnant remained to him   We also cap- 4
tured all his towns, in the same
campaign ,—there was not a city we
did not take,—from the sixty towns
in the district of Argob, to the capital
of Og in Bashan —All which towns 5
were fortified with high walls, gates
and bars, — beside a great many
towns of the Perizites   We devoted 6
them as we did to Sihon, king of
Heshbon ,—we devoted every city,
men, women and children , and all 7
the cattle, and plunder of those
towns we seized for ourselves   We 8
thus took, in the same campaign,
their country from the possession of
the two kings of the Amorites which
are this side of the Jordan, extending
from the vale of Arnon to the Hill of
Hermon [1]   All the towns of the 10
Uplands, and all Gilad, and all

---

[1] V 9 The parenthesis is the note of an
ancient commentator, probably Ezra's, not
part of the original text —F F

(The Zidonians call Hermon Shirion, 9
and the Amorites call it Senir.)

Bashan, to Salkah, and Adarai;—towns of the dominions of Og in

12 Bashan.[1] These countries you conquered in that campaign, extending from Aroer which is on the river Arnon. And the half of Mount Gilad was given to the Reubenites

13 and Gadites. But the remainder of Gilad and all Bashan, with the dominions of Og, I gave to the half tribe of Manasseh;—all the plain of Argob, and all Bashan which is called the land of the Rephaim.

14 Yair the son of Manasseh took all the district of Argob, as far as the borders of the Gheshurites and the Makathites, and he called them after his own

15 name;—Yair's Towns.[2]—But I gave

16 Gilad to Makir. To the Reubenites and Gadites I also gave a part of Gilad, to the middle of the vale of Arnon, the valley as a boundary as far as Jabok, with its valley to the

17 border of the Ammonites; and the plain of the Jordan as a boundary, from Kineroth as far as the Sea of the Plain,—the Dead Sea,—down to the hill-foot of Pisgah, from the east.

18 But I commanded you at the time, saying, "Your EVER-LIVING GOD has given you this country to possess, but you must march fully equipped in the front of your brothers the children of Israel, with all your forces.

19 However the women and children, and cattle, (for I know you have many cattle,) may remain in the

20 cities which I have given you, until the EVER-LIVING has settled your brothers like yourselves, and they are also in possession of the country which their EVER-LIVING GOD will give to them, beyond the Jordan; then you may each return."

21 I also commanded Joshua at that time, saying, "Your eyes have seen all that your EVER-LIVING GOD has done to these two kings;—the EVER-

LIVING will do the same to all the kingdoms which are over there.

22 Fear them not, for your EVER-LIVING GOD will fight for you."

23 And at that time I implored the EVER-LIVING, saying, "ALMIGHTY

24 LORD You have now begun to show to Your servant Your grandeur, and Your Strong Hand. What POWER in Heaven or on earth can do as You

25 have done with YOUR MIGHT? Let me, I pray, go over, and see this beautiful country that is beyond the Jordan;—those beautiful hills and

26 Lebanon!" But the EVER-LIVING was angry with me because of you, and would not listen to me, and the EVER-LIVING said to me,—" Let this be enough for you. Continue not to speak to Me again about this matter.

27 Go up to the top of Pisgah, and carry your eyes westward, and northward, and southward, and eastward, and see it with your eyes;—for you shall not pass over this river Jordan.

28 " Therefore command Joshua, and encourage, and strengthen him, for he shall go over before the people, and he shall conquer for them the country that you will survey."

We were then staying, in the valley near Beth-peor.

4 Consequently, now, Israel, listen to the constitutions and decrees which I will teach you to practise, that you may live, and go, and possess the country which the EVER-LIVING GOD of your fathers will

2 give you. You shall not add to the matter that I command you, nor shall you detract from it, but keep the commands of your EVER-LIVING GOD, as I have commanded you.

3 Your eyes saw what the EVER-LIVING did because of Bal-peor,—how the EVER-LIVING destroyed every man who went after Bal-peor among you.

4 But you who kept fast to your EVER-LIVING GOD are all of you alive to-day!

5 Attend to me as I teach you the constitutions and decrees which the EVER-LIVING, my GOD, commands you to practise when you arrive in the country which you are going to

6 possess, and guard them, and practise them;—for they will make you wise and intelligent in the eyes of the Peoples who hear of all these constitutions, who will say; "This is a wise and intelligent People—this

7 Great Nation!" For what nation is

---

[1] V. 11, in parentheses, is an ancient editor's note, probably Ezra's, not part of the speech of Moses.—F. F.

11 (Og, king of Bashan was of the remnant of the race of the Rephaim. He can be seen lying upon a couch of iron which is preserved in Rabath of the Ammonites. Its length is nine cubits, and breadth four cubits, by the common cubit.)

[2] The parenthesis is the note of an old Hebrew editor, not part of the oration of Moses.—F. F.

(As they are thus divided.)

so great as to possess gods in its breast? As our EVER-LIVING GOD

8 is to us in all we ask of Him? And what nation is so great? possessing institutions and decrees like these laws that I put before you to-day?

9 Only guard yourselves, and guard your lives carefully, from forgetting the events that your eyes have seen, and from turning your heart away all the days of your life, and teach them to your children, and to your children's children

10 Upon the day when you stood before your EVER-LIVING GOD at Horeb, when the EVER-LIVING commanded me, "Collect the People to Me, and I will let them hear what they must learn, so that they may fear Me all the time they live on the earth, and

11 teach their children" So you approached and stood below the hill, whilst the hill burned with fire up to the heart of the skies, with darkness,

12 cloud, and gloom There the EVER-LIVING spoke to you from the midst of the fire You heard a VOICE speaking to you!—but no Image ap-

13 pearing!—And it informed you of the Covenant which He commanded you to practise,—the Ten Commandments,—and wrote them upon two tables of stone

14 But to me, the EVER - LIVING ordered at that time to teach you the constitutions and decrees, which you were to practise in the land into which you would pass, to possess it

15 Therefore you must guard your minds very carefully,—for you did not see any SHAPE on the day the EVER-LIVING spoke with you in Horeb from the midst of the fire,—

16 from wickedly making for yourselves a carved SHAPE,—any Image, or

17 model of Man or Woman, or form of any beast that is upon the earth, form of any bird which flies in the

18 sky, form of any reptile on the ground, form of any fish that is in the waters lower than the earth,—

19 Or, if you raise your eyes heavenward, and see the sun, and the moon, or the stars,—all the host of the skies, — and bow to, and worship them, and serve those which your EVER-LIVING GOD has apportioned to all the nations under all the skies

20 —For the EVER-LIVING selected you, and brought you from the iron works of the Mitzeraim, to be a People for

21 Himself,—as you are to-day But

the EVER-LIVING was angry with me over your affairs, and swore to prevent me crossing the Jordan, and to prevent me arriving at the beautiful country which your EVER-LIVING GOD has given to you to possess!

22 For I must die in this country,—I may not pass over the Jordan!—but you will pass over, and possess that beautiful land!

23 Guard yourselves from forgetting the covenant of your EVER-LIVING GOD, which He contracted with you, for fear you should make for yourselves a carved image,—contrary to the command of your EVER-LIVING

24 GOD, for your EVER-LIVING GOD is a consuming fire,—HE is a jealous GOD!

25 When you have begotten children and children's children, and are in the country, and have corrupted yourselves, and make carved images, and do evil in the eyes of your EVER-

26 LIVING GOD, provoking Him,—I call to witness to-day the Heavens and the Earth to witness to you, that perishing you shall perish quickly from off the land which you pass over the Jordan to possess,—your time shall not be prolonged in it,—but you shall certainly waste away,

27 and the EVER-LIVING will scatter you among the nations, and your remnant shall die as a number among the nations where the EVER-LIVING

28 has driven you And you shall there serve gods made by human hands!—of wood, and stone, who cannot see,

29 or hear, or eat, or breathe! But if you should from there entreat your EVER-LIVING GOD, and decide to seek HIM with all your heart, and

30 with all your soul,—strengthen yourselves, and encourage yourselves with all these events, after long periods, and return to your EVER-LIVING GOD, and listen to His voice,

31 —for your EVER-LIVING GOD is a merciful GOD,—He will not desert you, and will not turn from you, and will not forget the covenant with your fathers, which He swore to

32 them —Therefore search, now, the former times that were before you,—from the time when GOD constructed man upon the earth,—and from one extreme of the heavens to the other extreme of the heavens,—has there ever been such a great event as this? —or has there been heard its like?—

33 a People who heard the VOICE of

34 GOD speaking from amid the fire, as you heard it,—and lived ? or that GOD attempted to go and take for Himself one nation from the breast of another nation, with trials, with miracles, and portents, and war, and with a strong hand, and a directing arm, and great manifestations, such as all those your EVER-LIVING GOD has made in your sight upon the Mitzeraim for you ?

35 Then see, and learn that the EVER-LIVING is GOD,—and except Him

36 NONE !—From the heavens you have heard HIS VOICE !—when He taught you,—and upon earth you have seen His Great Fire ! — and heard His commands from the midst of the

37 fire , because He loved your fathers, and chose their race after them, and

brought you by His great might to His PRESENCE from among the Mit-

38 zeraim, and will drive great and more powerful nations than you before your face, to bring you to,— to give you,—their country as a possession,—as at this day ! Therefore

39 learn to-day,—and fix it in your heart,—that the EVER-LIVING, He is GOD in heaven, and upon the earth, —and except HIM there is no other !

40 —So keep His institutions, and His commandments, which I commanded you to-day, that you may prosper, and your children after you,— and then your days will be long upon the land which your EVER-LIVING GOD will give to you for all time [1]

---

[1] Vv 41—43 are a note of an ancient editor not a part of the text of Moses This note was most probably written by Ezra —F F

41 (At this period Moses selected three cities over the Jordan towards the sun-

42 rise, for the man-slayer, who might kill his neighbour accidentally, whom he had not previously hated to fly to,—that he might fly to one of those CITIES OF GOD and live

43 They were Betzer in the desert in the district of Misher, for the Reubenites, and Ramoth in Ghilad, for the Gadites, and Golan in Bashan, for the Manassites)[2]

[2] Vv 44—48 are also a note of an ancient editor, probably Ezra, as the remark that Moses was on the Eastern side of Jordan indicates the commentator as looking from the Western side—say, Jerusalem All these are internal proofs, of the authenticity of the main text —F. F

(These were appointed there by Moses 44 for the children of Israel

45 The following are also Constitutional Enactments, and Decrees, which Moses dictated to the children of Israel at their

46 coming out from the Mitzeraim, at the ford of the Jordan, in the valley opposite Beth-peor, in the country of Sihon, king of the Amorites, who resided in Heshbon, whom Moses and the children of Israel defeated upon their coming out from the

47 Mitzeraim, when they seized his country, and the country of Og, king of Bashan, both kings of the Amorites, who were beyond the Jordan, toward the rising of

48 the sun, extending from Aroar, which is upon the bank of the river Arnon, to the Hill of Shian,—that is Hermon,—and all the plain beyond the Jordan towards the sun-rise, and to the Sea of the Plain, below the feet of Pisgah)

END OF THE FIRST ORATION

SPEECH II.

Upon the Covenant of Sinai.

5 Moses again assembled all Israel and said to them,—

Listen, Israel, to the constitutions and decrees which I proclaim in your hearing to-day,—both to learn them, and preserve them by practising

2 Our EVER-LIVING GOD contracted
3 a covenant with us in Horeb Not with our fathers did the EVER-LIVING contract that covenant, but with us, ourselves, those in this place,
4 all of us alive to-day The EVER-LIVING spoke face to face with you at the Hill, from the midst of the fire

5 I stood between the EVER-LIVING and you at that time to report to you the dictation of the EVER-LIVING, for you were afraid at the presence of the fire, and could not ascend to Him, and He said,—

6 I "I am your EVER-LIVING GOD Who brought you out of the land of Egypt,—from the house of bondage You shall have no other gods in My place

7 II "You shall not make for yourselves an Image,—any likeness of what is in the heavens above, or what
8 is on the earth beneath, or what is in the waters lower than the land
9 You shall not bow down to them nor serve them, for I, your EVER-LIVING GOD, am a jealous GOD, punishing the sins of the parents upon their children to the third and fourth generation, of those who hate Me,
10 but I show mercy to thousands of generations of those who love Me and keep My commandments

11 III "You shall not take the Name of your EVER-LIVING GOD in vain, for the EVER-LIVING will not hold him guiltless who takes His Name in vain

12 IV "Regard the Sabbath Day to keep it holy, as the EVER LIVING
13 GOD commanded you You may labour six days and do all your busi-
14 ness, but the seventh day is a rest to your EVER-LIVING GOD, you shall not do any business upon it,—you, or your son, or your daughter, or your servant, or your handmaid, or your ox, or your ass, or any of your

cattle, or your hired man, who may be in your house, — because your
15 workmen, and your maid servant shall rest like yourself Remember also that you were slaves in the land of the Mitzeraim, but your EVER-LIVING GOD brought you out from there with a strong hand, and a directing arm,—therefore your EVER-LIVING GOD commanded you to make the Day of Rest

16 V "Honour your father and your mother, as your EVER-LIVING GOD commanded you, so that your days may be lengthened, and that you may prosper upon the land which your EVER-LIVING GOD gives to you

17 VI "You shall not murder
18 VII "You shall not fornicate
19 VIII "You shall not steal.
20 IX "You shall not bring up false evidence against your neighbour
21 X "You shall not covet your neighbour's wife, you shall not long for your neighbour's farm, or his slave, or his handmaid, his ox, or his ass, or anything that is your neighbour's "

22 The EVER-LIVING dictated these commands to the whole assembly of you, from the midst of the fire, of the cloud, and of the gloom,—a GREAT VOICE,—and did not desist there, but wrote them upon two tables of stone, and gave them to me

23 But when you heard the VOICE from the midst of the darkness, and the mountain burning with fire,—then all the Chiefs of your tribes, and
24 your nobles approached to me, and said,—

"Now we have seen our EVER-LIVING GOD,—His Majesty and His Greatness,—and have heard HIS VOICE, HIS VOICE from the midst of the fire to-day We have seen that GOD can speak with mankind, and
25 lives Therefore, now, why should we die? For this Great Fire will consume us, if we ourselves remain longer to hear the Voice of our EVER-
26 LIVING GOD,—we shall die, for who is there of any race who has heard the Voice of the Living GOD speaking from the midst of the fire, like us,
27 and has lived? Go yourself near and listen to all that our EVER-LIVING GOD says, and then report to us all

that our EVER-LIVING GOD dictates to you, and we will listen to it, and do it."

28 And the EVER-LIVING heard the voice of your speeches when you spoke to me, and the EVER-LIVING said to me;—" I have heard the voice of this-People speaking to you. All

29 they have said is beautiful! What would I give if there were such a heart in them to attend to Me, and to keep all My commands for all time? Then there would be prosperity to them and to all their children for

30 ever!—Go! tell them to return to

31 their tents. But you, stay here, and I will dictate to you all My Commands, and the Constitutions, and Decrees, which you must teach them to prac- tise in the country which I will give

32 them to possess." Therefore you must practise them as your EVER-LIVING GOD commanded you;—you shall not turn away to the right or the left.

33 You shall walk in every way as your EVER-LIVING GOD commanded you, so that you may live, and prosper, and lengthen your days in the country which you shall possess.

6 And these are the commands, and constitutions, and decrees which your EVER-LIVING GOD commands you to learn to practise in the land to which you will pass over to possess.

2 So you must fear your EVER-LIVING GOD, and preserve all the Constitu- tions, and Commandments, which I command you;—you and your chil- dren, and the children of your chil-

3 dren, all the time of your life. Listen, therefore, Israel! and keep and prac- tise them,—so that you may prosper, and so that you may increase greatly, as your EVER-LIVING GOD promised to your fathers,—upon entering into the land flowing with milk and honey!

4 Listen, Israel! Our EVER-LIVING

5 GOD is a Single LIFE. Therefore love your EVER-LIVING GOD with all your heart, and with all your soul,

6 and with all your strength. And let these words that I command you to-

7 day be in your heart; and teach them to your sons, and speak about them when sitting in your house,— and in travelling on your journeys,— and when lying down,—and when

8 rising up. Bind them also as orna- ments upon your hands, and as front-

9 lets between your eyes and write them upon the doors of your house,

and upon your gates. And then when 10 your EVER-LIVING GOD brings you to the country which He promised to your fathers,—to Abraham, to Isaac, and to Jacob,—to give to you great and beautiful cities that you built not; and houses full of furniture that 11 you did not make; and many for- tresses which you did not fortify; vine- yards and olive yards which you did not plant;—where you may eat and be satisfied,—take care to yourselves 12 lest you forget the EVER-LIVING Who brought you from the land of the Mitzeraim,—from the house of bond- age!

Fear your EVER-LIVING GOD, and 13 serve Him, and swear by His Name. You must not go after other gods, 14 —than GOD;—those of the Peoples around you,—for your EVER-LIVING 15 GOD is a jealous GOD. Guard your- selves lest the anger of your EVER- LIVING GOD should burn against you, and He should destroy you from off the face of the land.

You shall not try your EVER- 16 LIVING GOD, as you tried Him in Masah. You shall carefully preserve 17 the commands of your EVER-LIVING GOD, and His proofs, and His con- stitutions that He ordered you. And 18 you shall practise Justice, and Right in the sight of the EVER-LIVING, so that you may prosper and possess that beautiful country where the EVER LIVING promised to your fathers to repulse all your enemies 19 before you;—as the EVER-LIVING will do.

When your son enquires of you 20 hereafter, asking; "Why did the EVER-LIVING GOD order these Proofs and Constitutions and Decrees for you?" You shall answer to your son; 21 —" We were slaves to Pharoh in Mit- zeraim, and the EVER-LIVING brought us out from among the Mitzerites with a strong hand. And the EVER- 22 LIVING produced great wonders, and portents, and inflicted sufferings on the Mitzerites, upon Pharoh and upon all his family in our sight; but 23 brought us from there, and brought us up to give us this country which He had promised to our fathers. Therefore the EVER-LIVING com- 24 manded us to practise all these con- stitutions, and to fear our EVER- LIVING GOD, for our benefit, all the time of our lives,—as at this day. And it is right for us that we should 25 continue to practise the whole of these commands before our EVER-LIVING GOD, as He commanded us "

7 For your EVER-LIVING GOD will bring you to the country which you are now going to seize, to plunder nations more numerous than yourselves,—the Khithites and the Ghergashites and the Amorites, and the Cananites, and the Perizites, and the Hivites, and the Jebusites — seven nations more numerous and stronger

2 than yourselves, whom your EVER-LIVING GOD will deliver up before you, and you will defeat them Destroy them, and make no treaty with them, and do not pity them!

3 Do not marry with them, give not your daughter to his son, nor take

4 his daughter for your son,—for it will turn your heart from following ME, and you will serve other gods, —when the anger of the EVER-LIVING will burn against you, and

5 He will destroy you quickly Consequently you shall do this to them,— you shall throw down their altars, and break their columns, and smash their shrines, and melt their cast

6 images in the fire, because you are a People devoted to your EVER-LIVING GOD Your EVER-LIVING GOD chose you to be a People for Himself,—separated from all the Peoples who are upon the face of

7 the earth!—Has He not increased you more than all the Peoples? The EVER-LIVING did not unite with you because you were the most numerous of the Peoples,—but chose you when you were the least of all the Peoples,

8 and the EVER-LIVING loved you because of keeping the oath which He swore to your fathers,—therefore the EVER-LIVING brought you out with a strong hand, and freed you from the House of Bondage, from the hand of Pharoh king of the Mitzeraim!

9 Therefore know that the EVER-LIVING IS GOD,—the GOD Who faithfully keeps His covenant, and shows favour to those who love Him and regard His commands, for a thousand

10 generations, but repays His enemies, those who hate Him, to their face, by destroying them He will not delay to repay those who hate Him to their

11 face Therefore preserve the Commandments, and the Constitutions, and the Decrees which I command you to-day, and practise them

12 For there will be a reward if you listen to these decrees, and preserve, and practise them,—for your EVER-LIVING GOD will keep the covenant, and the favour which He promised to your fathers, and will love you, and 13 bless you, and increase the fruit of your body, and the fruit of your grounds, your corn, your wine, and your oil,—your cattle shall breed, and your sheep bring forth upon the ground which He promised to your fathers to give to you! You shall be 14 more blessed than any People! Neither male nor female shall be sterile among you, nor your cattle barren And the EVER-LIVING will 15 turn from you every disease and sickness of the Mitzerites,—the sufferings that you know,—He will not lay them upon you, but will put them on all who hate you, therefore you shall 16 consume all the Peoples whom your EVER-LIVING GOD gives to you Your eye shall not have pity on them, —nor serve their gods, for they will be your snare

If, however, your heart should say 17 to you, " These nations are more numerous than I,—I am not able to dispossess them," fear them not! 18 Remember what your EVER-LIVING GOD did to Pharoh and to all the Mitzerites,—the great calamities that 19 your eyes saw, and the wonders, and the portents, and the strong hand, and the directing arm with which your EVER-LIVING GOD brought you out! Your EVER-LIVING GOD will do the same to all the Peoples before whom you are afraid! Your EVER-LIVING 20 GOD will also send upon them fever, to destroy the remnants who hide themselves from you! You shall not 21 be pursued by them, for your EVER-LIVING GOD is among you,—a GREAT GOD of LIGHT Your EVER-LIVING 22 GOD, however, will drive these nations before you little by little,—you shall not be able to master them quickly, for fear the beasts of the field should multiply upon you But your EVER- 23 LIVING GOD will displace them before you, and dissolve with much confusion until they perish And He 24 will deliver their kings to your hand, and you shall destroy their names from under the skies,—not a man can stand before you, until you have desolated them You shall burn 25 their carved gods with fire You shall not desire the gold nor silver they are made of, or take it for yourselves, for fear you should be ensnared by it; for you must serve the EVER-LIVING,—He is your GOD;—

26 therefore you shall not bring their foul practices into your house,—but you shall be pure,—for what contaminated them will contaminate you; and what defiled them will defile you.—Therefore be pure.

8 You must regard all the commands, that I order you to-day, in practice, so that you may live and increase, and go to seize the country that the EVER-LIVING promised to your

2 fathers. But remember how all the way your EVER-LIVING GOD led you these forty years in the desert, to try you, to prove you, to examine you, whether you would keep His Commands from your heart or not.

3 Therefore He afflicted you, and hungered you, and fed you with mana, which you had not known,—nor had your fathers known,—so that He might teach you "that man lives not by bread alone,—but that man lives by all that comes from the mouth of the EVER-LIVING."

4 Your clothes were not rags, nor your feet shoeless in those forty years;

5 and you knew in your heart that as a man instructs his son, your EVER-

6 LIVING GOD instructed you; therefore keep the Commands of your EVER-LIVING GOD, and walk in His

7 paths, and fear Him; for your EVER-LIVING GOD brings you to this beautiful land,—a land of brooks of water, springs, and torrents, coming out of

8 the valleys, and out of the hills;—a country of wheat and barley, and vines and figs, and pomegranates; a

9 land of olive oil and honey! A country where you will not eat from stores! Bread shall never fail at all in it. A land where the rocks have iron, and from whose hills you can

dig copper! Where you can eat and 10 fill yourselves, and bless your EVER-LIVING GOD over the beautiful land He has given to you!

Take care of yourselves lest you 11 should forget the EVER-LIVING, your GOD. Only keep His Commandments, and Decrees, and Institutions, which I command you to-day, for fear when 12 you eat and are full, and have built yourselves beautiful houses, and reside in them, and your cattle, and your 13 sheep multiply, and your silver and gold have increased, and all your possessions have grown,—and your heart 14 rises,—then you might forget your EVER-LIVING GOD Who brought you up out of the land of the Mitzeraim, —from the House of Bondage. Who 15 led you through this great desert where you saw the fiery serpents and scorpions, and the dry waterless land, —where He brought you water from the flinty rock,—feeding you in the 16 desert with mana which neither you nor your fathers had known;—so that He might try you, with the purpose of ultimately benefiting.

You, however, may say to your 17 heart, "I have obtained this power by my own courage, and the vigour of my hands."—Yet remember it was 18 your EVER-LIVING GOD Who gave you that courage, and granted that power, so that He might establish the covenant which He swore to your fathers,—as He does to-day.

But if ever it comes that you forget 19 your EVER-LIVING GOD, and go after other gods, and serve and worship them,—I bear witness to you to-day, that you shall perish, like the 20 nations the EVER-LIVING destroyed from before you,—thus you shall perish,—because you did not listen to the voice of your EVER-LIVING GOD.

END OF THE SECOND ORATION.

SPEECH III.

Why Israel was Chosen.

9 Listen, Israel! you are about to cross the Jordan to seize nations greater and more powerful than yourself, great cities fortified up to
2 the skies! A People great and tall, sons of the Anakim whom you know, and of whom you said, "Who can
3 stand before the sons of Anak!" But I bear witness to-day that your EVER-LIVING GOD, Who goes before you as a consuming fire, He will devastate them, and He will defeat them before you, and you shall drive out and destroy them from the hills, as the EVER-LIVING commanded you
4 When your EVER-LIVING GOD has driven them away from you, think not to say to your heart, "For my righteousness, the EVER-LIVING has brought me to possess this country, therefore the EVER-LIVING has driven out the nations who possessed it before me!"
5 Not for your righteousness, nor for the rectitude of your heart did you come to possess their country, but because of the wickedness of those nations your EVER-LIVING GOD drove them out before you, and for the same reason He established the covenant which He swore to your fathers,—to Abraham, to Isaac, and
6 to Jacob—Consequently learn that your EVER-LIVING GOD has not given you to possess that beautiful country because of your righteousness,—for you are a stiff-necked
7 people Remember! forget not how you have provoked your EVER-LIVING GOD in the desert, from the day He brought you out of the land of the Mitzeraim, until you arrived at this spot,—you have been rebels against
8 the EVER-LIVING! In Horeb also you provoked the EVER-LIVING, and the EVER-LIVING was angry with you
9 to destroy you, when I went up the mountain to receive the two tables of stone,—the Tables of the Covenant which the EVER-LIVING made with you,—when I stayed forty days and forty nights, eating no bread and
10 drinking no water, when the EVER-LIVING gave to me the two tables of stone, written by the finger of GOD,

and upon them, all the Commandments which the EVER-LIVING dictated to you on the Hill, from the midst of the fire, at the time of the public assembly And there, at the 11 end of forty days and forty nights, the EVER-LIVING gave to me the two tables of stone,—the Tables of the Covenant
When the EVER-LIVING said to 12 me, "Arise! Go down from this Hill!—for your People, whom I brought out from among the Mitzeraim, have gone to corruption! They have turned quickly from what I commanded them They have cast an Idol for themselves!'"
The EVER-LIVING also spoke to 13 me saying, "I have observed this people, and see that it is a perverse people Fly from Me, and I will 14 destroy and sweep their name from under the heavens, and I will make from you a powerful nation, and a greater than they"
I consequently turned and de- 15 scended from the Hill, and the Hill burnt with fire But the two tables of stone were in my two hands Then I looked and perceived that you 16 had sinned against your EVER-LIVING GOD, having made for yourselves a Cast-metal Calf,—turning yourselves soon from the path which the EVER-LIVING commanded you So I raised 17 the two tables, and threw them from my two hands, and broke them in your sight
I afterwards fell before the EVER- 18 LIVING, as at first, for forty days and forty nights, I ate no bread nor drank water, because of all the sin that you had sinned, in doing wrong in the sight of the EVER-LIVING, to provoke Him, for I was afraid in the 19 presence of the anger and indignation which stirred the EVER-LIVING against you to destroy you, but my EVER-LIVING GOD heard me again at that time The EVER-LIVING, 20 also, was very angry with Aaron, and would have destroyed him, but I prayed at the same time for Aaron himself, and your sin,—the calf that 21 you had made,—I took and melted in fire and beat it grinding as small as fine dust and threw the dust upon

the brook that flowed from the
22 Hill. At Thabarah again, and at
Masah, and Kibroth-Hathavah, you
23 were provoking the EVER-LIVING.
And when the EVER-LIVING sent
to you at Kadesh-Barnea, an order,
saying, "Go up and seize the
country which I have given you,"
again you rebelled against the order
of your EVER-LIVING GOD, and
were not true to Him, and would
24 not listen to His voice. You were
always rebels from the EVER-LIV-
25 ING, from the day I knew you!
I fell, however, before the EVER-
LIVING for those forty days and
those forty nights,—I fell down,—
because the EVER-LIVING said He
26 would destroy you. But I prayed
to the EVER-LIVING and said, "AL-
MIGHTY LORD, do not wreck Your
People, and Your inheritance, whom
You redeemed by Your greatness,
—whom You brought up from the
Mitzeraim with a strong hand.
27 Remember your servants Abraham,
and Isaac, and Jacob Turn not to
afflict this People for its wickedness
28 and for its sin; lest the country from
which You brought them should
say; "Because the EVER-LIVING was
not able to bring them to the land
which He promised, and because He
hated them He brought them out to
29 kill them in the desert. They are
also Your People, and Your Inheritance, whom You brought out by Your
Great Power, and with a directing
arm."

10   Then the EVER-LIVING said to me,
"Cut two tables of stone, like the
former ones, and come up to ME to
the Hill. Also make an ark of wood.
2 And I will write upon the tables the
Commandments that were upon the
former tables, that you broke, and
3 you can put them in the ark." I
consequently made an ark of acacia
wood, and cut two tables of stone,
like the first ones, and ascended the
Hill with the two tables in my hands,
4 and He wrote upon the tables the
same writing as upon the former
ones,—the Ten Commandments,—
which your EVER-LIVING GOD proclaimed on the Hill, from amid the
fire, on the day of the Public
Assembly. Then the EVER-LIVING
5 gave them to me. So I turned
and descended from the Hill, and
placed the two tables in the ark
that I had made.—and they are

there, as the EVER-LIVING instructed
me.[1]

I then remained on the Hill, as at 10
the previous time, forty days and
forty nights, and the EVER-LIVING
listened to me also again, that He
should not desire to wreck you. So 11
the EVER-LIVING said to me, "Arise!
Proceed! March before the People,
and let them go on and seize the country which I promised to their fathers to
give to them."

And now, Israel, what your EVER- 12
LIVING GOD asks of you is;—That
you should fear your EVER-LIVING
GOD, and walk in all His ways, and
love Him, and serve your EVER-LIVING
GOD, with all your heart, and all
your life; and to keep the command- 13
ments of the EVER-LIVING, and all
His institutions, which I have commanded you this day for your own
benefit.

Look! The heavens, and the 14
heaven of the heavens, — the earth
and all it contains, belong to your
EVER-LIVING GOD. Yet the EVER- 15
LIVING chose to love your fathers,
and He selected their race after them
from all the Peoples,—as at this day,
—therefore circumcise the flesh of 16
your hearts, and never stiffen your
necks, for your EVER-LIVING GOD is 17
a GOD of GODS, and ALMIGHTY of
ALMIGHTIES, the GREAT GOD, the
POWERFUL, and the ENLIGHTENER;
—Who will not regard appearances,
and will not take bribes! Who does 18
justice to the orphan and the widow,
and loves to give bread and clothes to
the stranger. Therefore you should 19

---

[1] Vv. 6—9 are a note of an ancient editor,
not a part of the speech of Moses. They are
probably a note of Ezra's, made after the return
from Babylon, but have been by a transcriber
widely misplaced, for they have not the least
connection with the subject of the text.—F. F.

(Afterwards the children of Israel 6
marched from the Wells of the son of
Yakan, to Moserah, where Aaron died, and
was buried, and Aliazer his son was made
priest in his stead From there they 7
marched to Gudgudah, and from Gudgudah to Yatbathah, a country of water
brooks. At that period the EVER-LIVING 8
separated the tribe of Levi to bear with
Aaron the Covenant of the EVER-LIVING,
to stand before the EVER-LIVING to
officiate, and to bless in His Name—
until to-day. Consequently there is not 9
a portion or an inheritance for the tribe
of Levi with its brothers. The EVER-
LIVING is its inheritance as your EVER-
LIVING GOD said to it.

love the stranger, for you were a stranger in the land of the Mitzeraim!

20 Fear your EVER-LIVING GOD, serve Him, and hold to Him, and

21 swear by His Name He led you, and He is your GOD, Who produced for you those great things, and the revelations that your eyes saw

22 Your fathers went down to the Mitzeraim as seventy persons, and now your EVER-LIVING GOD has collected you as a multitude like the stars of the heavens!

11 Therefore love your EVER-LIVING GOD, and carefully regard Him, and His Institutions, and His Decrees,

2 and His Commands for all time, and learn them to-day For you are not children who have not known, and have not seen the corrections of your EVER-LIVING GOD,—His greatness, and His strong hand, and His direct-

3 ing aim, and His wonders, and the events that He effected in the midst of the Mitzerites,—upon Pharoh, king of the Mitzeraim, and all his country,

4 and what He did to the army of the Mitzerites, to their horsemen, and to their chariots,—how the sea,—the Sea of Suf,—rushed over their heads when they followed after you,—how the EVER-LIVING destroyed them on

5 that day Also what He did for you in the desert, until you arrived at

6 this spot, and what He did to Dathan and Abiram, the sons of Ahab, the son of Reuben, — how the earth opened her mouth and swallowed them, and their homes, and their tents, and the whole of their supporters, slaying them in the centre of all Israel

7 For your eyes have seen all the great events that the EVER-LIVING

8 has done,—therefore attend to all the commands that I command you to-day, so that you may be hearty, and go and seize the country that

9 you are advancing to possess, and so that you may lengthen your stay upon the land which the EVER-LIVING swore to your fathers to give to them, and to their race,—a land flowing with milk and honey

10 For the country you are going to possess is not like the land of the Mitzeraim, whence you have come, where you sowed your seed, and watered it on your feet, like a

11 vegetable garden,—but the country you are advancing to possess is a land of hills and vales, and of rain from the skies refreshed with water

—a land that your EVER-LIVING GOD 12 visits,—the eyes of your EVER-LIVING GOD are continually upon it, from the first of the year until the last of the year —So it will happen, if you 13 attentively listen to my commands that I command you to-day, and love your EVER-LIVING GOD, and serve Him with all your heart, and with all your life, that I will give rain upon 14 your land at the season of sprouting, and of ripening, and you shall harvest your corn, and your wine, and your oil I will also give herbage upon 15 your fields for your cattle, that you may eat and be satisfied But guard 16 yourselves from seducing your hearts, and turning to serve other gods, and worshipping them For then the 17 anger of the EVER-LIVING will burn against you, and He will shut the skies, and there will be no rain, and the land will not give its increase, and you will soon perish from upon the beautiful country which the EVER-LIVING gave you Therefore fix these 18 words upon your hearts, and upon your souls, and bind them as ornaments upon your hands, and let them be as frontlets between your eyes, and 19 teach them to your children, to talk about in your homes, in your families, and in your journeys on the road, and at your lying down, and rising up! Write them also upon the doors 20 of your house, and upon your gates,— so that you may increase your days, 21 and the days of your children upon the ground which the EVER-LIVING promised to your fathers to give to them as long as the skies endured over the earth!—For if you carefully 22 keep all these commands which I command you to practise, and love your EVER-LIVING GOD, and walk in all His ways, and adhere to Him, then the EVER-LIVING will drive all 23 those nations from before you, and you shall possess nations greater and stronger than yourself,—every place 24 that the sole of your foot treads shall be yours,—from the desert to Lebanon, from the river, the river Frath [1] backwards to the sea, shall be your boundaries

None shall stand before you, you 25 shall terrify and chase them Your EVER-LIVING GOD will give all the country to you which you have travelled through, as He promised

1) 1, 12. 1 4

194

26 Attend! I will place before you
27 to-day CURSING and BLESSING. The
Blessing which you have heard in
the commands of your EVER-LIVING
GOD, which I command to you this
28 day; and the Cursing, if you do not
listen to the commands of your
EVER-LIVING GOD, but turn from the
path which I command to you this
day, to walk after other gods whom
you have not known.
29 So when your EVER-LIVING GOD
has brought you to the country that
you go to possess, you shall place the
Blessing upon the Hill of Gherizim,
and the Cursing upon the Hill of
30 Aibal. — Are they not over the Jordan, following the path of the
declining sun?—in the land of the
Cananites, who reside in the west
opposite Gilgal, at the side of the
31 Oakwood of Morah?[1]—When you
cross the Jordan to go to seize the
country which your EVER-LIVING
GOD will give to you,—you shall seize
32 it and settle in it. But take care to
practise the whole of the institutions,
and the legislation which I have
placed before you to-day;—

12 Which are the Institutions and the
Legislation which you shall carefully
practise in the land which the EVER-
LIVING, the GOD of your fathers, will
give to you to possess all the time
that you live upon the earth.
2 You must absolutely destroy all
the columns which the nations whom
you drive out, worship. Their gods
upon the hills, and heights, and upon
the mountains, and which they call
3 upon under every shadowy tree. You
shall also throw down their altars,
and break their pillars, and burn
their shrines in fire, and smash the
images of their gods, and destroy
their names from the places where
they are.
4 You shall not do so to your EVER-
5 LIVING GOD; for at the place which
your EVER-LIVING GOD may choose
from any of your tribes to place His
Name there, to fix it, you shall go
6 to it, and bring there your burnt-

offerings, and sacrifices, and your
services, and the presents of your
hands, and your vows, and the first
fruits of your herds, and flocks; and 7
you shall eat them there before your
EVER-LIVING GOD, and cheer yourselves in all the success of your
hand,—you, and your families, when
your EVER-LIVING GOD blesses you.
You shall not offer as we do here 8
to-day,—all that is right in your own
sight,—for you have not yet arrived 9
at the REST, and the Inheritance
which your EVER LIVING GOD will
give to you. But when you pass over 10
the Jordan, and occupy the country
that your EVER-LIVING GOD will
divide among you, and rest from all
your enemies around, and dwell
securely, then to the place where 11
your EVER-LIVING GOD shall choose
to fix HIS NAME, you shall bring all
that I have commanded you,—your
burnt-offerings, and sacrifices, your
gifts and the presents of your hand,
and all your free vows, that you vow
to the EVER-LIVING. You shall enjoy 12
yourselves there before your EVER-
LIVING GOD, you, and your sons and
daughters, and men servants, and
maid servants, and the Levite who
is in your village, for he has not a
share or estate among you. You 13
must guard yourselves from offering
your burnt-offerings in every place
you see, except in the place which 14
the EVER-LIVING may choose in one
of your tribes. —there you shall offer
your burnt-offerings, and there you
shall do all that I have commanded
you. However, you may, to all the 15
desires of your life, sacrifice and eat
flesh according to the blessings which
your EVER-LIVING GOD has given
you, in all your villages. Both the
clean and the unclean may eat of
them,—like as of the gazelle and the
stag,—except that they shall not eat 16
the blood;—that shall be poured
upon the ground like water. You 17
shall not eat in your villages from
the offering of your corn, and wine,
and oil, or of the firstlings of your
herd or flock, or of any vow which
you vow as free-will offerings, or of
presents from your hands,—you shall 18
only eat such in the presence of
your EVER-LIVING GOD, at the
place which your EVER-LIVING GOD
chooses to Himself; you and your
son and your daughter, and your
man servant and maid servant, and

[1] This poetic and striking indication of these
localities is an internal evidence that these
sublime orations are the work of Moses, and
written and spoken by him on the East of
the Jordan, and he pointed to the West as he
uttered the words. Had they been the work
of a forger in Jerusalem, as some modern
sceptics assert he would never have used the
words and gesture indicated. F. F.

the Levite who is in your village, shall enjoy yourselves before your EVER-LIVING GOD in all the prosperity of your hand

19 Take care that you do not forget the Levite all your time upon the
20 earth, for your EVER-LIVING GOD will extend your boundaries, as He promised you,—therefore I tell you to eat flesh, wherever you desire to live you may eat flesh, in all places you wish to live, you may eat flesh,
21 for the place where your EVER-LIVING GOD may choose to fix His Name may be far from you therefore you may sacrifice from your herd and from your flock that the EVER-LIVING gives you, as I commanded you, and may eat in your villages of all that your life desires,—
22 but only as the gazelle and the stag are eaten,—thus the clean and the unclean may eat, they may both eat
23 Only refrain from eating the blood, for the blood is the life, and you shall not eat the life with the flesh
24 You shall not eat it, you shall pour
25 it upon the earth like water You shall not eat it, for it is well to you, and to your children after you, that you should do right in the sight of
26 the EVER-LIVING Only what you have consecrated by yourself, and your vows, you shall take up and bring to the Place which the EVER-
27 LIVING has chosen, and you shall offer your burnt-offerings with the flesh and the blood upon the altar of your EVER-LIVING GOD, for the blood of your sacrifice shall be poured upon the altar of your EVER-LIVING GOD, and you shall eat the flesh
28 Listen attentively to all these words that I command you, so that you may prosper, and your children after you for ever, while you do fair and right in the sight of your EVER-LIVING GOD
29 When your EVER-LIVING GOD has defeated the nations where you are going, driving them before you, and you possess them, and reside in
30 their country, guard yourselves from enquiring about them,—from turning to enquire about their gods, and asking, "How did these nations serve their gods? for I would do the same
31 myself" You shall not do so with your EVER-LIVING GOD, for all the offerings to the EVER-LIVING which you take up to offer to your God as well as t   ...   r ... t ' ...

daughters shall be burnt with fire to your GOD

You must carefully practise all **13** the things which I have commanded you You must not add to them, nor shall you take away from them

When a Preacher arises among 2 you, or a dreamer of dreams, and gives you a proof, or an evidence, and the proof or the evidence which 3 he has declared to you comes, to persuade you to walk after other gods, whom you have not known, and to serve them,—listen not to the 4 words of that Preacher, or to that dreamer of dreams, for your EVER-LIVING GOD is trying you to learn if you are lovers of your EVER-LIVING GOD with all your heart, and with all soul You must walk after your 5 EVER-LIVING GOD, and fear Him and keep His Commandments, and listen to His voice, and serve Him, and adhere to Him Therefore that 6 Preacher, or that dreamer of dreams, shall be put to death, for advising to turn from your EVER-LIVING GOD, Who brought you from the land of the Mitzeraim, and freed you from the House of Bondage, for he would seduce you from the path your EVER-LIVING GOD commanded you to walk in,—so you must burn the evil from your breast

If your brother, the son of your 7 mother, should seduce you,—or your son, or your daughter, or the wife of your bosom, or your friend who is like your life,—should say privately, "Let us go and serve other gods," whom you have not known, nor your fathers,—some of the gods of the 8 Peoples who are around you,—close to you,—or far from you,—from one boundary of the earth to the other boundary of the earth,—do not incline to him, or listen to them Let 9 not your eye feel pity for them, and do not grieve or feel compassion for them,—but kill! Your hand shall be 10 the first to bring them to death, and the hand of all the people after you, who shall stone them with stones,— 11 for they shall die,—because they sought to seduce you from your EVER-LIVING GOD, Who brought you from the land of the Mitzerites, from the House of Bondage Then all Israel 12 will hear, and fear, and not continue to practise that sin in your midst

If you shall hear that at any city 13 e ... ' ... GOD has granted you to reside, it is said,

14 " There came men, sons of Belial, from our midst, and seduced the residents of our city, saying,—Let us go and serve other gods, whom

15 we know not," then you shall enquire, and investigate, and if the truth of the report is established, about that

16 abomination in the midst of you, you shall strike the residents in that town with the edge of the sword, and devote it with all that are in it and put the cattle to the edge of the

17 sword, and collect the whole of the furniture to the middle of its

market-place, and consume all its furniture completely to your EVER-LIVING GOD, and it shall be a ruin for ever,—it shall not be built again

18 And nothing of the accursed things shall stick to your hands, so that the EVER-LIVING may turn away from His burning anger, and grant you mercies and benefit you, and increase you, as He promised to your fathers,

19 so long as you listen to your EVER-LIVING GOD, and keep all His Commandments which I command you to-day, and do right in the sight of your EVER-LIVING GOD

END OF THE THIRD ORATION

SPEECH IV.

Laws against Sins and Self-Degradation.

14 You are the children of the LORD, you shall not cut yourselves, nor shave your eyebrows for the dead

2 For you are a People consecrated to your EVER-LIVING GOD, and the EVER-LIVING chose you to be a People separated from all the Peoples who are upon the face of the earth

3 You shall eat no filth

4 These are the beasts that you may eat, the ox, the sheep kind and the

5 goat kind, the stag and gazelle, and roebuck, and chamois, and antelope

6 and springbok, and bison, with all cattle that divide the hoof and chew the cud,—those animals you may

7 eat But of these who chew the cud you may not eat, although they divide the hoof, the camel, and the kangaroo, and the rabbit who chew the cud, but do not divide the hoof,—

8 they are unclean to you, with the hog, although it divides the hoof, yet it does not chew It is unclean to you You shall not eat of its flesh or touch its dead body

9 You may eat of these among all that are in the waters,—all that have

10 fins and scales you may eat, but of all that have not fins and scales, you may not eat They are unclean to you

11 You may eat every clean bird

12 But you may not eat of these,—the

13 eagle, and the osprey, the buzzard

14 and kite, with their species, and the

15 whole of the raven species, and the ostrich, and the night-hawk, and the sea-gull, and the cormorant, with

16 their species, with the pelican, and the

17 snake-eater, and the bittern, and the vomiter, and the eagle-vulture, and

18 the turkey-buzzard, with the stork, and the snorter, with their species,

19 and the hoopoo and the bat, and all the winged spawners are unclean to

20 you,—you may not eat them You

21 may eat every clean bird, but you may not eat any self-dying carcase,—give them to the foreigner who resides among you to be eaten, or sell to merchants, for you are a People consecrated to your EVER-LIVING GOD

You shall not boil a kid in its mother's milk

22 You shall tithe the whole of the produce of your grain, as it comes from the field year by year, and you

23 shall eat of it before your EVER-LIVING GOD, in the place that He chooses to fix His Name,—both of your corn, and wine, and oil, and of the blessings of your herd and flock, so that you may learn to reverence your EVER-LIVING GOD at all times

24 But if the journey is too long for you to be able to carry it because the place which your EVER-LIVING GOD has chosen to fix His Name in is too far from you,—then you shall bless your EVER-LIVING GOD, and convert

25 it into money, and take the money in your hand, and go to the place that your EVER-LIVING GOD has chosen for Himself, and expend that

26 money in all that your life requires,—in oxen, and sheep, and wine, and flesh, and in all that your life demands, and eat them there before your EVER-LIVING GOD, and enjoy yourself with your family But you shall

27 not forget the Levite who is in your villages, for he has no inheritance and share with you At the end of

28 the third year you shall bring the whole of the tithe of your produce in that year, and leave your villages The Levite shall also come, for he

29 has no share or inheritance, with you, and the foreigner, along with the fatherless, and the widow who are in your villages, and they shall eat, and be satisfied, because your EVER-LIVING GOD has blessed you in all the work of your hands which you have done

At the end of seven years, there 15 shall be a releasing, and this is the 2 kind of releasing —Every possessor of mortgaged land which his neighbour has mortgaged shall release it, he shall have no claim against his neighbour or his brother, because it is a Release by the EVER-LIVING You may have a claim against 3 foreigners, but you must release from your hand what belongs to your brothers for nothing, for you will not 4 be poor yourself, because blessing, the EVER-LIVING will bless you in the country which your EVER-LIVING GOD will give to you to possess —

5 That is, if you listen to the voice of your EVER-LIVING GOD, and continue to practise the whole of His Commandments, which I command you

6 to-day, for your EVER-LIVING GOD will bless you, as He has promised, and you shall lend to many nations, but you will not borrow, and you shall rule over many nations, but they shall not rule over you

7 Yet there will be poor among you one brother with another in your villages, in the country which your EVER-LIVING GOD gives you Harden not your heart, nor close your hand

8 from your poor brother, but open your hand to him, and lend, according to his necessity what is needful to

9 him Guard yourself from saying to your vile heart, "The seventh year, the year of release, is near,"—and your eye is cruel to your poor brother, and you will not lend to him,—when he will cry against you to the EVER-LIVING, and it will be a sin to you

10 Lend freely to him! and let not your heart grudge against lending, but rely upon this fact that your EVER-LIVING GOD will then bless you in all you do, and in all sent

11 from your hand! For the poor will never be wanting in the breast of the land,—therefore I have commanded you saying, "Open your hand freely to your distressed brother,—to your poor,—in the land!"

12 When your relative is sold to you,— a Hebrew man or a Hebrew woman,— he shall serve you six years, but in the seventh year you shall set him

13 free from you But when you set him free from you, you shall not

14 send him away destitute You shall reward him liberally from your flock, and from your corn, and from your wine vat, which your EVER-LIVING GOD has blessed You shall give to

15 him,—and shall remember that you were slaves among the Mitzeraim, and your EVER-LIVING GOD freed you,—therefore I command this thing to-day

16 But if it occurs that he says to you, "I will not go from you, for I like you and your house, for I have been

17 satisfied with you," then you shall take an awl, and fix him by his ear to your door, and he shall always be your servant that is, until your death. Thus also you shall do

It shall not be hard in your sight to 18 send him from you into freedom, for you shall only purchase your servant by the year for six years,—then your EVER-LIVING GOD will bless you in all your work

Every first-born which your herd, 19 or your flock bears, remember you must dedicate to your EVER-LIVING GOD You shall not work the first-born of your cow, nor shear the first-born of your ewe,—you shall eat them 20 year by year before your EVER-LIVING GOD, in the place that the EVER-LIVING chooses, you and your family But if there be a defect or 21 lameness in it, or bareness, or any disease, you shall not sacrifice it to your EVER-LIVING GOD, you must eat it 22 in your villages, the clean and the unclean together, as you do the gazelle and stag,—only you must not 23 eat their blood Pour it upon the earth like water

Regard the harvest month [1] and 16 offer the Passover to your EVER-LIVING GOD, for in the harvest month your EVER-LIVING GOD brought you out of the land of the Mitzeraim at night,—therefore sacri- 2 fice as the Passover to your EVER-LIVING GOD a lamb, and in the place which your EVER-LIVING GOD has chosen to fix His Name there

You shall not eat any ferment upon 3 it for seven days You must eat unfermented bread only, for you came out from the Mitzeraim in haste, therefore you shall remember the day you came out from the land of the Mitzerites, all the days of your life, and nothing fermenting shall be 4 seen in all your boundaries for seven days, and you shall not leave any of the flesh which you sacrifice at the beginning of the evening of that day until the morning You will not be 5 permitted to sacrifice the Passover in any of the villages which your EVER-LIVING GOD gives to you —but only 6 at the place which your EVER-LIVING GOD may choose to fix His Name there, may you sacrifice the Passover, at the afternoon as the sun declines, at the time you came out from the Mitzeraim So you shall 7 roast and eat it in the place which your EVER-LIVING GOD has chosen for Himself,—as you turned on that morning and went to your tents

You shall eat unfermented bread
8 with your GOD for six days, and on the seventh day you shall assemble to your EVER-LIVING GOD You shall do no business upon it

9 Count seven Sabbaths from the beginning of putting the sickle to the corn,—count to the end of seven
10 Sabbaths Then you shall make the Festival of Sabbaths to your EVER-
11 LIVING GOD, and enjoy yourselves before your EVER-LIVING GOD, you, and your sons, and your daughters, and man and maid servants, and the Levite who is in your village, and the foreigner, and the fatherless, and the widow, who are among you, at the place that your EVER-LIVING GOD has chosen to fix His Name in
12 For you must remember you were slaves among the Mitzeraim,—therefore preserve and practise these institutions
13 You must also make yourselves a festival of seven days after the harvesting of your corn and vintage, and enjoy yourselves in that feast, 14 you, your son, and your daughter, and your man and maid servants, and the Levite and the foreigner, and the fatherless, and the widow, who are in your villages You must feast for 15 seven days to your EVER-LIVING GOD in the place that the EVER-LIVING may choose, because your EVER-LIVING GOD has blessed you in all your products, and in all the work of your hand,—therefore you must be glad

All your men shall see the Pre- 16 sence of your EVER-LIVING GOD three times in a year, in the place He may choose, at the Feast of Unfermented Bread, [1] and at the Feast of Weeks, and the Feast of Tabernacles, and 17 you shall not see the Presence of the EVER-LIVING empty-handed

---

[1] Literally, "of biscuits' —F F

END OF THE FOURTH ORATION

SPEECH V.

Local Government

18 You shall appoint Judges and Recorders for yourselves in every village which your EVER-LIVING GOD gives to you, to control you, and to govern the People with honest
19 government. You shall not distort justice. You shall not regard stations. You shall not take bribes,—for bribes blind the eyes of the intelligent, and pervert the decrees
20 of justice. You shall follow perfect justice, so that you may live and possess the country that your EVER-LIVING GOD has given to you.
21 You shall not plant shrines, or any trees, at the side of the altar you make to your EVER-LIVING GOD,
22 nor shall you erect for yourselves columns, as standards, to your EVER-LIVING GOD.
17 You shall not sacrifice to your EVER-LIVING GOD an ox or a sheep in which there is any defect,—anything bad,—for that would be an insult to your EVER-LIVING GOD.
2 If there should come out from any of your villages which your EVER-LIVING GOD gives you, a man or a woman who does wrong in the sight of the EVER-LIVING by slighting His
3 Covenant and going and serving other gods, and worshipping them,— or the sun, or the moon, or any of the hosts of the skies contrary to my
4 command,—and it is reported to you, when you hear it, then you should enquire carefully, and if the truth of the thing is confirmed, that such an outrage has been done in
5 Israel, you shall bring out that man or that woman, who have done that wicked thing, in the village of the man or woman, and stone them to
6 death with stones. They shall be put to death on the evidence of two or three witnesses. Upon the evidence of one witness, they shall not
7 be put to death. The hands of the witnesses shall be first upon them, to kill them,—then the hands of all the People afterwards. You shall thus burn that wickedness from among you.
8 If a case should occur among you difficult to decide between blood and

blood, between right and right, and between stroke and stroke,—an affair of a contention in your gates,—you shall remove it, and take it up to the place which your EVER-LIVING GOD has chosen for Himself, and go to the
9 priests, to the Levites, and to the Judge who may be in your times, and appeal and report the matter to
10 the Chief Judge, and act upon the
11 decision which he pronounces. You shall not turn from the order that he communicates to you, to the right or
12 to the left. And the person who acts insolently against the decree of the priest appointed to serve your EVER-LIVING GOD there, and the Chief Judge,—that man shall die! Thus you shall burn that evil out of Israel
13 and all the People will hear, and fear, and no longer be contumacious.
14 When you arrive in the country which your EVER-LIVING GOD has given to you, and possess it and reside in it, and say to yourselves,— "Let us place a king over us, like all
15 the nations who are around," you shall only place over you the king whom your EVER-LIVING GOD may choose for Himself. You shall place a king over you from your brothers, you are not permitted to appoint a foreigner over yourselves, a man who is not your brother.
16 Further he shall not collect horses to himself, and he shall not take the People back to the Mitzeraim, because of its abundance of horses, for the EVER-LIVING has commanded you not to contemplate to return by that way for ever.
17 He shall not collect wives about himself, nor turn his heart to silver and gold, to accumulate them excessively.
18 When he is set upon the throne for his kingship, there shall be written out for him a Duplicate of the Law,
19 from the book in the custody of the Levitical priests, and he shall keep it with him, and read in it every day of his life, so that he may learn to fear the EVER-LIVING his GOD,—to guard the whole of the commandments of the LAW, and to administer
20 these Institutions, so that his heart may not rise above his brothers, and

that he may not turn from its commands to the right or to the left, so that he may extend his days in his kingship, he and his sons in the circuit of Israel　　　.

18 There shall be no share or inheritance to the Levitical Priests or any of the tribe of Levi with Israel　The EVER-LIVING is their inheritance and

2 feeder, therefore they shall have no inheritance among their brothers,—the EVER-LIVING is their inheritance,

3 as I said to you, therefore there shall be decreed for the priests something from each sacrifice sacrificed by the people, whether ox or sheep　There shall be given to the priest the fore

4 leg, jaws, and breast　You shall give to them the first-fruits of your corn also, the first-fruits of your oil, and

5 the first fleece of your flock　For your EVER-LIVING GOD chose them from all your tribes to stand to serve to the Name of the EVER-LIVING, they, and their children for all time

6 And when a Levite comes to one of your villages, in any part of Israel, although he is a stranger there, and comes from any village where he

7 formerly lived, he may serve to the Name of the EVER-LIVING, his GOD, like all his brothers who are fixed there in the Presence of the EVER-

8 LIVING　They shall eat share and share alike, of equal value on account of their ancestry

9 When you enter the country that your EVER-LIVING GOD has given you, you shall not learn the depravities of those heathens　You shall

10 not take with you your son or daughter to a throwing over a fire, to divinations, and enchantments, or

11 for witchcraft, or incantations, or enquiry of spirits, or fore-tellers, or

12 questioning the dead,—for the EVER-LIVING loathes all these practices, and to sweep away all these practices your EVER-LIVING GOD has driven

13 them from before you　You must be perfect before your EVER-LIVING

14 GOD,—for those heathens, whom you will drive out, listened to cloud-makers, and to diviners,—but you must not,—consequently give yourselves to the EVER-LIVING, your GOD

15 Your EVER-LIVING GOD will raise up a Prophet like me for you from among your brothers, after me,—listen to him

16 You all requested one from your EVER-LIVING GOD, at Horeb on the day of the Public Meeting, saying, " We cannot continue to hear the voice of the EVER-LIVING GOD, nor longer to see this great fire, for fear of death "　When the EVER-LIVING 17 replied to me, " What they have said is good　I will raise for them, from 18 amongst their brothers, ONE LIKE YOU, and will put words into his mouth, and he shall report to them all I command them　And any man 19 who will not listen to the messages which he delivers in MY NAME, I will drive out from My People

" But the Prophet who shall pre- 20 sume to deliver a message in MY NAME, which I have not commanded him to deliver, or who shall speak in the name of other gods — that Prophet shall die ! "

But perhaps you may say in your 21 heart,—" How can I distinguish such a message as what the EVER-LIVING has not spoken ?　When the Prophet 22 delivered it in the Name of the EVER-LIVING,—although he was not commanded ? "

When the event does not happen, —then the EVER-LIVING has not spoken　The Prophet has spoken it, in his presumption,—fear him not

When your EVER-LIVING GOD has 19 destroyed those heathen of whom your EVER-LIVING GOD has given you the country, and has driven them out, and you dwell in their cities and their houses, you shall separate three 2 cities to yourselves in the midst of the country that your EVER-LIVING GOD gives you to possess　You shall then 3 make roads for your use to these three cities, from the boundaries of the country which your EVER-LIVING GOD has divided amongst you, so that any man-slayer can fly to them

However, this is the kind of man- 4 slayer who may fly there and live,— he who has struck his neighbour unintentionally, when he did not previously hate him　—For instance one 5 who went with his neighbour to a wood to cut timber, and the iron flew from the handle of the axe in cutting the timber, or the iron flew from the tree and caught his neighbour, and he dies　He may fly to one of these cities, and live, lest the Avenger of 6 Blood pursue after the man-slayer, whilst his heart is hot, and overtake him, owing to the length of the way, and deprive him of life before he has been condemned to death,—for he

7 did not hate before the event. Consequently I command you to appoint three cities to be provided for yourselves. 8 But if your EVER-LIVING GOD extends your boundaries, as He promised to your fathers and gives to you the whole of the country which He promised to give to your fathers, 9 you shall also attend to all these orders, to do what I have commanded you to-day, and love your EVER-LIVING GOD, and walk in His ways, at all times. Therefore add three 10 other cities beside these three. Because you shall not shed innocent blood in the breast of the land that your EVER-LIVING GOD has given you to inherit, for that blood would be upon yourselves.

11 But if it happens that a man hates his neighbour, and waits for him, and arises against him, and strikes at his life so that he dies, and then flies to 12 one of those CITIES of GOD, the Magistrates of that city shall send, and apprehend him there, and deliver him to the hand of the Avenger of 13 Blood, and he shall be killed. Your eye shall not pity over him, for you must burn out innocent blood from Israel, that you may prosper.

14 You shall not remove the boundary of your neighbour, which your chiefs placed to your estate, when they divided the country which your EVER LIVING GOD gave you to possess.

15 A single witness shall not be received against a person for any offence, or for any sin. For every offence that may be committed, the evidence of two witnesses, or of three must establish it.

16 When anyone makes a quarrel with 17 a man, to do him an injury, both the persons between whom the dispute is, must appear before the presence of the EVER-LIVING, and before the Priests and Judges who may be in 18 their times, and the judges shall

enquire carefully to ascertain who is the false witness,—giving false evidence to injure his brother,—and shall 19 do to him as he intended to do to his brother,—and burn that wrong from their midst, so that when others hear 20 they may fear and not continue to do similar wrong amongst you. Your 21 eyes shall consequently not pity Life for life, eye for eye, tooth for tooth, hand for hand, foot for foot

1 When a corpse is found fallen in a 21 field in the land which your EVER-LIVING GOD gives you to possess, and it is not known how killed, your chiefs 2 and magistrates shall go and measure to the towns that are round about the corpse, to ascertain the town that 3 may be nearest to the corpse. Then the head man of that town shall take a heifer from the herd, which has not worked,—which has not drawn wheels, and the head man of that 4 town shall cause the heifer to be taken down to a vale with a constantly flowing brook, which has not been cultivated nor reaped, and break the neck of the heifer at the brook.

Then the priests of the sons of 5 Levi shall approach,—for the LORD your GOD chose them to officiate, and to bless in the name of the EVER-LIVING, and every contention and every dispute shall be decided by them, with all the Magistrates of the 6 surrounding towns,—to the corpse, and wash their hands over the broken-necked heifer at the brook, and as- 7 severate and say, "Our hands have not shed this blood, and our eyes did not see it. Cover it to the people of 8 Israel whom you have chosen, LORD, and lay not innocent blood on the breast of your People of Israel" Then the blood shall be covered for them, and you will burn the innocent 9 blood from amongst you,—for you must practise justice in the eyes of the EVER-LIVING

1 Ch. XIX.—XXI. These first nine verses of Ch. XXI have been evidently misplaced by some transcriber, and should be at the end of Ch. XIX, as I now place them, as they complete the subject dealt with by Moses. I therefore restore them to their proper position. The reader, however, will probably ask my reasons for these alterations which I make in the arrangement of the text in Ch. XIX—XXI. They are as follows. I had always felt that the accepted order of the matter had become confused by some very ancient transcribers, and therefore consulted scholars whom I believed to be fully competent to assist me in a rectification, by which I proposed to bring the thought of the speeches of Moses in those chapters to a perfectly consecutive current of meaning. All agreed with me that the old text had been confused, but would not venture to decide whether my new proposed arrangements were correct. I was disappointed, so at last appealed to my talented friend the Reverend John Bowen, B D, Rector of St Lawrence, Pembrokesh... who is an accomplished Classic and Oriental Scholar, and he kindly consented to co-operate with me, and I accepted his advice, careful and indeed to my suggestions, feeling convinced that he was right. The confusion of the text at the various points noted

in my margin, I think, arose at the time when our present text was copied on to a roll of skins, from the original stone plates or tablets upon which Moses engraved the Speeches for record in the Ark of Witnesses, as stated by Ahazer, his Editor, in Ch xxxii, v 24, of Deuteronomy. The Scribe then evidently confused the order of the plates. The fact that the various passages implicated contain about the same number of words, I take as an indication that my view is the right one. My learned and judicious friend, the Rev J Bowen, however, informs me that a previous commentator upon this part of Deuteronomy, who had noted the confusion in the records, has suggested an even earlier period for its origination. He believed, and Mr Bowen seems to agree with him, that it was made at the time when, in accordance with the command of Moses, the Law was engraved, "deeply cut," upon the pillars set up, and covered with some enduring chemical plaster, in the Vale of the Jordan, upon the passage of Joshua and his Army. That there the autographic tablets of Moses were in these paragraphs misarranged and subsequent transcribers failed to rectify the error. I leave my readers to decide which theory has the best weight of evidence to support it —F F

END OF THE FIFTH ORATION

SPEECH VI.

Laws of War.

20 When you go to war with your enemies, and see horses and chariots, —a people more numerous than yourselves, fear them not,—for your EVER-LIVING GOD is with you, Who brought you from the land of the Mitzeraim

2 And when you are preparing for the war, the Priest shall come forward and address the People and say to them,

3 "Listen, Israel! You are now preparing for war with your enemies Let not your heart shrink Fear not, nor be startled, nor terrified at them!

4 for your EVER-LIVING GOD marches with you, to fight for you against your enemy, and save you"

5 The Magistrates, also, shall address the People, saying, "What man is there who has built a new house, and not dedicated it? Let him go and return to his house, for fear he should be killed in the war, and another man should dedicate it

6 "And what man has planted a vineyard and has not reaped it? Let him go and return to his home, for fear he should be killed in the war, and another man reap it

7 "And what man is engaged to a woman, and has not married her? Let him go and return to his home for fear he should be killed in the war, and another man marry her"

8 The Magistrates shall even add to this address to the People, and ask,— "What man fears with a timid heart? Let him go and return to his house, and not depress the hearts of his brothers, like his own heart"

9 And when the Magistrates have ceased speaking to the People, then they should appoint officers to the regiments to command the People [1]

10 When you approach a city to war against it, you shall propose peace to

11 it, and if they will adopt peace, and open to you, then all the people found in it shall be subject to you, and serve

12 you But if they will not accept peace with you, but make war against

13 you, then assail them, for your EVER-LIVING GOD has given them into your hands, and destroy all the men by

14 the edge of the sword The women and children, however, and the cattle and all that may be in the city all

the booty, you may seize for yourselves, for you may use the booty of your enemies which your EVER-LIVING GOD gives to you

When you advance to war with your **21** enemies, and your EVER-LIVING GOD gives them into your hand, and you take them captive, and see amongst 11 the captives there is a beautiful woman, and you have a desire for her to take her to yourself as a wife, you shall take her into the sanctuary 12 of your house, and uncover her head, and pare her nails, and she shall put 13 off the clothing in which she was captured, and reside in your house, and weep for her father and mother the space of a month, and after that you can go to her and marry her, and she shall be your wife But if it then 14 happens that you do not like her, you shall free her for life,—you shall not sell her for money,—you shall not treat her as a slave, because you have degraded her You must do the same **20** to all the cities afar from you, which are not of cities of these nations here.

But in the cities of these Peoples, 16 that your EVER-LIVING GOD has given to you to divide, you shall not preserve a living breath, but devote 17 them,—the Hitites, and the Amorites, and the Cananites, and the Perizites, the Hivites and the Jebusites,—according to the command of your EVER-LIVING GOD The reason is,— 18 so that you may not learn from them to practise all the depravities which they practise against GOD, and thus you would sin against your EVER-LIVING GOD

When you besiege a city for a long 19 period, warring with it to capture it, you shall not destroy the fruit trees by assailing them with the axe, for you can feed from them, therefore you shall not cut them down, for the trees of the field sprang from the ground before you came to the siege However the trees that you know are 20 not trees for food, you may destroy and fell, and build towers with them against the city which is warring with you, until you subdue it

---

[1] Vv 10—14 of Ch xxi should come in, as I now put them, at Ch xx v 9, they having been misplaced into Ch xx by some old copier. See also note on Ch xxi. forward —F. F.

END OF THE SIXTH ORATION.

SPEECH VII.

Domestic Laws.

21 When a man has two wives, and loves the one and dislikes the other, and they bear children to him, both the loved and the disliked, and the son of the disliked one is the eldest,

16 when it comes to the time for his sons to inherit, he cannot make the son of his darling the eldest in place of the

17 son of the disliked, who is eldest, but he must acknowledge the son of the disliked, who is the eldest, and give to him two parts of all he possesses, for he is the first fruits of his love He is justly first-born

18 When a man has a disobedient and rebellious son, who will not listen to the voice of his father or the voice of his mother, but disobeys them and

19 will not listen to them, his father and mother shall take him and conduct him to the Magistrates of the town,

20 and to the open court, and say to the Magistrates of the city, "This son of ours is disobedient and rebellious. He will not listen to our voice He is depraved and drunken"

21 Then all the people of his town shall stone him with stones, and kill, —and that evil will be burnt out from your breast,—and Israel will hear and fear.

22 When a person has committed a crime condemnable to death, you shall kill him and hang him upon

23 a tree You shall not however leave him upon the tree, but bury him the same day, for GOD abhors the hung, consequently you shall not defile your country that your EVER-LIVING GOD has given you to possess

22 You shall not see the ox or sheep of your neighbour straying, and hide it from him You shall drive them

2 back to your neighbour But if you cannot find your neighbour in your vicinity, or do not know him, then you shall preserve them in your own premises, but if it occurs afterwards that your neighbour enquires for them from you, then return them to him

3 You shall also do the same with his ass, and the same to his clothing, and the same with everything, so that your neighbour,—which he has lost

and you have found You shall not use them secretly

4 You shall not see the ass or ox of your neighbour that has fallen on the road, and hide yourself from them Going to the spot, you shall lift them up for him

5 A woman shall not wear a man's dress, and a man shall not dress like a woman, for your EVER-LIVING GOD abhors all who do thus

6 When you find a bird's nest before you in the path, or on any tree, or chicks upon the earth, or eggs, and the mother sitting upon her chicks, or upon her eggs, you shall not take the mother with her young You must

7 drive off the mother, but you may take her young for yourself,—so that it may be well with you and you may extend your days

8 When you build a new house, you shall make a battlement on the circuit of the roof, so that you may not bring blood upon your house, if anyone falls from it

9 You shall not double-crop your farm, that would spoil the full development of the seed you sow, and the produce of the farm

10 You shall not plough with an ox and an ass yoked together

11 You shall not weave silk, wool, and flax together

12 You may make tassels upon the four corners of the cushions that you sit upon

13 When a man takes a wife, and on

14 going to her hates her, and puts insulting reports upon her, and brings a bad name upon her, by saying, "I married this woman, and when I approached her I found she was not

15 a maiden!'" then the father and mother of the girl shall take and bring the maiden, with the proofs of her maidenhood, to the Magistrates

16 of the village, and the father of the girl shall say to the Magistrates,— "I gave my daughter to this man as

17 a wife, but he hates her, and now he sets up insulting reports, saying, 'I did not find your daughter a maid,' but here is the proof of her chastity" Then they shall spread the garment of the Magistrates of the town,

18 and the Magistrates of the town shall

19 take that man, and punish him, and fine him a hundred silvers, and give them to the father of the girl, because he had brought a bad name upon a virgin of Israel, but she shall be his wife, he shall not be able to divorce her for his life

20 But if that report is true, the proofs of the chastity of the girl not being

21 found, then they shall take the girl to the outside of the house of her father and kill her, because she has acted disgracefully in Israel, by prostitution in the house of her father And thus you shall burn that evil from amongst you

22 When a man is found fornicating with a married woman,—they shall die, both of them The man who committed adultery with the woman, and the woman Thus you shall burn that evil from Israel

23 When a young maiden who is engaged to a man, meets a man in a town, and he fornicates with her,

24 bring both of them to the gate of the town, and stone them with stones, and kill the girl, because she did not cry out in the town, and the man because he has degraded the wife of his neighbour Thus you shall burn that evil from your breast

25 But if the man meets the betrothed girl in the fields, and the man overpowers her and ravishes her, then the man alone who has ravished her shall

26 die, and you shall do nothing to the girl The girl has committed no sin for death, for as a man rises against his neighbour and murders him, so

27 is this crime, for he met her in the field,—and the betrothed girl cried out, but none heard her

28 When a man meets a young maiden, who is not engaged, and takes her and seduces her,—when he is discovered, that man who corrupted her shall give to the father of the girl fifty silvers, and she shall be his wife afterwards Because he degraded he shall not be able to divorce her all his days

23 A man shall not marry the wife of his father, and not lift up the skirts of his father

2 A eunuch, and an emasculated man, shall not enter a public meeting of the EVER-LIVING

3 The child of incest shall not enter a public r ... ...
They sh ... ...

meeting of the EVER-LIVING'S for ten generations

4 An Ammonite and a Moabite shall not enter a public meeting of the EVER-LIVING'S, they shall never enter into a public meeting of the EVER-LIVING'S for ten generations,

5 because they did not supply you with bread and water upon the march when you came from among the Mitzeraim, and because they hired against you Balaam the son of Beor from the centre of Aram of the rivers[1] to curse you But it did not please your EVER-

6 LIVING GOD to listen to Balaam, so your EVER-LIVING GOD turned the cursing into a blessing, for the EVER-LIVING your GOD, loves you You

7 shall not seek their peace or benefit all your days for ever

8 You shall not exclude an Edomite, for he is your brother You shall not exclude a Mitzerite, because you were a foreigner in his country The

9 children that they produce may be naturalized with the EVER-LIVING after three generations

10 When you go to war with your enemy, keep yourselves from any

11 vile practice If there happens to be with you a man unclean from any accident at night, let him go outside the camp, and not come into the

12 middle of the camp, and at the approach of evening let him bathe in water, and at the decline of the sun he may enter the heart of the camp

13 You shall therefore provide a trench near your camp, where you can make a cesspool

14 You shall also have a spade with your weapons, so that when you turn yourselves to the cesspool and have evacuated, you can carefully cover up your excrement, for your EVER-LIV-

15 ING GOD marches in company with your camp to protect it, and to defeat your enemies before you, therefore your camps must be clean, that He may not see anything unsightly about you, and turn away

16 You shall not deliver up a slave who has taken refuge with you from his

17 master to his master Let him reside amongst you in the place he chooses, in one of your villages, to benefit himself You shall not drive him out

18 You shall not make a prostitute of a daughter of Israel

There shall not be a sodomite among the sons of Israel

19 You shall not bring the wages of a harlot, or the hire of a ruffian to the house of your EVER-LIVING GOD for any vow, for your EVER-LIVING GOD loathes both of them

20 You shall not take interest from your brothers, — interest upon money, interest upon food, interest upon anything which can be lent at in-

21 terest You may charge interest to foreigners,—but from your countrymen you shall not take interest, so that your EVER-LIVING GOD may bless you in every endeavour of your hand in the country which you are going to possess

22 When you vow a vow to your EVER-LIVING GOD, you shall not delay to pay it, for the EVER-LIVING your GOD will demand it from you,—

23 and that would be a sin to you But if you do not vow, it will be no sin

24 You must carefully perform the utterance of your lips whatever you vow to your EVER-LIVING GOD, you must give whatever you have promised with your mouth

25 When you go into your neighbour's vineyard, you may eat grapes to satisfy your wish, but you shall not put any into your basket

26 When you go through your neighbour's corn fields, you may pluck the ears with your hand,—but you shall not cut from your neighbour's corn with a sickle

END OF THE SEVENTH ORATION

SPEECH VIII.

Laws of Marriage and Domestic Life.

24 When a man takes a wife and marries her, if she does not find favour in his eyes, because there are found repulsive qualities in her,—let him write her a letter of divorce, and put it into her hand, and send 2 her from his house, so that she can go from his house and depart, and be 3 the wife of another   But if the other man hates her, then let him write her a letter of divorce, and put it in her hand, and send her from his house, or if the second man dies who took 4 her to him as a wife, she shall not be allowed to return to the first who divorced her, to be married as his wife, after she has sinned, for that would be loathsome in the presence of the EVER-LIVING   Therefore you shall not defile the land which your EVER-LIVING GOD gives you to inherit

5 When a man has recently taken a wife he shall not go out with the army, and no expedition shall be laid upon him for any thing   He shall be freed for his home for one year, and enjoy the wife he has married

6 You shall not take in pledge a mill-stone or its carriage,—for that would be to pledge a life

7 When a man is discovered stealing a person who is his brother of the sons of Israel, and has caused him to be bound and sold,—that thief shall be put to death   Thus you shall burn that crime from amongst you

8 Regarding contagious diseases, take especial care to do all that I have instructed you   The priests and the Levites must take care to do according to the rules I commanded them

9 Remember what your EVER-LIVING GOD did to Miriam on the march out of Mitzeraim.

10 When as a creditor you lend your neighbour anything, you shall not go into his house to advance upon the 11 pledge   You shall stand outside, and the man to whom you lend shall bring to you the pledge at the out-12 side, and, although the man is poor you shall not take his bed as the pledge   You shall return to him, 13 from his pledge, at the decline of the sun both his bed and blanket, that he may bless you,—and it will be righteousness to you in the presence of your EVER-LIVING GOD

You shall not oppress the poor and 14 helpless of your brothers in their wages, nor the foreigner who is in your country, or your villages   You 15 shall pay them their wages daily, when the sun shall set upon them, for they are poor, and their life depends upon them,—so that they may not cry to the EVER-LIVING against you, for it would be a sin against you

You shall not kill parents on 16 account of their children, nor children on account of their parents A man shall only be put to death for his own crimes

You shall not refuse justice to the 17 orphan of a foreigner, nor shall you distort it against the widow of a foreigner, but remember that you 18 were slaves to the Mitzerites, but your EVER-LIVING GOD released you from that, therefore I command you not to do those things

When you reap your harvest on 19 your farm, and have forgotten a sheaf in the field, you shall not return to take it   It shall be for the stranger, the fatherless, and the widow, so that your EVER-LIVING GOD may bless you in all the work of your hand

When you strip your olives you 20 shall not pick after yourself, that shall be done by the stranger, the fatherless, and the widow

When you gather your vineyard, 21 you shall not glean after yourself, that shall be for the stranger, the fatherless, and the widow, for you 22 must remember you were a slave in the land of the Mitzeraim, therefore I command you to do these things

When there is a dispute between 25 men, and they appear before the Judge, he shall examine between right and right, and wrong and wrong, and when he has decided between 2 the assailant and the assailed, he shall cause him to be punished in his own presence according to the extent of his crime   You may inflict 3 forty strokes,—not more, for fear if you strike him beyond these many lashes, your brother should become degraded in your sight

4 You shall not muzzle a bullock when thrashing

5 When brothers reside together and one of them dies, and does not leave a son, the wife of the dead man shall not be wife to a stranger Her brother-in-law shall go to her himself,

6 and marry his brother's wife, and the first son that she bears he shall bring up with his dead brother's name, so that his name may not be wiped out

7 from Israel But if the man refuses to marry his sister-in-law,—then his sister-in-law shall go to the court of the Judges and say to them, " My brother-in-law who could raise up a name to his brother in Israel, is not willing to do his duty "

8 The Judge of the town shall then summon him, and examine him about it, when he shall appear and say, " I am not willing to take her "

9 Then the sister-in-law shall approach to him in the sight of the Judges and pull the shoe from his foot and spit in his face and insult him and say, " So let them do to the man who will not build up his brother's house ! " And he shall 10 be nicknamed in Israel, " The Slipshod-man "

11 When men are fighting together, a man and his neighbour, and the wife of one approaches to help her husband by a stroke of her hand, and puts out her hand and seizes him by the genitals,—her hand shall 12 be cut off,—your eye shall not spare her

13 There shall not be in your bag weight and weight, full weight and short weight

14 There shall not be in your house measure and measure, full measure and short measure You shall have 15 a just and right weight, you shall have a just and right measure, so that your time may be extended in the land which your EVER-LIVING GOD gives to you, for the EVER- 16 LIVING your GOD abhors all who do those wicked things

END OF THE EIGHTH ORATION

SPEECH IX.

Upon Conduct in the Promised Land, and Ritual for Freewill Offerings.

17 Remember what Amalek did to you on your march, as you came from 18 the Mitzeraim. How he met you in the road and assailed your rear,—all the sick who were following you,—when you were weary, and harassed you,—and he did not regard the 19 ambassadors,—therefore when your EVER-LIVING GOD has given you peace from all your enemies around, in the country that your EVER-LIVING GOD has given you to divide into estates, wipe out the memory of Amalek from under the skies. Do not forget.

26 When you come into the country which your EVER-LIVING GOD has given you to divide, and possess, and 2 live in, you shall take the first fruit of all the produce of the ground that comes from the land which your EVER-LIVING GOD gives you, and put it in a basket and carry to the place where the EVER-LIVING, your 3 GOD, chooses to fix His Name, and go to the priest who may be in those days, and say to him ;

" I have to-day brought to the presence of the EVER-LIVING, your GOD, some of what the land which the EVER-LIVING promised to our fathers to give to us, has produced."

4 Then the Priest shall take the basket from your hand, and set it before the altar of your EVER-LIVING 5 GOD. You shall then kneel and say in the presence of your EVER-LIVING GOD ;

" My ancestor was a wandering Aramite and he went down to the Mitzeraim, as a foreigner, with a few persons ; but he became there a great, 6 strong and numerous nation. Then the Mitzerites wronged us, and oppressed us, and imposed a cruel 7 slavery upon us ; but we cried to the EVER-LIVING GOD of our fathers, and the EVER-LIVING heard our voice, and looked upon our affliction and our ...

and the EVER-LIVING brought us out 8 from among the Mitzeraim with a strong hand, and a directing arm, and with great signs and wonders, and revelations, and conducted us to 9 this place, and gave us this country ; a land flowing with milk and honey. So now, see ! I have brought some 10 produce of the ground which the EVER-LIVING has given to me, and have placed it before your EVER-LIVING GOD."

Then you shall bow down before 11 your EVER-LIVING GOD, and enjoy yourself with all the good things that your EVER-LIVING GOD has given you, and your family,—yourself, and the Levite, and the stranger who is amongst you.

Then afterwards fully tithe the 12 whole that is tithable of your produce in the third year. You shall tithe yearly, and give to the Levite, to the foreigner, to the fatherless, and to the widow, and they shall be fed in your villages, and be satisfied.

You shall also declare before your 13 EVER-LIVING GOD ;—

" I have eaten the consecrated part with my family, and I have also given of it to the Levite, and to the foreigner, and the fatherless, and the widow, according to all Your commands which You have commanded me. I have not passed over from Your commands, and I have not evaded. I have not used any part in self- 14 indulgence ; I have not consumed any part in depravity ; I have not given any part to the dead ; I have listened to the voice of the EVER-LIVING GOD ; I have done all that He has commanded me. Look down 15 from Your Holy Dwelling, from Heaven, and bless Your People of Israel, and the land that You have given to us, as You promised to our fathers,—the land flowing with milk and honey."

This very day your EVER-LIVING 16 GOD commands you to practise these institutions, and these decrees, and to preserve and do them with all your heart, and all of your soul.

17 The EVER-LIVING has told you to-day He will be your GOD, and that you must walk in His paths, and preserve His institutions, and His commands, and His decrees,—and

18 to listen to His voice. The EVER-LIVING has also told you to-day to be His Separated People,—as He commanded you,—and to preserve all His orders, and to fix yourself high 19 over all the heathen, so as to make yourself glorious, and famous, and beautiful, and that you should become a People sacred for your EVER-LIVING GOD — as He commanded you!

END OF THE NINTH ORATION

SPEECH X.

Confirming all Laws by the Parliamentary Consent, and Denouncing Punishments on Disobedience.

27   Then Moses and all the Judges of Israel commanded the People, saying,—

" Preserve all the commands which 2 I have ordered you to-day And at the time you pass over the Jordan to the country that your EVER-LIVING GOD will give to you, set up great stones, and spread them over with 3 plaster, and engrave upon them the whole of the commands of these laws, when you pass over and arrive in the country which the EVER-LIVING, your GOD, has given you,—a land flowing with milk and honey,—as the EVER-LIVING GOD promised to your fathers

4   " And when you have passed over the Jordan you shall set up those stones, as I command you to-day, upon the Hill of Aibal, and plaster 5 them with plaster You shall also build an altar there to your EVER-LIVING GOD,—an altar of stones,— you shall not use iron upon them 6 You shall build the altar to your EVER-LIVING GOD of whole stones, and shall offer upon it a burnt-offering to the EVER-LIVING, your GOD 7 You shall also sacrifice thank-offerings, and feast there, and enjoy your- 8 selves before the EVER-LIVING Then write upon the stones the whole of the words of this Law, engraved deeply "

9   (Moses and the Levitical Priests also proclaimed to all Israel, saying,—)

" To-day be silent, and listen, Israel You are to become the People of the EVER-LIVING, your 10 GOD ! Therefore listen to the voice of your EVER-LIVING GOD, and put in practice the Commands and Institutions that I command you to-day "

11   (And Moses further commanded the People at that time, saying,—)[1]

12   These shall stand upon Mount Gherezim to bless the People —

Simeon, and Levi, and Judah, and Issakar, and Joseph, and Benjamin

And these shall stand upon Mount 13 Aibal, for the cursing,—Reuben, Gad, and Asher, and Zebulon, and Dan, and Naphthali

And the Levites shall speak with a 14 loud voice and say to every man of Israel ,—

" Cursed be the man who makes a 15 statue or a casting, hateful to the LORD, the product of the hands of a mechanic, and sets it up in secret "

(Then all the People shall answer and say,) " He shall be "

" Cursed be whoever insults his 16 father or his mother ! "

(Then all the People shall say,) " He shall be "

" Cursed be whoever removes his 17 neighbour's land mark "

(Then all the People shall say,) " He shall be "

" Cursed be whoever misdirects a 18 blind man in his road "

(Then all the People shall say,) " He shall be "

" Cursed be whoever refuses justice 19 to the foreigner, orphan, or widow "

(Then all the People shall say,) " He shall be "

" Cursed be whoever commits 20 adultery with his father's wives ;— who raises the covering of his father "

(Then all the People shall say,) " He shall be "

" Cursed be whoever copulates with 21 any beast "

(Then all the People shall say,) " He shall be "

" Cursed be whoever fornicates with 22 his sister, the daughter of his father, or the daughter of his mother "

(Then all the People shall say,) " He shall be "

" Cursed be whoever fornicates with 23 his mother-in-law "

(Then all the People shall say,) • " He shall be "

" Cursed be whoever strikes his 24 neighbour in secret "

(Then all the People shall say,) " He shall be "

" Cursed be whoever takes a bribe 25 to kill an innocent person "

(Then all the People shall say, He shall be

---

[1] Ch xxvii v 1 9 and 11 are an editorial note of Aha ... Syhm th prcedings —F F

26   " Cursed be whoever does not stand
by the commands of this Law to practise them "
(Then all the People shall say,)
" He shall be."

28   But if you attentively listen to the
voice of your EVER-LIVING GOD, and
take care to practise all the commandments that I command you to-
day, then the EVER-LIVING, your
GOD, will give you superiority over
2   every nation on earth, and all these
blessings shall come to you, and surround you, because you listen to the
voice of your EVER-LIVING GOD.

The Blessings of Obedience.

3   You shall be blest in the city,
And blest in the field,
4   Blest in the fruit of your body,
And blest in the fruit of your farm,
And blest in the fruit of your cow,
And blest in the cast of your cattle,
And breeds of your sheep
5   Blest in your basket,
And blest in your cask
6   Blest in your going,
And blest in your coming.
7   JEHOVAH will make your opponents
To stumble before you,—
They shall advance by one path,
And fly from you by seven !
8   The EVER-LIVING will command
blessing to your barns, and to every
work of your hand, and will bless you
in the country that your EVER-LIVING
9   GOD has given you   JEHOVAH will
establish you as a People sacred to
Himself, as He promised, if you keep
the commands of your EVER-LIVING
10 GOD and walk in His paths.   Then
every People of the earth will see
that the NAME of the EVER-LIVING
has been fixed upon you, and they
11 will fear you, when the EVER-LIVING
causes you to abound in benefits, in
the fruit of your body, and the fruit
of your cattle, and the fruit of your
fields, in the land which the EVER-
LIVING promised to your fathers to
12 give you.   The EVER-LIVING will
open His best treasures from the
skies for you to give rain to adorn
your land, and to bless every work of
your hand
Many nations shall borrow of you,
13 —but you shall not borrow !—for the
LORD will make you the Head, and
not the Tail ! and you shall continually rise higher and not be depressed
—whilst you attend to the commands

of your EVER-LIVING GOD, which I
command you to-day to preserve and
practise — Therefore turn not from   14
any of the things that I have commanded you to-day, yesterday, and
before that, but walk after your
EVER-LIVING GOD, and serve Him
But if you will not listen to the   15
voice of your EVER-LIVING GOD, to
continue to practise the whole of His
Commands and Institutions, as I
instruct you to-day, then these curses
will come upon, and surround you,—

The Curses of Revolt from God.

You shall be cursed in the city,   16
And cursed in the field !
Cursed in your basket,   17
And cursed in your cask !
Cursed in the fruit of your body,   18
And fruit of your farms,
The cast of your cattle,
And breeds of your sheep !
You shall be cursed in your going,   19
And cursed in your coming !
The EVER-LIVING will send you   20
cursing, blundering, and blame in
every attempt of your hand, till you
waste and rapidly perish before the
evils assailing you, and become
desolate !
These things shall pursue, until   21
you cease from the land that you go
to possess !
The LORD will strike you with con-   22
sumption, and fever, and wasting, and
burning, and with sword, and blight,
and jaundice, and pursue until you
perish !   And the skies over your   23
head shall be brass, and the ground
beneath you iron !   The LORD will   24
rain powder on your land, and dust
from the skies shall fall upon you,
until you are a desert !   The LORD   25
will give you to defeat before your
enemies !   They shall meet you on
a single road,—but you shall fly
before them by seven roads, and be
in terror of every government on
earth !   And your carcases shall be   26
food to all the birds of the sky, and to
the beasts of the earth, and none
will drive them off !   And the EVER-   27
LIVING will inflict the ulcer of the Mitzeraim upon you, and tumours, and
scurvy, and the incurable itch, and   28
the EVER-LIVING will afflict you with
madness, and blindness, and bewilder-
ment of heart !   And you shall grope   29
'r n w dy s   '1 1 man
slopes i t i c r) ess   shall not

find your way,—and you shall also be wronged, and robbed, daily ; and

30 find no defender! You shall wed a wife, and another man lie with her! You shall build a house, but not dwell in it! You shall plant a vine-

31 yard, and not eat of it! They shall kill your ox in your sight, but will not allow you to eat of it! They will steal your ass before your face, and never return it! Your sheep will be given to your enemies, and no one

32 will help you! Your sons and your daughters will be sold to foreign nations,—your eyes shall see it,—and long for them every day, and possess them not!

33 A People whom you have not known shall consume the produce of your

34 farms, and all your acquisitions, and you shall be plundered, and oppressed at every time, and be maddened by the sights your eyes shall see

35 The EVER-LIVING will inflict you with a bad ulcer on your knees, and on your legs, which you cannot cure, from the sole of your foot to your

36 crown! The EVER-LIVING will make you, and the kings you have raised over yourselves, go to a nation which neither you nor your fathers have known, and there you shall serve

37 vile gods of wood and stone, and become a word of reproach and abuse among all the Peoples where the EVER-LIVING drives you!

38 You shall take much seed out to the field, and reap little, for the locust

39 shall destroy! You shall plant a vine-yard,—but not drink its wine, nor collect its grapes,—for the worm shall

40 consume them Olive groves shall be in all your fields, but you shall not refresh yourselves with oil,—for

41 the olives shall drop off! You shall beget sons and daughters,—but they shall not be yours, but shall go to slavery!

42 The caterpillar shall seize all your trees, and the fruits of your fields!

43 The foreigner who is amongst you shall climb up above you from station to station,—but you shall sink lower

44 and lower! He shall lend to you,— he shall be the head, and you shall be the tail!

45 And all these curses shall come upon you, and pursue, and hunt you to destruction, because you have not listened to the voice of your EVER-LIVING ⟨ ⟩ n ⟨ ⟩ H ⟨ ⟩ u mands ⟨ ⟩

ordained for you, and which should 46 have been a guide and instruction to you, and to your posterity for ever

But as you served not your EVER- 47 LIVING GOD with delight and gladness of heart in your abundance of all things,—therefore you shall serve 48 your enemies, whom the EVER-LIVING will send to you,—in heat and raging thirst, and nakedness, and want, and an iron yoke shall be put upon your neck, until you perish!

The EVER-LIVING will arouse against 49 you a nation from afar, flying like an eagle from the end of the earth,—a nation whose language you have not heard, a furious nation, who will not 50 respect the presence of the old, nor pity the young,—and it shall devour 51 the produce of your cattle, and the produce of your fields, until you are ruined, until you shall possess neither corn, nor wine, nor a calf from your cow, nor lamb from your sheep, until you are brought to ruin! And you 52 shall be oppressed in all your villages, and your walls, towers and fortifica-tions in which you trusted shall be thrown down in the whole country,— and you shall be harassed in every village of the land which your EVER-LIVING GOD gave to you! And you 53 shall eat the fruit of your body,—the flesh of your sons and your daughters, —whom your EVER-LIVING GOD had given you,—in the siege and distress with which your enemies shall distress you! The friend who was very dear 54 and delightful to you shall turn his eyes evil to his brother, and to the wives of his bosom, and to the re-mainder of his children who are left, to give one from amongst them as 55 food for his children, so that the rest may eat from the corpse with him in the siege and distress with which your enemies distress you in all your cities! The delicate lady who allowed 56 not the sole of her foot to touch the earth from delicacy and refinement, shall look with evil eyes upon the husband of her bosom, and her sons, and her daughters, and the new-born 57 child that comes on her lap, and her children whom she has borne, that she may eat them in the absolute famine in secret, in the siege and distress with which your enemies shall distress you in your gates.—If 58 you do not take care to practise the behests of the things of this Law, written in this book, and to reverence the

glory of this magnificent Revelation
59 of your EVER-LIVING GOD, for the
EVER-LIVING will make your own
punishments, and the punishments
of your posterity, astounding by these
great inflictions and diseases, and
60 sickness, and prostrations, and
will turn upon you all the maladies
of the Mitzerites which you feared
when present with them,—and they
61 shall stick to you,—besides numerous
diseases, and many plagues that are
not written in the record of this Law
The EVER-LIVING will bring them
62 upon you, until you are desolate, and
are a small remnant, instead of being
like the stars of the heavens for
number, because you have not listened
to the voice of your EVER-LIVING
63 GOD   And as the EVER-LIVING
was before delighting over you to
benefit you, and to increase you,—
then the EVER-LIVING will delight
to destroy, to desolate, and to bear
you away from the ground which you
64 have come to possess! And the
EVER-LIVING will scatter you amongst
all the Peoples, from one end of the

earth to the other end of the earth,
—and there you shall serve vile gods,
which neither you nor your fathers
knew, of wood and stone! And amid 65
those heathens you shall have no
quiet or comfort to the soles of your
feet, but the EVER-LIVING will give
you there a trembling heart, and
languishing eyes, and a wretched
spirit, and your life shall be in sus- 66
pense to you in the present, and you
shall tremble night and day, and
have no certainty for your existence
In the morning you shall say, "I 67
wish it were evening'" and in the
evening you shall exclaim, "I wish it
were morning," because of the fear of
your heart that terrifies you, and from
foreseeing what your eyes perceive!

The EVER-LIVING will also cause 68
you to return to the Mitzeraim, by
that mournful way, which I have told
you never to retrace, or to look upon,
—and you will there offer to sell
yourselves to your enemies as men
and women slaves,—and none will
buy you

END OF THE TENTH ORATION,

SPEECH XI.

Exhortation to Obedience, and Appointment of Joshua as Commander.

69 (The following are records of the Covenant that the EVER-LIVING commanded Moses to make with the children of Israel in the country of Moab, in addition to the Covenant that was recorded with them in Horeb.)

29 (Moses accordingly assembled all Israel and said to them;—)[1]

You saw all that the EVER-LIVING did in your sight, in the land of Mitzeraim, to Pharoh and to all his officers, and to all his country,

2 their great defeats which your eyes saw,—the wonders, and the great manifestations upon them.

3 But the EVER-LIVING did not give you a heart to understand, and eyes to see, and ears to hear, until to-day.

4 Although you wandered forty years in the desert, you were not deficient in clothing upon yourselves, and your shoes were not stripped from your

5 feet. You did not eat bread or drink wine or beer, so that you might learn that I am your EVER-LIVING GOD.

6 Then you came to this place and met Sihon king of Heshbon, and Og king of Bashan, and you advanced to

7 fight, and slew them, and took their country, and give it to be divided by the Reubenites, and Gadites, and the

8 half tribe of Manasseh. Therefore remember the contents of this covenant and practise them, so that you may reflect upon all you are bound to do,

9 You are to-day all of you stationed before the EVER-LIVING, your GOD;—your nobles, your governors, your judges, and your officials, every man

10 of Israel; your children, your wives, and the foreigners who are amongst you;—the hewers of wood, and

11 drawers of water for you;—to assent to the Covenant of your EVER-LIVING GOD, and to swear to what the EVER-LIVING, your GOD, has agreed with

12 you to-day, so that you may rise up

from to-day to be a People for HIM, and HE may be a GOD to you, as HE promised you, and as HE swore to your fathers,—to Abraham, to Isaac, and to Jacob. Since it is not I 13 alone who made this Covenant and this confirmation with you, that is 14 established here with us to-day before the EVER-LIVING our GOD, and which is confirmed to us here to-day. For 15 you know that we resided in the land of the Mitzeraim, and that you were slaves amongst the heathen whom you served; and you saw their cor- 16 ruptions, and their idols, of wood, and stone, of silver and gold, that they have! Take special care to 17 yourselves, man or woman, or family or tribe, who has a heart, from turning to-day from our EVER-LIVING GOD, to go and serve the gods of those Heathen,—lest there should be a root bearing poison and anguish amongst you.

But should anyone listening to the 18 words of this oath say to himself in his heart, "I shall prosper, although I walk in the ideas of my heart, for my cup is full when I am thirsty!"— the EVER-LIVING will not be ready 19 to forgive him, but the LORD's anger and indignation will smoke at that person, and HE will heap upon him all that is written in this record, and the EVER LIVING will wipe his name from under the skies, and the LORD 20 will set him apart for evil, in every tribe of Israel, for all the curses of the covenant written in the record of this Law. And the future genera- 21 tions of your sons, who may arise after you, and the strangers who come from distant countries and see the afflictions of the country, and the curses with which the EVER-LIVING has cursed it, shall exclaim, 'Brim- 22 stone and salt burn all the country! It is not sown—does not grow,—and produces no vegetation, like ruined Sodom and Gomorah, Admah and Tzeboim, whom the EVER-LIVING destroyed in HIS anger and in HIS wrath!"

And all the nations shall ask, 23 "Why has the EVER-LIVING afflicted this land? Why should His great indignation burn so? When they 24

---

[1] V. 69 of Ch. xxviii., and v. 1 of Ch. xxix., are an editorial note, probably by Minzer the Priest, when outing the Master's Orations for the Ark of WHD ___ I J

will be answered, "Because they rejected the Covenant of the EVER-LIVING, the GOD of their fathers, which He made with them when He brought them out of the land of the

25 Mitzeraim, and they went and served other gods, and worshipped them,—gods whom they knew not, and who

26 could not benefit them." Therefore the anger of the LORD burnt against the country, and He caused all the affliction written in this record to come upon it.

27 The EVER-LIVING will also pluck you up from the ground with violence, and with great wrath, and fling you into other countries [1]

28 The Secret Reasons are with our EVER-LIVING GOD, but the revelations are with us and our children for ever, that we may practise the whole of the Decrees of this Law!

Rewards of Return to God.

30 Consequently when these events come upon you, the blessings and the cursings which I have put before you, and you cause your heart to turn back in every nation where your EVER-LIVING GOD has scattered you,

2 and you return to your EVER-LIVING GOD, and listen to His voice in all that I have commanded you to-day, you and your children, with all your

3 heart and with all your soul,—and return to your EVER-LIVING GOD,—your rest and your comfort,—then the EVER-LIVING, your GOD, will come again and collect you from every People where He had scattered

4 you If you have been drawn to the limits of the sky, your EVER-LIVING

5 GOD will collect you from there,—the EVER-LIVING, your GOD, will take you and bring you to the country your fathers possessed, and you shall possess it, and will cause you to prosper, and increase more than

6 your fathers And the EVER-LIVING GOD will mould your hearts, and the hearts of your posterity, to love your EVER-LIVING GOD, with all your

7 soul, so that you may live, and the EVER-LIVING will put all those afflictions upon your enemies, and on those who hated and persecuted you,

8 when you repent and listen to the

voice of the EVER-LIVING, and practise all His commands, which I command you to-day Your EVER-LIVING GOD also will cause you to 9 excel in every work of your hand,—in the fruit of your body, in the produce of your cattle, in the beautiful produce of your farms,—for the EVER-LIVING will come to rejoice over you in delight, as He rejoiced over your fathers,—because you listen 10 to the voice of your EVER-LIVING GOD, to preserve His Commandments and Institutions which are written in this record of the Law,—when you return to the EVER-LIVING, your GOD, with all your heart and with all your soul For these laws which I 11 command you to-day, will never depart, or go far from you They 12 are not in the heavens, that you should say,—"Who can go up for us to the heavens, and bring them to us that we may listen to and practise them?" Nor are they across the sea, 13 that you should say, "Who can cross over for us, and bring them to us, that we may hear and practise them?" —for the matter is very close to you, in your mouth, and in your heart to 14 practise

Look! I put before you to-day 15 Life, and Prosperity,—and Sin, and Death! What I propose to you 16 is Life,—to love the EVER-LIVING, your GOD,—to walk in His ways, to preserve His Legislation, and Institutions, and Decrees, when your EVER-LIVING GOD will increase you, and bless you in the land which you are going to possess!

But if your heart revolts, and you 17 will not listen, but degrade yourselves, and worship vile gods, and serve them, I announce to you to- 18 day that perishing you shall perish,—your time shall not be long on the ground which you are passing the Jordan to go and possess! Bear 19 witness to me, now, Heavens and Earth! I place Life and Death before you,—the Blessing and the Curse! Therefore choose for yourselves the Life,—that you and your posterity may live! Love your EVER- 20 LIVING GOD, listen to His voice, and hold to Him,—for He will give you life, and extend your time, to rest upon the land that the EVER-LIVING promised to your fathers,—to Abra-le : to Israel, and to Jacob to give them

---

1 End of v 27 ... ... note, not part ... th ... st ... ...

Peroration to the Parliament of Israel.[1]

31 (Then Moses proceeded to conclude his speeches to all Israel, and said to them.)

2 "I am the son of a hundred and twenty years to-day! I am no longer able to go out far, or to come back, and the EVER-LIVING has said to me, 'You shall not pass over this

3 Jordan.' The EVER-LIVING, your GOD, Himself will pass over before you! HE will destroy those heathens from before you, and drive them out! The Saviour Himself will pass over before you, as the EVER-LIVING has

4 said, and the EVER-LIVING will do to them as He did to Sihon and to Og, kings of the Amorites, and to their country which you destroyed.

5 The EVER-LIVING will thus deliver them to your face, and you shall do to them, exactly as you were com-

6 manded. Take courage! Be strong! Fear not! Tremble not before them! for your EVER-LIVING GOD HIMSELF marches with you! HE will not forsake or desert you."[2]

---

[1] Ch. XXXI, v. 1 is an editorial note undoubtedly contemporary with Moses, probably by Ahazer the priest.—F. F.

[2] Ch. XXXI, vv. 7, 9, 10, are original introductory notes to the last addresses of Moses probably by Ahazer.—F. F.

(Moses then called to Joshua and said to him in the sight of all Israel.)

"Be strong and bold! for you shall bring this People to the land which the EVER-LIVING promised to Abraham, to give to them, and you must

8 divide it amongst them, and the EVER-LIVING HIMSELF will march before you,—HE will be with you! HE will not forsake or abandon you! Fear not! Shrink not!"

9 (Moses afterwards engraved this law, and gave it to the Priests, the sons of Levi, who carried the Ark of the Covenant of the EVER-LIVING, and to all the Judges of

10 Israel, Moses also ordered them saying.)

"At the end of every seven years, at the year of release, and at the Feast of Tabernacles when all

11 Israel goes to see the Presence of your EVER-LIVING GOD, in the place which He chooses, you shall read this Law to all Israel, in their hearing, at a Public Meeting of the People,

12 of the men, the women, the children, and the foreigners who are in your villages, so that they may hear, and learn, and fear the EVER-LIVING, your GOD, and take care to practise all the commands of this law, and

13 that their children, who know it not, may hear and learn to fear the EVER-LIVING, your GOD, all the time of their life upon the land that you are crossing the Jordan to possess."

END OF THE ELEVENTH ORATION

SPEECH XII.

Being the Public Song of Moses, and Appointment of Joshua.

14   The EVER-LIVING afterwards said to Moses, "Now that your days approach death, summon Joshua, and station him in the Hall of Assembly, and I will instruct him"

(Moses and Joshua therefore went and stationed themselves in the Hall of As-
15 sembly, and the EVER-LIVING appeared in the Hall of Assembly in a Pillar of Cloud, and the Pillar of Cloud stood at
16 the opening of the Hall, and the EVER-LIVING said to Moses)[1]

God foretells the Apostasy of Israel.

"You are now to sleep with your fathers, when this People will arise and whore after the foreign gods of the country where they are going to reside, and they will revolt from ME, and break the Covenant that I made
17 with them! But My anger will burn against them at that time, and I will turn from them, and hide My face from them, and they shall meet many miseries and sufferings to devour them, when they will exclaim, 'Is there no GOD near me to bring me
18 out from these miseries?' But I will hide My presence carefully at that time, because of all the wicked-ness which they have done when
19 turning after other gods! Therefore, now, write for them this song, and teach the children of Israel to put it into their mouths, so that this song may be a witness for ME with the
20 children of Israel, for I will bring them to the land, which I promised to their fathers, flowing with milk and honey, which they will eat, and be satiated, and fatten, and revolt to vile gods, and serve them, and despise
21 Me, and Break My Covenant But when these many miseries, and dis-tresses, and troubles meet them, then this song will be before them as an evidence,— for it will not be forgotten from the mouth of their

race,—that I knew to-day the distress which they would then suffer, before they arrived in the country which I had promised"

Moses consequently wrote the song 22 on that day, and taught it to the children of Israel

(Afterwards he instructed Joshua the 23 son of Nun, saying,—)[1]

" Be strong and bold! for now the children of Israel are going to the country which I promised to them and I will be with you"

(When Moses had finished engraving 24 the commands of this Law in a record to its end, he commanded the Levites who 25 carried the Ark of the Covenant of the LORD, saying,)

" Take this Book of the Law, and 26 place it inside the Ark of the Cove-nant of the EVER-LIVING, your GOD, and it shall be there as a witness to you, that I knew your rebelliousness 27 and your stiff neck,—here, whilst I lived with you, to-day, you are mur-muring against the EVER-LIVING, and will be so after I die! Assemble all 28 your Judges, Princes, and Governors to me, and I will recite in their hear-ing these words, and I will call as witnesses to them Heaven and Earth, that I knew that after my death you 29 would corrupt, and turn yourselves from the path which I commanded you, and acquire for yourselves misery in the future,—for you will do evil in the eyes of the EVER-LIVING, and provoke Him by the fabrications of your own hands'

(Then Moses repeated the words of 30 this song in the hearing of all the Assembly of Israel to their end)

SONG OF MOSES

STANZA I.

The Invocation.

Listen, Heaven, and I will speak,   32
And hear my utterance, Earth!
My teaching shall drop like rain,   2
My utterance spread like dew,—

---

[1] This introduction is clearly from the pen of Aliazer the Priest, who edited these Ora-tions of Moses and is another internal proof of the authenticity of these Speeches of Moses —F. F.

P.

[1] Ch xxxi, vv 23, 25, and 30 are an . . . . t . . st, upon the . . . . k Witnesses All . . . .

26J   P

Like showers upon the herbage,
And like sprinklings on the grass

3 For I proclaim Jehovah's Name,
I exalt our Glorious GOD!

4 Whose fort is a perfect refuge,
For all His lines are straight!
A GOD of Truth, and not unjust,
Righteous and upright, HE.

STANZA II

The Revolt from God.

5 Corrupt, you have not His Son's form,—
You wayward and fickle race!—

6 Repay not thus to the LORD,
You stupid, and unwise clan
Is HE not your Forming-Father?
Who made and constructed you?

7 Remember the Times Everlasting,—
Reflect on the ages of years,—
Ask your father, who will inform you,
Your elders, and they will relate,

8 How the Highest allotted the races,
When He divided the sons of Man,
Fixing the bounds of the nations,
With a place for Israel's sons!

STANZA III.

How God pities His People.

9 For the LORD is kind to His People,
To Jacob He measured his share!

10 Whom He met in a desert country,—
When he strayed in a howling waste,
He turned him, and He directed,
He watched as the ball of His eye,

11 He guarded his nest, like an eagle,
He fluttered over his prey,
He spread His wings to support him,
He carried him by their strength,—

12 He was led by JEHOVAH alone,—
He had no strange god with him

STANZA IV

How God prospered Jacob, yet how his Sons were wicked.

13 He raised him high in the country,
And he ate of the fruits of the field
Sucked honey out of the cliff,
And oil from the flinty rock!

14 Cows' cheese, and butter of sheep
Along with best of the lambs,
And of Bashan's rams and goats,
With the fattest grains of the wheat!

15 Drank the foaming blood of the grape —
Yet to ... ... kick!—

You were fat, you were stout and bloated,
And forsook your Maker,—your GOD!

And fell from the Rock of His 16
safety,
And by Strangers raised His wrath,
By Depravities raised disgust, 17
And Godless worshipped Demons,—
Gods that they never knew,—
Fresh from abroad imported,
Whom your fathers never feared,— 18
And neglected the Power that made you,
And forgot your GOD in your lust 19

STANZA V

How God sorrows over Man's Sins.

But the LORD will see—and will sorrow,
Be sad for His daughters and sons, 20
Say, 'My face I will veil from them,—
I will see what it is they pursue!
For they are a race that is faithless,
They never will build on the truth, 21
They provoke Me with fictile gods,
They insult with the idols they make
So I vex by an Unknown People,
By a nation unthought I provoke! 22

STANZA VI

The Punishment upon Sin.

Then a fire shall go from My presence,
And burn down to the pit below,—
And consume the land and its produce,
And, igniting the base of the hills, 23
It shall rush to their top with a roar!—
I will feed My arrows upon them,— 24
Mad with famine and fever's rage,
As a bitter force of destruction,
I will send fierce beasts upon them
With the venomous snakes of the 25
dust,—
Without the sword shall devour,
And Terrors invade their homes,
Alike on the youth and the maiden,
The suckling child, and the grey 26
beard —
I declare I would blow them away,
I would blot from the memory of 27
man,—
Unless on account of their foemen,—
Lest their oppressors should see,
And say, 'Our own hand has conquered!' -

28 But did not JEHOVAH do it?
For the race was bereft of its senses,

29 And had no understanding left

STANZA VII.

God grieves at Man's Irreflection.

30 I would they were wise to reflection,
That they understood its results,
Then one should chase a thousand
And two could repulse a host,—
Except for the POWER Who sold
them,

31 And the LORD Who delivered them
up!
For their Rock is not like our Rock,

32 Our foes being judges themselves
For their vine is a true stock of
Sodom,
From Gomorah's blasted farm,
Its bunches are bunches of
poisons,—

33 Bitter clusters of grapes it yields
Their wine is the venom of serpents,

34 And the poison of deadly asps —
Is it not stored up beside Me,

35 And well sealed up in My barns,
A means of avenge and requital,
When the time of their punishment
comes?
When their day of distress ap-
proaches,

36 Its agents are ready prepared

STANZA VIII

God will redeem His repentant People.

Then the LORD will redress His
People,—
For His servants He deeply grieves,
When He sees their power depart-
ing,

37 And fail, and fade, and decay
Then He asks, "Where now are
their godlings?

38 The powers upon whom they
trust,—
Who ate the fat of their offerings,
And drank up the draughts of their
wine?
Can they now arise and help you?

39 Can they now be your hope?

STANZA IX

God is our only Refuge, our true Helper.

Look! I only Myself am THAT!
And there is no GOD but Me,—
I am the TRUTH and the LIFE,—

I wound, and I can restore,
And none can tear from My
hand!

So I lift up My hand to the heavens, 40
And declare, as for ever I live,

I will flash My sword as the light- 41
ning,
And Justice stands on My right!
I will put distress upon tyrants,
And repayment upon My foes!

My darts will be drunk with their 42
blood,
And My sword will devour their
flesh,
Drink the blood of the slain and
captives,
And the chiefs who lead on My
foes!

STANZA X

God promises Salvation and Freedom to the Heathen and His People.

You Heathen, rejoice with His 43
People!
For He raises the blood of His saints,
And upon their oppressors does
justice,
And the land of His People pro-
tects [1]

(Moses came forward and recited all the 44
words of this song in the hearing of the
People, and of Hoshea the son of Nun

When Moses had finished reciting all 45
these verses to Israel, he said to them,)

"Fix upon your hearts all the ideas 46
which I have commanded to you, and
to your children, from the first until
to-day, and take care to practise the
whole of the purport of this legislation, for I have not merely spoken 47
myself to you, but He Who is your
Life has spoken it, to extend your
times upon the land which you pass
over the Jordan to possess" [2]

(The EVER-LIVING afterwards spoke to 48
Moses on that very day saying,—)

[1] Vv 44, 45, are an editorial note of Ahazer
the Priest, for the Sacred Copy of the Ark of
Witnesses —F F

[2] Vv 48, 49 The words in brackets are an
editorial note of Ahazer, not part of the text.
—F F

(It is in the country of Moab, opposite 49
Jerikho)

All these statements that these speeches
were recorded in writing on the east of
Jordan, in Moab, are conclusive proof that
they are the production of Moses —F. F.

49   "Go up the hill by the ford,—to Mount Nebo,—and survey the land of Canan, which I will give to the chil-

50   dren of Israel for possession, and you shall die upon the mountain that you ascend, and be added to your people, as Aaron your brother died on the Hill of Hills, and was

51   added to his people,—because you did not exalt Me among the children of Israel at Meribah of Kadesh, in the desert of Tzin, where you did not sanctify My presence among the

52   children of Israel Therefore you shall survey the country near it, but you shall not enter the country which I will give to the sons of Israel "

STANZA I

The Blessing of Moses.

33   (And having been thus spoken to, Moses, the Man of GOD, blessed the sons of Israel before his death and said,—) 1

2   "The LORD came down from Sinai,
And on them shone from the Tempest,
He blazed from Paran's hill,
And brought ten thousand Saints
His flaming right-hand ruled,

3   For love of His sacred tribes

STANZA II.

The Almighty's Decree.

"On your hand let them trust,
At your word rise and march,

4   Let Moses give them Laws,
As Prince of Jacob's Host,

5   And be Yeshurun's Leader,
Controlling the Nations' Chiefs,
Uniting Israel's Tribes

Moses Blesses the Tribes.

"Let Reuben live,—not die,—
And let his number be great!"

7 (He then said to Judah,)
"Let the LORD hear Judah's voice,
And His hand go out with his men,
As a power and help from his foes "

8 (And then to Levi he said,)
"You have the SWEETNESS and LIGHT,—
You are with the one with a trust,

For at Massah you showed your truth,
And fought at the Waters of Strife,
Who said to his father and 9 mother,
' I have no reverence for you,'
And as brother he recognised none,
And had no regard for his son,
When he was the guard of Your TRUTH,
And stood in defence of Your BOND,—
Let them teach Jacob Decrees, 10
And in Israel settle Your laws,
And offer the incense to You,
On Your Altar presenting the Gifts
Bless, LORD, their power, and 11 work,
And break through the strength of their foes,
And their enemies when they arise "

(He said to Benjamin,) 12
"The Beloved of the LORD rests secure,
Relying on Him all the day,
And borne safe up in His arms "

(Then to Joseph he said) 13
"May the LORD give bliss to His land,
By the gifts of the skies and the dews,
And with fountains bubbling below,
And the bounties produced by 14 the sun,
And the gifts that increase with the moon,
And gifts from the hills of the 15 East
And the wealth of the ancient 16 hills,
And the gifts that burst from the ground,
And delights of the shadowing palms,
Come all upon Joseph's head,
And crown him his brothers' Prince
Like a noble and splendid 17 prince,—
His horns are the horns of a bull,
With them he will conquer nations,
And unite the Land into one,
For the ten thousands of Ephraim,—
And Manasseh's thousands are his'

---

1 Ch xxxiii, v 1, was a note undoubtedly by Ahazer the first Priest in the original copy of the Ark of Witnesses —J L

18 (Then he said to Zebulon,)
   "Zebulon be glad in your Ports;
   And Issaker in your Halls!
19   They are called the Men of the
     Hills,
     Where they feast in a noble
     feast,
     For they suck of the wide
     spreading seas,
     And the treasures that hide in
     the sand!"
20 (Then turning to Gad, he said)
   "Let the horseman, Gad, be
    blest,—
    Like a tiger he crouches down,
    And tears with his arms and
    jaws!
21   But he thought at the first for
     himself,
     So was granted a princely home,
     And produced the leaders of men,
     Who did the work of the LORD,
     And first led My People right"
22 (Then he exclaimed to Dan,)
   "Dan is the whelp of a lion,
   Who leaps up out of Bashan!"
23 (Then he said to Naphthali,)
   "Naphthali loves to take rest,
   And be filled with the gifts of the
    LORD,—
   He possesses the tides of the
    sea"
24 (Then as to Asher said,)
   "Let Asher be blessed with his
    sons,

By his brothers let him be
   loved,
And dabble his footsteps in oil!—
Your bars shall be iron and 25
   bronze,
And your wealth like the tide of
   the seas"

The Last Psalm of Moses to God.

   "There is none like the GOD of 26
    Yeshurun,
   Who rides on the heavens to
    your aid,
   And floats on the heights of the
    clouds!
   His GOD is above from of old,   27
   And beneath, the Eternal Arms,
   Who sweeps out the foe from
    your face,
   And gives the command to
    destroy

   Israel dwells alone, and secure,   28
   Jacob's spring in a land of the
    corn,
   And his skies drop dews of wine!
   Blest Israel! who is like you?   29
   A Victor Race for JEHOVAH,—
   Your shield, your help, and your
    sword!
   You shall grow, and subdue your
    foes,
   And advance on their hills like a
    road"

END OF THE BOOKS OF MOSES

Aliazer's Concluding Narrative.

34 1 Moses then ascended the Hill of Nebo, from the fords of Moab, up to the peak of Pisgah, which is opposite Jeriko, and the EVER-LIVING showed him all the country [2]

4 For the EVER-LIVING had said to him, "This is the country that I promised to your fathers, to Abraham, to Isaac, and Jacob,—saying I will give it to your race Look at it with your eyes, for you shall not pass over to it "

5 Moses, the servant of the EVER-LIVING, consequently died there before JEHOVAH, in the land of Moab,

6 and was buried in a valley in that country behind Beth-peor [3]

7 Moses was one hundred and twenty years old at his death His eyes were not weak, and his strength had not gone

8 The children of Israel, however, wept for Moses at the Fords of Moab, thirty days, until the time of mourning the loss of Moses was completed

9 But Joshua the son of Nun was full of spirit and intelligence, for Moses

---

[1] Ch xxxiv, v 1 This chapter is an editor's note, undoubtedly that of Aliazer the High Priest, as a record of the death and burial of Moses —F F

[2] 2 [from Ghilad to Dan, and Naphthali, and the country of Ephraim and Manasseh, and all the land of Judah to the Western

3 Sea, and the south plain of the valley of Jeriko, the City of Palms, as far as Tzur (Tyre)]

Vv 2, 3 The above words in brackets are not part of the original text, but the note of an ancient editor, probably Ezra, when he edited the Books of Moses after the return from the Babylonian Captivity, as the geographical indications are clearly from the standpoint of Jerusalem, not like the rest of the chapter, from the Plain of Moab, east of the Jordan — F F

[3] (But no one knows his grave at this day)

---

had laid his hands upon him, so the children of Israel listened to him, and he acted as the EVER-LIVING had commanded to Moses [1]

Envoy by Ezra or some Old Transcriber.

"The Fifth of the Fivefold Law is done ,—
Thank GOD the Great and Enlightening Sun "

"Courage "

(There never, however, arose a prophet 10 again in Israel like Moses, who saw the EVER-LIVING face to face, with all the 11 signs and wonders which the EVER-LIVING sent him to effect upon the land of the Mitzeraim, upon Pharoh and his Ministers, and all his country, and with 12 so strong a hand, and with such great revelations as Moses produced in the sight of all Israel)

[1] Vv 10, 11, 12 These bracketed lines are a note of Ezra probably, or some ancient editor of his period, and do not form a part of the original text Such notes were formerly usually bracketed in the original matter, the ancient plan of writing upon a long roll of skin or leather affording no space to put them at the foot of the page, as we now do I have, however, in this translation, put them in their proper place for our day,—at the foot of the page These ancient notes are a strong proof of the authenticity and great age of the Text as we still have it, as they must have been added before the use of papyrus paper had introduced the plan of folding books and records into leaves Layard's discoveries at Nineveh prove that as late as the time of Ezra (500 years before Christ) clay tablets, written or engraved upon, and then baked, were the ordinary materials used for records and correspondence, although the Jews would seem also to have begun to write upon skins, then or shortly after, and hence the interlining of these notes Papyrus paper seems to have been invented not much earlier than 400 before Christ, and not thousands of years as modern sceptics assert Consequently all papyri pretending to greater antiquity are forgeries —F F

END OF VOLUME I

ST. PAUL'S EPISTLES IN MODERN ENGLISH.—*Continued.*

H. B. COLLINS, Esq., London, wrote:

"This morning brings me not only your letter, but also one from a friend (a bookseller), a man of good sound judgment. He writes: 'I am much struck with the ability displayed, and give expression to my own admiration of the strikingly clear presentment of St. Paul's meaning.' He desires me to send him a dozen copies. Will you please send them to me."

The Rev. H. S. CHAMPNEYS, Rector of Epperstone, Notts., wrote:

"I am delighted with your translation of Paul's Epistle to the Romans."

KESHUB CHUNDER SEN, the Native Apostle of India, wrote:

"SIMLA, *15th June, 1883.*

"You would certainly do a great work if you could spread a knowledge of Paul in the east and the west, and by translating his Epistles into modern and intelligible English, create a deeper and more appreciative interest in his teaching. Here, in India, the number of educated natives who understand English, and are at the same time interested in theological literature, is small. However, I shall try to publish from time to time in our press organ 'The Liberal and New Dispensation,' the more striking passages of your excellent version of the Epistle to the Romans, which may be of particular interest to my countrymen. Trusting you will persevere, &c."

THE BOOK OF JOB

TRANSLATED DIRECT FROM THE HEBREW, AND IN THE SAME METRE AS THE ORIGINAL.

PRICE, 4to. Art Edition, **3 6.** In Paper Cover, 8vo, **8d.**

The Right Reverend E. H. BICKERSTETH, D.D., Lord Bishop of Exeter, says:

"I think it a very able version."

St. Paul and the Book of Job are published for the Translator by

MESSRS. HORACE MARSHALL & SON,

TEMPLE HOUSE, TEMPLE AVENUE, LONDON, E.C.;

And Sold by all Booksellers.

THE BIBLE IN MODERN ENGLISH.

(TO BE ISSUED IN FOUR VOLS.)

VOL. I.—THE FIVE BOOKS OF MOSES.

Direct from the Hebrew.

VOL. I., PRICE **2 6** nett, Cloth. In Leather, Gilt. **6 ·** nett, per Vol.

Published for the Translator by

MESSRS. S. W. PARTRIDGE & CO.,

8 & 9, PATERNOSTER ROW, LONDON, E.C.;

And Sold by all Booksellers throughout the World.

Pantè ... ...

page 156
118
$\overline{.07}$?
$\underline{\text{Pte}}$?

212